Popular Music Autobiography

Popular Music Autobiography

The Revolution in Life-Writing by 1960s' Musicians and Their Descendants

Oliver Lovesey

BLOOMSBURY ACADEMIC
NEW YORK • LONDON • OXFORD • NEW DELHI • SYDNEY

BLOOMSBURY ACADEMIC
Bloomsbury Publishing Inc
1385 Broadway, New York, NY 10018, USA
50 Bedford Square, London, WC1B 3DP, UK
29 Earlsfort Terrace, Dublin 2, Ireland

BLOOMSBURY, BLOOMSBURY ACADEMIC and the Diana logo are trademarks of Bloomsbury Publishing Plc

First published in the United States of America 2022
This paperback edition published 2023

Copyright © Oliver Lovesey, 2022

For legal purposes the Acknowledgments on p. 207 constitute an extension of this copyright page.

Cover design: Louise Dugdale
Cover image: Paul Thek, Nude, Astride Zebra, 1965 © 1987 The Peter Hujar Archive, LLC; courtesy Pace/MacGill Gallery, New York and Fraenkel Gallery, San Francisco

All rights reserved. No part of this publication may be reproduced or transmitted in any form or by any means, electronic or mechanical, including photocopying, recording, or any information storage or retrieval system, without prior permission in writing from the publishers.

Bloomsbury Publishing Inc does not have any control over, or responsibility for, any third-party websites referred to or in this book. All internet addresses given in this book were correct at the time of going to press. The author and publisher regret any inconvenience caused if addresses have changed or sites have ceased to exist, but can accept no responsibility for any such changes.

A catalog record for this book is available from the Library of Congress.

ISBN:	HB:	978-1-5013-5583-7
	PB:	978-1-5013-8591-9
	ePDF:	978-1-5013-5585-1
	eBook:	978-1-5013-5584-4

Typeset by Integra Software Services Pvt. Ltd.

To find out more about our authors and books visit www.bloomsbury.com and sign up for our newsletters.

Contents

Introduction: Generation Audio-Biography		1
1	Disenabling Fame: Rock 'n' Recovery Autobiographies and Disability Narrative	47
2	"A Cellarful of Boys": The Swinging Sixties, Gay Managers, and the Other Beatle	73
3	Performative Identity: Cosey Fanni Tutti, Brett Anderson, Moby	93
4	Performative Identity: Patti Smith, David Wojnarowicz	137
5	The Invention of Bob Dylan and the Archival Autograph	171
Conclusion		199
Acknowledgments		207
Works Cited		208
Index		237

Introduction

Generation Audio-Biography

The rock star imaginary has become one of the defining myths of our time. Its apparently eternally youthful creative energy is conjured in everything from energy drinks to political campaigns, and like musicians' lives, it has become one of the vital cultural and multimedia contexts that inform listening to music. The image on the cover of *Popular Music Autobiography* is a photograph by Peter Hujar, who also took some of the best early portraits of punk pioneer Iggy Pop. This cover image is Hujar's 1965 photograph of Paul Thek, an iconic artist in his own right, a painter, photographer, and performance artist, who may be the originator of installation art. This image may embody the notion of the rock star as a vulnerable child and also an "erotic politician," in Jim Morrison's phrase (qtd. in Didion 22). It is a surrealist fantasy evoking the spirit of the revolutionary musical experimentation of the 1960s. Popular music autobiographers are naked and vulnerable, riding on the exotic expectations of readers for revelations about celebrity and fame. The image is distinctly anti-militaristic and anti-patriarchal, a parody of a general riding into battle, naked and swordless. The stuffed zebra is a *memento mori* of a psychedelic variety. Musician autobiographers recount their lives in popular music fully aware, often for the first time, that soon the music will be over. The image may also stand against interpretation and misinterpretation of artists, art, and musicians, as the actual rider here inspired Susan Sontag's 1966 essay collection *Against Interpretation* which called for a serious examination of contemporary popular culture, including camp. An often acerbic public intellectual with omnivorous appetites, Sontag recorded in her journals in 1965 that "[m]y biggest pleasure [in] the last two years has come from pop music" (*Consciousness* 139), and confessed in a *Rolling Stone* interview in 1979: "[r]ock and roll literally changed my life" (*Complete* 35).

Popular Music Autobiography addresses the exponential growth in the number, diversity, and quality of life writing produced mainly over the past three decades by musicians associated with the 1960s, the nexus of the revolution in popular music performed by the post-war generation,[1] amid demographic upheavals and seismic shifts in technology. It tackles these figures in the representative autobiographies of Eric Clapton and Marianne Faithfull, for example, but it also looks at their "descendants," those generational cohorts who recognized and often predictably rebelled against the giants on whose shoulders they were standing, partly because of the truism that rock stars were first fans or star fuckers. Recent critical interest in life writing, particularly since the twenty-first-century memoir boom, largely has overlooked the growth in autobiographies by artists of popular music.[2] These autobiographies are dismissed as "facile" in a 1994 study of "aesthetic autobiography" (Nalbantian 1) or as "break[ing] little ground in terms of genre" in Patrick Madden's 2013 scan of "new memoir" (222) or overlooked altogether in Linda Anderson's 2011 or Laura Marcus's 2018 surveys of autobiography as well as in the admittedly somewhat "arbitrary" list of sixty life writing genres, including "jockography," in Sidonie Smith and Julia Watson's influential *Reading Autobiography* of 2010 (127, 272, 253–86).[3] However, in a pioneering study in the field of popular music life writing, the forthcoming *Music, Memory and Memoir*, though narrowly focused on the sub-genre of memoir by artists in multiple disciplines, Robert Edgar, Fraser Mann, and Helen Pleasance consider the reception of life writing as being somewhat solipsistic ("Introduction," 1–9).[4] Readers, presumed to be fans, read the memoirs while simultaneously revisiting their own pasts, for which the musician writers have provided a soundtrack. Hence, popular music life writing serves to provoke readers' own memory work, and its own qualities tend to be overlooked. There has been great resistance to reading popular music autobiographies as part of autobiography's ever-expanding counter canon or as being of significance in understanding popular music. Such resistance persists despite this music's power as a technology for constructing people's "sense of themselves" (Frith, "Music" 156),[5] and the ever-expanding multimedia fields from MTV to YouTube and social media platforms in which listening now occurs.[6] Moreover, popular music autobiographies and auto/biographies have won the National Book Award (2010) and the Norman Mailer Prize (2011), and popular music itself has been afforded the Pulitzer Prize for Music (2018), and Bob Dylan has been honored with the Nobel Prize for Literature (2016).[7] New York's Metropolitan Museum and London's Victoria and Albert Museum have exhibited rock object d'art and instruments, part of a more general acknowledgment of the significance and immersiveness of popular music culture.

Popular Music Autobiography situates its examination of this largely ignored explosion in life writing by musicians (in sites such as formal autobiographies and memoirs, diaries, auto-fiction, songs, and self-fashioned museums) in the context of the recent growth of critical interest in autobiography, disability, celebrity, and popular music studies, using the somewhat vexed term "autobiography" because of its familiarity.[8] It argues that these writings have a vital presence in the textual and digital mediascapes in which listening to popular music now takes place. These popular music autobiographies, however, frequently seek to dispel their writers' well-known celebrity status and particularly its association with a lack of seriousness. In a number of cases, they are witness narratives of addiction, an addiction pursued to mitigate the rigors of fame. These works, as a result, often constitute a meditation on the nature of postmodern fame itself within a celebrity-obsessed culture, in an age of confession, identity politics, and the selfie.[9] Due in part to the long shadow of the youthful dead in the late 1960s as well as the realities of age and disability, these works are also often a meditation on mortality, if not exactly nostalgia.[10] Paradoxically, they aim to reclaim the private self in a public forum. They sometimes aspire, however clandestinely, to a more traditional, achievement-based renown, of a less controversial literary variety. They often narrate their emergent and also performative selves in relationship with others—constructing a relational self—acknowledging origins and sources, and sometimes seeking atonement. Taken together, they represent a kind of generational autobiography of the revolutionary 1960s music people as well as some of their descendants, and also, inevitably, a history of the present.

There are many types of popular music autobiography, according to their governing idea or method, though there is often overlap. Some are primarily logbooks of tours and recording sessions, or song-by-song breakdowns of albums, while others are essentially "gearhead" tech manuals, such as those by certain prog or prog-metal rockers. Others seek to set the record straight, as when Shirley Collins explains the loss of her voice for nearly four decades, or set out to settle scores and obtain "retrospective justice" (Michael Holroyd qtd. in Smith and Watson, *Reading* 213). Donovan Leitch, for example, aims to demolish his early image as a Dylan clone, laying claim to having enabled world or New Age music and Celtic rock, and pursuing his muse. Individual volumes are sometimes part of a series as with those of David Crosby, including his recent biopic,[11] or Patti Smith, works which increasingly mash up history and fiction. Others are accounts of addiction, as a consequence of childhood trauma, as in the case of Mark Lanegan, or mental health concerns, as with

Richard Lloyd, or from being a closeted "metal god" like Rob Halford (229).[12] Some are paratextual or illustrative memoirs such as Tom Morello's *Whatever It Takes* (2020), a "photo memoir" by the highly articulate former exotic dancer and Harvard-educated son of a Kenyan Mau Mau freedom fighter, who presents himself with illustrious colleagues such as Bruce Springsteen and Chris Cornell. Others use the occasion of the memoir to advance other interests, as when Lenny Kravitz advances his philosophy, Bruce Dickinson focuses on fencing and flying, and Neil Peart narrates his motorcycle travels, or Neil Young's *Waging Heavy Peace* (2012) attends to obsessions with automobile technology, building and collecting, and offering advice such as that "old rocker[s]" should write memoirs (223). Meta-popular music autobiographies characterize the jokey, hyper-self-conscious perspective, found in works by Moby and Jeff Tweedy, which appears to be engaged partly to deflect autobiography's implied self-importance or the deadening effects of gratitude-laden recovery speak. Chris Frantz's *Remain in Love* (2020) shows an amalgamation of types. An anecdotal logbook of tours and recordings with vignettes about the self-regard of Brian Eno, James Brown, Ziggy Marley, Lou Reed, Patti Smith, and the Happy Mondays, for example, it also seeks to settle scores on two fronts: a disregard for the musical abilities of Talking Heads' bass player and Frantz's wife Tina Weymouth and also what Frantz calls the "lies of omission" of David Byrne who has taken and been widely given credit as the band's creative mastermind (275).[13] Frantz details Byrne dismantling Talking Heads via media interviews. The best revenge, however, as he suggests, may be living well, wintering in France with his family and two corgies, and being inducted into the Rock and Roll Hall of Fame.

While not a taxonomy, certain distinctive tenets or principles of popular music autobiographies may be offered provisionally for what is an evolving and dynamic sub-genre of life writing. 1) Anti-memoir: There is often an upfront denial of catering to the sex, drugs, and rock 'n' roll, name-dropping stereotype,[14] with the exception of the rock 'n' recovery works examined in the next chapter. As even Peggy Seeger in her eighth decade puts it ironically, "[a]s everyone knows, musicians are short on reliability and long on drugs, alcohol and random sex" (*First* 212). 2) Anti-apology: Unlike traditional autobiography which, however briefly and formulaically, sets out its reasons for existing, popular music autobiographies often omit this self-justification. There is a strong sense, however, that the writer's music is a type of pre-text, which may or may not assume a knowledgeable reader. 3) De-celebritification: Unlike conventional celebrity memoirs (L. Marcus 88), they are usually written not at the height of fame when the musician is young, but, like traditional autobiography, at a later moment of reflection. They often address the unwelcome arrival of celebrity and a negotiation with perceptions of themselves as entertainers (and not musicians and songwriters). 4) The Authenticity Nexus: The relationship of their work to musical tradition, the bugbear of authenticity, and their work's originality are addressed. Sometimes, discussion of the specifics of songwriting, recording, and performing supply the needed contexts. 5) "That David Copperfield Kind of Crap": As in traditional autobiography and autofiction, but usually from a very different socio-economic perspective, popular music autobiographies offer a portrait of growing up (Salinger). Often, childhood trauma has a significant role, and there is thus a narrative of escape or salvation amounting to a type of spiritual transformation, or the narrative of an alternative meritocracy.[15] 6) Performative Identity: There is commonly an address to the negotiation of private and public selves, image, and staged identity. 7) Relational Selves: This is an acknowledgement of the aid of others, and a reaching out in terms of crediting sources and influences. Sometimes, there is also an expression of failures and a desire for atonement and reconciliation. 8) Paratextuality: Frequently, photographs are included, though, as with Dylan's *Chronicles*, this is not always the case. In Patti Smith's life writing of different types, creative photography has become increasingly central. There may also be companion playlists and song-by-song rehearsals as if directing the reader back to the recordings. Increasingly, there are tie-ins or spin-offs, such as companion music compilations.

Autobiographical contexts

Critical autobiography studies—in which "autobiography" itself has increasingly become the cringe-worthy "a" word[16]—have expanded massively in scope since its emergence in the 1950s, questioning inherited notions of homogeneous selfhood in life writing and embracing difference in gender, race, class, and other terms. In particular, it has questioned notions of a unitary, stable self embedded within some historical constructions of the genre of autobiography. This written, autographed self, "ideological subject" or ideological "I" (P. Smith 105, 100–16) carries traces of the homogeneity of the Eurocentric, bourgeois, humanist, paternalistic, all-knowing and universal "Enlightenment 'self'" (Watson and Smith, "De/Colonization" xvii). This self is also freighted with the baggage of homophobia and xenophobia. Autobiographical homogeneity has been countered by elaborations of what Édouard Glissant addresses in a postcolonial context in *Poetics of Relation* as a relational self. Paul John Eakin's *Living Autobiographically*, Amy Culley and Rebecca Styler's "Lives in Relation," and Bart Moore-Gilbert's *Postcolonial Life-Writing* are among recent works advancing the centrality of such a relational identity, which increasingly has been accepted as a component in most autobiography (Smith and Watson, "Personal" xlii).[17]

Autobiography has been a very open, free form from its fifth-century origins to its more recent myriad of digital forms including online and social media confessions and graphic memoirs[18]—such as the comic book autobiography of David Wojnarowicz—despite what might appear to be the tyranny of chronology. Music has an important and often overlooked place in some of the classics of the genre, which show that music has not always and only been for professionals in terms of its making and reception. They also display discrete features that we will see in popular music autobiographies, indicating they are less autobiographical outlier than they might appear to be. These canonical and counter-canonical autobiographers often seek to establish their authority as writers within a tradition—whether biblical, classical, autobiographical, or that of women's genealogy—similar to popular musicians' positioning their work's authenticity and originality against the roots of the folk heritage. If not exactly the rock star of autobiographers, Saint Augustine (354–430 CE), in addition to being a saint, was or has been embraced as almost certainly the originator of the genre and a celebrity of a sort in his own time. He would eventually be the subject of a song by Bob Dylan.[19] A North African who wrote down his *Confessions*, Augustine was well-established in the Church establishment and well-known for his writing, including works on music, throughout European and oriental Christendom. Garry Wills translates Augustine's title as "Testimony,"[20] the term used for the much more recent autobiography by Robbie Robertson (2016). Augustine was writing primarily for an audience of one (God) who knew his story and his motives, justifications, prevarications, and duplicity far better than he did himself. A kind of religious lie detector test, Augustine's *Confessions* resemble the life writing of famous popular musicians in that they tell an apparently well-known story often to a fandom which seeks the real, private story. While most popular musician autobiographers explicitly disdain the "sex, drugs, and rock 'n' roll" tale of excess that is anticipated in their life writing—but may or may not be part of their personal story—Augustine drills down on his sinfulness. Delaying his acceptance of salvation, rather than partying and having affairs, however, is his main grievance with himself. He says, famously, "[g]ive me chastity ... but not yet" (169). He confesses "both what I know of myself"—including stealing pears (enticed by the sin, not the fruit), visiting the theatre, and adhering to the Manichean heresy—but he also confesses "what I do not know" (211). He recognizes the danger of spiritual pride, even in "the very process of self-reproach," though the written confession is intended in part to disabuse those "who know me [or] ... have heard of me or read my books" and consider him the epitome of sanctity (247, 209).

Before his conversion, Augustine wrote a number of books on the philosophy of music, and particularly the aesthetics of rhythm (*De Musica*), and his curiosity was boundless: in *The City of God*, for example, he refers to those who can sing with their anuses (626–7).[21] Both the climax of his spiritual journey and a later temptation are signaled by music, as when his conversion follows hearing a child singing and after his baptism,[22] "hymns and canticles" are performed, a recent innovation (190–1). Obsessed later with annihilating all temptations from gluttony to intellectual curiosity, he considers renouncing music, "the pleasures of sound," but he pardons it due to music's encouragement of piety, especially among "weaker spirits" (238, 239). Montaigne will say humorously, though not directly in reference to the *Confessions*, "[t]here is a great difference between a man who does not want to sin and one who does not know how to" (74). In his confession, Augustine anticipates one of the major seventeenth-century developments in life writing, which in turn will influence the psychological novel, the spiritual autobiography, such as John Bunyan's *Grace Abounding to the Chief of Sinners*, in which the autobiographer compares his dastardly life to that of Christ and longs for a "happy death." When in 1966, John Lennon, in an unguarded moment in an interview, equated the Beatles with Jesus—referring to the intensity of their fans' adoration—he would provoke one of the major checks to the band's global popularity,[23] though his iconoclasticism may have paid dividends over time in securing his reputation as a folk philosopher or self-styled "working class hero." When Patti Smith in punk guise referred to a "rock-n-roll Jesus" in her co-written *Cowboy Mouth* and shouted that "Jesus died for somebody's sins but not mine" in "Gloria" from *Horses*, the reaction would be far different though her audience was much smaller and anticipated being pleasantly scandalized (Smith and Shepherd qtd. in Shaw 60–1; Smith qtd. in Shaw 2–3).

The first autobiography by an English woman may be the medieval *Book of Margery Kempe*, the record of an oral recounting of the illiterate Kempe's life, a text of much significance for Throbbing Gristle's Cosey Fanni Tutti, whose autobiography is addressed in Chapter 3. Kempe (1373–1440), like former West Indian slave Mary Prince four hundred years later,[24] dictated her recollections to different scribes, including a priest, and their modifications of her words render her text highly unstable. Kempe's book is recorded oral history, recounting a life, though not, like Augustine's or Rousseau's, beginning with a description of childhood. Mediated or collaborative authorship[25]—when a text's composition involves others directly, as in Keith Richards' *Life* written "with James Fox"—is not only associated with recent autobiographies by performing artists. Kempe creates her book as directed by divine promptings with the strong implication that understanding the resulting text, "badly set down, and written quite without reason" as the work's "Proem" explains, may also require divine assistance (36). She recounts intense spiritual experiences accompanied by extreme, prolonged, and disturbing vocalizations. Kempe's vocal performance of loud, copious weeping, sobbing, and shrieking was elicited by her mystical transports. She records them as signs which confirm her divine inspiration,[26] though these holy fits of tears, sometimes accompanied by Kempe's hearing heavenly music, raised suspicions among her hearers about their heretical or demonic origin; reading her work as hysterical has until fairly recently dominated critical discourse (Aers 74–5). Kempe interprets such "contempt and reproof for her weeping and her crying" as further indications of her spiritual authority (250). Kempe composes within a type of feminist genealogy, a line of European holy women such as Julian of Norwich, whom she knew, or St. Bridget of Sweden, whose writings she heard recited (Windeatt 16–19). She thus belongs within a lineage of women who spoke out when their voices were silenced by the Church establishment, as if their voices were scandalous, the open mouth signifying an open womb. She recounts her journey as a woman in the world—not a recluse or anchorite—from being a wife with fourteen children and a very different, patriarchal heredity to being a bride of Christ. Her first mystical experience followed severe postpartum depression after the birth of her first child. She traces her life from her marriage and her fraught attempt for it to be a non-sexual union, her establishment of a brewing business, as well as her temptations to fine dress and even adultery, and finally to her international pilgrimages. She uses direct speech to report conversations with God and erotic language for spiritual matters, with its precedents in the Bible and wisdom literature,[27] but generally Kempe's frankness about sexual matters is more commonly associated with later male autobiographers like Rousseau.

St. Teresa of Ávila (1515–82), from a wealthy Jewish and Christian family, wrote her *Life* under duress, pressured by her confessor who, like many others, suspected that her mystical raptures, ecstasies, and visions were the devil's work. She wrote during the Inquisition and risked denunciation as a heretic. While she begins with an account of her early addiction to books of chivalry and ends with her energetic reform of the Carmelite order, much of her autobiography recounts her out-of-body spiritual experiences, which she sometimes uses music to describe. Music, in these instances, embodies a rebellion against patriarchal, institutional control. Sonic Youth's atmospheric "Teresa's Sound-worlds," claims Romeo Hontiveros, may have been inspired by her.[28] While she reads Augustine's *Confessions* and consults broadly, her authority in the *Life* mainly derives from the evidence of her transports and visions themselves, including one in which Christ gives her pointers to silence priestly scepticism. Though obsessed with a sense of her own wickedness, she resists some of her confessor's suggestions such as that she just snap her fingers should she feel a rapture coming on. A more sympathetic confessor suggests she incorporate a hymn in her prayers, but "as I was reciting it a rapture came on me so suddenly that it almost carried me away …. I heard these words: 'I want you to converse now not with men but with angels'" (172). The feelings of King David "when he played on the harp and sang the praises of God," she refers to in another instance of "heavenly madness" when she felt "bewildered and intoxicated with love," and her soul longed "to be all one tongue with which to praise the Lord" (112–14). This reference to David's playing appears in Leonard Cohen's hymn-like "Hallelujah," an instance of a hit song with Old Testament allusions and an easy way with the sacred, like Dylan's "Jokerman," that would go on to achieve a degree of immortality.[29] "Hallelujah"'s most famous cover, itself based on John Cale's—not Cohen's—version, is probably that by Jeff Buckley whose journals were published in 2019, and who admired the song as a celebration of sexual—not spiritual—ecstasy.[30] St. Teresa's celebrity stature was recognized in her lifetime. One might say, moreover, that she was fast-tracked for canonization, and those souvenir hunters who wanted a piece of her literally took one after her death when her corpse was dismembered by relic seekers, a manifestation of popular regard for her sanctity and the celebrity she always resisted.

Michel de Montaigne (1533–92) suggests that to portray himself, as befitting a unique subject, he requires a new genre, and he demonstrates the potentially highly experimental nature of writing one's life as we will see in Patti Smith's innovations. While performing "musical compositions" requires "skill," he explains that his qualification for writing his autobiography is merely that on the subject of himself he is "the most learned man alive" (Montaigne 236). He sets out not a chronology of life events but instead his reflections on various subjects, in a series of digressive experiments or "essays" as an indirect and also more authentic and revealing method of picturing his character and disposition. He implies that character exists in a person's mental and emotional processes, and that tracing mental wandering as triggered by impressions and involuntary memories is the best way to reveal oneself. Like *Tristram Shandy* (1759–67), Laurence Sterne's autobiographical novel, which begins at the very beginning in his parents' bed with Tristram's conception, Montaigne says that his book is the anatomy of himself, and "[w]ho touches one, touches the other" (237). In this respect, his *Essays* anticipate a range of autobiographical fiction including stream of consciousness works like Marcel Proust's *Remembrance of Things Past* (1913–27) and Patti Smith's *Year of the Monkey* (2019). He writes for "the pleasure of my relatives and friends" and paints himself "in all my nakedness," and he recommends that other readers abandon the "frivolous and unrewarding" book at the outset (23). He does not justify his project as an account of his unusual education, though he was permitted to speak and read only Latin, not French, till he was six years old (J.S. Mill justifies his autobiography for this very reason, as a documentation of his highly unusual—today it might be regarded as a species of child abuse—utilitarian education). He also maintains that it is only possible to judge a life after death, and hence he anticipates the ideal "posthumous" autobiography such as *The Posthumous Memoirs of Brás Cubas* (1881) by the descendant of Brazilian slaves Machado De Assis (1839–1908).[31] Over the course of his three volumes, Montaigne becomes more forthcoming about himself, and less devoted to making self-deprecating allusions to classical and wisdom literature. However, he concludes with a hope for a healthy old age when he may listen to music and, echoing a Horacian prayer, be "no stranger to the lyre" (406).[32]

Romantic Genevan philosopher and political scientist Jean-Jacques Rousseau (1712–78), for much of his career, as his posthumously published autobiographical *Confessions* (1782) reveals, considered himself to be primarily a musician, though largely self-taught. He composed operas, such as *The Village Soothsayer*, penned the *Dictionary of Music*, devised a system of numerical musical notation, and sustained himself by working as a human photocopy machine reproducing musical scores (359–78). Rousseau presents himself as an eccentric, quixotic figure on a picaresque vocational quest, and before his later operatic success, his volatile temperament created internal dissonance: "[i]t was as though my brain, raised to the pitch of some foreign instrument, were tuned far outside its usual register" (127). For example, on one occasion well before his later success as a composer, he fabricates an identity upon arrival in Lausanne as an accomplished singing master and composer from Paris seeking pupils, and though at this stage his ignorance of reading, writing, and performing music is almost total, he convinces people of his virtuosity and assembles musicians who perform a concert of "insane music" (145). His *Confessions*, beginning with a famously extended narrative of his childhood, tells the warts—or sexual peccadilloes—and all story of his life to confound his enemies, to witness before God, and to justify why someone who had himself suffered abandonment as a boy would adopt out his five children. Rousseau's might be the closest to an eighteenth-century sex, drugs, and rock 'n' roll narrative (minus the drugs), given his attention to masturbation and his love of being flogged, and his encounters on the straight–gay continuum. He claims to deliver "the most secret history of my soul" ("Preface" 648), punctuated by incidents of intense shame, and also an anatomy of his society in that he has lived within all its ranks, despite being a self-perceived outsider and natural aristocrat in his feelings. Unlike Wordsworth's poetic autobiography *The Prelude* (1850), Rousseau's *Confessions*, he insists, is a faithful portrait of the growth of not his mind, but his senses. In the autobiography's second half, however, he shifts from an almost masochistic self-mortification, as if the shamefulness of episodes guarantees their veracity, and presents himself as a paranoid hypochondriac with a persecution complex living in a hostile age.

Without music, says Nietzsche in his autobiography *Ecce Homo* (1908), sounding a little like a modern teenage fan, "I could not have endured my youth"; Wagner, he maintains, was his hashish (31).[33] *Ecce Homo* is an eccentric, philosophical autobiography,[34] like Carlyle's *Sartor Resartus* (1833–34), in which Nietzsche assumes the constructed persona of a braggart or narcissist[35] to play with and parody the notion that all autobiographies are vanity projects. It does not address his own sense of personal failure as a composer of music, however. While he summarizes his books as if to say that essentially he is these books or their ideas, just as many popular music autobiographers do in their anecdotal logbooks of recordings and concerts, he emphasizes that everyone must live his or her own life and not imitate others. Like some popular music autobiographers, in addition, he is at pains to admonish readers not to worship or mimic their idols. He advises being oneself and living so as to have no regrets[36] even if one does not become a rock star or superman. He compares living well to playing music: "Let the instrument be what it will, let it be as out of tune as only the instrument 'man' can become out of tune—I should have to be ill not to succeed in getting out of it something listenable"; after that, "the rest is silence" (13, 12).

Nietzsche's "disciple" Michel Foucault,[37] who was a celebrity intellectual before his death from complications from AIDS, two months before Rock Hudson's, in 1984, claimed that all of his works were "fragment[s] of an autobiography" or an "autobiographical allegory" that responded to *Ecce Homo*'s challenge "to become what one is" (Miller 31, 112, 5).[38] Foucault's embrace of the moral imperative of authenticity, of such concern for popular musicians in a decidedly different register, partly resulted from his intimate association with "serialists and deodecaphonic musicians" like Jean Barraqué who regarded musical reception as a limit experience in which the listener may be "trembling on the verge of suicide" (qtd. in Miller 79, 80). Hearing Barraqué's music aided in Foucault's liberation from universal categories and dialectical reasoning (Macey 53-4, 216), and he claimed that music itself had been as important in his development as reading Nietzsche (Eribon 67). For Foucault, such extreme experiences included the use of LSD and also play with "self-cancellation" or other forms of extreme self-renunciation.[39] Such concerns inevitably, and ironically for a free thinker, brought him close to the writings of early Christian apologists like Augustine, though they also drew on the ancients' concern with the care of the self in a process that, in Foucault's formulation, leads the individual to become a "self-interpreter" (Foucault, "Technologies" 39).[40] Rock music for Foucault, as he says in a discussion with Barraqué's associate Pierre Boulez, is tied to performative rites and spectacle, and fosters group identification. Appreciating rock music displays a self-affirming immersion in "a way of life," but Foucault suspects, perhaps echoing Adorno, that listeners' ready access through multiple media channels, dulls and commodifies rock's radicalism (Foucault, "Contemporary" 316, 317).

Popular musicology and autobiography/biography

Popular music autobiographies have been dismissed by some scholars of music as being merely manifestations of sub-cultural ephemera related to an inferior, amateur art associated with a disembodied cultural tradition, and popular music itself has not always been taken seriously. Simon Frith and Howard Horne in

Art Into Pop, for example, point to a tendency to discount popular musicians themselves as untaught non-professionals whose production has value only as a sociological curiosity. There is a need "to pay proper attention to the music-makers" in studies of popular music, and by extension to their lives (169). In his influential *Studying Popular Music*, Richard Middleton notes the more widespread resistance to popular music itself within musicology and cultural studies. As a more self-critical "new musicology" developed in the 1990s, with an interdisciplinary, global focus and a shift from the exclusive analysis of musical scores—utilizing a notation system carrying "its own ideological and aesthetic baggage" (Brackett 19)—Middleton's remarks about academic hostility to popular music study became increasingly common, and have almost become an expected rhetorical gesture, as are apologies for the use of the term "autobiography" as we have seen.[41] Middleton advocates for theoretical—particularly materialist—muscle while also effecting reform in the field,[42] a position elaborated further in his *Voicing the Popular*, predicated on the notion of popular music as the voice of the folk (23–4). His critique of Adorno's writings on popular music notes their dismissal of performance as mere mechanical reproduction of recordings and their disregard for popular musicians and their compositional artistry. Adorno falsely universalizes and homogenizes the modes of production of popular music, creates a false dichotomy between popular music and the avant-garde, and ignores the voices of resistance and the diverse roots of American popular music. He also polices reception of music that must be a detached, cerebral undertaking, and he is suspicious of aesthetic pleasure rooted in the subconscious and the body.

In *On Popular Music*, Adorno attacks the false individualism of popular music composers or singer songwriters who produce pseudo-individualized, "pre-digested" songs in hit factories like the Brill Building (Adorno 445). Adorno's condemnation of robotic, assembly-line creativity is radically different, however, from the later dismissal of popular musicians' creativity as the "primitive savage" modes of those distinguished by their "musical illiteracy" (Brackett 158). For David Brackett, though popular music has a "participatory aesthetic," its creator is usually not a collective but an individual who combines "singing voice, body, image, and biographical details" (22, 2). Knowledge of the performer influences interpretation of popular song, he maintains, by referring to the influence of Billie Holiday's collaborative autobiography *Lady Sings the Blues* (1956) (34–74), which is as much a critique of the anti-African American and misogynistic justice system as a deep dive into things musical.[43] Listening to and understanding music, as Frith argues in *Performing Rites*, take place in the broader context of a "musical culture," and popular music's "meaning" lies in attending to its musicians, who are "performers with bodies and personalities," and taking pleasure in their voices (249, 210). Musicians' autobiographies, while not exactly "language about music," inform the "narrative modes" of listening, as Lawrence Kramer points out in a different context (396, 397). He elucidates five theses on "the cultural study of music," illustrated with reference to George Sand's autobiography and its remarks about four of Frédéric Chopin's Preludes (400–6).

Life writing and biography have had a vexed place in ethnomusicology, but a more assured importance in the tradition of actual field collection. Philip Bohlman explains that in folk music scholarship, the music itself is frequently anonymized and rendered "voiceless" and "devoid of individual personality"; the performer as a result becomes merely a "curator" of an "artefact" (69, 80). Dynamic creativity, variation, and innovation by individual musicians within or just outside the tradition are similarly discounted as not fitting prescribed theories or systems of classification, a practice sometimes amounting to white-washing.[44] It is worth remembering that a reviewer attacked John and Alan Lomax's 1934 *American Ballads and Folk Songs* for its suggestion that the nation's rich folk heritage was dependent on "'Niggah' convicts and white 'bums'" (qtd. in J. Becker 38). In his 1964 study of ethnomusicological field collection, however, Kenneth S. Goldstein—who mentored musicologist and folk singer Paul Clayton who in turn mentored Bob Dylan—draws on the pioneering work of the Lomaxes, who would discover Leadbelly and retain half the royalties for "Goodnight Irene" to finance Alan's own international folk music collecting. Goldstein recommends the collector obtain "the story of the life" of the "individual folklore informant" or "tradition bearer" in order to determine "the many factors which go into the making of a traditional performer" and to adjudicate what renders "one performer a star among lesser figures in the community of tradition" (121, 125). Goldstein's collecting of folksong in North America and particularly in sites such as Appalachia was predicated on the idea that it represented a survival of the last trace of an extinct tradition of Elizabethan plainsong. Field work represented oral history, demonstrating the roots of ethnomusicology in anthropology and English studies, the first American professor of English at Harvard University being Francis James Child.

Autobiographical writing, however, has had an important place in the popular folk tradition, its documentation, and its revival. Dylan said that reading Woody

Guthrie's partly fictional autobiography *Bound for Glory* (1943) partly inspired him to become a folk singer poet, in at least one of his origin stories, and he later wrote a memoir. Guthrie was encouraged to write his autobiography—a John-Steinbeck-meets-Will-Rogers-style comic epic of the Great Plains—by Alan Lomax, and he received a $500 advance from E.P. Dutton, reaping more money from his writing than from his songs (Klein 184, 238-39). Like a novel, *Bound for Glory* is mostly written in the form of dialogue in a distinctly Oklahoma idiom which Guthrie abandoned for his sexually-explicit novel *House of Earth* (2013), which he had hoped would be turned into a film script (Brinkley and Depp xxxix). The romance of Guthrie's troubadour-on-the-road account as well as that of folk song field collection, of the sort undertaken by Lomax, eventually attracted Dylan to musicologists like Carl Sandburg and Paul Clayton, whom we shall return to in the last chapter. Dylan heard some of the rural, vernacular musicians recorded on Harry Smith's famous *Anthology*—an archive of recorded songs and not field recordings—first in person at Lomax's apartment in New York when Lomax's assistant, Carla Rotolo, was Dylan's girlfriend's sister (Szwed 338). Dylan's early mentor and later partner and still later sparring partner Joan Baez would write two volumes of memoir. Alan Lomax's father John Lomax wrote his autobiography, *Adventures of a Ballad Hunter*, a homey account of finding his vocation as a field researcher musicologist with an Edison phonograph and wax cylinders in 1908 after being raised in "the upper crust of the 'po' white trash'" (1). The Harvard Shakespeare scholar George Kittredge, the student and successor of Francis Child, had encouraged John Lomax's collecting of original cowboy songs—not survivals of English ballads—to preserve "from extinction this expression of American literature," which an Anglo-Saxon philologist at the University of Texas dismissed as "tawdry, cheap and unworthy" (J. Lomax 29, 27). When published in 1910, *Cowboy Songs*, for which he had solicited submissions through the news media, included lyrics and also—somewhat unusually—musical notation, a pattern followed in his second book which Macmillan's reader, Charles Seeger, considered "simply god-awful" (qtd. in Pescatello 135).[45] Lomax details how he and his son Alan later began collecting African-American songs, uninfluenced, so they hoped, by pop radio, church hymns, or jazz. "[O]ur best field was the southern penitentiaries," where they encountered Leadbelly (J. Lomax 97); they sometimes used the execution chamber as a recording studio. Comparative musicologist Alan Lomax expanded his father's work, collecting "oral autobiograph[ies]" as when he recorded Jelly Roll Morton's musical history, in line with Russian folklorists who compiled "the autobiographies of folk performers, bringing the singer … up to the level of importance of the song" (Szwed 69, 123). The politically engaged Alan Lomax considered his work a way to give "a voice to the voiceless," an "outcaste people" whose work in lucrative state penitentiaries merely perpetuated pre-Civil War slavery and resembled the production in Nazi concentration camps, as he wrote in *The Land Where the Blues Began* (1993) (xv, xix, 258).

Pioneering American musicologist Charles Seeger did not write an autobiography, but he began a co-authored narrative of his life and ideas with Ann Pescatello drawing heavily on his recorded reminiscences. A theorist of ethnomusicology and a frustrated classical conductor and composer as well as a dyed-in-the-wool contrarian, who had serious hearing problems, Seeger generally downplayed the importance of individual creators of folk or popular music and hence their autobiographies. After 1935, however, he would become an academic prostlezer for folk music itself, abandoning his early position that folk music was a type of opium for the downtrodden and a dead or dying branch of culture on the evolutionary tree. Later, he acknowledged that "in much non-Western music the performer, rather than a 'composer,' is the main creator or re-creator" (Pescatello 246). He did have a lofty regard for the life stories of classical composers such as Erik Satie, and he rated the folk song "Barbara Allen" so highly that he believed it must have been "transposed by some English composer" (Pescatello 134), indicating his underlying classist assumptions about originality in folk music. Similarly, Francis Child regarded the creators of ballads as an illiterate, anonymous mass, an anonymity reinforced by Child's use of numbers to distinguish ballads; he didn't inquire into living "native" informants or oral knowledge keepers when assembling his data; and his research on textual variants ignored his ballads' social and historical contexts.[46] Cecil Sharp documented the singers or performers of Child ballads and other songs in his field collection trips to Appalachia with Maud Karpeles between 1916 and 1918, and he also transcribed tunes (pointedly excluding African-American material),[47] convinced that from these folk roots "trained composers" would create a new music of the future (Filene 20–2). Such salvage ethnography is a kind of musical necrophilia, valuing the parasitic nourishment of art music from a repository of cultural artifacts, often from the global south (Lovesey, "Decolonizing" 1).

In line with the stance of the Communist party, though he was not a party member,[48] Seeger, early in his career, similarly dismissed folk music as voicing melancholy or frivolous themes and being incapable of igniting revolutionary outrage (Pescatello 125, 132). True "proletarian music" or "music for the masses," he felt, required a presumably classically trained and "disciplined composer" who could elevate hearers' musical taste while inspiring their natural zeal though his own attempt at a propaganda song, "Lenin, Who's That Guy?" showed the limitations of this approach (Pescatello 118, 110, 112). If musical "[a]rt was to be a weapon in the class struggle," it presumably required something resembling Seeger's esteem for modern classical music's polytonality or dissonant counterpoint, and it was to be listened to and studied—not sung—by the masses (Pescatello 110). In an early version of the "British Invasion" of the 1960s, it would require the introduction in the 1930s of a European regard for folk music as an untapped reservoir for art music to inspire the respect for the form that would appear in works by Copland and Bernstein (Pescatello 111–12; Seeger, "Tradition" 415–16, 422–3). Seeger valued the apparent "anonymity of the folk idiom" which demonstrated its role as a social function or a representative of broader cultural norms, and he was incensed by individuals copyrighting traditional folk songs unless the material had been massively transformed (Pescatello 168, 231).[49] As would become much better known through his son Pete Seeger's rousing quasi-Pentacostal singalongs of socialist hymns, Charles Seeger regarded all people as "inherently musical" and music making itself as "a group activity" in which everyone must participate (Pescatello 145). Seeger would come to deplore the colonized minds at work when ethnomusicologists elevated the search for surviving traces of English ballads over the hunt for original songs of domestic production, maintaining that "the musical soul of America is in its folk music … and … its popular music to the extent popular music has borrowed, stolen and manhandled folk music materials" (qtd. in Pescatello 164).

Peggy Seeger, like the most famous Seeger descendant, Pete, voiced political concerns in innovations within the traditional folk songbook, but also like her brother Mike Seeger—perhaps the most virtuosic musician in the well-regarded Seeger dynasty and idolized by Dylan (*Chronicles* 69–71)—regarded the music of the folk, "those at the bottom of the social heap," as by definition political (Freedman 279; Seeger, *First* 407). Peggy Seeger's *First Time Ever, A Memoir* (2017) is a self-described "companion" volume to Jean Freedman's biography. Seeger also credits her partner Irene Pyper Scott, with whom she entered a civil union in 2008, for urging her to write the memoir "as therapy" (49). In a powerfully frank, feisty style, Seeger relates her part in the saga of a family of gifted bohemian intellectual musicians, evoking a different world and a more innocent America, centered on a living community of song. She unflinchingly describes her parents' unorthodox sexual education, her retrieval of her own aborted fetus from a toilet, her stoma which she names Sydney, and the indignity of hearing Ewan MacColl's famous song, from which she derives her book's title, in the ubiquitous "aural wallpaper" surrounding her in the "loo" of a British department store (197). Her energetic family was politically engaged, but it also embodied society's structural racism. They had African-American servants, including the musician Elizabeth Cotten, and there was a button below their dining table to ring and alert the kitchen servants when to present or remove dishes. She shares Pete's commitment to the notion that "a real revolution" can be "achieved with arts" which "can leap over barriers of words, barriers of religion, barriers of politics"; like other patriarchs in this usually long-lived family, as Bruce Springsteen said at Pete's ninetieth birthday celebration at Madison Square Garden, Pete resembles "your granddad, if your granddad could kick your ass" (qtd. in Freedman 285, 275). The Seegers' use of traditional folk materials was not the product of "geriatric sentimentality," as Clive Davis said of Peggy's work,[50] or nostalgic kitsch, but derived from a regard for the song itself and the oral history it contains. It did not subscribe to the cult of the singer or the songwriter. However, Peggy is sufficiently savvy an entrepreneur to issue a two-CD set of her songs to correspond with her memoir's launch (xiv).

First Time Ever shows Peggy Seeger's ear for the idiom of speech in her remarkable account of her childhood. She describes the family practice of having "sick toys" to be played with only by a sick child, her own initializing the lid of a new baby grand piano and being spanked while her mother transcribed Ozella Jones' recording from a state penitentiary, "I been a bad, bad girl," and leaving colored footprints around the house after Jackson Pollock made an action painting in their living room (15, 19). Living in a television-free home, the resourceful Peggy made most of her own clothes, and learned banjo with her brother Mike using Pete's instructional book and studied guitar with one of Segovia's students, and played music with house guests like Woody Guthrie and Leadbelly. She was closest to her father and recalls his devotion to yoga, healthy diet, and nude swimming, but she clearly regrets her distance from her mother who moved from writing classical music to "composing babies" (9), and died from cancer just when Peggy might have found "mending time" with her (68). Seeger in surprising detail traces her raggle taggle adventures over continents, including meeting Chairman Mao and sharing a Paris apartment with a Ravensbrück survivor, and then her shared career with Ewan MacColl writing and performing BBC Radio Ballad documentaries, making field recordings with Roma and Scots Travelers, and producing yearly Festival of Fools musicals with critiques of the year's events. The memoir then shifts, becoming increasingly shadowed by the specters of the dead and dying, and adding admittedly unmemoir-like digressions, advice, and rants on, for example, how to prevent your 1907 Martin guitar from being stolen, how to play the English concertina, how to teach a university course on songwriting, and how to drink vodka shots in Moscow, with ranting asides about "these treacherous days" "of ruthless capitalism" (404, 409). In passing, she gives an extended account of her ill health and recounts "grassroots touring" horror stories which resemble an unplugged pseudo-amateur folk circuit version of 1984's *This Is Spinal Tap* (300). While she was always ready to participate in political action from writing a song for Obama's 2008 campaign and for Occupy Wall Street, in addition to her touring and steady record production, she was particularly engaged with feminist issues, understating that in traditional ballads "[w]omen don't get very good press" (4). She sang "Reclaim the Night" and "Winnie and Sam" about domestic violence, "I'm Gonna Be an Engineer" about equity employment, and "The Judge's Chair" on abortion rights. The memoir recounts her attempt to discover her true identity divorced from the powerful men and women around her, and it details her evolution from being an almost academic relayer of the folk tradition to being an adapter, editor, and translator of traditional song.

Muses and muse-axes

While Peggy Seeger may still be best known as the face that launched a thousand songs or cover versions, as the subject of her husband Ewan MacColl's classic "The First Time Ever I Saw Your Face," she has been far more than a muse. She adds Ewan's embarrassing erectile dysfunction to her demythologized account of that song's genesis unlike the recollection in MacColl's own autobiography,[51] noting with mock solemnity that "*second time ever I lay with you* doesn't really cut it, metrically or otherwise" (101). She is adamant that in her relationship with her "comrade lover," "I was too young and Ewan should have known better," in line with her repeated refrain "I was not a feminist back then" (335, 101, 302). She makes clear that Ewan's second wife's being pregnant with the baby who would become the famous singer of "Fairytale of New York," Kirsty MacColl, when Seeger herself is pregnant with her first child with Ewan nearly terminated their relationship. Her coined word "muse-axes" voices her ambivalence about the castrating potential of the muse and the legacy of being always associated with someone else's song (437). However, the $75,000 royalty cheque following Roberta Flack's soulful, Grammy-winning version of the song after years of being "professionally idiotic," puts a certain crimp in her and Ewan's anti-commercial, anti-appropriation, more-authentic-than-thou, purist credentials along with their "snobbish," "tunnel-visioned" ignorance about even politically engaged popular music; this financial windfall nourished a taste for the finer and fattier things of life that proved fatal for the songwriter (349, 280, 283, 285, 355). She does warn of the dangers of traditional singers being swept up in the commercial enticements of the folk revival, citing the Clancy Brothers as an ensemble who escaped (244), though Liam Clancy's memoir presents a different picture.[52] She has recently re-recorded Ewan's iconic song (422), just as Joni Mitchell has re-recorded "Both Sides Now"—her pure soprano voice now damaged from a lifelong devotion to cigarettes—in line with a number of other artists revisiting their most famous work from the perspective and with the voice of age.

Like Patti Smith whose youthful ambition was to be the artistic muse of a great man, or like Mitchell who was humiliated by a notorious article in *Rolling Stone* tracking her romantic relationships with famous songwriters and later naming her "Old Lady of the Year" in 1972 as if she were a groupie (Hagan, *Sticky* 225–6), women's position in 1960s and 1970s popular music has often been assessed according to their muse-like proximity to men. Famously, Marianne Faithfull rejected the role outright, and her efforts to distance herself as muse from Mick Jagger, as she relates in her memoirs, contributed to her self-refashioning as a heroin addict. While more a "pinup" or object of the male audience gaze than muse, Blondie's Debbie Harry recognized that in rock's "macho game" in the 1970s women were "window dressing," but there was no rulebook for building a career, unlike today when rock gets "taught in school" and "it's all about being famous" (191, 105, 108, 173). In her memoir *Face It*, Harry, a former Playboy bunny and later Barbie doll model, attempts to present herself as a knowing purveyor of a Marilyn Monroe-like male fantasy—while somehow also projecting signs of the "androgynous" and the "transsexual" (105)—in a relentlessly predatory culture in which sex sells everything. The memoir is packed with fan art and elegant portraits of Harry, and walk-ons by a gun-toting Phil Spector, serial killer Ted Bundy, Andy Warhol, and David Bowie's—but not, she makes clear, Iggy Pop's—penis: "[s]ince I was in an all-male band, maybe they figured I really *was* the cock-check lady" (154). The memoir is partly a love song to her former partner and bandmate Chris Stein, whose million-dollar debt mandated Blondie's reformation in 1997 (296). Despite her bravado, Harry still seems more immersed within this culture of exploitation than an active agent empowered by turning the tables, noting distressingly that "even as a little girl, I always attracted sexual attention" (19).

A less fraught use of the term "muse" appears elsewhere, such as with alt-rockers Throwing Muses, who formed in the early 1980s. Muse Kristin Hersh's memoir *Paradoxical Undressing* (2010) is based on her teenage diary after a serious car accident left her with a variously diagnosed dissociative affective disorder manifesting as often discordant music playing uncalled-for in her brain. She bases songs on the synesthetic, other-inspired "sonic haunting" of her post-concussion syndrome (77), paradoxically composing music to exorcise involuntary sound. She confronts notions such as that "you can't play guitar 'cause you don't have a penis" (27). The memoir resembles young adult fiction and offers an often distressing, anti-hippy, anti-entertainment, anti-music industry celebratory gesture to alt music and alt scenes. Non-musician Suze Rotolo, in her memoir *A Freewheelin' Time* (2008), says within an often scathing portrait of Bob Dylan that "I served as muse during our time together," but she refused to be the seventh string on his guitar (290), and she declines to name songs she might have inspired. Model and photographer Patti Boyd, in her autobiography *Wonderful Tonight* (2007), does present herself as the inspiration for George Harrison's "Something," Eric Clapton's "Wonderful Tonight," and Clapton and Jim Gordon's "Layla." Rita Coolidge's memoir *Delta Lady* (2016) asserts her claim to have not only inspired but also written the "counter-melody" for "Layla," though she is still uncredited (122). Leon Russell wrote "Delta Lady" and the much covered "A Song For You" about Coolidge (54–5), and she also claims to have originated the idea for his "Superstar" (131). This instance may resemble Yoko Ono's until recently uncredited contribution—a contribution originating in her prose poems in *Grapefruit* (1964)—to Lennon's iconic "Imagine" (Rogers). Ono, of course, wanted to be not merely a muse but a contributing artist in the Beatles.[53] Anti-muse Marianne Faithfull similarly battled for "at least 20 years" for a "Sister Morphine" co-writers' credit (qtd. in "Sweet" 64). Rose Simpson, of the extraordinarily inventive Incredible String Band (ISB) (1966–74), however, embraces her role as "muse" in her recently published memoir,[54] *Muse, Odalisque, Handmaiden: A Girl's Life in the Incredible String Band* (2020).

Simpson's memoir offers an intelligent insider's account of the utopian, communitarian ethos and the DIY aesthetic of the 1960s' counterculture along with their obvious and hidden dangers. From 1968 to late 1970, Simpson was a member of and participant observer in the ISB, much admired in the mid- and late 1960s by the Beatles, the Stones, and Led Zeppelin, a band which followed an uncompromisingly eccentric, quixotic musical and philosophical path of "deliberate chaotic amateurism" in which "[e]xpertise was considered an unnecessary restriction on innate creativity" (73, 82). Their sometimes wildly inventive songs—though typically refusing to perform their most popular ones, even at Woodstock—drew on British and American roots and world music, while often advancing a smorgasbord of esoteric and "half-understood spiritual pretensions" (89). It is a divided memoir, split between an attempt to provide a sympathetic, explanatory portrayal of the fey, twee idealism of the "ISB ethos" and its cultural contexts (80), and an exposé of the egotism, irrationality, and sexism lurking behind mantras of free love, psychedelic experimentation, and convention flaunting. Rejecting an unhappy upbringing in a working-class family and faced with a disillusioning university course and the likely prospect of a conventional post-graduation married life, and perhaps unwilling to participate any longer in the meaninglessness of "growing up absurd," Simpson inadvertently accepts the role of "muse," one of the few allowed for women by Paul Goodman.[55] She is attracted by the creative, liberating aura of the band as well as the beauty and kindness of one of its founders, Mike Heron, a former accountant with a middle-class background. A non-musician, she becomes an unpaid participant who, while also sewing many of Heron's clothes, plays instruments and sings parts learned by rote in concerts and on records—her bass playing expert enough to attract the admiration of Steve Winwood—as the band veers from near global fame to near-total obscurity. Her vague role in the band—along with that of its other female member, Licorice McKechnie, initially the girlfriend and "muse" of the other founding member, Robin Williamson (168)—annoyed the band's record producer and manager Joe Boyd, who championed Nick Drake in the period, but also puzzled outsiders. Passing encounters enhance this impression, as when Sandy Denny is indifferent, Nico and Vashti Bunyan ignore the "girls," and Joan Baez is openly contemptuous, and Joni Mitchell is encountered only at parties or across a hot tub with CSN at Esalen and Janis Joplin across a store's clothing rack.

The ISB's touring and recording, and also its communal living—which allowed for "sexual chaos" and was designed to facilitate Williamson's interest in multimedia musical theater (158), if not Heron's interest in rock music— are surrounded by darker shadows of the counterculture. On the periphery of their celebrity orbit, there are drug casualties of "aristocratic hippies" and "'fuck a 14-year-old' parties" in London (76), and a brief encounter with Boston's notorious Fort Hill Community, a mecca for jug band music, messianism, bank robbery, and misogyny, the East Coast equivalent of the Family, whose Charlie Manson wanted to be a rock star. Within the ISB, tension is generated by creative incompatibilities; a stridently anti-showbusiness ethic; stubborn resistance to compromise; subtly and not-so-subtly maintained financial, emotional, and creative dependence; and also an entrenched unwillingness to communicate problems openly and hence a weird, British, anti-establishment, hippy version of keeping a stiff upper lip. The ISB's demise, however, shifts into high gear with its devotion to Scientology whose embrace of the band as "psychedelic celebrities" and whose unfamiliarity in the counterculture lead the ISB's core members to believe they can utilize it to become spiritual avatars (147). We have an insider's account of the hierarchical, dictatorial, and paranoid corporate cult with its "simplistic psychology and bad science fiction" and its dismissal of criticism as the expression of "the sufferings of past lives" (116). Arrogant hypocrisy enters the band as the qualities which endeared the ISB to fans are anathema to Scientology, and members' need for money to feed the cult's appetite transforms them into insincere hippy posers and Scientology propagandists as their audience loses interest. "[C]onvinced that Scientology was nonsense and … [having] no intention of following its theories and rules," Simpson faces an ultimatum from the band no doubt from "fear that evil forces embodied in other people might injure their eternal purity" (215, 120). While rejecting Scientology, she suffers "a lurking sense of betrayal" that she also has rejected "ISB's original nature" (231). Simpson departs suddenly and forever in December 1970, clearly profoundly traumatized and realizing that her experience with the band was a paradise that is now forever lost (9).

Shirley Collins's *All in the Downs* (2018), published when she was eighty-three, is her third work of autobiography after her biopic *The Ballad of Shirley Collins* (2017) and her first volume *America Over the Water* (2004), which mostly recalls her song collecting between 1959 and 1960 in Appalachia (which was like "going back in time") with Alan Lomax, who later proposed to her (Collins, *America* 86). Rather than becoming his muse, Collins recognized that marrying Lomax would make her a non-entity: "I would be living his life, not mine" (*All* 105). Thus, defying convention, she conjures a more radical inner version of *Jane Eyre*: "Reader I didn't marry him" (*America* 20). Amid omnipresent racism and the threat of the KKK, they record at Parchman prison farm and discover Mississippi Fred McDowell. *All in the Downs* was written during Collins's recent "renaissance" after "my time in the wilderness," the nearly four decades when she was silent, following the humiliations she suffered when singing in concerts during the collapse of her marriage to Ashley Hutchings of Fairport Convention and Steeleye Span (187, 217). Rediscovering her voice around 2014 with the assistance of David Tibet of Current 93 led to her successful album *Lodestar* (2016) and a cascade of honors from the MBE, honorary degrees from the Open and Sussex universities, and BBC awards, one presented by Blur's Graham Coxon. Even with her now aged, deepened voice, she is confident in knowing "how to 'tell' a song," and feels in solidarity with generations of singers who were mostly poor, rural women (217), though she does not consider the inventedness and manipulation of the Victorian folk revival (Colls and Heathman 751–69). Collins's sense of being a "conduit," "a link in a mysterious chain," however, had been challenged earlier by folk purists like Peggy Seeger and Ewan MacColl (156), and she includes what may be the obligatory account of MacColl's inept attempts at seduction. While keeping to an unforced, affectless, almost ethnographic style of singing, Collins's willingness to experiment with instrumental accompaniment, including the raga embellishments of Davy Graham on *Folk Roots, New Routes* (1964), drew the ire of the folk preservation purists: "the knives were out from the MacColl gang" (119). She refused respected producer Joe Boyd's recommendation that she "*sell* the song a bit more," but she welcomed the new tone colors added by the ISB's Mike Heron and Robin Williamson, who have produced their own autobiographical works[56]: "They played percussion on Indian finger cymbals, African drum, Japanese finger sticks, and Robin on whistle and chanter," and "you couldn't help but love them and their music; beautiful, fey, Celtic, funny, and perhaps above all, wise" (127). While Shirley's sister Dolly added flute-organ on the ISB's masterwork *The Hangman's Beautiful Daughter* (1968), extra-musical suggestions created tension as "when Robin tried to persuade her [Dolly] to take some LSD, telling her that she couldn't see trees properly until she took the drug" (128). In this period, Collins also met with a flirtatious Jimi Hendrix, "handsome, playful, teasing, sweet and graceful" who whispered "I can see why John married you" (138). A little later, she would associate with less successful bands such as the Sussex Pistols—not to be confused with those other Pistols—at a time when audiences called for covers of folk hits, such as those by Pete Seeger and Judy Collins, when Scottish or Irish, rather than English, traditional music was most popular. Traveling solo to out-of-town gigs, even with a banjo in hand, she was sometimes accosted by the police and accused of being a prostitute.

The respected polymath artist and avant-garde noise musician Kim Gordon titles her memoir *Girl in a Band* to critique such assumptions about women in the popular music industry, where the woman onstage benefits the music label if she "sucks in the male gaze" rather than being independent and "kick-ass" (4, 127).[57] Looks, not musical chops, also garnered media attention initially for the all-female Go-Go's, according to Belinda Carlisle's memoir, *Lips Unsealed*.[58] Like *Girl in a Band*, *The Only Girl*, the title of Robin Green's memoir, sub-titled *My Life and Times on the Masthead of Rolling Stone*, points to the sexism in the popular music publishing industry at a time when "my relations with men were, in large part, how I experienced the world" and "I slept with almost every man I met" (146, 144), until her refusal to publish a story in which a Kennedy penis had a cameo got her fired.[59] Gordon touches on what might have been a moment of female solidarity when she was invited to produce the "car crash" Courtney Love and her band Hole's album *Pretty on the Inside* (1991), recognizing that Gordon brought genuine indie cred to the project (9, 189–91), but she mainly details her years in Sonic Youth whose duration reflected that of her marriage to co-founder Thurston Moore. Her memoir may resemble the popular music autobiography equivalent of revenge porn,[60] after the end of her nearly three-decade-long marriage following her discovery of Moore's extra-marital affair. The memoir offers an apologia to fans about the demise of an eccentric and much-loved band. Gordon and Moore were the Bacall and Bogart, John and Yoko, or Sid and Nancy of the indie rock scene, a role Love attempted to reproduce with Kurt Cobain. Gordon especially resents Moore's post-breakup "rock star showboating"—anathema to Sonic Youth's indie ethos—in the band's final shows, and she adamantly rejects the "supportive, stand-by-your-man role" (3, 6). She seems to blame herself for being surprised by Moore's betrayal, while being hypersensitive to the therapy-industry's and pop psychology's assessment of "self-blame." She acutely resents their romance, which inevitably mimics the story of Sonic Youth, being transformed into a celebrity marriage cliché. While she details her seemingly conventional middle-class upbringing in California—despite her brother's worsening schizophrenia and her acute awareness of "the darkness shimmering beneath the shiny quilt of American pop culture"—and relates her notes about Sonic Youth's career, Gordon's focus obsessively returns to a kind of self-therapy, questioning the misinterpreted relationship pattern of the "codependent woman" and "narcissistic man" (141, 113). Like Chrissie Hynde, since the writing of her memoir Gordon has also been increasingly involved in graphic art.

Chrissie Hynde's memoir *Reckless* is presented with disconcerting facetiousness as a Pretender's "reckless life" by "your hapless narrator" (117). Her pose of daredevil defiance, like some aspects of her portrayal of punk as a "bluff" or of rock as requiring "gimmicks," is leavened by her self-portrayal as an often "obnoxious" "idiot," "dummkopf," "phony" "public loser number one," and "complete pain in the ass" (256, 218, 295, 180, 187, 235, 229, 296). She does live up to her own billing in descriptions of dangerous acts such as accepting a ride from a stranger in Cleveland, "[h]aving no previous engagements in my social calendar for the afternoon," and then being dosed with mescaline, robbed, possibly raped, and threatened with murder (180). Her potty-mouthed self-assertion as an under-achiever—"I was a total prick when I was drunk" (297)—belies her regret at disregarding her parents or offending them with her language but primarily her guilt at the overdose deaths of her bandmates James Honeyman-Scott and Pete Farndon which cast a shade over the memoir's madcap hilarity. Hynde led a peripatetic life prior to creating a band resembling a "motorcycle club with guitars" (237). She was a rock music journalist for *NME* and clerked at Vivienne Westwood's SEX shop in London, learning of fashion's incestuous relationship with popular music, the wisdom of not dating members of your own band or bringing significant others on tour or performing stoned, and that "a shitty original is still better than a good cover" and that "song-writing credits are the number-one reason bands break up" (216, 242).

Hynde presents an unsentimental portrait of the gutting of community in her hometown of Akron, Ohio to be replaced by mindless materialism and social conformity. However, she points out that the popular version of a counterculture critique of such values among weekend hippies or wanna-be punks from the suburbs was mainly some shared, half-understood reference points and an excuse to be self-indulgent with sex and drugs. Hedonism grew from nihilism—not idealism. Far more than a celebration of rock music or rock icons or even veganism, "in the end, this story is a story of drug abuse" (115). She falls in love with a fantasy of England as a wacky, old-fashioned, socialist paradise, while recognizing that her true object of desire, 1960s London, is extinct. Her fantasy resembles in reverse the Americana obsession of the Kinks' Ray Davies, as detailed in some of his life writing.[61] Hynde had a child with Davies, though her plan for their wedding "should have been enacted only onstage in the theatre of the absurd" (305). She witnesses the birth of British punk and the rise of the Clash, the Damned, the Slits, and the Sex Pistols, whose Johnny Rotten and Sid Vicious both offer to marry her so that she can remain in England, though she earlier had declined Malcolm McLaren's offer to join a band. There are walk-ons by Johnny Thunders, John Belushi, and Timothy Leary. For Hynde, as for Debbie Harry, rock is distinctly male, and the closest approximation to being a guy is to be in a rock band (117).[62] The memoir thus narrates a weird type of penis envy or in this case Iggy Pop-envy, with equal measures fantasy and ambition. Here, the phallus is a power symbol and also the emblem of the trickster, clown, or lord of disorder and misrule.[63] Hynde comes to see that her role in a rock band would have to foreground "[m]y natural androgyny" and "be something that transcended gender" (167, 193).

Popular music celebrity

Popular music's development since the 1950s has kept pace with the growing ubiquity of celebrity culture and may even have electrified its frenzy. Celebrity itself may be the loose baggy monster of cultural studies and other interdisciplinary offshoots due to its ever-changing and paradoxically self-important ephemerality and also its broad reach. Celebrity studies tackles questions of celebrity's genealogy, rationale, and social consequences; its manifestations in creative cultures from celluloid to vinyl and in individuals from political leaders to death row inmates; and the phenomenology of fan identification and star persona as well as the apparently universal desire to be famous if only for a quarter of an hour (Halpern).

Academic study of celebrity began in the mid-twentieth century (Marshall and Redmond 2–3), but while celebrity itself has classical origins, as Leo Braudy shows in *The Frenzy of Renown*, its modern form developed in the eighteenth and nineteenth centuries. Chris Rojek regards celebrity—whether achieved, ascribed, or attributed—as a consequence of modernity's questioning of religious faith and the fall of absolute monarchies, and also as a contingent component of late capitalism in that it caters, via an "ideology of heroic individualism," to alienated consumer citizens' desire for compensation and for something or someone to emulate (*Celebrity* 33, 198–9). Rojek isolates James Boswell's *Life of Samuel Johnson* (1791) as demonstrating "the birth of modern fandom" (*Celebrity* 121), and Joe Hagan even claims that *Rolling Stone* became Bob Dylan's Boswell, "whether he acknowledged it or not" (*Sticky* 135). Rojek points to *The Newgate Calendar* (1774) as constructing the rogue as notorious celebrity (*Celebrity* 119–20). He also examines a nineteenth-century version of present-day celebrity lifestyle gurus. Samuel Smiles' *Self Help* (1859) is an instructional, inspirational work, advocating self-discipline to ensure success by breaking through class barriers all the while illustrating its injunctions with anecdotes from the lives of celebrities in different fields who display distinctive national characteristics (Rojek, *Celebrity* 117–20).

The first international celebrity, however, may have been Lord Byron who possessed attributed celebrity as an aristocrat, achieved celebrity as a songwriter and poet especially after *Childe Harold's Pilgrimage* (1812) made him a star, and attributed celebrity due to his notoriety for rumored incestuous and same-sex affairs, as well as revolutionary adventures.[64] Byron's fame as a poet more than survived both the publication of his quasi-sexual autobiography *Don Juan* (1819) and the burning of his memoirs. Some celebrity scholars regard Byron as "the model for future popular music icons" (Marshall, "Introduction: Celebrity in the Digital Era" xvi), and the director of *Dont Look Back*, D.A. Pennebaker, said, "I saw Dylan as a Byronesque pop figure" (qtd. in Hajdu 249). In the late nineteenth century, Oscar Wilde created himself as a celebrity by deploying both photography and parody (of the Aesthetic movement) before earning fame through his plays, descending into infamy after his conviction for same-sex acts, and rising again more recently and more brilliantly than ever as the embodiment of the Irish colonial subaltern and Britain's most beloved gay martyr.[65] In this period, despite its surfeit of scandalous and supremely creative literary celebrities, Victorian Britain labored under a distinct musical inferiority complex that was possibly a reaction to musical great man-ism (or celebrity obsession) and particularly Beethoven or Wagner envy, though it did not affect the dominance of the piano in middle-class parlors. An earlier nineteenth-century guitar craze, however, witnessed a move from domestic to professional performance with interventions in guitar composition or concerts by celebrities like Paganini, Weber, and Berloiz, though it was popularized by Catalan virtuoso Fernando Sor (1778–1839) just prior to the peak of interest in 1835. Like Niccolò Paganini, Sor generated as much heat on the concert stage for his sexual allure as for his impassioned guitar playing, perhaps providing a model for later phallo- or pyrotechnic displays (Lovesey, "The Victorian Guitar" 491–9).

Contemporary popular music stars' association with celebrity has a long history, extending to at least Frank Sinatra and enhanced by glamour photography and links with Hollywood star power.[66] Focus on the star musician followed the early twentieth century shift from sheet music and direct participation in music making to recordings and passive solitary listening, and hence the perception of a definitive recorded original (Marshall, "Meanings" 196–205).[67] This process accelerated in the 1960s when popular musicians began both performing and writing their own songs. The phenomenon of the Beatles would create a new type of celebrity (Marshall, "Celebrity" 163–75). The popularity and cultural capital of Sinatra would resemble that of later rock stars in terms of the importance of career longevity as well as back catalog and album (vs single) sales than might appear to be the case in the emphasis on seismic shifts according to the orthodoxy of "boomer historiography" (Keightley 376). Dylan has not only covered Sinatra's hits in a career stretching over half a century, but he also has recently sold his own back catalog of about six hundred songs to Universal Music for a rumored $300 million, though the wizards of back catalog marketing and repackaging must be the Beatles both collectively and individually. The 2021 "Uber Deluxe" fiftieth anniversary limited edition of George Harrison's *All Things Must Pass*, for example, includes gnome figurines and prayer beads. Dylan and the Beatles appealed to the developing rock market's taste for lengthy careers as "a kind of multi-faceted totality, in which each album may function as a quasi-autobiographical 'statement' in a longer star narrative" (Keightley 388). A critical distinction between older and newer versions of popular musicians' celebrity appears, too, in newer performance styles drawing on the folk tradition valuing authenticity, naturalness, and sincerity, as displayed by singers like Dylan and Joni Mitchell,[68] who wrote their own songs, and figures like Judy Collins and Joan Baez, who mostly drew from the traditional folk repertoire. Such performers

> constructed their authenticity around naturalness and the rejection of performance codes. Folk performers such as Joan Baez eschewed the concept of spectacle in dress and appearance to be more closely affiliated with the audience. Barefoot, without makeup, and wearing simple clothes, Baez would sing with only the accompaniment of an acoustic guitar. The stylistic configuration she portrayed was emulated by a generation of women.
>
> (Marshall, "Meanings" 204)

Baez was a star before she met Dylan, and she appeared in November 1962 on the cover of *Time* magazine.

Popular music celebrity took a great leap forward in acquiring a public face, however, with the covers of *Rolling Stone* as rock stars became like religious icons to fans. Rock stars assumed the notional "Jesus Christ Pose," however much that pose was designed, according to John Lennon and, later, Beatles' fan Chris Cornell, Soundgarden's "Errol Flynn of rock," to be a critique of rock star narcissism and overreaching celebrity culture itself.[69] Joe Hagan's recent biography of Jann Wenner, produced at his instigation and with his cooperation, shows how under Wenner's editorship *Rolling Stone* was engaged in a process of "reframing rock and roll as a celebrity culture" (508–9, 228). Hagan presents Wenner as a frustrated novelist and a closeted gay man with an overarching ambition and naked greed, who recognized his limitations as a rock critic and his need for the respectable stability of a straight marriage/business partnership, and later a private jet. His story embodies the rise but mostly the fall of 1960s countercultural idealism. Hagan traces the career of the fame-addicted Wenner, who would go on to purchase and transform the celebrity magazine *Us Weekly*, with its regular features such as "Stars: They're Just Like Us." Wenner developed from being a rock "groupie" or "starfucker" to being something of a celebrity in his own right, promoting and associating as an equal with his big three: Jagger, Springsteen, Bono (Hagan 479, 485). During Wenner's tenure, the magazine moved from being a politically radical, counterculture flagship to being a reflection of the celebrity status quo, as is evidenced by the subjects of its much coveted cover. On its one-year anniversary, *Rolling Stone* reprinted Lennon and Yoko Ono's nude "Two Virgins" self-portrait, and as Wenner gloated, "print a famous foreskin and the world will beat a path to your door" (qtd. in Hagan 168). Lennon himself, however, would take debonair cinema celebrity David Niven's autobiographical reminiscences as his model for an aborted life writing project as Kenneth Womack explains, though a version of this project eventually may have surfaced in his unfinished musical, ultimately published as "The Ballad of John and Yoko" in *Skywriting by Word of Mouth* (*John Lennon* 44–9).[70] By the end of Wenner's tenure, *Rolling Stone*'s cover would feature the populist Donald Trump, whose election "signaled the complete triumph of celebrity culture over every aspect of American life" (Hagan, *Sticky* 503). Unwittingly or otherwise, the magazine witnessed or helped to curate the shift in politics and popular music's celebrity fortunes.

Andy Warhol, who was the Velvet Underground's self-appointed manager despite Brian Epstein's interest (DeCurtis, *Lou* 104), may have anticipated celebrity's contemporary ubiquity in his koan-like utterance "[i]n the future everybody will be world famous for fifteen minutes" (qtd. in Gopnik 605). It was one of a series of disembodied epigrams in the catalog of his retrospective exhibition in Stockholm in February 1968 at which the Velvets were scheduled to perform. There is profound ambivalence in Warhol's apparently democratic idea, because if in the future everyone will be famous, then no one will be really famous. Mechanically reproduced, fame itself will cease to exist. Warhol's *Diaries*, which originated as a logbook of expenses,[71] frequently refer to people's misremembering and misquoting the famous statement (162), and its own provenance is questionable, given that Warhol was surrounded by articulate courtiers who voiced his thoughts, his books were ghostwritten, and everything emerging from the Factory, regardless of his input, displayed the "Warhol" label. Moreover, Warhol's remark about fame is just one of his ex-cathedra pronouncements, such as that in the future "everything will be art" and that the artist is also a work of art (qtd. in Gopnik 472), a project to which he dedicated himself as celebrity artist. To a degree, even his society portraits were expensive autographs, allowing sitters to display the instantly recognizable Warhol brand. Moreover, his own never-satisfied celebrity obsession—he'd written fan mail as a child—was tied to a fawning regard for blue-blooded Americans with pedigrees and famous names. Associating with them potentially might just create a different genealogy from that of a descendant of impoverished immigrants from Ruthenia in the Carpathian Mountains near Transylvania.

Warhol's name ensured that the Velvet Underground secured a record contract, and, as even the notoriously curmudgeonly Lou Reed acknowledged (DeCurtis, *Lou* 87; Cale and Bockris 92), Warhol empowered the band's adherence to radical artistic integrity or to being "un-user-friendly" in their participation in Warhol's multimedia total work of art, the Exploding Plastic Inevitable (Gopnik 503).[72] Warhol's rock album covers added avant-garde cache, and those for the Velvets' first album and the Rolling Stones' *Sticky Fingers* evoked the "Power of the Penis," as one of Warhol's circle at Max's Kansas City framed it (Corey Tippin qtd. in Gopnik 542). Warhol's cover for the Stones' *Love You Live* hints at S&M. As with Warhol's early films, these album covers participate in the mainstreaming of homoerotic imagery and pornography, the latter as in some more recent films by Lars Von Trier, for example.[73] In other areas, too, Warhol's was the art of the voyeur, moving from reconstructions of omnipresent commercial design and representations of divas of stage and screen to human "landscapes" or "still lives" of genitals and anuses, as well as paintings made with urine, semen, or feces. The Velvets' John Cale recalls asking Warhol for a post-Velvets' album cover and Warhol responding, "I'll get Yoko Ono to pose naked with you and we'll call it John and Yoko" (qtd. in Gopnik 448). For a quintessentially gay artist, like Little Richard, Liberace, or Elton John, however, Warhol was surprisingly homophobic. His diaries, mostly written as AIDS was emerging, obsess over others' sexual orientation and whether they are fairies, fags, nellies, or those with "a problem" (Colacello 42), and his personal objects of desire were young, straight all-American males. His aspirational amours appear in striking contrast to his envy of the "modern marriage" of photographer Christopher Makos and artist Peter Wise (*Diaries* 523, 526, 528). The real "queering of Pop Art" would be accomplished less by Warhol than by artists like David Wojnarowicz, whom we shall consider in Chapter 4 (Blinderman, "Conversation" 80).

Warhol was a conceptual artist provocateur whose Duchampean work questions the nature of art, the value of originality versus repetition, and the notion of the artist as a genius with a muse-inspired vision versus one obsessed with money and celebrity. He created an instantly recognizable anti-art image which in hindsight represents the psychedelic decade of post-abstract impressionism, though he grandly declared Pop Art finished in the early 1960s and retired as a painter in 1965. Warhol's portraits and even his most famous album covers are religious icons for a secular age when celebrities such as Elvis or Marilyn and even Mao are worshipped and pop stars are more popular than Jesus. Making repetition central to his celebrity image production echoed the multiplication of icons in the Eastern Orthodox Church, challenged the uniqueness of the original work of art, and almost undermined celebrity itself. Warhol's *Diaries* read like pages from a celebrity magazine, such as his own *Interview* which was modeled on *Rolling Stone* (Colacello 5–6), or a gushing, confidential high school social calendar. A good party, as he says, is one where "[e]verybody was somebody" (*Diaries* 344), and though he was obsessed with transvestites, the Factory's "superstars" were in his terms "nobodies." He meets people and notes who they're wearing, whether they have gained or lost weight, the state of their complexion and make-up, their relationship status, and what drugs they're on. His frantic social life was mandated by a desire to star gaze, to attract $25,000 commissions for his society portraits, and to gauge others' reactions to him as a measure of his own status and whether he's being invited to act in a TV show or reduced to being a TV game show question (*Diaries* 277). While it made him rich and fed his hoarding instinct, Warhol's mid-1970s concentration on celebrity and commerce alienated the art world (Colacello 266).

Popular music's association with celebrity triggered a disregard for popular music autobiographies within both musicology and autobiography studies as we have seen in earlier sections of this introduction. Autobiography, moreover, is largely ignored within celebrity studies itself (DeAngelis and Desjardins

489). If popular musicians are perceived as circulating only within a closed celebrity orbit, popular music autobiographies are readily dismissed. These autobiographies become merely vehicles to garner publicity for promotion, and in effect they become monograph-length extensions of the celebrity autograph. Perhaps most damning of all, they can be viewed as existing for fans only. In his memoir, Wilco's Jeff Tweedy humorously undercuts the "fans only" caution directly. Perhaps channeling a more ironic, self-aware Holden Caulfield or a version of the self-deprecating persona Moby adopts as we shall see in Chapter 3, Tweedy notes preposterously that "if you're a fan of mine, then you've presumably been enticed to read this book by the hypersexual nature of Wilco's oeuvre, and you've probably been wondering when I'm going to get around to the scintillating details of my sex life and, in particular, how I lost my virginity" (128). This is particularly ironic for a post-recovery frontman of a rootsy band of everyman alt-rockers and a memoir which as the *Times Literary Supplement*'s review put it "is like hanging out with a super-smart friend you used to get high with but who, now that he's on the wagon, is even funnier and wiser" (Winters 30). However, whatever expectations readers bring to music people's autobiographies, there is an attempt to cater to their requirements for the full back story or back catalog. Cross-marketing has been part of the sales pitch, and the perception of popular music autobiography as a type of supplementary souvenir or "merch," like the concert T-shirt, is promoted by the spin-offs advertised with some autobiographies. Robbie Robertson's *Testimony*, for example, appeared in 2016 at the same time as a compilation of his songs for the project. Elton John's 2021 8-CD *Jewel Box* set includes tracks discussed in his 2019 memoir *Me*. Bruce Springsteen's memoir *Born to Run* of 2016 has developed in the two years since its publication into something resembling "my life, the musical." Springsteen's autobiography has multiple paratexts or extra-textual epitexts, moving it from between the covers of a book into performative readings at bookstores, an audiobook with musical transitions, a Broadway show, and a Netflix biopic (Laura Watson). The Broadway show revealed a warts and all portrait of or confession by Springsteen as an individual who very deliberately invented his image as everyone's favorite working class hero and reluctant rock star.[74] Although his autobiographical project lies somewhere between Wagner's total art or *gesamtkunstwerk* and a Kardashian-worthy product diversification branding exercise, significantly, Springsteen's fan base resembles a religious cult, and they dance in the dark but also pray and presumably pay together.

In celebrity studies terms, popular music autobiographies constitute or aim for a type of "reality-effect" as when the celebrity attempts to step out from the realm of his or her celebrity image (Marshall, "Introduction" 3); however, as Rojek points out, this sleight of hand is impossible because the celebrity's public face or mask cannot be removed to expose the real life within, given that "wearing a 'front' is the inescapable condition of celebrity" (*Celebrity* 83–9). While in *Pop Music, Pop Culture*, Rojek reminds us that behind every rock star, as for Springsteen, there is a steadfast fan base, a music industry, and an innovative sound technology, and that popular music is created within well-established modes and often collaboratively, he tends to disregard individual music composers as functionaries or situated operatives within networks of production, exchange, circulation, and consumption. He ignores popular music autobiographies even in his discussion of "textual avatars" or of internet celebrity sites selling books (190, 202), but importantly he does allow that composers' lives can provide a "cultural biography" of their era, and that they can operate along with their music "as lightning rods channelling much wider questions of culture, economy, politics and society" (19, 152, 213). He suggests, moreover, that the "digital revolution" has reduced the importance of or even disappeared the rock star, and that one of the outcomes of this change has been "the liberation of fans" or at least the recognition of "fan labour" in creating the star in the first place (148, 213). However, as other celebrity scholars have noted, the digital economy may have enabled even closer connection between producers and consumers. Popular musicians have engaged with the contemporary, interactive model of the "presentational self," characteristic of the new social mediascape as Marshall makes clear ("New Media" 634–44). This new technology also has created, among the Beatles' fandom, for example, an emerging generation of "fan-scholars," as Jeffrey Roessner argues (223). Toija Cinque, in addition, considers how the perception of a celebrity musician's virtual, online presence affects the experience of listening to digital music. While music's digitization "deterritorializes the star performer," it may also enhance the listener's awareness of the music's creator (441). For members of the "'it should be free' generation" (Peter Green qtd. in Cinque 449), it may be more "possible to 'absorb' the essence of the star, by a kind of 'osmosis' or cultural identification" (449).

The popular musician as a rebel with three chords—or Pro Tools—and the truth is as much a part of the rock star mythology as the sex, drugs, and rock 'n' roll stereotype and perhaps equally as questionable. Popular musicians, however, have traded on a guise of authenticity, however constituted, along with a type of notorious, shamanistic, transgressive, or scandalous image associated with an anti-heroic, bohemian outsider status. Part of this "alternative" posture is disdain for celebrity and celebrity culture itself as an entrenched, manipulative aspect of the status quo, and a perception of their own celebrity as an unwanted by-product rather than a goal of musical apprenticeship. Some musicians, of course, have used their celebrity platform to raise funds for worthy causes, as in the case of George Harrison's 1971 Concert for Bangladesh, or to harness social activism. Popular music autobiographies, in fact, often aim at de-celebrification, though their writers will remain celebrities whose own youthful images retain their selling power as witnessed by their placement on the covers of their life writing. Sometimes, as the next chapter explains, rock stars attempt to escape the rigors, indignities, and distortions of celebrity or fame within the entertainment industry juggernaut by pathways leading to drug addiction. Addiction thus becomes a way to disenable the incursions of unwelcome celebrity.

As this book argues, popular music autobiographies sometimes aspire to cross the line between twenty-first-century acquired or attributed celebrity and an older model of achievement-based fame. This model distinguishes celebrity, as indicating a highly temporary and insubstantial recognition, and fame, as indicating lasting renown within established fields such as military victory or recognized achievement in literary or artistic fields (Braudy; Wesołowski). Popular music autobiographies sometimes demonstrate a desire to transform celebrity—its cost the forfeiture of seriousness—into lasting fame in traditionally sanctioned forms. Despite its deep roots, as we have seen, autobiography itself is a fairly recent literary genre, and no area of cultural production is now immune from celebrity's encroachment. Moreover, even literary seriousness has registered negative impacts in postmodern celebrity culture (G. Davidson 293–308), and respected writers like Salman Rushdie "have extended the cult of personality, so that their public image arguably has more public recognition than their work" (Rojek, *Celebrity* 129). Moreover, popular music autobiographies, like virtual interaction with songwriters and the images of MTV and YouTube, are now an inalienable part of the experience of listening to popular music.

Overview

Popular Music Autobiography aims to show the significance of life writing by musicians and writers of popular music, an overlooked aspect of the memoir boom of the past three decades. This first chapter has attempted to introduce the broad contexts of this examination. The project's inevitably preliminary and selective interventions in this field will unfold in the following chapters.

Chapter 1, "Disenabling Fame: Rock 'n' Recovery Autobiographies and Disability Narrative," argues that a number of popular music autobiographies claim that drugs were a resource to mediate the outrageous demands of fame in the entertainment industry for individuals who did not become musicians to gain celebrity. While the writing of a post-addiction narrative may have become part of a popular musician's career trajectory and it may even serve to enhance celebrity status, the seeds of addiction itself often were planted earlier with the romantic myth of the artist and the aura of the rock star. In the context of an examination of the place of addiction within disability and autobiography studies, this chapter tackles the rock 'n' recovery narratives of 1960s musicians like Eric Clapton and Marianne Faithfull and their later echo in the rock 'n' recovery narratives of the stars of the Hollywood bands Red Hot Chili Peppers, Mötley Crüe, and Guns N' Roses.

Chapter 2, "'A Cellarful of Boys': The Swinging Sixties, Gay Managers, and the Other Beatle," considers Brian Epstein's *A Cellarful of Noise* (1964), ghostwritten by Derek Taylor, as a quasi-Victorian autobiography that masks as much as it reveals its subject. It does inadvertently expose the internalized homophobia in the period between 1957's Wolfenden Report and 1967's Sexual Offences Act in the ostensibly sexually liberated 1960s. This chapter explores the queer gaze of Epstein and managers such as Joe Meek and Kit Lambert in assessing potential pop star clients against the expectations of fans and the dangers of associating too closely with stars.

Chapter 3, "Performative Identity: Cosey Fanni Tutti, Brett Anderson, Moby," argues for the centrality of a constructed persona of different types in popular music autobiographies by post-punk, post-glam musicians of the late 1970s, 1980s, and early 1990s whose music often intersected with other arts and displayed a theoretical self-consciousness. The writers address their own image as performing artists in works of life writing in which there is also a performative identity in play. While they reject being spokespersons for a generation, they do situate their creative expression among cultural sub-groups within particular, localized scenes, and they are forthcoming about their involvement with prostitution, domestic abuse, and addiction, and in their responses to charges of fascist or queer posturing.

Chapter 4, "Performative Identity: Patti Smith, David Wojnarowicz," explores performative identity in two hugely creative artists whose work emerged in New York's cultural renaissance of the 1970s and 1980s. In punk and no-wave manifestations of post-1960s rock, Patti Smith and David Wojnarowicz embraced a confrontational, DIY aesthetic, melding their interests in poetry, photography, and painting with the violent immediacy of anti-pop music forms. Both Smith and Wojnarowicz were influenced by the lives and work of Arthur Rimbaud and William Burroughs, and also by photography which was gaining recognition as an art form. Each was both a photographer and a subject of one of the two most famous and even infamous American photographers, Robert Mapplethorpe and Peter Hujar, both of whom died during the AIDS plague of the 1980s and 1990s. Smith and Wojnarowicz experimented freely in their music and their autobiographical writings, but while Smith would become an esteemed figure in the literary establishment, Wojnarowicz may be best remembered for his final artistic interventions in ACT UP.

Chapter 5, "The Invention of Bob Dylan and the Archival Autograph," argues that autobiography is central to Bob Dylan's work in his self-creation as "Bob Dylan," and in the construction of his Archive, his songs, his auto-fiction *Tarantula*, and his memoir, *Chronicles*. To differing degrees, these autobiographical sites demonstrate a multiple identity as in Rimbaud's "Je est un autre" (qtd. in White, *Rimbaud* 185, but they also indicate the significance of relational identity in his work. Dylan increasingly seems committed to acknowledging sources and influences—unlike the previously sparse acknowledgment for which he has sometimes been criticized—and even making reparations. His memoir perhaps uniquely sets out the sources and well-springs of particularly his extraordinary creativity in the 1960s. While remaining true to his roots in popular music, Dylan has gone on to achieve fame in the field of literature as Nobel laureate.

Notes

1 Theodore Roszak refers to "generation" as "the most unwieldy of social categories" (*Elder* 22).
2 While, as Maria DiBattista and Emily Wittman noted in 2014, "autobiography has become more hospitable to the ludic, the relativistic, the patchwork, the highly experimental, and the highly self-conscious" (14), the general absence of attention in autobiography studies may attest to ambivalence about popular culture, a

lingering regard for formal innovation, and an uneasiness about popular musicians in particular as being tainted by commerce, celebrity, kitsch, and the jouissance of ludic performance. In a study of the memoir boom in terms of its modes of industrial production which commodified identity, Julie Rak briefly mentions musicians' life writing as part of celebrity culture, and she refers to Keith Richards' autobiographical *Life* as a ghostwritten memoir (207–8).

3 Elsewhere in the volume, they briefly refer to works by musicians as "celebrity autobiographies" or "self-advertisements," though making a partial exception of Dylan's "genuinely innovative" *Chronicles*: "In 2007, a veritable barrage of narratives by musicians whose fame was earned in the 1960s and 1970s hit the bookstores in time for holiday shoppers. Bob Dylan is one of the luminaries whose autobiographical stories have become best-sellers. In the contemporary commodification of culture, the growth industry in self-advertisement ensures that celebrities can cash in on the memoir boom. Some satisfy readerly desires for gossip and vicarious immersion in a fantasy world of drugs, sex, and rock and roll. Many are written only to capitalize on fleeting fame and possibly rejuvenate it" (162–3).

4 Within academic journals, Thomas Swiss's brief article from 2005 in *Popular Music* on the "neglected" subject of "rock autobiographies" (287), notes their collaborative authorship, identity construction, and relatability, concluding that interpreting rock autobiographies resembles interpreting rock songs. Daniel Stein and Martin Butler's 2015 edited special issue of *Popular Music and Society* offers a broadly based survey of the field, including jazz and hip-hop.

5 See, too, Andy Bennett's "Identity: Music, Community, and Self" and Tia DeNora's influential *Music in Everyday Life* as well as her more recent research on music and self-therapy in *Music Asylums*. An extensive overview of the notion of musical identities appears in the recent *Handbook of Musical Identities*, edited by Raymond MacDonald, David J. Hargreaves, and Dorothy Miell.

6 Persona Studies may suggest ways of conceptualizing the relationship of life writing and music. In addition to listeners' awareness of a work of music's author and performer, and because music is embodied social communication, listeners personify or persona-fy music, affording it an "emotive persona": "music pushes people to discern an emotional meaning relating to a character-like persona as they interpret music and its affective formations into sentiments" (Fairchild and Marshall 5).

7 Patti Smith's *Just Kids* won the 2010 National Book Award, Keith Richards' *Life* won the 2011 Norman Mailer Prize, and Kendrick Lamar won the 2018 Pulitzer Prize for Music.

8 Laura Marcus notes that "'[a]utobiography' continues to be used as a generic marker and in book titles" (7), though the field has extended far beyond Philippe Lejeune's classic 1975 definition of autobiography as a "retrospective prose

narrative written by a real person concerning his own existence, where the focus is his individual life, in particular the story of his personality" (4). G. Thomas Couser distinguishes the more "selective" memoir from the more "comprehensive" autobiography (*Memoir* 24, 15–32). Despite their misgivings, Smith and Watson, the well-established and revered "Smith and Wesson of autobiography studies," according to Tim Adams, continue to use the term ("Personal" xlv).

9   In "an age of narcissism," William Gass in 1994 lamented the proliferation of banal life writing. Nancy K. Miller explained the memoir boom as "voyeurism for a declining, imperial narcissism" (qtd. in Rak 15).

10 In this context, see Simon Reynolds' insightful *Retromania*. See, too, a discussion of this phenomenon in association with the retro band par excellence in Lovesey's "Pop Art at Woodtock: Sha Na Na." Kristin Hersh evokes something similar in her phrase "a syringe of déjà vu" (12).

11 *David Crosby: Remember My Name* demonstrates Crosby's contrition and is a gesture of reconciliation but also a marketing ploy for his latest albums, extracts from which in the biopic show how much they might have profited from Stephen Stills' gifts as producer, arranger, and musician. Crosby laments: "All the main guys that I made music with won't even talk to me. … One of them hating my guts could be an accident. McQuinn, Nash, Neil, and Stephen all really dislike me strongly."

12 Halford has trademarked this phrase and also used it for his heavy metal clothing line (316–17). With camp bravado, he also refers to himself as "the stately homo of heavy metal" due to his admiration for Quentin Crisp, or as a "gay-metal-pop-tart" due to his love for divas (3, 324).

13 David Byrne gives a brief account of the band's career as part of the story of his musical evolution in *How Music Works*, though it is not an autobiography (36–59).

14 Some compendiums or extracts from popular music autobiographies and interviews cater to this appetite. See, for example, Jacob Hoye's *Smoke, Snort, Swallow, Shoot: Legendary Binges, Lost Weekends, and Other Feats of Rock 'n' Roll Incoherence*; Jim Driver's *The Mammoth Book of Sex, Drugs and Rock 'n' Roll*; Jake Brennan's *Disgraceland: Musicians Getting Away with Murder and Behaving Very Badly*; and Lizzy Goodman's *Meet Me In The Bathroom: Rebirth and Rock and Roll in New York City 2001–2011*.

15 A notable exception demonstrating the breadth of the field is Salman Ahmad's *Rock & Roll Jihad, A Muslim Rock Star's Revolution*, detailing the unusually privileged, if sometimes terrifying, migratory upbringing of the Pakistani-American musician whose Sufi *qawwali* rock was inspired partly by Led Zeppelin. However, Ahmad would inspire others' "rags-to-raja" narratives (96).

16 Smith and Watson's introduction to their 2016 collection *Life Writing* notes that their "reliance on the term 'autobiography' in essays from the 1990s now makes us cringe" (xxi), and they point to a wider problem relating to terminology: "[n]ow, of course,

even the terms 'life narrative' and 'life writing' seem too limited for the ever-increasing modes of presenting, performing, imaging, and circulating a 'life' in the multimedia of graphic memoir, performance art, visual art, and online platforms" (xxii).

17 See, too, Smith and Watson's *Reading Autobiography* (215–16, 248, 278–79).
18 Recent expansion in modes of self-representation has stretched the boundaries of terminology to where it may reinforce Paul de Man's self-interested scepticism ("Autobiography as De-Facement") or that of other pioneers in the field such as James Olney (DiBattista and Wittman 2). In addition to life writing in a myriad of blogs, documentary forms, and social media platforms (Anderson, *Autobiography* 114; Hayes 233–56; Cappello 246), there are widely circulated interviews such as the notorious one with virtuoso guitarist and songwriter John Mayer, who regards Eric Clapton as a mentor, referring to his penis as a "white supremacist" ("John Mayer's Penis Speaks!"), as well as collective documentary-style biographies such as Metallica's *Some Kind of Monster* (2004). David McCooey's introductory "The Limits of Life Writing" provides a brief overview of the recent expansion of the genre and its critical interventions.
19 Dylan's 1967 "I Dreamed I Saw St. Augustine" recasts the protest song "I Dreamed I Saw Joe Hill" (Hampton 114), which Dylan discusses in *Chronicles* (52–4).
20 Adam Becker suggests "Acknowledgments" for the title (23). Wills cautions against other common misinterpretations of the *Confessions*, in addition to its title (xiii–xx), noting that Augustine reads his own past accompanied by a tissue of biblical reflections, because "[f]or Augustine, the recovered self is a transcended self" (95).
21 While perhaps anticipating Burroughs' usage in *Naked Lunch* and the stage shenenagans of Canadian pop band Bare Naked Ladies, Augustine does not blame such practices for the fall of the Roman empire, though elsewhere in this massive tome, he does blame the gruesome and licentious performances of the Roman arena and circus, highly addictive to viewers, as well as a more general devotion to pagan religious beliefs, for the decline.
22 See Wills on this incident (47).
23 See Kenneth Womack's *Long and Winding Roads* (152–3), William Northcutt's "The Spectacle of Alienation" (130–2), and Marshall's "The Celebrity Legacy of the Beatles" (507) on the nearly catastrophic effect of Lennon's remark.
24 "[T]he first black British woman to escape from slavery" (Ferguson 1), Mary Prince (1788–1833?) in England dictated her story of being born a slave in Bermuda, her brutal treatment, and her work to emancipate herself to Susanna Strickland who acknowledges that she "pruned" and refined the text, though it remains "essentially her [Prince's] own" (Pringle 55). Strickland and others used Prince's autobiography, *The History of Mary Prince* (1831), for the work of the Anti-Slavery Society, and as

a result they may well have eliminated typical female slave testimony such as details of sexual exploitation and collective resistance.
25 Regarding "collaborative" life writing, in which the "collaborator" may function as editor, researcher, co-producer, censor, transcriber, interviewer, or coaxer, see Smith and Watson's *Reading Autobiography* (67–9, 240–1, 264–5).
26 As a woman, Kempe required authorization for her treatment of spiritual subjects, an "authority which literate authors derived from texts" (Lochrie 34–7, 39).
27 For example, Christ tells her "I must be intimate with you …. [Y]ou may boldly, when you are in bed, take me to you as your wedded husband …. [Y]ou can boldly … kiss my mouth, my head, and my feet as sweetly as you want" (126–7).
28 Kim Gordon's autobiography makes no mention of the song from 1992's album *Dirty*, which may be because it was sung by her ex-husband Thurston Moore, and the band was usually more concerned with contemporary celebrities and popular culture figures like Madonna.
29 Cohen—whom Dylan called the "Kafka of the blues" (qtd. in Light xiv) and who became a rock star in his eighties—finally wanted to restrict cover versions of the song, because its fame was apparently making him an incongruous version of the one-hit wonder, overlooking "Bird on a Wire," covered by Joe Cocker, and "Democracy," with its prescient line, "democracy is coming to the U.S.A." See Alan Light's extensive treatment of the song and its contexts in *The Holy and the Broken*.
30 In the collection of "journals, objects & ephemera," *Jeff Buckley: His Own Voice*, there is a list of Buckley's books including one volume by Cohen and autobiographies by Chuck Berry and Ray Charles (49). See, too, Lovesey's "Anti-Orpheus."
31 Being dead allows the life writer to "confess plainly what we were and what we failed to be," and has the "great advantage" that "while it leaves no mouth to laugh, nor does it leave eyes to weep" (Machado 69, 153). The highly self-conscious, metafictional, and allusive novel is a Brazilian *Tristram Shandy* with South American characteristics.
32 Cicero noted that "Socrates learned as an old man to play the lyre, that favourite instrument of the ancients" (57).
33 Wagner accepted Nietzsche initially as a disciple or acolyte, but later broke with him violently (Kaag 88).
34 John Kaag suggests, in his own autobiographical reflection, that all of Nietzsche's last books were partly autobiographical (144).
35 *Ecce Homo* may belong to what Michael Tanner calls "Nietzsche's self-mythologization" (90).
36 Loving one's fate or "*amor fati*" in his Latin phrase, is, he says, "my innermost nature" (94).

37 Foucault's friend, the philosopher Paul Veyne, to whom Foucault gave "the title of 'honorary homosexual,'" refers to Foucault as a disciple of Nietzsche's *The Gay Science*, and maintains that "Foucault's entire *oeuvre* is a continuation of Nietzsche's *Genealogy of Morality*" (138, 118, 110).

38 A year before his death, Foucault put this slightly differently: "Each of my works is a part of my own biography. For one or another reason I had the occasion to feel and live those things" ("Truth" 11). Foucault scholar Gary Gutting is suspicious of Miller's biographical "speculation" about Foucault (23–4).

39 Mathieu Lindon who belonged to Foucault's inner circle in Paris along with Hervé Guibert, "inventing new bonds of love and sex, bodies and feelings," gives evidence of Foucault's use of LSD in his memoir *Learning What Love Means*: "[t]hinking differently was … what he hoped to find in acid" (121, 235). See, too, Simeon Wade's *Foucault in California*.

40 Foucault's "Technologies of the Self" traces a movement from the classical admiration for knowing oneself via "self-exercise[s]" such as writing and dream analysis to Christian confession's emphasis on disclosure of thoughts and "bad intentions" and ultimately "self-renunciation" (27, 33, 22). Hence, a "Christian hermeneutics of the self" entails that "self-revelation is at the same time self-destruction" (46, 43).

41 The influential, nearly eight-hundred-page *Cultural Studies* anthology from 1992, edited by Lawrence Grossberg et al., devoted only one of forty essays to popular music. In this essay, Simon Frith noted that despite "the deep desire of intellectuals not to be intellectual," "pop music-making is deemed somehow less 'cultured' than classical music-making" partly because it is produced by the "proudly untaught and semi-skilled" ("Cultural Study" 182, 175). John Shepherd in 2012 lamented the disregard for popular music studies within Sociology, in the form of an autobiographical reflection (240–2). "Popular music," Charles Fairchild and P. David Marshall reminded us in 2019, "is still posited as a kind of subaltern, aesthetic 'other' to a European classical tradition" (12). Reconsiderations continue within musicology. Henry Stobart, for example, in 2008, emphasized the need to reform and de-exoticize ethnomusicology (2–20).

42 Charles Hamm calls Middleton's portrayal of musicology an "ahistorical" "caricature," and he intimates that Middleton fails to understand American popular music (389, 396).

43 Holiday does detail the evolution of "Strange Fruit," for example, as well as the myopic reactions of her audience such as when she is asked to "sing that sexy song you're so famous for … about the naked bodies swinging in the trees" (84).

44 Bohlman relates this tendency to sanitize or white-wash folk traditions to the construction of the myth of Appalachia as a *sprachin seln* or isolated "speech

island," an isolated remnant of European song (58): "The initial assertions that English ballads and dance genres were the archetypes of folk music in the Appalachians quickly became a surrogate tradition, spurring collectors to discover songs that would justify the appropriate classification systems, especially the system devised by [Francis] Child. As a result, many of the same collectors ignored the more popular black-influenced styles that were flourishing in the same region. Under Nazism in Germany during the 1930s and early 1940s, folk music classification declared a sort of independence from ethnography, thus allowing the establishment of claims that Germanic and Nordic folk music was somehow central to European folk music in general" (50).

45 Child included no musical notation in his groundbreaking five-volume *English and Scottish Popular Ballads* with its primary focus on textual variants. The challenges of transcribing folk and non-Western music accurately would preoccupy Seeger for much of his career (Rees 98–101) as would the relationship of music and language, "the linguocentric predicament" (Pescatello 280). Seeger's second wife, the composer Ruth Crawford Seeger later assisted Lomax with transcriptions, and she profoundly influenced Seeger's ideas about folk song transcription (Tick 112–21).

46 Child's research was based on a romantic sense of the ballads' original milieu as being undivided by class or print culture. The ballads for Child constituted a type of pre-history of written poetry, a "primitive" stage in the evolution of civilized culture, a view in line with that elucidated by Victorian anthropologist Edward B. Tyler. See Jill Terry Rudy on disputes over the ballads' origins in "the ballad wars," and her account of the pre-history of formalist English studies in folklore (535, 524–44).

47 Peggy Seeger who stayed with Karpeles briefly in Europe, recalls hearing that Sharp's assistant and advance guard entering Appalachia between 1916 and 1918 would announce: "Mr Sharp doesn't want to hear nigger music" (*First* 148).

48 Charles Seeger was investigated by the FBI in the 1950s due to his left-wing associations (Rees 104), and Pete Seeger appeared before HUAC (1947–57), led by Senator Joe McCarthy, whose lawyer Roy Cohn would mentor Donald Trump. Due to folk music's guilt by association with communism during the Red Scare (1947–57), "country" music would prevail over "folk" as a moniker for the music now associated with Nashville (Peterson 198–9). See, too, Jesse Jarnow's *Wasn't That A Time*.

49 Peggy Seeger shared her father's opinion, detailing an instance when she taught "Freight Train" to a couple who then copyrighted the song as if they had written it (104–5).

50 Speaking at Queen Elizabeth House in London at Peggy Seeger's eightieth birthday celebration, Davis noted her sons' participation, saying that she "responded to their

teasing by recalling the circumstances in which they were conceived. Game, set and match" (qtd. in Freedman 304).

51 MacColl, who was encouraged to write his autobiography by Alan Lomax, is far more detached in his recollection of meeting the woman who would eventually become his third wife: "Within six weeks Peggy and I had become close friends and during the next six months we worked together on a series of projects" (270).

52 In *The Mountain of the Women, Memoirs of an Irish Troubadour*, Liam Clancy recounts an impoverished Irish upbringing, but his primary ambition was to be an actor, and he became a successful folk singer almost by accident. He was virtually collected himself by the unstable, infatuated American heiress Diane Guggenheim who wanted "my body and my soul" and may have attempted "a kind of rape" followed by a suicide attempt (164–7). Together, they made field recordings of "waulking" songs in the Hebrides and later, with Paul Clayton, in Appalachia. Liam emerged with his brothers and Tommy Makem as well as figures like Dylan in the Greenwich Village scene prior to their appearance on *The Ed Sullivan Show*.

53 Ono told Lennon at their first meeting in November 1966 that she needed a "patron," according to Frederic Seaman (5). According to Lennon's lover May Pang, Ono later resented that her fame and fortune had come to depend totally on an emotionally unstable, sometimes abusive pop star, and that her artistic achievements were reduced to a cartoonish John and Yoko, peace and love caricature (242–5). Pang also claims that Lennon told her that Ono had pressured him to leave the Beatles and blocked a possible reunion at the Concert for Bangladesh (275, 45–6). Despite his later reunion with Ono after their separation, Lennon lacked inspiration in his final years, as he often had in the Beatles until impelled by McCartney's productivity and contractual demands. As Lennon's Dakota neighbor Rex Reed noted: "All he did was lie around stoned watching television" (qtd. in Womack, *John* 9). *Double Fantasy*, with Lennon's contributions initially inspired by envy for McCartney's "Coming Up" (Womack, *John* 98–100, 197), would require the scandal of Lennon's murder to become a hit. With the aid of *Rolling Stone*'s Jann Wenner, Ono successfully re-made the legend such that the Beatles' artistically restricted the avant-garde Lennon and that in his last years he willingly abandoned music for house husbandry (Hagan, *Sticky* 397–401).

54 An earlier account of her appearance with the ISB at Woodstock appears in "Scattered Brightness."

55 This is Goodman's phrase for the meaninglessness of growing up in the technocratic society of the late 1950s, but he addresses American young men, feeling that motherhood alone, with the provision for the role of muse in certain sub-cultures, supplies women meaning in society (*Growing* 21), and notoriously his educational program included sexual exploitation. He maintained, as he put it

elsewhere, "[t]he teacher-student relation is almost always erotic" ("The Politics" 223).

56 In his co-authored autobiography, *You Know What You Could Be*, Heron remarks on the ISB's idealistic view of America as the land of uninterrupted song: "We knew you couldn't take three strides without tripping over a rural bluesman, every church had a gorgeous gospel choir and families sat round in the evening singing Carter Family songs" (66). For Williamson's autobiographical works, see Lovesey's "The 'World' Before Globalization" (130).

57 While, in the band's early days, Gordon "had no technical ability to speak of" in playing music, she "did everything possible to maintain an identity as an individual within the band. I had no interest in being just the female half of a couple" (146).

58 Carlisle cites an early review noting her merely "adequate" voice, but gushing over her as "an energetic beauty with bee-stung lips and a Monroe-esque vulnerability" (58–9). The band in its underwear, photographed by Annie Leibovitz under the headline "Go-Go's Put Out," graced the cover of *Rolling Stone* in August 1982 (91). She details the band's trouble getting a record deal because they were considered a novelty act, though their first album would be number 1 on Billboard's album charts, the first by an all-female group, writing and performing its own songs. Some members bonded over antics like slipping menstrual blood into the drinks of desirable young men (71). Carlisle's memoir deals less with the band's music than with their in-fighting as well as her own cocaine addiction, spiraling from an abusive upbringing, eating disorder, panic attacks, and imposter syndrome.

59 Green's account is revealing about sexism in the 1960s, even in the underground, counterculture press, when pressures for sex, particularly after the Pill, and especially in a self-consciously bohemian, radical milieu, were ubiquitous, and refusal appeared old-fashioned, uptight, and even selfish. The memoir quickly becomes an autobiography as sexual history from masturbation and STDs, seducing professors and editors, and writing porn, to the quest for the Big O; but she refuses *Rolling Stone*'s desire for an account of her night with Robert Kennedy Jr. (13, 139–44). Green's story recalls John Cooke's memoir of Janis Joplin's desperate and sad interpersonal modus operandi, in which sexual conquest established control and reinforced a sense of self-worth (93, 111–15, 126, 170–1, 222–3, 333–5).

60 She refers to the interpersonal tension onstage, "this raw, weird pornography of strain and distance" (9).

61 See Lovesey's "The British Invasion of the Wild West" (172).

62 "Becoming a woman," Hynde writes, "was an obstacle that had horrified and dogged me throughout my teens, but I wasn't a guy and I was never going to be a

guy, which I had to accept. That meant I'd probably never play guitar in a band" (88).
63 Obsessed with Iggy Pop and Lou Reed, Hynde writes of her "sexual fantasies about … my rock-star heroes. I wanted to be them, not do them" (87). She details her encounter with Iggy, "the Big Daddy Jackpot," "this Class A piece of tail," "the Swedish-colored lord of sex and rock-and-roll" (286).
64 See Loren Glass's consideration of Byron as a brand (39–43), and Clara Tuite on Byron as a scandalous celebrity.
65 See Matthew Sturgis's remarkable biography *Oscar, A Life* and also Michèle Mendelssohn's *Making Oscar Wilde* which shows how America and Wilde's tour there made Wilde. Laura Lee's *Oscar's Ghost* demonstrates the struggle for Wilde's legacy.
66 See Chris Rojek's *Frank Sinatra*, Richard Dyer's *Stars*, and Leo Lowenthal's "The Triumph of Mass Idols."
67 Rock music's live performance has a secondary status to that of recordings which themselves mimic live performance and in effect perform authenticity, as performance scholar Philip Auslander argues, drawing on the insights of Simon Frith and Keith Negus (*Liveness* 74–7).
68 Mitchell in 2020 released her archival recordings as far as "Both Sides Now"; Dylan covered her hit "Big Yellow Taxi" on his 1973 album *Dylan*.
69 Later, Lennon would announce to the Beatles that he was Jesus Christ, as Womack points out (*Long* 218). Reiff discusses Cornell's interpretation of his song "Jesus Christ Pose" (136–7) and refers to photographer Jesse Frohman's remark about Cornell's charismatic resemblance to Flynn (qtd. on 153).
70 See, too, Womack's "Reconsidering Performative Autobiography: Life-Writing and the Beatles."
71 They were first designed for the IRS because Warhol's business had been audited in 1972, a procedure he believed was politically motivated, and the original typescript had receipts stapled to its pages (Hackett xviii). The diaries were written out by Warhol's secretary Pat Hackett based on her notes from daily phone calls with her boss (xix). The published diary of nearly 850 pages was edited down drastically from a document of twenty thousand pages (xx).
72 The *Diaries*' remarks on music are minimal, though Warhol obsesses about earning no money as producer of the Velvets' first record, and he's baffled by Lou Reed's contempt.
73 See Stephen Koch's *Stargazer* (47–51, 114–31).
74 Pamela Fox examines the conflicted self-construction and conflated life writing sub-genres in Springsteen's text, the memoir of a bipolar, multi-millionaire "poet laureate of the American working class" (123–4).

1

Disenabling Fame: Rock 'n' Recovery Autobiographies and Disability Narrative

Recent rock 'n' recovery autobiographies of addiction reveal a meditation on the pathology of fame. The writers' addictions inevitably belong to what has become a celebrity career trajectory of conspicuous excess leading to illness, rehab, and often relapse and then dramatic recovery that both valorizes artistic integrity and distracts from the muse. Increasingly, the autobiography of recovery is part of the celebrity cycle, though one of the most famous former addicts, Keith Richards—a former adman who turns on and off his wasted persona at will—has been notoriously contemptuous of recovery confessions, and his hyperbolic aphorisms about drugs and health have been collected in Mark Blake's *Stone Me: The Wit and Wisdom of Keith Richards*, and his own autobiography has appeared. Recent autobiographies by Eric Clapton, Marianne Faithfull, Ronnie Wood, Anthony Kiedis, and Slash, as well as the autobiographical works of Nikki Sixx and Kurt Cobain among others, are predicated on a romantic myth of the artist conspicuous for extreme excess that morphs into a shadow dance with death. The ideal of the heroic rock star—exploited in energy drinks, video games, and even presidential campaigns—is fit, youthful, and supremely abled, perhaps most famously exemplified in Joel Brodsky's "young lion" photograph of Jim Morrison. This stance of usually testosterone-driven virility is the equivalent of normalcy in illness narratives. To be a rock star is to live with blinding intensity as the object of universal envy, perhaps especially for those like John Lennon and Kurt Cobain with a fascinated dread of the physically disabled. The lust for life and passion for anarchy that celebrates the body electric, however, is an industry-driven and socially sanctioned pose, partly accepted, like ubiquitous celebrity culture itself, as a social cure for postmodern malaise.

These celebrity autobiographies of addiction, many appearing just as disability studies entered the mainstream, have an uncomfortable location within the "unstable" category of disability (Davis 23) and also a/b studies. In the context of a consideration of the cultural contexts of addiction, this chapter argues that the quantity and distinctive qualities of these rock 'n' recovery autobiographies suggest a distinct subgenre, given the complexity of altruistic and self-serving motives lying behind their creation, their hybrid genre, their construction of self, and perhaps most importantly, their highly ambivalent relationship to fame. These autobiographies attempt to reclaim their writers' lives from addiction and from the illness of fame.

Addiction as disability

Addiction has an uneasy location within disability studies, itself perhaps defined by instability and indeterminacy (Bérubé 338) and a close connection to narrative (Garland-Thomson 77). Like illnesses such as HIV/AIDS stigmatized as being acquired through sexual behavior, addiction—perhaps particularly celebrity addiction—is widely dismissed as "a calamity one brings on oneself" through a perverse lifestyle (Sontag, *Illness* 114). Drug addiction itself, however, is a fairly recent category of illness. The "invention" of drug addiction—the first usage of "addiction" relating to drugs in the *OED* appeared in 1906—at the turn of the century was concurrent with the rise of widespread anxieties about various "others": the deviant, the foreign, and the homosexual (Redfield and Brodie 3–6). Addiction has from the early twentieth century been associated with vice and criminality, and Nazi eugenicists grouped alcoholism with a vast range of "'defective' conditions" in their euthanasia campaigns (Muzak 256–7; Snyder and Mitchell 102, 122). The "pathologization and criminalization of habit" (Redfield and Brodie 4) grew out of the Victorian medicalization of private life, a process that Virginia Berridge has traced in *Opium and the People*, making habitual drug use into a disease. The psychiatric disease model of addiction as deviance, itself a liberation from earlier demonizations of addiction, gave way in the 1960s and 1970s in the face of "recreational" drug-using behavior and especially the reality of returning drug-dependent Vietnam vets in America. This disease model of addiction, however, rooting normative addictive behavior in the brain, liver, DNA, or personality type, has come at a cost. The creation of a stable addict identity demands the radical reconstruction of the individual's life story in terms of the later addictive behavior. If addiction is perceived to be a chronic behavior that brings to the fore a defining component of personal identity, then the addict who has been placed in a toxic environment must for ever more reside in a state of suspended recovery and seek prophetic signs in all past life experience. As with breast cancer survivors like Marianne Faithfull, the addict's having been once afflicted entails being forever liable to recurrence or relapse, and the necessity of perpetual self-surveillance.

Celebrity addiction carries its own myths and metaphors, as if genius or beauty is abnormally fragile and fame's proximity to death explains the high-stakes danger pay. The rock star, even more than film stars like Marilyn Monroe, performs a spectacle of flirtation with death, from stage diving to risking electrocution or assassination, as the price of attempting to steal fire from the gods, a metaphor used in so much heavy metal mythology. The nearness of death is the sign of authenticity, rejection of conventional life in all its forms, and the drive of genius. There is the constant spectacle of groupies, contract riders demanding the finest wines and M&M's, and drugs, but also unscrupulous promoters hiring unsafe helicopters, demanding overwork and the presence of guns, knives, and organized crime. Death is a well-respected career move in rock, in a culture in which even celebrity murder is a category of fame. However, rock's famous dead, Janis Joplin, Jimi Hendrix, Jim Morrison, and Brian Jones, and even Keith Moon—that Kurt Cobain's wise mother labeled the "stupid club" she begged him not to join (Cross 227)—were mostly far from being beautiful young lions when they died in distinctly unglamorous settings, at a time when addiction and rehabilitation were not well understood in clinical discourse. Morrison and Jones had donned fat suits to murder their rock star images,[1] aided by rampant alcoholism and drug abuse, and stars like Hendrix and Moon choked on their own vomit in bed, or, like Joplin, walking across a motel room, or like alcoholics Sandy Denny, walking down a flight of stairs, or Morrison and Humble Pie's Steve Marriott, taking a bath. The glamorization of rock star fatalities and the sensational attention given copycat suicides as followed the death of Cobain, through tourist dead rock star tours and books like *Stairway to Heaven: The Final Resting Places of Rock's Legends*, allow rights holders to profit from endless recirculation. Rock star deaths create an impossible standard for other rockers,[2] and Morrison widely announced his coming death in the wake of those of Hendrix and Joplin. Even young cult stars like Jeff Buckley—himself a dabbler in heroin to medicate his probable bipolar disorder (Browne 326–30)—was intensely aware of the heroin overdose death of his father, Tim Buckley, and his audience's expectation of his own early death, and would perform celebrity death scenes as part of his stage act.

The rock 'n' recovery autobiographies considered here labor under this mythology of immortality and also under a related derring-do attitude to addiction itself. Two important cultural figures, William Burroughs and Keith Richards, are the virtual godfathers of these accounts and their attitudes to addictive practices have been widely influential. Richards is cited as an addict role model by Slash and Sixx (and indirectly by Wood), and Burroughs is similarly cited by Faithfull, and he had a quasi-mentoring relationship with Cobain with whom he later recorded. Similarly, in the perhaps classic version of copycat addiction, Miles Davis succumbs to the prevailing notion that "heroin might make you play as great as Bird" (96). Dickie Pride, discovered by Larry Parnes, however, may have been the first rock casualty who succumbed to copycat addiction, and he died, aged twenty-seven, in 1969.[3] Early in his career, Richards adopted the drug-taking of musical mentors (156–7), and he recognized the value of a reckless, naughty public persona as a Rolling Stone, though this image was partly the creation of the band's first manager, Andrew Loog Oldham, to distinguish his "boys" from the Beatles. Richards' statements about addiction are full of rakish bravado, as if he styled himself a bohemian aristocrat gone to seed: "I don't know if I've been extremely lucky … but I've never turned blue in someone else's bathroom. I consider that the height of bad manners" (qtd. in Blake 98). His flippant witticisms about narcotics, quoted with affection by Ronnie Wood, include his adage about having no "problem with drugs, only policemen" (214). A more strident version appears in the memoir of MC5 founder, political activist, and former federal prisoner on "drug-related" charges Wayne Kramer: "[d]rug prohibition has killed more people than drugs ever could" (296).[4] The self-satirizing pose of gone-to-seed rock god dispensing medical and lifestyle advice also has been taken up by Ozzy Osbourne and David Crosby.

Burroughs and his fellow Beat writers were iconic rebels to 60s rockers (his photograph appears on the cover of *Sergeant Pepper's Lonely Hearts Club Band*), and his credo that addiction is "a way of life" in the autobiographical "Prologue" to *Junky* gave addiction itself legitimacy and at the same time an automatic identification with an artistic tradition and the authenticity of street culture. Moreover, Burroughs, an erstwhile philosopher of addiction, framed addiction as an anthropological adventure. Like stoic philosopher Marcus Aurelius who in his *Meditations* warns against the dangers of pleasure or anything that will "habituate you to dependency" (62),[5] Burroughs maintains that addiction is an afflicting virus, though resistance to it fosters "cellular stoicism" (xli). The delights of the "kick" for Burroughs pale before the strenuous but presumably virtuous resolve needed to endure the horrors of drug withdrawal. When *Junky* was first published, a nervous publisher's note was added drawing attention to the novel's purpose as a deterrent to "discourage imitation by thrill-hungry teen-agers" (qtd. in Harris xxi), a caution not duplicated on the covers of the rock 'n' recovery autobiographies.

Richards' *Life* is a very well-rehearsed "life" as Richards has covered many of the incidents in multiple interviews over six decades. He regards his music as belonging to the tradition of African American blues, but also country and reggae, each with its own traditions of borrowing, mentoring, and theft. Far from acknowledging that there is "a vampiric relationship between the white rock and rollers and the black people who inspired all their music" (Hagan "Question"), Richards self-identifies as black. As he says, "[t]o the Jamaicans, the ones that I know, I'm black but I've turned white to be their spy," or at least he is in a process of "transition from white man to black" (346). He is abundantly aware of his partly self-created image and the myths surrounding him and his infamous drug use. A conflicted focus on heroin addiction—perhaps the key feature of Richards' media persona—occupies *Life*'s middle portion. This subject goes along with his equally famous elegantly wasted insouciance and his self-designed haircut, imitated by everyone from Patti Smith to Izzy Stradlin. He acknowledges the ravages of dependence and his many failed withdrawal regimes (one on the advice of William Burroughs); but he can't part from the swaggering bravado of his stance as a successful addict who chose addiction to keep himself grounded and resist the ego-perils of superstardom. Heroin was fame or rock stardom's analgesic: "I never particularly liked being that famous. ... I was doing it [heroin] not to be a 'pop star' ... That was very difficult to handle, and I could handle it better on smack" (285). He mainly used pharmaceutical-grade heroin, injecting directly into muscle tissue and not veins. He also has had some legal good fortune as when the penalty for his 1977 Toronto bust was reduced to giving a concert for the blind (391–414), which some in Canada quipped should have been for the deaf ("Silence"). Richards suggests the weak paternal figures in his hard-bitten, lonely, working class upbringing as well as persistent bullying at school may have contributed to his vulnerability. He reveals unwittingly, however, that Brian Jones—teenage father, flamboyant dandy, possibly homoerotic sadist, who probably suffered from an undiagnosed bipolar condition exasperated by ingestion of near-suicidal quantities of narcotics—may well have originated the Rolling Stones' dangerous image now so widely associated with Richards.

The confessional motive

The motives behind these rock 'n' recovery autobiographies are often deeply conflicted. It's "not very rock 'n' roll" to write a confessional autobiography for the benefit of others as Sixx notes, though he claims rock's very rebelliousness allows him to confront the stereotype (413). Celebrity disability autobiographies, such as Michael J. Fox's *Lucky Man* and Christopher Reeve's *Still Me*, often are designed to use celebrity visibility to draw attention to the realities of disability and offer hope. The literary celebrity memoir by Susan Cheever, *Note Found in a Bottle: My Life As A Drinker*, that takes its epigraph from F. Scott Fitzgerald's *The Crack-Up* and includes details of her famous father, John Cheever's alcoholism—to which we shall return in Chapter 3—is motivated by a desire to help others understand the disease of alcoholism that she says is "still invisible" (188). The motives of rock 'n' recovery autobiographies, however, while ostensibly altruistic, are sometimes much more ambiguous. A rock 'n' recovery autobiography, as in the case of John Phillips' *Papa John, An Autobiography*, while drawing attention to addiction, may be a staged performance of contrition designed to seek an advantage in coming legal battles, as his daughter Mackenzie Phillips later realized, as she writes in her own narrative of addiction and sexual abuse *High on Arrival* (145), or it may seek to justify a liver transplant, as in the case of David Crosby's *Long Time Gone*. Eric Clapton and the more recent autobiographers examined here all claim to write for others' benefit, even to fund rehab centers or children's charities, but their accounts clearly glamorize their rock 'n' roll lifestyle, with inflammatory dust-jacket promises of sex, drugs, and rockin' writing in sometimes cartoonish formats replete with nude photographs (Sixx; Kiedis). While most acknowledge the absolute helplessness in the face of addiction demanded by some recovery programs, it was probably publishers' advances and the subjects' own pop cultural savvy about the public's addiction to fame that dictated attending to debauchery at least as much as contrition.

These riff and tell books are also highly competitive in their desire to outdo or "out-Mötley" others (Sixx 330).[6] The humor of Alice Cooper's renunciation of alcoholism for "golf addiction" or Clapton's confession that before heroin and alcohol he was addicted to chocolate is highly unusual. Sixx's *The Heroin Diaries: A Year in the Life of a Shattered Rock Star* and the Guns N' Roses guitarist's *Slash* emerged in the aftermath of Anthony Kiedis's autobiography and seem partly designed to compete for the crown of most deranged, depraved rocker while ostensibly being billed as cautionary tales. Sixx writes somewhat formulaically: "If one person reads this book and doesn't have to go down the same road as me, it was worth sharing my personal hell with them. I'm also donating profits from this book to help runaway kids" (8). Sometimes, there is even a conflict between competing addictive practices and disabilities. For example, the bipolar disorder that Adam Ant self-medicated via his sex addiction, as his 2006 autobiography explains, takes a side seat to his mania for pop stardom and workaholism,[7] and Grace Slick's 1999 alcoholism narrative details sexual exploits with various lizard kings, as both symptom and benefit of her illness.[8] Canadian Celtic-rock fiddler Ashley MacIsaac's crack addiction can't bypass the internalized homophobia that fired his self-destructive exhibitionism as he writes in his 2003 autobiography *Fiddling with Disaster*. Rock 'n' recovery narratives designed to close a chapter on excess, or recover agency over the illness narrative itself (Couser, *Recovering* 191–2; Linton 162), inevitably re-launch the rockers' often stalled careers, and attempt to raise the curtain on a second act to feed the public's insatiable celebrity obsession.

The impetus behind many of these autobiographies extends from the 12-step programs of many rehab centers and in particular the emphasis on public confession or the so-called "drunkalogue." They all unwittingly represent an unambiguous endorsement of residential recovery, group therapy, and the 12-step program. This approach to recovery provides not only a way to live but also a way to narrate, and some of the writers, such as Kiedis, unconsciously slip into somewhat clichéd, jargon-riddled recovery speak. A number of the autobiographers recount a litany of failed "cures" before they accept the 12-step approach: trips to the Caribbean or even the Sahara to recover; acupuncture; cocktails of fruit juice, vitamins, and Valium; or regularizing the supply of heroin in lockdown clinical settings to exhaust the drug's appeal; or using unlimited supplies of alcohol to control the symptoms of withdrawal and thus trading heroin addiction for alcoholism. The recovering addict—and former addicts usually must accept that they are forever in a state of recovery—is forced to acknowledge a powerlessness to resist drugs, accept responsibility for past irresponsibility, and express a willingness to make amends. Recovery is directly related to reading or hearing others' accounts of enslavement to drugs or alcohol, and to drafting and retelling one's own narrative. Recovery is thus textual, an act of telling and retelling. As Robyn Warhol has demonstrated in a study of the "rhetoric of addiction" in a different context, there is a close similarity between recovery and Evangelical conversion narratives (106).

Generic hybridity

The very different rock 'n' recovery autobiographies considered here belong to a genre distinguished by its very hybridity. These texts are "postmodern morality tales" (Coyle 18) that present addiction and celebrity's disabling effects as a "moral test" (Quayson 37). Their stoical laments for past hedonism sometimes employ the rhetoric of spiritual autobiography as their writers survive the torments of ghostly demons en route to humility and understanding; Brian "Head" Welch's *Save Me From Myself* is a conversion narrative as well as a pathography. These are also unusual *bildungs* narratives in that the writers, often encountering advanced middle age, must acknowledge their mortality and their previous licensed irresponsibility within the enforced infantilism of a celebrity "culture of invalidism" to use Maria Frawley's phrase in a different context (6). The very act of writing, often "with" a professional coauthor, a type of facilitated communication, acknowledges the difficulty of articulation. The role of these coauthors appears to be the jogging of memory or the organization of events into a coherent narrative for authors whose main education has been in show business. It may be, too, that these coauthors at the prompting of publishers advocate for the recounting of celebrity encounters that can electrify ad copy and inflate sales. All of these rock 'n' recovery autobiographies include celebrity walk-ons, but whether due to reticence or amnesia, such revelations are minimized.[9] Ronnie Wood's autobiography in this regard is closest to celebrity fluff, an extended series of pub yarns, supplying fellow fans with the inside story, until addiction nearly ruins everything and famous underworld drug dealers overtake film, comedy, sports, music, or political stars (from Tony Curtis, with obligatory remarks about Marilyn Monroe's promiscuity, to Groucho Marx, Muhammed Ali, Jimi Hendrix, and Margaret Trudeau), leading to his injunction: "never holiday with a dealer, or the mafia" (244). Faithfull includes a detailed account of Bob Dylan's nervous and inept attempted seduction in the mid-sixties, though this is genuinely revealing about the reactionary sexual politics of the pop world.

Part of the trajectory of the conventional illness narrative traces a movement towards the recognition of the value of personal growth or spiritual insight gleaned from the somatic experience. This model of recovery reconstructs the illness itself "as the occasion finally to behave well. At the least the calamity of disease can clear the way for insight into lifelong self-deceptions and failures of character" (Sontag, *Illness* 42). The ritualized and highly effective AA conception of addiction as a treatable but incurable disease, in the face of which the addict is utterly powerless save for the intervention of a higher power, offers another deterministic narrative denying personal agency (Muzak 260). These deterministic narratives of addictive personality type and addiction as incurable illness are opposed in rock 'n' recovery addiction autobiographies in which the autobiography takes authority over the story of addictive calamity in an effort to achieve what G. Thomas Couser in a different context calls "self-destigmatization" (*Recovering* 92). The movement from autopathography to full autobiography in these texts is an attempt to resist prescriptive narratives of illness and identity.

The writers extend their life story beyond the disability memoir by delving into childhood memories. Frequently, as in the case of Clapton, Kiedis, or Sixx, the writers uncover a repressed Oedipal narrative of child abuse or abandonment that fueled the hunger for the drug of fame.[10] Clapton, for example, uncovers a childhood trauma, discovering that his "parents" were really his grandparents; his "sister" was his mother. Faithfull locates her tendency to self-criticism and self-diagnosis in her family. She was the daughter of a Second World War British spy and an Austro-Hungarian baroness—who traumatized her daughter with tales of her own incest and rape—and great granddaughter of Leopold von Sacher-Masoch, author of sexual-enslavement classic *Venus in Furs* (1870), after whom Richard von Krafft-Ebing in *Psychopathia Sexualis* (1886) coined the term "masochism." Both Kiedis and Sixx were the children of addicts, and Sixx unknowingly participated in the institutionalization of his music-loving sister Lisa—her Down's syndrome possibly caused by her mother's drug use—in a sanatorium the family was advised not to visit, a pattern of abandonment he repeated with his own children.

Clapton is closest to what Charles A. Riley has called the "antidisability memoir" (40–2), in which the story of addiction and disability is emphatically not the focus of the account until the maelstrom of addiction, rehab, and relapse overwhelms any attempt to focus on music or the cultural revolution of the second half of the twentieth century. "Clapton is God" is a slogan notably downplayed in his story of heroin addiction and alcoholism that makes a virtue of gentlemanly or Garboesque reticence and of devotion to artistic integrity, though its reserve appears to go against its aim of confession. Clapton attempts to expand the autopathography, almost certainly begun during his stints at various rehab centers (he refers to a diary), into a fully-fledged autobiography. He is particularly disdainful of fame and its trappings, as well as any type of self-pity. His stance is that of many 60s rock celebrities and the 1990s "alternative" musicians for whom absolute artistic authenticity cannot sustain promotional fabrication or celebrity association, though the Beatles showed how this could be done (Marshall, "The Celebrity of the Beatles" 170). Ironically for a future rock god, Clapton from the beginning desired to be "anonymous" (9), but his steady descent into addiction, recovery, and relapse, paralleled his rise into the British rock aristocracy. In its relentlessly fast-moving, breezy pace, his autobiography also reads like a social calendar and publicist-supplied event itinerary. It may be that Clapton, like his former bandmate in Blind Faith Steve Winwood, simply can't remember, the amnesia of the Woodstock generation being proverbial (Street 30).

Part of a generation of youthful English rockers who accompanied the elder statesmen of the blues, like Sonny Boy Williamson and Howlin Wolf, when they toured Europe with pick-up bands in the early 60s, Clapton had early exposure to addictive practices to withstand grueling tours, organized crime's involvement in the entertainment industry, and the disability of age. In his initiation into the music industry, he encountered the mythologies of the blues: the need to live the blues in order to play the blues, to make a deal with the devil at the crossroads, to be African American, and to have a deep contempt for fame. Striving for the ideal of absolute dust-bowl artistic authenticity in performance and recording is especially difficult in an age of vinyl and digital reproduction, and his extended virtuoso improvisations in Cream and his solo middle-of-the-road, blue-eyed reggae blues (miraculously combining shifting baby boomer tastes with his own awareness of diminished artistic capacity) have been more successful than his attempt to channel Robert Johnson. In the wake of Clapton's autobiography, both of his bandmates in Cream have published either an autobiography (Ginger Baker's *Hellraiser*) or contributed to a biography "written in collaboration with the subject" (Jack Bruce's *Jack Bruce: Composing Himself, the Authorised Biography*, 21) containing details of their own much less well-known heroin addictions into which they were seduced in part by the "romance of heroin" in the jazz tradition (Shapiro 172), as we saw with Miles Davis.

Clapton avoids writing a kiss-and-tell celebrity autobiography, though he catalogs a long line of model and aristocratic girlfriends. His spare remarks about his wife Pattie Boyd, the former wife of Beatle George Harrison about whom he co-wrote his famous "Layla," particularly in light of her generally sympathetic portrait of him in her autobiography *Wonderful Tonight*, are restrained to the point of coldness and his admissions of serial infidelity are remarkably untroubled. Boyd embraces the role of muse, titling her autobiography after one of Clapton's best-known songs, a hoarse-voiced ode to his lover's make-up. She recalls her first husband George Harrison's fondness for cocaine, as well as Clapton's harrowing heroin addiction and then alcoholism, but she gives far less attention to her own alcoholism and to the very meagre settlements from both divorces, like that of Cynthia Lennon from John Lennon as she writes in *John* (306–7), that may well have driven her to write. Clapton generally avoids any odor of unpleasantness or the scandalous stories of his comrades such as Jim Gordon of Derek and the Dominoes, credited co-writer of "Layla," who in a bout of psychosis, triggered by cocaine and heroin excess, murdered his mother. Clapton's addiction exacerbated his typical response to conflict or crisis through emotional withdrawal, and he became a virtual recluse in his mansion. He sketches a portrait of the rock star as drug addict: constipated, sexless, and fat, due to his diet of junk and junk food. Without an AA or NA support system after his first recovery, he merely traded addictions and became an alcoholic. Clapton's narrative is one outcome of his therapy for alcoholism: peer support counseling and ultimately his establishment of a treatment center in Antigua, where wealthy American and European clients pay for treatment and Caribbeans are free. *Clapton*, both pathography and autobiography, has a bourgeois and heteronormative comic closure with his return to work in the music industry, a new family, and a new luxury yacht.

Fashioning the self

One of the central tenets of 12-step recovery programs is the addict's acceptance that addiction constitutes an identity and not merely a repeated behavior. While more broadly addressing the social construction of "the pathologizing mythologies of compulsion," Eve Kosofsky Sedgwick traces the implications of widespread "addiction attribution" for an understanding of the self (*Tendencies* 138). She suggests that the renewal of earlier denunciations of drug-using behavior as a type of moral insanity has elevated "the unitary self" as an ethical absolute (139). The anxiety about a total loss of personal autonomy, with its ethical implications, as a result of enslavement to a variety of obsessions is what Timothy Melley calls "agency panic" (39). In various ways, the rock 'n' recovery autobiographies resist such a deterministic prognosis. They shift from autopathography to full autobiography in part to resist the determinations of the disability memoir, and to foreground creative drives and accomplishments.

Moreover, they frequently construct the self as radically divided. In some cases, this divided self is presented as in a modern psychomachia; Sixx, for example, distinguishes between his healthy and sick identities as Nikki and "Sikki." Kiedis in his autobiography appears to be addressing himself, reminding himself to continue psychic work, as if he were a New Age life coach strengthening his resolve against addiction, with a "palette of spiritual principles" always at his side (289). His writing self, reflecting on the past, appears to address a future reading self who may be tempted to relapse. In addition, he writes of being inhabited by an alien presence, "the eight-hundred pound gorilla" (437), and Mackenzie Phillips similarly refers to a sleeping monster that will reside within her forever. More commonly in the rock 'n' recovery autobiographies, however, the fault line of the bifurcated self divides a remembered identity and a media image.

Faithfull's account in particular presents her addiction as the result of identity confusion due to her obsession with her shifting, distorted media image. She resents the role of muse that she was assigned by the British media early in her career when she was regarded as the official consort of the "bisexual" Mick Jagger (*Faithfull* 103, 128). Her therapy was later to teach her that her own life narrative was not simply an adjunct to the saga of the Rolling Stones. Her initial descent into full-blown heroin addiction when she was homeless in London was "a form of self-medication, an act of self-preservation" (221) after enduring a series of traumas, a number involving witnessing fractured versions of herself: seeing her life portrayed in the film *Performance*, feeling an overwhelming identification with Ophelia whom she played in Tony Richardson's production of *Hamlet*—preparing for the mad scene with a "jack" of heroin—but especially seeing "my self-portrait in a dark mirror" in the song "Sister Morphine," co-written by Jagger, overlooked (240).

Faithfull is an unusual, and unusually literary, rock 'n' recovery autobiography. Like Joan Baez and Judy Collins, Faithfull is a popular singer who has written more than a single autobiography, though the impetus behind her work is clearly advancing the process of recovery. Her autobiography's 2007 sequel, the fragmentary *Memories, Dreams and Reflections*, is a more conventional disability narrative, recounting Faithfull's experience with breast cancer as well as detailing her family's history. As a devotee of the Shelly Circle, Faithfull fashions herself in a somewhat theatrical, self-mythologizing way. Faithfull writes with keenly observed detail primarily about her heroin and cocaine addictions and her many attempts at rehab, but her account is never far from the Gothic. She calls "Sister Morphine" her "pop *Frankenstein*" (240), and judges the disregard for her work as a creative artist to be one of the major causes of her descent into full-blown addiction. *Faithfull* is a harrowing account of her long "romance with drugs" as she calls it, quite unlike the novelistic gesture of De Quincey's *Confessions of an English Opium-Eater* that was a kind of Bible for the Rolling Stones. De Quincey in turn had "modelled himself on Coleridge, whose public persona was closely associated with opium dependence" (Morrison 209), but his *Confessions* did not make him into "a social outcast or criminal" but "turned him into a celebrity" (Black 145). Faithfull does come inevitably to rehearse the Gothic metaphor of bodily invasion, though in her case it is the sensation that insects are crawling under her skin during fits of cocaine psychosis. Like her mentor William Burroughs, Faithfull says somewhat aphoristically that she searched for addiction's cure within the disease itself (301), a diagnosis and "cure" that become yet another self-rationalizing justification to delay rehabilitation.

Faithfull's destructive perception of her divided self, as well as her interest in self-diagnosis and self-criticism, fostered earlier in her life, was reinforced in the 1960s pop milieu. In her early career as a pop starlet, she was surrounded by fabricated people. She became muse and wife of rock impresario John Dunbar, "a great fabricator of selves" (38), at whose art gallery Yoko met John. She was easily exploited in a rock 'n' roll milieu in which declining sexual invitations was considered bad manners. She later becomes Jagger's girlfriend, directed into this role by Keith Richards (109), and watches Jagger's developing incapacity to separate his flamboyant public celebrity image and his private self. She comes to recognize that "[a]ll celebrities become burlesques of themselves in the end" (270). A suicide attempt ending in a six-day coma provides her with a new image in the press as a mad woman much to her dismay, though when she is jailed in London and later New York suffering the first stages of heroin withdrawal, she is asked for her autograph by police, and encounters yet another hybrid role as pop diva, drug addict, and criminal. She describes two years of living in a bombed ruin in Soho as a period of grace because "nobody knew who I was" (301), but eventually she returns to her obsession with destroying her earlier public image as "flawless consort" possessed with endless "money, fame and adulation" (305, 308), and she slashes her face with a razor blade. She relapses again and again, until she accepts that her new fame as the "Marlene Dietrich of pop" and her "self-hatred" are linked (380, 378). She attempts a type of self-psychoanalysis until she relapses yet again and makes yet another suicide attempt. Finally, after treatment at the Hazelden Clinic in Minneapolis and partly as a result of reading her own biography, she sees her media image as "a series of caricatures" and recognizes her self-loathing (416). She enters intensive therapy, joining AA and NA, a process not without a peppering of celebrity encounters, most ending with sexual propositions. Publishers' insistent demands for such "salacious" details about the Rolling Stones led sibling in the "dysfunctional Rolling Stones family" Anita Pallenberg to refuse to write an autobiography: "[i]f young Posh Spice can write her autobiography, then I don't want to write one!" (Barber).[11]

Ronnie Wood's autobiography is the account of a fan of the Rolling Stones who became a Rolling Stone himself, but his self-perception is so tied to his identification with Rolling Stones guitarist Keith Richards that he must become an addict. Like his idol, Wood is typically dismissive of treatment, though he has been a rehab junkie at various celebrity centers. His near-death as a Rolling Stone when Jagger threatens to fire him for his addiction, rather than any of his near-fatal overdoses, drives him to commit to rehabilitation. His autobiography appears to be part of his rehabilitation program at Cottonwood in Arizona: "It was here that I was asked to draw my life to put it in some sort of perspective" (307). His autobiography begins with his first Stones concert in 1964, and he recounts Andrew Loog Oldham's construction of the group's bad boy image later modified into the Satanic aura that Jagger adopted from his role in *Performance*. Wood is almost a clone of Richards, and he appears to relish being mistaken for his fellow guitarist. Like members of Guns N' Roses later, Wood wants to copy an image and lifestyle. Richards, however, has a mythically hearty constitution, a knowledge of his limits, a refined eclecticism in drug-taking, and a knowledge of his image that has preserved him, though he has been surrounded by collateral damage. Wood descends into addiction "through freebase, coke, heroin, booze, more freebase and finally sobriety" (103). He marvels seeing his second wife self-detox, though he still offers her a celebratory line of coke in the delivery room. A similar offer—"[c]elebrating the birth of my daughter with a bottle of wine and a gram of coke"—brought home to punk pioneer John Cale the selfish destructiveness of his drug behavior, as he writes in his autobiography (212). Kurt Cobain perversely topped them both by offering Courtney Love a mutual suicide pact in the delivery room (Cross 106). Wood recognizes his obsession with freebase (he provides a recipe) is a yearning to relive his initial euphoria, and that trying to live like a Rolling Stone is a ploy to chase his ecstasy as a fan watching the band perform. Like Clapton's, however, Wood's autobiography ends comically with the launch of his new career as a successful celebrity portrait painter and entrepreneur with Sir Andrew Lloyd Webber as patron and clients like Prince Charles and Bill Clinton. He somewhat implausibly assesses the "privileges associated with fame" as those of a prisoner in a "golden jail" haunted by the "demons" of his drug cravings, but he is still cocky enough to promise a novel for his next literary adventure (336, 355, 357).

Living with fame

Over the past three decades with the growing power and ubiquity of celebrity culture, fame or the desire for fame has had a major role in constructing identity. Rock stars like Clapton disregarded fame as an unwanted side effect of a devotion to musical authenticity and artistic integrity. Their second generation imitators, many from Hollywood, however, sought legitimacy via a connection to 60s rock stars, not realizing the constructedness of their idols' public images. Like the 60s rockers—now in their seventies and eighties—the 1980s and 90s glam rock stars often sought acceptance and recognition in public as a salve for deep psychic wounds, but they also wanted fame at any cost, and partly by design they became postmodern parodies.[12] Like Wood, who is a transitional figure in this development, these musicians are rock star fans who made themselves into famous rock stars. They are the "ready-made" rock stars and "clones" identified by Baudrillard (*Paroxysm* 48)—his example is Michael Jackson—who imitate the hairstyles, lifestyles, and addictions of their heroes.

Being identified as *Spinal Tap* imitators designated the 1980s and 90s hair rockers' and cross-dressing glam rockers' greatest fear. They initially at least did not want to be ridiculous parodies of earlier metal bands, well before the self-consciously, self-commercializing reality TV antics of drug casualty Ozzy Osborne and his antithesis, drug-loathing Gene Simmons, would relaunch long-stalled careers. Eventually, however, members of Mötley Crüe, for example, would themselves become reality TV participants and a band like Metallica would make a video of group therapy, *Some Kind of Monster*, after its cofounder, James Hetfield's treatment for alcoholism. Such self-conscious parody was not always a successful strategy, as in the case of Adam Ant who embraced what he calls "rock 'n' roll pastiche" (82).[13] He was considered a poseur by punk rockers, a movement that he felt was created by fashion merchandising. He takes criticism for his own image's S&M and Nazi references lightly because for him—unlike Joy Division who were similarly and more justifiably criticized—punk was never political: "the look was the most important statement" (96).

Adam Ant's *Stand and Deliver: The Autobiography* is not a rock 'n' recovery autobiography but rather a memoir of his father's physical abuse, his mother's poverty, his ambivalence about his Roma heritage, and his bipolar disorder, self-medicated with relentless rounds of work and sex.

The Hollywood bands, Red Hot Chili Peppers, Mötley Crüe, and Guns N' Roses, had a much less ambivalent attitude towards the manipulation of image and the promotion of entertainment over total artistic authenticity. For Kiedis in his autobiography *Scar Tissue*, the fact that drummer Chad Smith auditioned with "a really bad Guns N' Roses hairdo" and partied at "the Mötley Crüe bar" discounted him immediately (233, 238); he initially did not want clones in his band. Smith, however, eventually did replace Jack Irons, fired for his addiction, and soon the new band would even have a *Spinal Tap* impersonator opening their shows, though they increasingly resented their fans' demands for yet more outlandish cartoon displays, from performing with blow torches on their heads to wearing nothing but socks on penises to an all-naked show at the Woodstock reunion. Their video for 1989's "Knock Me Down" featured "the psychedelic, morbid image of dead rock stars on the walls" (242). They were able to embrace the self-parodying circus of late-twentieth-century rock performance partly because their Funkadelic musical mentor, crack-addicted George Clinton, pioneered outlandish, outer-space costumes in the disco days of the 1970s. However, jazz-loving Chili Pepper Flea would only let his funk flag fly after first dismissing rock as "a dumbed-down form … [all] haircuts and advertising," pop as resembling "a TV commercial for salad dressing," and the musical mainstream as "pabulum" (196, 303). Being the child of addicts and alcoholics presumably drives his resistance to the faux-romance and "false Eden of junkiedom" which he suggests would claim first guitarist Hillel Slovak, but Flea also refuses to "wind up dead in a bathtub like a sixties rock star" (195, 315).[14] Between speedball binges, Flea's dear friend, the Hollywood-raised Kiedis, was always able to briefly self-detox and once again, as he says in a different context, "Mickey Moused my way through" (Kiedis 445). Kiedis explains how the success of his band's *Blood Sugar Sex Magik* led to an unexpected consequence: guitarist John Frusciante loathed "the star-making machinery" so much that, to be true to his perception of the William Burroughs-style artist who is "at war with the world," he quit the band to embrace five years of heroin addiction (284–5). Frusciante exemplifies the reluctant rock star who chooses addiction to fight fame. Fame became a test of Kiedis's ego-driven "entitlement" (293), an opportunity to see if he could handle "this weirdness" of adulation (294), and he relapses again and again until he adheres to each of the 12 steps of recovery and admits he has not "outwitted drug addiction" (459).

Raised within the entertainment industry in Laurel Canyon, Slash of Guns N' Roses learned to refashion himself as an extra in *Sid and Nancy*, a fictional documentary about the Sex Pistols' most-famous drug casualty, and to chase heroin from books about "my rock-star heroes ... all junkies" (244). Recalling the stance of Keith Richards, Slash's autobiography locates heroin's appeal in its darkness that exorcises the "vapid" nature of "success and fame" (246). Slash contributed anecdotes about drug binges to his friend Nikki Sixx's rock 'n' recovery narrative. Sixx's *The Heroin Diaries* attempts to create a type of autobiographical text from very sketchy diary jottings repetitively recounting the warm blanket comfort of heroin, the paranoid psychosis of cocaine, and an uncontrollable obsession with fame itself. The text usually delivers what its cartoonish format and cover promise: a fragmentary series of ink-splattered jottings, the graphics designed to replicate Sixx's blood-spattered bedroom closet, "my junkie wonderland" (31), fully stocked with drugs, syringes, guns, and presumably pens. His diary reveals his obsession with the lives of famous rock stars. He takes heroin "[b]ecause my heroes [Keith Richards, Johnny Thunders, Sid Vicious] did it ... because I idolize my heroes because they didn't care; and I really don't care about anything" (30). He was "determined to get hooked on heroin," because, as his addict buddy Slash recalls, Sixx was "all about the attitude and the image" (73–6). Like an obsessed fan, he habitually phones famous people, like Keith Richards, and leaves voicemail messages that are never returned. Sixx's diary entries are supplemented by extensive retrospective exegesis from Sixx himself, his bandmates, family, and music industry insiders. One of the most disconcerting voices belongs to his former lover Vanity, who is now Evangelist Denise Matthews; her fuzzy recollections of her time with Sixx unleash tirades against idolatry, demonism, and fornication. Despite perpetual conflict and Sixx's deep-seated misogyny, the couple stayed together because of Sixx's attraction to her proximity to fame: she was once Prince's backup singer and "[r]ock stars are star-fuckers" (45).

Fame's pathology

The obsession with fame, as we saw briefly in the last chapter, is a distinctly modern disease, as Leo Braudy, Jean Baudrillard, and Susan Sontag have shown.[15]

It entails the fundamental fracturing of identity displayed in some of these rock 'n' recovery autobiographies. In his autobiographical works as we shall see, the 90s rocker Kurt Cobain displays the most tortured relationship to fame, having both a Clapton-like devotion to creative authenticity as well as an enhanced and ironic awareness of postmodern media saturation. Braudy, like Baudrillard, points to this postmodern shift from earlier designations of fame used to create an imagery of centralized political power to later conceptions of "media fame" lacking national or even temporal specificity. He also projects towards "the end of fame" (596–7), due to the democratization of access to fame and a mass audience's absorption of the very identity of the famous person as witnessed in an extreme form by the copycat suicides following Cobain's death. The Victorian valorization of self-made people, evidencing a new social mobility, has become in the post-Second World War era, he argues, a willing self-exposure in which "a victory over alcoholism" is more important than "a Lincolnesque rise from poverty" (595). Being famous, divorced from any artistic or heroic achievement, is the goal. As Susan Hopkins points out, for young girls who idolize Kylie Minogue or Madonna, "fame is replacing romance as the dominant female fantasy": "every girl will be famous, it's just a question of when" (qtd. in Turner, *Understanding* 67). The most recent shift in the conception of fame results from the global saturation of the celebrity industry, celebrity's commodification, new technologies of reproduction and distribution, and the disappearance of the famous person into the gaze of a mass audience. Increasingly, "the medium is the audience" (Gamson 113). The modernist suspicion of fame's fabrication and commercialization has shifted to a celebratory embrace of postmodern self-reflexive parody. In the twenty-first century, we approach post-fame, the demise of the cult of celebrity that Andy Warhol famously anticipated. The willingness to accept "fabricated celebrity" on reality TV, wanna-be music celebrity competitions, and has-been celebrity shows, as well as with manufactured rock bands may indicate the beginning of the end of fame.

Rock stars, as these autobiographies indicate, are perhaps the perfect, transparent image of this phenomenon, banal in its very ubiquity. They live within images and have disappeared into the simulacrum of themselves. Their fame is produced via mass-consumption art, itself a gateway product used to fuel a desire for additional consumption of fashion, fragrances, jewelry, guitars, technology, ice cream, or memorabilia. In Baudrillard's terms, rock stars exist as postmodern subjects within media images of themselves. If they first sought fame to "confer a reality that they lacked," they quickly discover "their sense of unreality has only increased" (Braudy 589). In the mass public spectacles of rock stardom at which the audience performs a well-known part before rock stars who were themselves once fans—with chemical preparation, sounds, movements, phones aloft, and gestures of adulation—the audience like the performer loses a sense of individual identity. The famous rock star thus is less a person than "a story about a person" who becomes "part of the audience's story about itself" (Braudy 593).[16] The extreme fan addicted to fame, or "fame junkies" (Halpern 191), only represents the outer limits of the fandom that is a critical part of a globally saturated celebrity culture. Increasingly, the rock star show, barely visible to most of the audience, is "performed" on close-up screens above the stage and then recorded and watched by the live audience on cell phone reproductions of the event. In Baudrillard's terms:

> Nothing escapes this kind of image—recording, sound-recording, this immediate, simultaneous consciousness-recording, any more. Nothing takes place without a screen. ... What we get now isn't really our own image, but an instantaneous recording in real time. In real time, there isn't even the distance of an image. But, merely to exist, you need distance from yourself. The abolition of that distance condemns us to indefinite reproduction, to a kind of derisory immortality which no longer has anything in common with the immortality of destiny.
>
> (*Paroxysm* 50)

Rock 'n' recovery autobiographies are attempts to proclaim mortality and fallibility,[17] and, however conflicted, to escape this kind of "disembodied ideality" (Baudrillard, *Fragments* 6).

Kurt Cobain, the rocker with perhaps the most self-conscious, ambivalent, and finally tortured relationship to fame, produced a type of autobiography or at least a series of psychic self-portraits in his visual and plastic arts projects as well as his posthumously published *Journals*. Courtney Love, Cobain's actress, rock star wife, published her *Diaries* in 2006, though they are closer to miscellany or commonplace book, and aim less at autobiographical or drug rehabilitation than a kind of reputational rehab.[18] While he may have been the quintessential image of the slacker junkie rock star—as he was intensely aware—and contemptuous of macho hair bands like Guns N' Roses, Cobain was also a savvy self-marketer and self-promoter, as well as a visual artist who wanted fame but also street cred. He signed with Geffen, but was forever associated with indie SubPop, played music industry awards shows, and changed *In Utero*'s cover illustration of fetuses to accommodate Walmart. He crafted every shot of Nirvana's breakthrough video for "Smells Like Teen Spirit," as well as every detail of the design of every other video, CD cover, and T-shirt the band produced. He appeared on the cover of *Rolling Stone* in a T-shirt emblazoned "Corporate Magazines Still Suck" as if winking at his different audiences and nailing to the wall his radical, indie credentials for the mass market. As he writes in his *Journals*, "I've always felt it was kind of necessary to help out the 'Now Generation' internally destroy the enemy by posing as or using the enemy" (269). His awareness of his famous persona as a media creation was only matched by his self-conscious attempt to use the media as an artistic medium. The result was his inevitably conflicted sense of identity.

His art of urban disturbia is a deliberately "anti-star" self-exposure (Cross 134), showing his knowledge of and his contempt for his own skilful manipulation of his media image. Perhaps more clearly than his journals, Cobain's art works, some collected in Charles Cross's *Cobain Unseen*, reveal an elaborate private mythology of disturbed childhood from which he was unable to escape: his early exposure to Ritalin; his parents' divorce; an exploitative experience of disabled sex; witness of suicide by hanging; his embarrassment about his own early infatuation with heavy metal hair bands; and a lifelong obsession with suicide.[19] Cobain blamed his anxiety about his rock star status on fame itself, "the weirdness of always being recognized" (Cross 223), and he justified his heroin use as self-medication for stomach pain, back pain, and childhood trauma, and also as normal behavior needing no justification, citing the sanction of William Burroughs. He resisted the authority and banality of anti-drug messages and treatment programs. He hated, for example, what he considered the manufactured insincerity of "the AA rap" (Cross 223) or "becoming a slave to another drug the 12 step program" (*Journals* 284), and he rejected multiple attempts at therapy and rehab. He committed suicide shortly after an intervention led him to the Exodus rehab center. Conspiracy theories after Cobain's death, however, judged that his fame had killed him given that his suicide note was interpreted as a doctored farewell to the music industry and his fans. While he attempted to control or terminate his own celebrity narrative in the manner of his death, he finally left himself powerless to confront misinterpretations of his motives.

Rock 'n' recovery autobiographies of the twenty-first century are a special type of postmodern autobiography, a distinct subgenre of celebrity disability autobiography. While many celebrity autobiographies are attempts at self-promotion, settling scores, or reclaiming lives from tabloid gossip, rock 'n' recovery autobiographies make some attempt at effecting a cure. Not only are they driven by a desire to demedicalize their life narratives (Frank, *Wounded* 10), but through the redrafting of a life script by collaborators in group therapy (in some cases the rock star's first direct contact with common folk since adolescence), the writers' attempt to reclaim their lives from addiction. Their notions of self-identity in some cases have been so caught in the hyperreality of media representations of themselves along with drug-generated delusions and hallucinations that they have been unable to distinguish between self and image. The rocker addicts must unpack the myths of invincibility, transcendent genius, and demonic excess that they have helped perpetuate and that have fed the public's celebrity addiction.

Notes

1   Morrison had been an overweight child, and had many anxieties about his appearance and even his voice (Babitz, "Jim" 221–34). The Sinatra-loving Morrison of the early Doors' years was lithe and beautiful after a precarious existence as a "brilliant, penniless bard on the beach" in Venice, California when he "never wanted to be a rock star," as his friend Bill Cosgrave remembers (164, 185). He would become an alcoholic, retaining an explosive, Oedipal hatred of all authority.
2   Bands like MGMT confront this toxic legacy with comic irony in facetious, faux-autobiographical songs like 2009's "Time to Pretend."
3   A trained choral singer, Pride [Richard Kneller] loved jazz and began using heroin in London's jazz scene in the mid-1960s. Underlying mental problems, career frustration, and addiction contributed to his depression "treated" with a lobotomy in 1967, two years before he died of an overdose. See Bullock (54–6).
4   Abandoned by an alcoholic father and sexually abused by another father figure, Kramer in his 2018 memoir subscribes to a quasi-Freudian view of addiction as the underdeveloped ego acting out (267). Influenced by reading of the "brilliant bullshit" marketing outlined in the Rolling Stones' *Our Own Story* (46), Kramer pushed the MC5 to advocate "Dope, Rock & Roll, and Fucking in the Streets," though for Kramer this became "addiction, prison, and rock & roll" (83, 294). The MC5's idealistic if naive revolutionary agenda combined anti-war slogans and endorsement of youthful hedonism with admiration for Black Panther fashion and notions such as that "revolutionaries don't wear underwear" (101). Kramer's conflicted motives appear in his desire "to destroy the power structure with the force of the electric guitar and be as high as possible in the process" and simultaneously "be famous and wealthy and have all the sex I could handle" (270). The band ran afoul of their former

manager John Sinclair, about whom John Lennon wrote a song, and Up Against the Wall Motherfuckers who dismissed the MC5 as posers adopting radical politics for marketing purposes. See Osha Neumann's account (104–11). Former Weather Underground member Jonathan Lerner ironically references the MC5's most iconic song in a self-deprecating remark about bourgeois college students styling themselves "kick-out-the-jams revolutionaries" (57) in his autofictional novel *Alex Underground* which details going underground and discovering his gay sexuality in Cuba and Europe—the latter via prostitution—though elsewhere Lerner details a sexual relationship with famous Weather Underground leader Bill Ayers (*Swords* 119–22), who later married Bernardine Dohrn (Ayers 219). Kramer justified his later career of burglary as if he were "some kind of Robin Hood," though it only funded his decades-long addictions to heroin, alcohol, and crack and landed him in federal prison for over two years (269).

5   Like the rock 'n' recovery autobiographies, Aurelius asks how he can live a public life with integrity and balance. He also reflects on fame's ephemerality, though he would likely have regarded the fame of a rock 'n' roll musician as a brand of infamy.

6   Mötley Crüe appears to be a very competitive group even in writing autobiographies. In what may be a desire to "out-Mötley" his bandmate Nikki Sixx, at least in the self-promotion and cross-marketing departments, singer Vince Neil has recently published his autobiography, part of a promotional package with a CD and cross-marketed with his tattoo parlour chain and signature line of tequila as well as tie-ins with his clubs and his aviation company (281). The child of alcoholic parents, Neil battles his own alcohol and cocaine addiction and other obsessions with sex, fans' adulation, fighting, and almost pathological recklessness that he has pursued to seek oblivion and escape from deep-seated insecurities. He is a rehab- and celebrity-rehab junkie and yet someone who denies being an alcoholic. For such a remarkably inarticulate account—a transcription of the subject's reluctant, obtuse, faulty, and inarticulate remembering—it is highly evocative particularly due to his ex-wives' testimony and to his sweeping denials of responsibility.

7   Similarly, Rick Springfield's memoir details his lifelong depression that led to a suicide attempt. He attempted to self-medicate via what became a sexual addiction; his distorted body image led him to plastic facial surgery for the first time at age twenty-three.

8   Belinda Carlisle of the Go-Go's *Lips Unsealed* similarly recounts celebrity encounters with James Belushi and Michael Hutchence and her eventual husband, the son of actor James Mason, but it is less a kiss-and-tell Hollywood memoir than a surprisingly flat, clichéd attempt to make amends. Raised "Belinda Kurczeski from the Valley" in an abusive, alcoholic household (150), she details a steady descent into anorexia and addictions to cocaine and alcohol.

9 MacKenzie Phillips' autobiography, which Augusten Burroughs declares somewhat disingenuously on the dustjacket blurb as "no celebrity addiction memoir," appears typical in this regard. For example, she recounts being invited to the suite of Keith Richards' partner, model and actress Anita Pallenberg, a heroin addict, and encountering a scene that Phillips' boyfriend Peter Asher considered bizarre. Phillips stayed the entire night but provides no details, because "I don't remember … I can't tell whether my memory lapses are the fault of years of drug use or whether they mark memories so painful that I've hidden them from myself" (104).

10 Anthony Elliot argues for psychoanalytic theory's relevance for contemporary cultural critique in *The Mourning of John Lennon* (8).

11 Similarly, Billy Joel received an advance for his autobiography, but returned it when "[t]here wasn't enough sex, drugs and rock & roll in it for the publisher" (qtd. in Greene, "The Mix" 38).

12 For Linda Hutcheon, as for Fredric Jameson and Baudrillard, parody is a makeshift and deeply conservative aesthetic strategy arising from alienation. While Hutcheon reads parody as a potentially transgressive Bakhtinian "intertextual dialogism" (72), she recognizes its "aesthetic institutionalization" (72–5). For Jameson, parody, "the play of random stylistic allusion," is depthless and affectless, a sign of "the high modernist ideology of style" (17–18). For Baudrillard, parody is the aesthetic of a "world controlled by the principle of simulation" (*Simulacra* 123). In a period when "art has become fashion," the artist plays "a game with the vestiges of what has been destroyed" (*Baudrillard Live* 95). He suggests that parody is a type of postmodern narcissism lacking the qualities of the mythic or the imaginary (*Baudrillard Live* 83).

13 Jameson reads pastiche as depthless parody: "Pastiche is, like parody, the imitation of a peculiar or unique, idiosyncratic style. … But it is a neutral practice of such mimicry, without any of parody's ulterior motives …. Pastiche is thus blank parody" (17). Even wildly successful punk-reggae pioneers the Police faced criticism for inauthenticity. Sting, though never an addict, structures his memoir as a hallucinated retelling of his life story inspired by his participation at a Brazilian sacred ceremony at which he ingested the psychedelic drug ayahuasca. Similarly, rap hybrid Eminem's 2009 release was *Relapse*, though the singer, according to his autobiography, is addicted less to alcohol or narcotics than workaholism and junk food. In interviews, he admits addictions to prescription pills (Ambien, Valium, Vicodin, Methadone), Big Macs, and celebrity rehab reality TV shows (Eells, "Eminem" 50–4).

14 Flea also claims to lack the "hard-core addict gene" "that makes someone keep doing drugs when they consciously understand that it's destroying their life" (166, 318). He found "insta-family" with Kiedis and Slovak (209), which assuaged his

deep-seated insecurity and panic attacks, and eventually distanced him from daredevil antics with Kiedis like jumping from roofs into strangers' swimming pools, fishing naked with bait in the anus, shoplifting, freebasing crack, and sharing needles. He's a strident anti-hippy who believes in the hippy values of love, peace, and environmentalism, as well as in music's spiritual transcendence and social empowerment, and he wishes to make amends for resenting his bandmates' addictions and their threat to the band's success rather than offering effective help.

15 Braudy conceptualizes the frenzy for celebrity as a distinctly modern illness (590), and Baudrillard locates the ultimate modern disease in the total loss of identity in a world of images (*Transparency* 37). Sontag identifies a similar malaise: "People themselves aspire to become images: celebrities. Reality has abdicated. There are only representations: media" (*Regarding* 109).

16 Celebrity discourse unites diverse national, cultural, and generational groups; moreover, decoding celebrity fabrication has become part of postmodern entertainment (Gamson 155–7). Part of the exchange for fame is that the celebrity can never be taken seriously, a risk especially for "celebritising politicians" (Turner, *Fame Games* 134).

17 The place of mortality and disability, the intersection of the public and the private, in a celebrity culture is the meditative subject of Annie Leibovitz's "autobiographical" display "Annie Leibovitz: A Photographer's Life, 1990–2005," published as a volume by Random House in 2006. Her black and white photographs of her beloved Susan Sontag in her last months and just after her death are perhaps almost as painful to view as Leibovitz's commentary indicates they were to create. "Ever since cameras were invented in 1839," Sontag wrote in *Regarding the Pain of Others*, "photography has kept company with death" and been considered "superior to any painting as a memento of the vanished past and the dear departed" (24). Leibovitz's portraits of Sontag were created by the celebrity photographer with the full permission of the modern philosopher. The stark documentary photographs of the dying Sontag surrounded by huge, bright, sensual spectacles of the Hollywood and Washington glitterati take on an acute, reflected poignancy. They are a *memento mori* in the market of vanity fair which is what the rock 'n' recovery narratives considered here, at their very best, aim to become.

18 The drummer of Love's band Hole, recommended for the post by Kurt Cobain, was Patty Schemel, the gay daughter of "professional recovering alcoholic[s]" who, via the "genetic link," would become a "heroin-addicted crackhead" tied to "the hamster wheel of detox," recovery, relapse, and sabotaged relationships (21, 262, 264, 75). She details the minutia of drug usage and detox, leading to homelessness and prostitution, presumably to demythologize "[h]eroin, my heroine" (104). Her often harrowing, deadpan memoir says little about her musicianship save that

drumming channels anger, mandates pain, and for the savvy, may involve receipt of "publishing royalties" (160, 220–1). She details Courtney Love's dictatorial and chaotic handling of Hole, resenting Love's high-handed insistence on tough love rehab for others, including Cobain and Schemel, while pursuing her own use.

19 As a child, he said he had "suicide genes" and in his suicide note he referred to himself as a "death rocker" (Cross 19, 153). His art began with found objects that he would prepare by various types of manipulation, dismemberment, or juxtaposition. These works reveal a haunted world of childhood, replete with small cardboard boxes customized to resemble coffins, and repeated juxtapositions of baby dolls with desiccated corpses and medical procedures.

2

"A Cellarful of Boys": The Swinging Sixties, Gay Managers, and the Other Beatle

In a study of the cultural location of popular music, Simon Frith writes that "the absence of gays from the subcultural pop myth reflects ... the fantasy involved [in] ... a utopia of innocence" ("Cultural" 181). The absence of gays from the autobiography of one of the most famous, closeted gay Englishmen of 1960s Swinging London is especially notable. Brian Epstein's autobiography, *A Cellarful of Noise* (1964), was named after the Beatles' manager's first major encounter with the group in Liverpool's Cavern Club, and the beginning of his own meteoric ascent into the intoxicating world of celebrity, drugs, and sexual opportunity, where he was often regarded as the "fifth Beatle" and outside of which increasingly he wanted to establish his own independent fame before his death, probably from an accidental drug overdose on August 27, 1967. Epstein belonged to Liverpool's "assimilated" Jewish community, a fact of which the Beatles were fully aware and about which Epstein was often uneasy.[1] Paul McCartney later wanted Linda Eastman's father as the Beatles' financial manager, but his name-change from Epstein was styled a cover-up by the Beatles' later Jewish manager Allen Klein to win John Lennon's endorsement.[2] The renown of Brian Epstein's nearly miraculous achievement with the Beatles would diminish after his death, accompanied by the Beatles' descent into the clutches of Klein with his street-fighter aggression, well-researched flattery, and million-dollar promises ending with decades-long renditions of the "Sue Me, Sue You Blues." Epstein's initial fascination with the Beatles was partly a masochistic obsession with Lennon, the epitome for him of leather-clad "rough trade," the dangerous object of a style of homoerotic desire that nearly created a scandal on the eve of the Beatles' American invasion.[3] Lennon was fully aware of his hold over Epstein. Asked for a title for Epstein's autobiography, Lennon, recently celebrated author of the instant bestseller *In His Own Write*, suggested brutally "Queer Jew" (qtd. in Brown and Gaines 130). This phrase exemplifies Lennon's famous cutting humor issuing from his sixth sense for other people's—particularly other outsiders'—vulnerabilities that perhaps veiled his own deep-seated insecurities.[4] After the book's release, he called it "A Cellarful of Boys," drawing attention to the nature of Epstein's initial attraction to the Beatles.

This chapter examines Epstein's autobiography as an example of a distinctly late-Victorian genre of life writing which conceals or masks as much as it reveals its subject[5] and in this case exposes internalized homophobia at a time when acts of "gross indecency" between men in "public or private" were criminalized under the provisions of 1885's Labouchere Amendment. Epstein managed the Beatles in the period between 1957's Wolfenden Report recommending decriminalization and the Sexual Offences Act of July 27, 1967 legalizing this recommendation, though consent provisions were not equalized until 2003. The decade from 1957 to 1967 was a period highlighted in "novels" and "autobiographies": "congratulatory narratives that defined post-war Britain as the 'permissive society'" but that ignored the "abject, immoral, and dangerous" (Houlbrook 241, 243). Epstein's attraction to dangerous rough trade—itself a species of "sexual colonialism" (Weeks, *Against* 56)[6]—may express his unhappiness with being gay and his internalized homophobia which rendered Epstein and many others subconsciously unable to enter "a successful homosexual relationship" (Peter Brown qtd. in Geller and Wall 27).[7] Epstein's object of desire, however, also may anticipate a refusal of the heteronormative narrative of domesticity, marriage, and parenthood[8] later embraced by iconic figures like Elton John. John's autobiography details his difficult upbringing—his aunt was born in a workhouse (14)—and losing his virginity to his manager, John Reid, who turned out to be unfaithful, violent, and financially unreliable, and recently installing as manager his husband, David Furnish.[9]

Pop stars like Marc Almond would reject such accommodations and the celebratory myth of inclusion they promoted. Almond's *Tainted Life* of 1999 declared that "coming out as gay is still a luxury of the privileged" in a still homophobic music industry (121). Scissor Sisters' Jake Shears in his 2018 memoir laments the "insidious" homophobia in the media and even among the three gay members of his band (233, 266), and Judas Priest's Rob Halford in 2020's *Confess* acknowledges "a lot of homophobia still exists in the music world" (288).[10] The triumphant narrative of Elton John's *Me* suggests that fabulous wealth, glittering celebrity, and an aura of benevolence may neutralize or at least mitigate anti-gay vitriol. In this respect, Epstein's autobiography challenges congratulatory narratives of an earlier period of gay popular music history, questioning homogeneity in same-sex practices. Epstein's autobiography was a calculated, dangerous performance of apparent self-exposure and concealment resembling his fascination with high-risk "dangerous situations" (Nat Weiss qtd. in Geller and Wall 87).[11] He was more frank in unpublished diaries, sadly resolving to use "will-power" to "overcome" his homosexuality.[12] In light of a consideration of other gay members of rock's management establishment in the ostensibly sexually liberated 1960s,[13] this chapter examines early rock autobiography and its use of mediated authorship in celebrity self-promotion, the often paradoxical construction of the self in Epstein's text, and the relationship between rock autobiography and addiction memoir as well as the revelation of the queer gaze in Epstein's account of his first encounter with the Beatles.

Epstein came to maturity in a period blighted by the "queer panic" after the highly publicized trials, conviction, and two-year imprisonment at hard labor of Oscar Wilde under Labouchere's provisions (Cornwall 489).[14] This law broadened the scope for prosecution of male same-sex activity, that was in legal terms the crime that dared not speak its name, focusing particularly on consensual relations (Cook 43).[15] Predicated on religious sanctions and assumptions that "unnatural," non-procreative same-sex acts manifested moral insanity and involved coercion and violence, Victorian anti-gay laws had a draconian influence. While all legislation relating to same-sex acts from 1533's anti-sodomy laws was understood to encourage blackmail, the vague nature of the newly defined acts constituting criminal activity or what might be interpreted as attempts to commit them further enabled extortion. Moreover, in the post-Second World War, Cold War period, there was increasing surveillance due to a belief that homosexuality was a contagion spread in homosocial military environments, as well as paranoia about the vulnerability of those engaged in espionage. As Lord Montagu would remember in his autobiography, acknowledging his bisexuality, the early 1950s imagined "reds under every bed" and "*in* every bed as well" (81, 98). One prominent target of this paranoia was Alan Turing, the subject of Neil Tennant's recent *A Man From the Future*. A founder of computer science, Turing broke the Nazis' Enigma Code, but was charged with gross indecency in 1952. Accepting chemical castration rather than imprisonment, Turing committed suicide by eating a poisoned apple on June 7, 1954.

The most scandalous instance in this period was the so-called Montagu Case of 1953 that led indirectly to the Inquiry into Homosexual Offences and Prostitution (Wolfenden Commission) because of public disgust about the use of entrapment, searches without warrants, denials of access to legal counsel, and virtual coercion of witnesses. To crush homosexuality out of existence, a judicial spectacle was made of a prominent peer. Lord Montagu, Michael Pitt-Rivers, and Peter Wildeblood, the *Daily Times*' Diplomatic Correspondent, were charged for events allegedly occurring at Montagu's beach hut, which as Wildeblood notes have "achieved more notoriety, than any other since the days of Nero" (40). There was a strong feeling that Lord Montagu's crime lay primarily in his association with people who were "infinitely his social inferior" (Wildeblood 26). The charge was issued the day after another, similar prosecution against Montagu was dismissed. The trial was ground-breaking because Wildeblood, while denying all charges, admitted under oath he was an "invert." This admission, however, and affectionate expressions in Wildeblood's letters to a young corporal, as well as the judge's leading summation of evidence, led to convictions. In his autobiographical account, Wildeblood deplored the dehumanizing conditions in decaying Victorian prisons, which, as in Wilde's assessment in *De Profundis* (155–63) and in his letters to *The Daily Chronicle*, housed the uneducated, elderly, disabled, and mentally ill. Wildeblood served twelve months in Wormwood Scrubs, where Keith Richards would be remanded after his 1967 Redlands' bust, which provoked William Rees-Mogg's famous indictment of British cultural intolerance, *The Times*' July 1, 1967 editorial, "Who Breaks a Butterfly on a Wheel?" Upon his release a decade earlier, rejecting hormonal "cures" (144, 186)—in the late 1950s, Lou Reed, on the other side of the Atlantic, would be subjected to electro-shock therapy as a homosexual cure (Doggett, *Lou* 18–19)[16]—Wildeblood spoke before the Wolfenden Commission. He claimed "the right to choose the person whom I love" (175), incensed that existing laws made same-sex expression safer for the "promiscuous homosexual, who seeks his lover in the street," than for "the man who lives with another in affection and trust" (176).

The Montagu Case exposed the injustice of England's anti-gay laws, but the resulting public disgust at the police-state methods used to entrap and coerce, as well as the law's injustice, failure to act as a deterrent, and encouragement of blackmail, mental illness, and suicide, led to the Inquiry headed by John Wolfenden. Wolfenden's son Jeremy, born in the same year as Epstein, lived as a young man on the fringes of the emerging rock community, but his father ironically could not accept his homosexuality. Jeremy would have a precocious, if brief, career in journalism, and he was open in his circle about his desires for boys, confident about acting within the limits of tolerance. At Oxford he was the sometime lover of Kit Lambert, with whom he later shared accommodation in Chelsea, before becoming the *Daily Telegraph*'s foreign correspondent in the Soviet Union in 1961 and informally joining Britain's Secret Intelligence Service. While a correspondent, he was photographed *in flagrante delicto* with a "delicious" Polish youth, a KGB plant, by agents bursting from a closet. Wolfenden's louche, reckless attitude is evident in his reaction to incriminating photos: he requested enlargements (Faulks 268). Finally married in America, he was the plaything of the SIS, MI5, KGB, and FBI, pressures he managed via soon-to-be fatal alcoholism and benzedrine addiction. Wolfenden must be one of the few people with tickets to see the Beatles at Carnegie Hall, who decided not to attend (Faulks 283).

While the anti-gay cold war of the 1950s thawed a little in the early 60s show business world, homosexuality remained "strictly taboo" (Repsch 45) and "scandalous" as the Rolling Stones' manager Andrew Loog Oldham recalled (qtd. in Myers 104). Oldham embraced camp flamboyance and later encouraged the same in the Stones. Well before Television's Richard Lloyd could describe himself as "try-sexual"[17] or hyper-macho metal bands could name themselves Queens of the Stone Age, British blues singer Long John Baldry called his band Ada Baldry and the Hoochie Coochie Ladies but only in private, recognizing that the music industry remained "homophobic" (Myers 67, 198). Baldry, however, was sufficiently savvy as to convince Elton John in 1968 that he was gay and shouldn't marry a woman even though "[w]e'd ordered a cake," an incident later inspiring "Someone Saved My Life Tonight" (John 53). Like Epstein, Baldry had an erotic predilection for "straight kids" and often was blackmailed (Myers 105). Barry Gibb has recently recalled landing in London in the mid-1960s and being managed by the gay Robert Stigwood, who tried to take over the Beatles: "this was a gay world .... We were heterosexual boys in a homosexual business .... Larry Parnes ... Robert Stigwood, Brian Epstein. It was a gay scene, you know, and so we had to always be on the lookout. There was always somebody that wanted to jump all over you" (31). Like Epstein and Stigwood, record producer and manager Joe Meek was drawn to youthful—and straight—men, though Meek preferred blonds (Bullock 197, 245). Meek turned down Epstein's request to record the Beatles, but like Epstein he developed his own stable of artists, sometimes chosen for their good looks.[18] Like Larry Parnes,[19] Meek developed a reputation as a seducer on the music industry's 60s version of the "gay casting couch" (Hofler 53, 92; Repsch 227). Johnny Gustafson, described as "very good-looking" in *A Cellarful of Noise* (136), claimed a drunken Epstein made a sexual approach (Geller and Wall 105), and Epstein signed his lover John "Diz" Gillespie and propositioned his contracted artist Paddy Chambers (Coleman 256–9). Though longing for a domestic life with children and having a partner in Lional Howard, Meek, like Epstein, was enticed by the frisson of dangerous sexual encounters. Howard was mortified by Meek's cottaging, because "there was never any need to go out looking; it would always come to him anyway" (Repsch 223). Meek finally descended into paranoia and depression, dying in a murder/suicide six months before Epstein's death.

"[I]t is the fate of rock and roll managers to attract less attention than performers," Andrew Motion writes of the Who's manager Kit Lambert (2). Like Epstein, Lambert knew he was famous only for his proximity to the stars he helped create, and he also faced pop management's greatest temptation: wanting to be a star in his own right. Like Epstein, Lambert was approached by a literary agent about writing an autobiography, but, in collaboration with John Lindsay, he only published a few sketches in *The Sun* in 1981. At this point, Lambert was deeply in debt, an alcoholic addicted to heroin and cocaine. He claimed credit for the Who's auto-destructive aesthetic, Mod clothes, and even windmill guitar gestures. His aura of gentility, like Epstein's, opened doors for the Who into the entertainment industry, and he similarly denied any homoerotic attraction, though Roger Daltry's angel-headed fawn persona before their testosterone-driven set at Woodstock enabled their global reach. Pete Townshend is more discriminating on Lambert's intimations of their appeal: "because he was a homosexual and the audience were ninety per cent boys, he picked up that the link between our audience and the band was a sexual one …. We treated our boy audience like thirteen-year-old girls" (qtd. in Motion 309). This may be an instance of early gay managers' instilling a confrontational "anti-establishment attitude" and even a "new masculine archetype" in emerging rock culture (Petridis, "Straight"). Townshend is more ambivalent about himself in *Who I Am*, self-identifying as "probably bisexual"; his gay encounters are usually drink- or drug-fueled, ill-remembered "experiments" initiated by others and punctuated with the disclaimer, "I didn't let him actually fuck me" (135–6). Townshend was jealous of Lambert's "sexual dalliance" with Mick Jagger due to his appreciation of Jagger's anatomy (88), differently assessed, to Jagger's enduring mortification, in Richards' autobiography: Richards claims Jagger has a "tiny todger," but "an enormous pair of balls" (Richards 256; Hagan, *Sticky* 485–6). Lambert's discomfort with his homosexuality may partly explain his masochistic "desire to be physically abused" (Motion 316). Finally, nearly derelict, Lambert lodged with acquaintances, his last hostess allowing him male prostitutes but "only in the afternoon, when the children were at school" (369–70). Here he died of a cerebral haemorrhage after a fall, though, like Epstein and Wolfenden, due to his depression, self-destructiveness, and addictions, insiders were not really surprised.

Epstein's autobiography, commissioned by Ernest Hecht, English publisher of *Venus in Furs*, in late 1963 just before the Beatles' arrival in America, had paradoxical motives. Hecht recognized early the appetite for books on popular culture, and was irritated by what he regarded as Epstein's vanity and arrogance, but especially his procrastination; he perceived that for Epstein, the project was designed to boost not his revenues—though obsessed with promotion and distribution, later beginning an audiobook version—but his ego (Coleman 173–7). Appearing in August 1964, this celebrity autobiography, pre-destined to be a bestseller, was remarkably prescient in anticipating the Beatles' distinctly new, uncontainable global fame that would only accelerate after their demise, a few years after Epstein's death, and arguably continue expanding until the present, with repackaging of Beatles' product, interpretation, and reminiscences, feeding a financial empire of monstrous complexity (Doggett, *You* 349–50). Well before "Yesterday" or "Something," *A Cellarful of Noise* celebrates the Beatles' unique melange of Tin Pan Alley tunesmithing, Goon-era comedy, and charmingly heretical, provincial insouciance. Epstein advances his own genius in nurturing artistic talent and his uncanny ability as someone who disliked popular music to hear a pop hit. His autobiography was a pre-emptive strike against sensation journalism, forestalling inquiry into his private life that could damage the carefully cultivated image of his wholesome, lovable mop tops. While a celebrity autobiography—too readily dismissed as "frothy" or "vapid" (Brown and Gaines 131; Coleman 177)—it styled Epstein as an independent artist in a more traditionally respectable medium as a writer, theater impresario, or actor.

The autobiography was ghostwritten by Derek Taylor, an entertainment reporter from Manchester and later the Beatles' press officer—who previously ghosted a short piece for George Harrison—based on interviews at the Imperial Hotel, Torquay, in April 1964. Taylor would come to recognize how fame "distorted everyone who came within its orbit" (Savage, "Introduction" 6). Taylor was not Epstein's first choice; he had suggested gay writer Beverley Nicholls (Coleman 173–4). At one point in the interviews, Epstein tearfully revealed his homosexuality, the "one thing I had to censor. … He couldn't have anything in there that implied or hinted at homosexuality because of the dangers of jail.

This was only ten years after the Lord Montague thing, which was a frightening, horrible witch-hunt" (Taylor qtd. in Geller and Wall 85). Epstein was also anxious during these interviews about the longevity of the "beat-group bubble" (Epstein qtd. in Bramwell 144), and while he was engaged in psychotherapy at the Priory clinic in London in this period—sometimes entering for short stays for chronic insomnia and addiction—Epstein's autobiography is not clearly confessional (Bramwell 152). Taylor remembers Epstein's acceptance of robbery and violence as the price of his sexual preference, but he dreaded blackmail. Epstein may have told Taylor at that time of a particularly brutal assault, robbery, and blackmail in Liverpool. Much to his shame, Epstein's affluent parents intervened and police apprehended the culprit when Epstein was delivering payment.[20] Other than somewhat incongruous literary allusions and formulaic promotional-package references to the "four long-haired lads from Liverpool" (52), the stylistic tenor and voice of the autobiography appear to be largely Epstein's. Surprisingly frank in detailing his early failures and some of the Beatles' foibles, it is silent on sex, drugs, and possible assault charges, VD treatments, paternity suits, or anti-Semitic and homophobic jibes.[21]

Epstein repeats his anxiety about the dangers of entertainers' overexposure, lamenting having himself become "almost a professional interviewee" (185), but the autobiography clearly aims to stop—while answering—ubiquitous questions about the Beatles' talent and character, and the secret of his own success. Despite his acute vulnerability, he proclaims with breath-taking bravado:

> I don't mind people delving deep into me, searching for reasons and secrets, because there is nothing too bad there. Even if there were something to be ashamed of, if it were true and it were known and it were published, I could not complain. I am extremely fond of the truth and I wish I could find it as often as I find the reverse in my day-to-day contacts with people.
>
> (202)

While rhyming off the Beatles' triumphs in northern England, the Royal Variety Show, and America, and the already-mythic narrative of his response to requests for "My Bonnie" (which Joe Flannery, his old friend and pop management mentor, calls a phony myth, resulting from Epstein's detachment from the creation of the autobiography [157]), Epstein downplays any artificial contrivances such as chart manipulation. He inadvertently advances the specter of his own extraordinary good fortune as the refined, theater- and classical-music-loving, genteel, eldest son of a wealthy Jewish mercantile family with an eye for a star. Epstein discovered his own identity through the Beatles' success, and while his autobiography is his public life story, it is also the narrative of those others through whom, and by whom he now exists. If he is the fifth Beatle, he is also not a Beatle at all, making yet more poignant his discomfort that people only want to know him because of his association. Horrified at contemplating the relief of selling the Beatles to reduce his stress, he backs away from the decision, with the whole-hearted endorsement of the Beatles. Before his death three years later, Epstein again was fretting over the renewal of his managerial contract and the prospect of relinquishing his magical but haunting property when the Beatles, in their post-touring career, were withdrawing from him socially and professionally.

In his self-fashioning, Epstein is both the active agent of the Beatles' success as well as an almost passive recipient of good fortune, and he is acutely aware of the media's power in maintaining interest in his properties while potentially destroying him. There may have been a tacit understanding that, like the British royal family, the Beatles and by extension Epstein were off-limits for scandal journalism,[22] but Epstein maintained close, frank relations with some journalists to prevent exposure (Coleman 255-6), and occasionally used more draconian measures (Flannery 161-2). Image-control and self-fashioning had always been a part of the Beatles' phenomenon from the late collective autobiography of the *Anthology* project to Harrison's *I, Me, Mine*, Lennon's extensive post-Beatles' interviews (*Lennon Remembers*) and autobiographical plans (Norman 771-7), and McCartney's participation in Barry Miles' revealing biography. Epstein is ambiguous about financial practices, holding with gentlemanly disdain that he doesn't know his net worth and stressing the uncharted terrain of pop management, recording, publishing, and mechandising practices in the early 60s. Some mis-steps breezily glossed over here would later draw the ire of the Beatles and became part of his legacy. The protracted merchandising lawsuit, for example, settled in January 1967, would profoundly embarrass Epstein, when he was overextended in new enterprises and still micromanaging everything, if increasingly erratically.

A Cellarful of Noise is a divided narrative, and not only because of its mediated, textual "self" or Epstein's "double life" as a gay man. As in Edmund Gosse's late-Victorian *Father and Son*, that is both autobiography and biography, and inadvertently a story of the schism between Modernism and late-Victorian pieties, this text is an insider's narrative of the Beatles as well as Epstein's story. While dismissing a paternal role (preferring to designate himself as guide [202]), Epstein assumes the position of explaining these very young men, as would "a father of four children" (158). Most of these portions of the autobiography are highly conventional, as in celebrity puff pieces, with repeated references to the "boys'" naturalness, instinctiveness, naivete, and humility, as well as their music's remoteness from rock and roll "savagery" (144). He downplays his styling of the Beatles and anticipates what would become heated retellings of originary narratives about haircuts and suits. While mentioning their fondness for Scotch and coke, he insists that "audience response is their only stimulating drug" (193), and he refers to female fans' frenzy as an expression of maternal possessiveness. He notes the Beatles' awareness of the inadvisability of marrying while in the spotlight, but he says he allows them total freedom. He says little about Lennon's wife and son, and nothing about the circumstances of the hasty marriage.

Epstein's account of himself is less a *Prelude*-like inquiry into conscience, motive or even origins, or a Victorian act of self-interpretation, than a somewhat picaresque, performative anti-*bildungs* narrative of failures in education, military service, and career, the personal story as negative curriculum vitae. Save for feeling like an outsider—perhaps a coded reference to his homosexuality—and having little interest in subjects other than art, dress designing, or window dressing, Epstein does not explain his expulsions and withdrawals from various schools, the main effect of which is Epstein's shame at disappointing his parents. The fiasco following his conscription into the army displays his flair for reckless, self-wounding drama. He is discharged following his impersonation of an officer, narrowly avoiding a court martial. He had "hated the 'hideous' uniform and had his tailor run up an elegant officer's outfit which he wore in order to cruise bars in search of young men" (Miles 86). Referring to the mental crisis that later made him consider selling the Beatles and worsened catastrophically before his death,[23] Epstein saw a psychiatrist and was discharged on medical grounds, though a "diagnosis" of homosexuality probably was involved (Brown and Gaines 55). Contrite, he returned to the Liverpool family business, opening the small record section that would lead him indirectly to the Beatles, but he despairs at becoming "a doomed middle-aged businessman" (87). Patrons of the Liverpool Playhouse encourage his audition at RADA (Royal Academy of Dramatic Art), but his motive appears to be the lure of stardom. His parents are as distressed by his interest in the "unstable and unmanly" theatrical profession as they were earlier by his desire to design dresses, when, as his teachers warned, there is "nothing less manly than dress designing" (76). He soon abandons acting, however, abhorring fellow acting students' "narcissism" and acting itself as the art of hypocrisy (88). He omits having been arrested outside a public toilet for "persistently importuning," and being sentenced to two years' probation and medical treatment, as well as "possibly electric shock therapy" (Lewisohn 263).[24] Again contrite and weary of disappointing his parents with further dilettantish adventures, he returns to Liverpool and cultivates record merchandising. Just prior to the mythic requests for "My Bonnie" that would lead him to the Beatles, he once more is becoming "a little restless and bored" (94).

While this pattern of enthusiasm, boredom, and accelerating stress upsets Epstein and his parents, he never equates his emotional imbalance with having been a Jewish child of the Second World War. Born on Yom Kippur, the Jewish day of atonement, in September 1934, shortly after Hitler declared the Thousand-Year Reich at the Nuremberg Rally, Epstein makes no reference to the Holocaust, his extended Lithuanian and Polish family, or contingency plans in case of a German invasion. This silence may reflect the traumatized post-war attitude to the genocide before the aftermath of Eichmann's trial in 1961. He notes the bombing of Liverpool only in connection with his family's relocation within the city. He makes little of the location of the Beatles' early success in Hamburg, though Flannery recalled his main interest in 1962 as being equated with rumors that "anything went sexually" there (211–12). He records that "Paris fell" to the Beatles without remarking on the overtone of 1940 (146), just as he ignores the predominance of "effeminate boys, rather than over-excited girls" at French shows (Sounes, *FAB* 96). Epstein only briefly acknowledges encountering English anti-Semitism that "[e]ven now … lurks round the corner in some guise or other and though it doesn't matter to me any more, it did when I was young" (72–3). The oppression of anti-Semitism was matched no doubt by Epstein's perception of being the closeted gay son of a Jewish family, at a time when homosexuality was not only illegal but widely conflated with pedophilia (M. Miller 19–20), and generally understood to render family life and even personal happiness impossible.

Epstein makes a half-hearted attempt to present himself as heterosexual. He refers to having "lost a girlfriend" on a night out with the Beatles (118–19), and to being ready to marry "if I can get two days off" (203), a remark with an air of campish, music hall banter. He follows speculation about the Beatles' nearly inevitable marriages and his own probable marriage ("they will marry and so … may I") with an oddly ambivalent statement: "when this happens I must be sure that my own organization is strong enough to endure the changes" (203), indicating the strength of his roster of artists or his psychic endurance of the heteronormative. Epstein may have felt marriage was his fate, though he was known among eligible women as "the Immaculate Deception" (Coleman 34). He likely felt pressure to marry to appease his father following his disastrously quixotic early years; after his father's death on July 17, 1967 and a period of consolation for his mother, he "dropped the charade" and embarked on a type of sensual compensation with a reckless abandon that probably contributed to his demise (Bramwell 214–17). Epstein's autobiographical narrative, however, omits not only his homosexuality, but also his desire for high-stakes, anonymous sexual encounters with straight or apparently straight men, that his gay friends warned him against. Epstein's attraction to rough trade—usually male prostitutes posing as hyper-masculine straight men, with an overtone of danger due to the practice's illegality as well as the implicit degradation in the "gay for pay" dynamic, real or performative—was perhaps an unconscious, dramatic protest against a perpetually disguised, conformist identity. His desire for rough trade and the specter of heterosexuality in macho bullfighters may also have expressed his internalized homophobia, a feeling that the frank display of homoeroticism is offensive. While Epstein had gay friends in Liverpool—some brought into the Beatles' organization—he generally did not find lovers in this circle.

There were, however, other ways to be gay even in the Swinging Sixties.[25] A very different account of same-sex activity and its acceptance appears in the autobiography of the Kinks' Dave Davies. Davies recalls sexual adventures with men drawn from his circle of friends and acquaintances, including Baldry and *Ready, Steady, Go!* host Michael Aldred (51–3): "It was fashionable at the time, especially in show-business, to be adventurous and try different things, and there was never any stigma attached to my interest in other young men" (52).[26] Publicist Allan Warren would concur: "[i]n the sixties it was practically compulsory to be bisexual! … If you weren't … then you were not very trendy" (qtd. in Bullock 161–2). Davies makes no reference to the legal climate or to the "heavily butch" values of the pop world as Epstein's sometime lover, the actor and gay activist Peter (Bette) Bourne recalls (qtd. in Coleman 209), but Davies' occasional encounters took place among friends. Moreover, his attitude to the law and his confident "hetero-credentials" already may have been established by being expelled from school with his pregnant girlfriend. In a recent interview, Davies recalls that Epstein contemplated managing the Kinks, but while he "fancied" Ray Davies, Epstein considered the band too "scruffy" ("Kinks Legend"). Epstein's friend and the object of an unrequited infatuation, Joe Flannery, himself in a long-term gay relationship, was alarmed by Epstein's risk-taking, and after the violent assault mentioned earlier, "I tried to tell him that he could have love in his life without endangering his life" (qtd. in Geller and Wall 25). Perhaps Epstein's most long-term series of encounters involved Diz Gillespie, briefly installed in Epstein's Belgravia home, who abused and robbed him. Lonnie Trimble, Epstein's manservant, himself in a stable gay partnership, recalls chiding Diz: "You're not playing your role. You don't have to love him but at least you ought to sleep with him once a week and give him a kiss when he comes home in the evening" (qtd. in Geller and Wall 95). Nat Weiss describes Gillespie as "the garden-variety type hustler. If you wanted to keep your beer cold you'd put it next to his heart" (qtd. in Brown and Gaines 176). The affair would briefly revive before the Beatles' final performance at Candlestick Park in San Francisco on August 29, 1966, but Epstein was soon confronting Gillespie's theft of Beatles' contracts, money, black market pills, and Polaroids of young male lovers. Weiss, whose briefcase was also stolen, hired a detective, recovering some of the blackmailer's stash. Epstein's resulting depression led to a suicide attempt (Brown and Gaines 200).

The titular scene in Epstein's autobiography describes his descent into the Cavern to see the Beatles, and he instantly recognized the band's "star quality" if not their potential for creative "daring" (Womack, *Maximum* 68, 264). They also embodied the performative version of Epstein's rough trade ideal as leather-clad, would-be hoodlums—though even Lennon's street fighter, Teddy boy persona was a mask taken from "the macho school of pretense" as he later admitted (Cott 120) and this posing may have made him the target of violence (Bramwell 20–2).[27] The Beatles at the Cavern were the "personification of his secret sexual desires" (Brown and Gaines 60). The band's star "face" in the parlance of the day was drummer Pete Best, with his matinee idol good looks, and he would be subjected to Epstein's seduction attempt (Bullock 146). The autobiography reverts to the passive voice in describing Best's firing (Best "had been replaced" 123), or it refers to his "disappearance" (155). Best's firing is one of the variously-interpreted, mythic Beatles' narratives, probably resulting from the other Beatles' unspoken animosity, Epstein's suspicion of Best's enterprising, would-be manager mother, Mona, and the potential scandal of her affair with Neil Aspinal.[28] Recounting his first Beatles' performance in the autobiography, Epstein ignores the young men's physical attractions, which he notes in almost every other reference to his boy bands. As in Lambert's dismissal of any attraction to members of the Who, Epstein deflects attention from the queer gaze tabulating the Beatles' appeal.

Elsewhere, however, Epstein refers to Lennon's "low husky voice" and to the Beatles as "rough," disdainful, and "very attractive" (105, 99). Lennon famously would accompany Epstein to Spain, though McCartney also accompanied the openly gay Robert Fraser to Paris (Sounes, *FAB* 191). Spain was one of Epstein's favored European destinations, a virtual homotopia for gay sexual tourism due to its greater tolerance of same-sex activity. Speculation continues about what might have taken place, and Epstein clearly was infatuated with Lennon,[29] who was violently hypersensitive to suggestions of an erotic dalliance as was Epstein himself about any intimation of his homoerotic attraction to the band (Lewisohn 574–5). Lennon was forthcoming about other, uncomfortable elements in his sexual history, such as a possibly incestuous desire (Norman 778), but it is unlikely that Epstein got Lennon into anything resembling the "unnatural postures" to which he maintains he would never subject "my artists" (195), though, as mentioned earlier, there were instances when the professional and personal overlapped.

While silent on the strain of leading a double life and gambling with exposure, Epstein's autobiography frequently returns to the stress of managing the Beatles, a condition he likens to "a malignant disease" (184). While designed to short circuit inquiry into his private life, *A Cellarful of Noise* is a cry for help, however unconscious. Like a number of recent rock 'n' recovery autobiographies, as we saw in the last chapter, Epstein's is partly a disability narrative focused on the pathology of fame, though his extreme mood fluctuations may have indicated an undiagnosed bipolar disorder (Geller and Wall 93). While only later would Epstein succumb to his unregulated intake of amphetamines and Tuinals, Seconals, and Nembutals, supplemented with LSD and alcohol, the autobiography establishes the conditions leading to his demise. Chronic insomnia, for which he was hospitalized, afflicted Epstein when he was obsessed with becoming steadily less needed by the Beatles, and his deluded thinking would render monumental the delay of male prostitutes coming to his country home on a long weekend or his latest infatuation's failure to return calls. At the end of his life, Epstein's object of desire was the later manager of the Yardbirds and Wham!, and co-writer of "You Don't Have to Say You Love Me," Simon Napier-Bell.[30] Writing in early 1964, Epstein recognized the destructiveness of his nervous tension and his inability to delegate responsibility or tolerate boredom, as well as his dread of failure, but offers no solutions.

While written at the apex of his success, Epstein's autobiography responds to the chorus of questions about his and his "boys'" post-Beatles' life. With only the evidence of songs like "I Want To Hold Your Hand," the media assumed the Beatles were a boy band—however extraordinary—with a distinct sell-by date. Epstein anticipates their future in films, after the storied success of *A Hard Day's Night* and before the catastrophe of the post-Epstein *Magical Mystery Tour*. For their third film in 1967, Epstein and producer Walter Shenson contracted Joe Orton, who found his voice in socially subversive farces after his incarceration for defacing library books, a severe sentence "because we were queers" (qtd. in Lahr, *Prick* 86): "the boys, in my script, have been caught *in flagrante*, become involved in dubious political activity, dressed as women, committed murder, been put in prison and committed adultery" (Orton 83). His screenplay rejected without comment, Orton dismissed Epstein as an "amateur," a "thoroughly weak, flaccid type" (Orton 126), an assessment which may refer to his perception of Epstein's pretentious, closeted existence when Orton was an active cottager who also maintained a strained domestic partnership with Liverpudlian Kenneth Halliwell, who tragically would murder Orton just weeks before Epstein's death. Epstein's autobiography was partly attempting to raise the curtain on a second, post-Beatles' act for himself. While constantly growing his stable of artists from Gerry Marsden to the "very handsome" Tommy Quigley—renamed Quickly, in the style of Rock Hudson's manager's repackaging (Hofler 189)—Epstein was seeking a more conventionally respectable medium for his talents, away from the fickle entertainment world and "savage" music. He suggests returning to the theater, and Epstein would score some success, like impresario—and Holocaust survivor, whose mother died in Auschwitz—Bill Graham, staging rock concerts in a fixed venue and signing popular Liverpool performance poets, the Scaffold.

The Beatles were embedded in Epstein's self-perception, and *A Cellarful of Noise* was titled after the locale that witnessed the creation of his identity. As insiders noted, the Beatles were the projection of Epstein's "alter ego" (Weiss qtd. in Geller and Wall 42), and through them he lived "vicariously" (Flanning 161). As ambivalent rock star Lou Reed recognized, Epstein, having "only come to life" through the Beatles, was fated to be one of those who discovered that "the self [he] … wanted to become is occupied by another body" (83, 87). Epstein wanted to be a Beatle and a star himself, and may have taken drugs to fit into their world, but he was also intoxicated with the Beatles' charisma like a fan. The pronoun trouble (slippage from "they" to "we" when discussing the Beatles in *A Cellarful of Noise*) is one indication of his ambivalent identification, as is the autobiography's mixture of monomania ("that curious grandiloquence that Brian emanated" [Brown and Gaines 131]) and abjection. While distressed that his only interest as a person was contingent on his association, Epstein paradoxically exploited it to secure sexual contacts and to terminate relationships. He felt exceptionally vulnerable for his ability to harm the Beatles, but also that his proximity made him untouchable. He was obsessed with the macho image they displayed at the Cavern, an ideal he impossibly desired to imitate, as well as the element of danger which they or his desire for them manifested. This dangerous desire may have been related to a wished-for, utopian transgression of hetero-normative codes. Napier-Bell, for example, recalls Epstein's confession about joining the audience at one of the Beatles' concerts: "[o]ne night I pushed my way into the middle of ten thousand screaming kids, right into the middle of the chaos, and let myself go in a falsetto voice. I went absolutely berserk and it was the most erotic thing I ever did in my life" (*You Don't* 120). Epstein was the über-fan—desiring fame at any price—whose identity was fractured by his obsession. The Beatles were his children or his sons, but in the weeks prior to his death, his stability undermined by insomnia, depression, self-medication, and loneliness, he would repeat more ominously, invoking the monstrous impresario of the late Victorian classic *Trilby* (1894), "I am Svengali that has created a monster" (Barrett qtd. in Geller and Wall 153).[31]

Notes

1 See Jon Stratton on Jewish culture in post-Holocaust popular music (165–219).
2 Klein earlier had attempted to work with the Beatles, but was rebuffed by Epstein (Womack, *Solid* 67–8).
3 On the Beatles' first trip to America, publication of a story and photograph of Epstein with a male prostitute in New York's Plaza hotel was narrowly averted (Sounes, *FAB* 99–101).
4 See Sounes on Lennon's mocking the disabled and the loss of drummer Colin Hanton (*FAB* 28).
5 Oliver Buckton uncovers diverse forms of "secrecy as a narrative strategy" in Victorian same-sex life writing, focusing on potentially self-incriminating "confession" (1, 12). By the mid-twentieth century, homosexuality was considered pathological (Hocquenghem 69–72), a conception informing Epstein's strategy of secrecy.
6 Acknowledging gay prostitution's complexity, Weeks refers to an attraction for a lower-class, "manly" male prostitute as a type of colonialism, though he doesn't consider the masochism in the sort of violent encounters Epstein sought out, (*Against* 56).

7   Shortly before his death, Epstein in an interview—in which he mentions earlier thoughts of suicide—equated recent changes to anti-gay laws and likely relaxation of drug regulation (Bullock 264), though Epstein's friend, the gay Jewish entertainment lawyer David Jacobs said of Epstein after his death: "He was incapable of any lasting physical relationship with anyone. He was incapable of love" (qtd. in Bullock 265).

8   See Weeks on critics of the "surrender to heteronormativity" (*The World* 169).

9   His accomplished autobiography *Me*, written for his children (352), shows Elton John in touch with his—partly inherited—inner diva and inner wounded child as he surveys his extraordinary career, and details avoiding AIDS by being more sexual "voyeur" than participant (128), though making no attempt to explain his miraculous facility with melody or his synergy with Bernie Taupin's lyrics. His detailed post-retirement "plans" suggest that "work" could be added to his cocaine, alcohol, food, and possibly shopping or hoarding addictions (353). Edmund White gives a perceptive, if unflattering, portrait of the superstar's post-recovery self-fashioning (*Arts* 349–60). Elton John is the subject of a kiss-and-tell memoir by a disgruntled ex-lover, Gary Clarke, who details the retainers, courtiers, and favorites of Elton's quasi-Renaissance court, and his manipulative pattern of acquiring and discarding lovers, as well as his devotion to "celebrity biographies" (58). Clarke's Elton John is "self-centered," controlling, jealous, and vengeful (243). Clarke comes to resent being a "young piece of flesh to be used and discarded by old queens and self-destructive celebs" (140).

10   Much of Halford's humorous autobiography addresses his reluctance to come out as gay due to metal fans' famously macho intolerance. However, as he shows, he hid in plain sight with lyrics, clothing, and stage antics broadcasting his homosexuality for those who could interpret the signs. He largely ignores AIDS, presumably as *Confess* isn't designed, he says, to be a "misery memoir" (11), but he also overlooks the hyper-masculine camp posing of heavy metal with its satanic or fascistic overtones. He acknowledges Judas Priest's parodic qualities as if it were a *Spinal Tap*-style send-up of heavy metal conventions, though Judas Priest probably influenced *Spinal Tap*'s creation directly (181–2, 334, 349). Halford's heavy metal is less electrified, bombastic delta blues than a response to an upbringing in coal country in the industrial wasteland surrounding Birmingham.

11   Geoffrey Ellis arranged Epstein's encounter with a "thoroughly respectable-looking young man" in New York to restrict Epstein's risk-taking, but Epstein told him he later went to Central Park for more excitement. Ellis says drolly, "[t]hereafter, I distanced myself from his nocturnal activities" (17–18).

12   Extracts appear in Geller and Wall's *The Brian Epstein Story* (4, 20). It appears that these diaries and other personal papers were sold at Christie's, London on April 27, 2000 (Lewisohn 827, n.8).

13 See Napier-Bell on the gay sensibility's influence on 60s pop management (*Black* 77, 344). Darryl Bullock more recently details the intersection of gay pop management in the 1960s with the worlds of theater and movie celebrity, politics, and organized crime as rock bands took the spotlight from solo singer entertainers. There may be an echo of this situation recently in the cluster of gay music and music media moguls such as David Geffen, Clive Davis, and Jann Wenner. See Edmund White's portrait of Geffen (*Arts* 333–48), Davis's autobiography's discussion of his bisexuality (545–48), and Joe Hagan's biography of Wenner.
14 See Sinfield on the trials' effect on subsequent perceptions of gay "identity" and relationships.
15 On the complexity of anti-gay criminal laws in the period, see Cocks (7–39) and Cook (6–7, 42–55). Cocks notes that in the Victorian context, homosexuality's "unspeakable status" "produced paradoxical opportunities not only for representation, but also for self-making" (199), and regarding post-Stonewall gay history, Halperin discusses the complex relationship between "gay shame" and "queer resistance" (41–6).
16 Reed's Velvet Underground bandmate John Cale, in his autobiography, attributes Reed's notoriously confrontational nature to his parents, but not his shock treatments: "It wasn't until he gave me a few sexual nudges that it finally clicked that Lou [Reed] was gay, or at least bisexual. ... Lou used to talk about his sexual prowess just for shock value. ... In those days the very suggestion that you would be sexually interested in a man was enough to make you feel that there was something wrong with you. ... In retrospect, I realize he was just doing this to upset me, that it was part of the endless mind games endemic to his personality. ... The intention to shock with everything he did seemed to be so gratuitously vicious that the trail must have begun long in the past" (74–5).
17 Lloyd in his autobiography calls himself a "try-sexual," meaning he "would try anything. I had tried homosexuality, and I tried it a lot, but I was coming to a place where I realized that I would never really be comfortable continuing that exploration" (151). Wanting to be known as one of the hardest if not the largest men in rock, as attested to by the Plaster Casters and others, Lloyd worked as a male prostitute in New York and Los Angeles, and lived with older gay managers Danny Fields and Terry Ork, though he claims no sex was involved (150–1). Walter Lure from Johnny Thunders & the Heartbreakers—in his memoir of his life from CBGBs to Wall Street and his choice between "[h]eroin or finance"—identifies as "bisexual," mentions having a threesome with Lloyd, and stresses the punk scene's tolerance (130, 223, 180).
18 Believing good looks were essential for pop success and voicing an anxious anti-Semitism, Epstein rejected Paul Simon as "a bit small and Jewish-looking," "[n]ot

real pop star material" (qtd. in Bramwell 152). Later, Apple would pass on Crosby, Stills, and Nash, and also David Bowie.

19 Entertainment entrepreneur Parnes notoriously had a stable of renamed male stars, which an early version of the Beatles attempted to join by auditioning to back Billy Fury, though they would briefly back Parnes' artist Johnny Gentle on a Scottish tour in May 1960, with Paul recast as Paul Ramon (Bullock 71–3; Lewisohn 298–302). Parnes was "impressed at Lennon's bullishness," but disliked Stu Sutcliffe's musicianship (Bullock 72).

20 See Flannery (117–23), Brown (Brown and Gaines 50–2, 58–9), and Lewisohn (269–70).

21 See Coleman for Lionel Bart's description of a "master-slave relationship" between Epstein and Lennon, and Lennon's adaptation of "Baby, You're A Rich Man": "Baby, You're a Rich Fag Jew" (319–20). George Martin noted that Lennon "was a very tender person at heart. He could also be very brutal and very cruel" (qtd. in Womack, *John* 13). Lennon exploded in violence when he was teased about a gay relationship with Epstein, like his violent attack on Stu Sutcliffe; later, he would attack Epstein (Bullock 257–8). Lennon's lover May Pang recounts a number of violent attacks against her, noting that "murderous rage … was a permanent part of his personality" (201). Lennon anticipated a violent death to repay his own karmic debt for acts of violence and violent fantasies (Seaman 206–7, 275).

22 See Napier-Bell on dangers to journalists outing favorite stars (*Black* 290–1). Bullock notes that "[t]he British press had little interest in outing celebrities, unless their names came up in court cases" (77–8).

23 Epstein also may have been approached by Colonel Parker in 1966 to manage Elvis, and the infamous Kray twins considered blackmailing Epstein for the Beatles' management (Bullock 235, 209).

24 See Epstein on this episode in unpublished diaries (Geller and Wall 18–21).

25 See Weeks' and Porter's *Between the Acts* and Duberman's autobiographical *Cures*.

26 The Sex Pistols' Steve Jones is similarly open about his "geezer-on-geezer" experiences in this period (63), though he is also frank about his abuse from pedophiles, including his step-father, his voyeurism, sex and food addiction, and inability to sustain affectionate relationships. He becomes devoted to 12-step programs, and to make amends he details his thefts of instruments and clothes from famous musicians. His heroin addiction and alcoholism, eventually reducing him to selling his plasma in New York, he blames on inheriting the "gene" for addiction (244, 13), but also "my shit upbringing" (7).

27 While acknowledging Epstein's homoerotic attraction, Lewisohn downplays its importance (498–502).

28 See Flannery (183–91) and Larry Kane (245–63). Kane remembers Epstein's "brief but classy pass" (224–6).

29 Trimble said Epstein told him "he and John Lennon had been lovers" (qtd. in Geller and Wall 107) as is confirmed by Brown (Brown and Gaines 85, 205). While also noting Lennon's homoerotic interest in McCartney, Norman concurs that in Spain, propositioned by Epstein, Lennon "may fleetingly have reciprocated" (669, 306–8). Apparently prepared to be the receiving partner in sodomy and encountering Epstein's disinterest, Lennon told his friend Pete Shotton, according to Darryl Bullock, "I let him toss me off," using the slang terminology for masturbation (146). Doggett refers to Lennon's erotic fantasy about Harrison expressed in a diary entry (*You* 258).

30 Napier-Bell suggests that the desperate voicemail messages left for him by Epstein before his death, some apparently addressed to John Lennon, were part of Epstein's attempt at seduction (*You Don't* 123–4). The bisexual Napier-Bell had explained that he felt no reciprocal attraction for Epstein being wary of someone whose "emotional relationships were notoriously unstable" and who remained obsessed with Lennon (*You Don't* 124). "[D]rawn into the competitive world of pop music for erotic reasons," Epstein remained closeted, Napier-Bell believes, because "[h]e was afraid of being thought of as a lucky dilettante, a naughty school-master playing around with the choirboys" (*You Don't* 127, 119). For Napier-Bell, the Beatles' charisma rested in the "secret … [of] how four tough working-class lads had come to accept the benefits of acting coquettishly for a wealthy middle-class homosexual. People said their image was that of the boy next door, but … [it was really] the cool, cocky brashness of a kid who's found a sugar-daddy and got himself set up in Mayfair" (*You Don't* 118).

31 On the Jewish Svengali in George Du Maurier's anti-Semetic novel *Trilby*, see Lovesey's "The Victorian Guitar" (507–8).

3

Performative Identity: Cosey Fanni Tutti, Brett Anderson, Moby

Performative identity in popular music autobiography appears especially in life writing by post-punk, post-glam musicians of the late 1970s, 1980s and early 90s whose music often intersected with other arts. These musicians skilfully manipulated both avant-garde and popular forms in a variety of artistic expressions, though this facility may reflect and update 1960s musicians' debt to the milieu of art school.[1] Importantly, as musicians, these autobiographers resisted representations of themselves as voices of a generation. While refusing genealogical designations as spokespersons for new versions of "my generation," the "Woodstock generation," the "blank generation," or the later "generation like" or "generation RX," for example,[2] they still situate their creative authority in particular, local scenes or movements tied to specific times and places, and within distinct genres from industrial to electronica.[3] In addition, they display a consciousness of their own second order or parodic "rock" roots by flaunting a constructed inauthenticity.[4]

They also share distinctly literary or theoretical associations whether, for example, to rebellious French theorists or symbolist poets, Victorian or Beat godfathers, or monuments of the literary establishment such as the creator of *Moby Dick*. Their performative identity appears in the self-consciously created self of these works which mimics in some cases the more theatrical persona of these musicians' stage identities, and in some cases their performance art or artistic "actions." As Simon Frith writes in a different context, their writing selves are "involved in a process of *double enactment*," engaging both their celebrity or aspirational rock star personality and its flamboyantly parodic or deliberately anti-heroic reflection (*Performing* 212). While autobiography always renders the writer a self-observer, self-dramatizer, and even self-vivisector, and all autobiography is to some degree a performance,[5] identity is performative in these popular music autobiographies in terms of their narrators' embodiment of different onstage and promotional selves or personas as lived within the collective, embodied consciousness of performance space itself. We find this deliberate self-construction in the comic persona in Moby's autobiographies, the self-objectivization in Cosey Fanni Tutti's, and, as we shall see in the next chapter, the self-mythologizing in the life writing of David Wojnarowicz.

Performative rock itself in its marriage of the avant-garde and a street-wise sensibility in its post-punk, post-glam manifestations may draw from earlier happenings and performance art. Happenings,[6] argues Jeff Nuttall, were a Duchampian development by American action painters and pop artists who "found" art in everyday objects and human action (124). "Happenings were simply three-dimensional paintings in which the movements of painter and public were incorporated into the design," eventually complicated by drugs and "the principle of transformation by destruction" (Nuttall 124, 125). Performance art, that would go on more directly to influence popular music performance, unlike popular forms such as burlesque, drag shows, music hall, and vaudeville, is associated with the museum and the theater. The performance artist, explains Frith, poses as both subject of the performance as well as its medium, playing with the boundary between private and public, and placing the performer at risk (*Performing* 205–6). In practice, however, the solemnity of its theoretical heritage was sometimes absent. A "street" view of performance and its interpretation in the early 70s appears in the diaries of novelist and musician Jim Carroll.[7] He recounts his own performance near Max's Kansas City in New York, when he released a cockroach and then sprayed it repeatedly with "malodorous insecticide": "The audience loved it." The next week *The Village Voice* called it "a non-verbal demonstration on the horrors of Vietnam" (62, 63). Elements of provocative performance or "guerrilla-theater action," as Mark Rudd calls it (45), also belonged to the work of a number of the period's anarchist and communist anti-war groups such as the Yippies, the Weathermen, and the SDS-associated Up Against the Wall Motherfuckers (whose leader Ben Morea was associated with the Living Theater and other members with Comedia del Arte) (Rudd 44, 188–9; Neumann 54, 89–99, 114).[8] Among the many madcap 1960s precursors of performance rock, the early Grateful Dead's involvement with Ken Kesey and the Merry Pranksters' acid tests, rock operas like the Who's *Tommy*, and conceptual performance pieces like the Incredible String Band's *U* are notable. Another significant development was 1966's Exploding Plastic Inevitable, a "new" hybrid art form, created by Andy Warhol from a blend of the rock concert, the happening and freak out, and emerging installation art, incorporating the conceptual forms of John Cage and La Monte Young, with whom the Velvet Underground's John Cale had worked.[9]

Cosey Fanni Tutti

Sex work in the hard core pornography industry is unconventional research for a rock 'n' roll or even an experimental, industrial music project,[10] and Cosey Fanni Tutti (Christine Carol Newby) of industrial rock band Throbbing Gristle (TG) refers to her autobiography as a re-entry into "the lion's den of my past," "the tainted past," based on her diaries, in order to set "the record straight" (ix, 306, 331). Revisiting the past is performed in a surprisingly detached, affectless fashion, ostensibly motivated by a more general desire to archive and monetize the remnants of art action pieces due to contemporary interest in the interaction of art and pornography, before pornography's twenty-first-century mainstreaming, as well as rock 'n' roll nostalgia. The autobiography was also designed to settle scores and distance Tutti from the eloquent Genesis (Breyer) P-Orridge (Neil Megson), who self-identified as s/he. P-Orridge, who died in early 2020, has often been credited—not least by him/herself—as the originator, theorist, spokesperson, and ultimately the terminator of TG (P-Orridge, *Sacred* 212–14). P-Orridge regarded him/herself as primarily a writer (Reynolds, *Rip* xxvii; Tessitore 140)—not a musician—but later s/he may have aspired to start or revive a neo-pagan, quasi-occult religion but ended up leading a cult. Along with other self-aggrandizing notions, P-Orridge was committed to destroying socially programmed personal identity, a plan carried much further in 2003 in the gender-erasing Pandrogyne project, with his/her second wife, the nurse and dominatrix Jacqueline "Lady Jaye" Breyer P-Orridge, a transformation involving daily injections of ketamine for nearly a year and radical body modification through plastic surgery. S/he described his/her artistic performances as self-therapy (S. Reed 77), though there may have been more than a little S&M at play, and s/he worked for six months as a female dominatrix (P-Orridge, *Sacred* 153). One of TG's legacies is the jarring or at least radically different discursive registers of Tutti and P-Orridge in their accounts of the band's history. Given their antagonistic stance to much of 1960s and 1970s popular music and prevalent notions of art itself, Tutti's *Art Sex Music* by extension may be an "unpopular" music autobiography,[11] though in his critique of industrial music,

S. Alexander Reed suggests that attention to background and biography, if of a gender essentialist variety,[12] may be the best means to grasp TG's significance. Simon Reynolds even suggests that TG mainly embodied an artistic concept or aesthetic philosophy, and that one "could almost skip the records and read" the lucid explanations of P-Orridge (*Rip* 240).[13]

TG between 1976 and 1981 was a Vienna Aktionists-inspired, George Bataille-like transgressive art band engaged in "breaking down preconceived ideas of what was 'music'" as Tutti puts it or, in P-Orridge's words, in conspiring to "create something that really fucks music" (Tutti 237; P-Orridge, *Sacred* 214). The Vienna Aktionists movement of the 1960s criticized art's entrapment in generic boundaries, its commercialism, and, in the work of Valie Export, its violence against women, and its members utilized staged happenings or actions, focused often in grotesque ways on the body and bodily fluids, as well as on the destruction of art objects, such as guitars; Pete Townshend's inspiration would come from auto-destructive art theorist Gustav Metzger (Townshend 64). The Aktionists' transgressive autopsy art may be best known in J.G. Ballard's 1973 novel *Crash* (Reed 24), though pre-TG COUM Transmissions demonstrated its ability to shock. One such action had P-Orridge "placing severed chicken heads on top of his penis and masturbating" and "for a pièce de résistance, he might give himself a blood and milk enema and then fart out the liquid" (Reynolds, *Rip* 227). TG's transgressive ethos also resembles that of radical philosopher and artist Georges Bataille who in a variety of works explored the interaction of violence with the sacred and the erotic. Tutti participated in a festival on Bataille in 1984, "Violent Silence Festival—Arts of Transgression," at London's Bloomsbury Theatre, and she had previously engaged with his narrative of incest, *My Mother* (303, 304). The band was designed from its outset to be a non-band playing non-music in order not to commercialize its creations. Initially self-styled as makers of a species of Fluxus-style "anti-art," if not "wreckers of civilisation" as controversial Conservative MP Nicholas Fairbairn notoriously declared in 1976 (Kellein 73; Tutti 208),[14] TG—like 3TK4 as we shall see in the next chapter—began as performance artists with a twist. They may have been an unusual post-psychedelic band which described itself as a purveyor of performance art largely to secure state funding (Reynolds 226), though applying for funding and archiving performances were major parts of its modus operandi, in line with the practices of more conventional performance artists. TG would become one of the most uncompromising and dysfunctional, if ever playful and facetious, bands of the late 1970s. They ended, however, after a brief rebirth in the twenty-first century, as *Art Sex Music* details, with the sad spectacle of a spirited a cappella version of the "Sue Me, Sue You Blues," perhaps the most conventional, bathetic rock 'n' roll finale.

TG was associated, as was their precursor COUM Transmissions, with the Fluxus movement, which grew from composer John Cage's musical experiments as set out in a manifesto by George Maciunas in 1963. Maciunas had been stunned to hear Cage's *Music for Prepared Piano* using his aleatonic methods in the early 1950s (Kellein 21). Fluxus was an international group of artists and others, primarily in the 1960s and early 1970s, committed to democratizing art itself and access to it, collaborative artistic production, and upending the art and culture industry's commercialization. While Fluxus works often have a "light-hearted playfulness," they engage with a "difficult politics" (Thompson 53). Its best-known manifestation may be in the work of Brion Gysin, La Monte Young, and Yoko Ono. Ono's famous performance piece, "Cut-Dress," in which audience members are invited to cut off the clothes of a seated woman, indicates the seemingly teasing but provocative gender politics involved; Ono's early recorded song "Why"—the B-side of John Lennon's "Mother"—explores vocal dissonance or sonic noise over a driving blues rock rhythm track. While its maker was not a member of Fluxus, Gil Scott Heron's "The Revolution Will Not Be Televised" similarly was very much engaged with its anti-commercial, playful, and politically pointed spirit. TG's precursor art collective mounted a piece entitled "This Machine Kills Music," engaging Fluxus's anti-art sentiments, and by extension questioning the assurance of Woody Guthrie's famous "This Machine Kills Fascists'" guitar slogan. TG band members later will record Fluxus-associated novelist William Burroughs in New York and Kansas, and Tutti will transcribe his collaborator Brion Gysin's work, and later P-Orridge will publish a series of interviews with Gysin.[15] TG's most direct association with Fluxus may have been its engagement with mail art, a practice that led to P-Orridge's conviction for distributing pornography through the post,[16] Tutti's moniker Cosey Fanni Tutti, and their reception of Jerry Dreva's "'Wanks for the Memories,' a masturbation book, full of his boyfriend's semen" (211), anticipating Tutti's own interest in bodily fluid art. P-Orridge noted that some of the tampon art at the *Prostitution* action "was a real Fluxus game" (qtd. in Savage, *England's Dreaming* 251).

TG emerged in part, like Manchester's Joy Division,[17] from the sub-culture of dispossession in the violent housing estates and working-class factory environs of England's embittered northern industrial cities, with the Second World War rationing only ending in 1954. "[P]ost-war dereliction" demanded a focus on bare survival accompanied by "a confrontational and uncompromising attitude" within a culture of violent tension between different social, economic, and generational sub-groups (1): "There was a schism between those who fought in the war and the teenage children who were breaking away from the traditions their parents had defended with their lives" (31). Tutti recounts a precocious upbringing[18] in a topsy turvy wonderland of bombed buildings and detritus dumps from the Second World War in Hull, one of the most bombed cities in the UK. TG echoed this sonic environment rather than striving to interpret it or distract from it. In this context, the band's occasional use of Nazi imagery was highly provocative. Like Joy Division, its name taken from Nazi concentration camp brothels and its clothing style from the Hitler youth, TG used Nazi imagery in some of its early performances, referred to "Zyklon B" in a song title, and placed "Music from the Death Factory" on an early poster. Later, as Reynolds notes, the band's fascist flirtation would shift uneasily toward identification (*Rip* 234, 239). Voicing the unspoken and exposing the hidden, as with the horrors of the Holocaust, also led to a fascination with medical experimentation and celebrity murderers like Manchester's "Moors Murderers," Gary Gilmore, and Charles Manson—an obsession later taken up by deathcore bands like Whitechapel—and TG also covered Manson's music. TG and particularly P-Orridge were influenced by the occult magus Aleister Crowley, of whom Jimmy Page is the best-known rock devotee, and took William Burroughs and Brion Gysin as mentors. While appearing to oppose the joyful transcendence offered by groups like the Beatles, however, TG's work still manifested some of the same radical experimentation, graphic-design and multimedia savvy, and heavily produced vs acoustic qualities as well as the hippy undertones of the "second flowering of an authentic psychedelia," and in turn the band spawned its own descendants (Reynolds, *Rip* 224–44). Like punk bands of the mid-1970s in conceptual terms, TG was more directly associated than much of 1960s popular music with the avant-garde and experimental music as well as the aesthetics of parody. Cosey Fanni Tutti's name, for example, was derived via a mail art exchange from Mozart's 1790 opera *Così fan tutte*. The name was coined by Les Maull, an early COUM Transmissions associate: "doing the five-knuckle shuffle with his eight inches of throbbing gristle" (Tutti 105, 157). With a few exceptions, such as the references to their music's evolution "[f]rom a limp, post-coital COUM penis to a fully erect Throbbing Gristle, up and ready for action" or "Throbbing Gristle's final spurt coming to a sticky end," Tutti's autobiography avoids penis jokes (241, 399).

TG's music in Tutti's account emerged from the sonic experimentation of COUM Transmissions, facilitated by Chris Carter's innovative technological expertise and enthusiasm for creating sonic gadgets and particularly the sound-mangling analogue special effects unit, the Gristleizer.[19] While they also played more conventional rock instruments, they conscientiously rejected virtuosity or even competence, modeling their playing instead on the notion of a child's first encounter with an instrument, and in concert sometimes inviting audience members to play (Reynolds, *Rip* 230). Tutti played cornet—Sleazy having passed on the instrument because "All I get is a fart" (qtd. in Daniel 47)—and also a modified, prepared guitar routed though a distortion box with a variety of pedal-controlled effects, often striking the strings with different objects. Her radical approach and its distance from the "mindless indulgences and spoon-feeding" of the contemporary music scene appear when she purchases a new guitar: "The other guitarists were all doing renditions of 'Stairway to Heaven' and there was me saying to the assistant, 'No, I don't need to tune my guitar first—I'll just plug in. I kind of know what sound I'm looking for'" (241, 244). The resulting music was antagonistic to contemporary punk rock, disco, or rock 'n' roll. Keenan points out that TG "fully deliver[ed] on punk's failed promise to explore extreme culture as a way of sabotaging systems of control—beginning with rock music itself. Where punk ranted against rock while playing a debased version of the same, TG might have assumed rock's classic quartet format, but they were very consciously anti-rock 'n' roll" (20). In the manner of Fluxus, TG made a virtue of being almost a cottage industry for its various members rather than a viable commercial enterprise, refusing to capitalize on the ascent of electronic music or record industry interest.[20] Moreover, given its fraught interpersonal dynamics, the band virtually began breaking up or threatening to from its outset, accompanied by regular technical malfunctions in concert. Moreover, the "aural assault" of the band's soundscapes was designed to "hit people between the eyes .... A sound that caused an involuntary physical response in the body" (241). As Reynolds points out, "[t]hey were fascinated by military research into the use of infrasound as a non-lethal weapon, with certain frequencies triggering vomiting, epileptic seizures, and even involuntary defecation" (*Rip* 235). Their performances attacked popular music conventions and aggressively terrorized audience expectations, and they transformed "the concert place into an interrogation room where the audience's complicity in rock idolatry was broken down and ridiculed. With all exits for rock's Dionysian energies blocked, TG's audiences would inevitably turn on each other, the group or the hall for release" (Keenan 27). In practice, however, over its short career, the band's music evolved from ambient sound based on prepared loops without rhythm or vocals to more rhythmic, percussive tracks and finally to more melodic songs. While TG's music has "passages of astonishing intensity," it also relied on "an arsenal of riffs and tricks as predictable as any musical language ... [and] the palette of sound-colours could start to feel somewhat samey" (Reynolds, *Rip* 231).

The band's creation coincided with Tutti's and Chris Carter's romance—partly signaled by the representation of Carter's castration in *Cease to Exist*, their "kind of home-made, dark snuff movie" (230)—and the beginning of the end of Tutti's relationship with P-Orridge, though he first insisted they form a ménage a trois. She postponed a final break to preserve TG. Significantly, this romance also ends her career making hard core pornographic films, though she continues nude modeling and stripping, the latter sometimes accompanied by her favorite "Because the Night" by Patti Smith, who had sometimes performed a striptease parody in early shows (284). Like others who had warned her or expressed outrage, Carter was shocked by P-Orridge's treatment of Tutti. Other pressures on band unity were Peter (Sleazy) Christopherson's graphic work for Hipgnosis, which designed album covers for Pink Floyd. Sleazy also made quasi forensic crime scene designs for the window of John Krivine's BOY boutique which caught the attention of the police. BOY and its flagship band Chelsea/Generation X rivaled Malcolm McLaren and Vivienne Westwood's SEX shop: "each [shop] had a brand and a band to help sell it" (199). For Tutti, punk from its very inception was primarily "commercial" in orientation (qtd. in Daniel 23–5). Sleazy took some of the first publicity photos of the Sex Pistols, though McLaren considered them "too extreme" for promotional purposes (199). Another pressure came from P-Orridge's seduction by punk rock and rock star posturing.

The *Prostitution* action of October 19–26, 1976 at London's ICA (Institute of Contemporary Arts) was the official launch of TG, their performance being followed by a striptease and the band LSD featuring Billy Idol, and it galvanized media and even parliamentary outrage at the explicit and confrontational nature of the work on display.[21] Giving widespread public exposure to performance art for the first time (Savage, *England's Dreaming* 250), it provoked "concern about the subsidized avant-garde ... at a time of recession and public spending cuts" (Reynolds, *Rip* 229), similar to the later hysteria surrounding David Wojnarowicz's exhibition in America as we shall see. The inclusion of used, bloodied tampons and of pornographic magazine photographs in the show's art installation attracted the most negative attention. The barrage of censorious newspaper articles was then displayed as part of the show's interactive engagement with its audience. Tutti's tampon art was associated with her highly personal, body-centered aesthetic, rather than a Warhol-style oxidation painting or Damien Hirst-style animals-preserved-in-formaldehyde intervention, though it never extended to the preserved remains of her miscarried fetus (345–6). It was also not a quasi-punk rock gesture of defiance as when at 1992's Reading Festival, Donita Sparks of Los Angeles's L7 band, frustrated at being pelted in the rain with mud balls, "pulled out her tampon onstage and threw it at the audience" (Lanegan 99). There may have been a whimsical if grotesque side to Tutti's tampon art, however, given that "[f]or fun we had Sotheby's value one of my soiled tampons: £80" (209). The virulent press coverage disproportionally targeted Tutti, ending her modeling jobs (Ford 6.24), but it had a more personal cost. It severed all contact with her parents whom she would never see again, though that would not dissuade her from a final tampon art action at the Queen's country estate Sandringham. As a now post-menopausal woman, Tutti incorporated her "last tampons … crushed and pulped into papier-mâché. The different sizes, shades of white, spots of pale blue (tampon string) and varied hues of dried red blood looked beautiful" (384). As one of the final gestures in her *Self*lessness series, it was a radically autobiographical "imprint of my*self*" (384).

The voice and style of *Art Sex Music* are aggressively unliterary, perhaps an outgrowth of a Fluxus-tinged anti-art ethos. Given her dramatic, eccentric artwork, Tutti's autobiography is in many ways almost blandly impersonal if not exactly industrial in its colloquial matter-of-factness. This presentation may have been designed to register her distance from the highly articulate, charming, and educated voice of P-Orridge who had assumed the role of trumpeting TG's philosophy and also taking credit for most of its work, much to Tutti's annoyance. The unusual impersonality of Tutti's voice may also have been designed to resemble that of probably England's first female autobiographer, Margery Kempe (1373–1438) who, being illiterate, dictated her life story to an amanuensis.[22] The mediated distancing of the personal voice in these works links an otherwise improbable mash-up of the sacred and the profane. Tutti's autobiography's insistently unpretentious, oral, anti-art voice may also be deployed to keep prurient interest and moral censure about her work in the porn industry at bay, and perhaps less obviously to contextualize the autobiography's other story: Tutti's horrifically abusive relationship with P-Orridge. It also may be aligned with a version of "*Self*lessness," her art project series, including her tampon art, a project relating more directly to the annihilation of subjectivity than to altruism or transcendence (341).

Given the avant-garde associations of TG's mixed media work and its controversial engagement with the sex industry, the affectless presentation is at once both off-putting and authenticating, and also performative in presenting a distinctly working-class, northern English point of view. Its plain spoken toughness demonstrates the street-smarts inculcated by and required in order to withstand the post-war urban wilderness and its abusive domestic arrangements. Clichés and northernisms abound as when Tutti is "gobsmacked," "gutted," "knackered," or "brought … up sharp," or doesn't "give a toss" or when she is "blagging" [using deception] or "playing gooseberry" [chaperoning] or looking for the "bog-standard" [average] or when "it wasn't the done thing" or "some people grassed each other up" [betrayed them to the authorities] (63, 35, 164, 425, 252, 44, 239, 120–1). There are myriad cliché-ridden and occasionally slangy "'What the fuck?!' moment[s]" when "the shit hits the fan" (438, 121), as when it's "the last straw" or "par for the course" or "didn't cut the mustard" or became "tough going" "outside my comfort zone" or, more happily and circularly, when "we were like kids in a candy store" and things go "smooth as silk" or "come full circle" (46, 78, 409, 137, 162, 461, 496, 498). While rhetorical or kitchen sink clichés convey a degree of authenticity or inadvertently provide explanation—as when "shouldering the responsibility for Gen's tantrums" is described blandly and revealingly as part of life's "regular ups and downs" (162)—they do flatten delivery and obscure the idiosyncrasies of the individual voice. While irony or tone-deafness may be involved in describing porn work as contributing "a purity" to her art (172), at moments when aesthetic appreciation is involved, the results are deadening, as in the description of Jimi Hendrix's performance as being "unlike anything I'd seen or heard before" (35). However unwittingly, this colloquial propensity with its occasional, incongruously wide-eyed endorsements—"I was feeling a little deflated that I hadn't been invited to join in the orgy" (118), or "I found it exciting hunting for my artworks on the top shelves of newsagents and in Soho sex shops" (152)—reinforces the portrayal of Tutti as a self-taught, instinctual artist, though one, as the latter sections of the autobiography reveal, who justifiably seeks credit and also institutional approval for her groundbreaking artistic work.

Art Sex Music has a marked retrospective intelligence particularly in its account of Tutti's nearly pathological relationship with P-Orridge, many of whose misrepresentations of their life and work she only uncovered "years later" (83). As with her later surprise at her naive involvement in the illegal, dangerous, and "unpredictable" porn industry (141)—where she is sometimes regarded as a non-entity on set, strippers commonly are motivated by "self-hate" and called "dogs" by promoters (288, 289), she is pressured to have her pubic hair shaved by a male magazine editor (150), and she witnesses others' sexual degradation[23]—she seems only very slowly to recognize P-Orridge's abuse though this may be part of a conventional pattern of denial. Tutti initially was attracted by P-Orridge's nonconformist, bohemian, creative spark, and perhaps his interrupted formal art education and his somewhat more genteel background, and his similarly somewhat inflated account of his own artistic achievements.[24] However, as others point out at the beginning of their relationship, s/he uses his/her extreme narcissism and sense of personal exceptionalism to justify manipulations, that resemble the actions of a would-be guru or cult leader. P-Orridge, in Tutti's account, soon possesses and controls virtually every aspect of her life as if she were a possession, servant, or slave.[25] P-Orridge claims divine inspiration and blames his/her rages on medical conditions, while insisting that Tutti inflames them. S/he also refuses to wear condoms, resulting in her pregnancy and subsequent abortion. S/he also renames her, clothes her (while modeling his/her own clothes on the droogs from *A Clockwork Orange*), reads her diary and adds disparaging comments, dictates her involvement in group sex, and enforces a strict double standard regarding their open sexual relationship, her freedom to be away from home, and the retention of secrets. In addition, she performs all the cooking, cleaning, washing, and ironing, and P-Orridge resents her waking him/her when she rises early for paid employment, sometimes factory work, to support P-Orridge's artistic endeavors. P-Orridge even engages in a NXIVM cult-style co-opting of the language of feminist self-empowerment to humiliate women. For example, at one stage, he insists on her having sex with men he chooses, and in so doing to "hurt myself for him [to] … prove my love and dedication to him beyond doubt. These 'tests' were a self-serving play presented to me under the twisted notion that submitting to his demands was a way for me to gain strength" (196). He stresses that she is replaceable, and that disobedience could lead to expulsion. Despite her attempts at compliance, her isolation increases and she realizes that "nothing pleased or appeased him for long" (99, 103), but, as in a classic case of spousal abuse, she says "I still adored and loved

Gen" (88). He is also physically abusive, which includes punching her in the face and kicking her in the crotch, actions which concern her only if marks on her body will interfere with her sex work. When she finally determines to leave and after she finally departs, there are three attempts at murder, though "I felt guilty for making Gen so unhappy" (248). P-Orridge attempts to strangle and later threatens to stab her, and he throws a concrete block at her head while she is sunbathing. He has threatened ominously, "[i]f I can't have you, nobody can" (246). She normalizes these incidents, concluding glibly after the latter, for example, that it "put a halt to any more sunbathing for me when Gen was around" (255).

There is a similar if more extreme story of domestic abuse within the slightly earlier "working class revolution" of the 1960s popular music scene recounted by Beverley (Kutner) Martyn in her autobiography *Sweet Honesty* (14). Born into a Polish Jewish family in Coventry in 1947, Beverley became a rising folk music star. While she played at the Monterey Pop Festival in 1967, co-wrote songs with Nick Drake, and may have inspired "Bridge Over Troubled Water" by Paul Simon (34–5), with whom she had a relationship (34–5; Hilburn 110), her career was derailed by abusive men beginning with her father. Her boyfriend Bert Jansch, later of Pentangle, persuaded her to turn down a recording contract with EMI, and though a drama school graduate, she rejected a position with London's Royal Shakespeare Company.[26] She signed with Joe Boyd's Witchseason Productions, which included the Incredible String Band in its roster, before she met the "enchanting, ethereal" John Martyn, virtuoso guitarist and songwriter (41). Significantly, Boyd warned her about Martyn, who had a volatile "Jekyll and Hyde" personality (Dave Pegg qtd. in Munro 132), and an unquenchable appetite for drink and drugs; Boyd may have hoped that a romance between Beverley and Nick Drake might have saved both of them (Munro 58). Martyn soon ends her career, taking over offers extended to her, and they marry and have two children. Martyn's physical abuse begins in 1969 when he is jealous of her meeting with Bob Dylan in Woodstock. She initially feels sorry for and forgives him, a pattern replicated by Tutti, not realizing "how many times that scenario of violence followed by remorse would be played out" (47). Others notice but don't investigate her "tell-tale bruises" (68), and "[o]ver the years I received a broken nose, a fractured inner ear and hairline fractures of the skull," and he threatens violence against their children, and the abuse induces her psychosis (71). She blames herself for this abuse and even when she finally leaves, divorce proceedings extending over a decade, she receives no alimony, and though continuing to feel terrified of him, she finally allows Martyn back into her life for the sake of their children.[27]

Powerful women in the music business like Carol King would experience similar spousal abuse (Weller 395–8), and even Carly Simon was a victim of the music industry's version of the Hollywood casting couch as she explains in her memoir (165–70). Peggy Seeger relates a similar story about Dylan's manager Albert Grossman (*First* 112). Rock diva Tina Turner sadly has become almost as famous for her soulful music as for her witness to domestic abuse suffered at the hands of Ike Turner that progressed from beatings with coat hangers to choking and punching (144). More recently, Inuit throat singer and Polaris prize-winning world music artist Tanya Tagaq in her raw, fictionalized memoir *Split Tooth*—dedicated to "the Missing and Murdered Indigenous Women and Girls, and survivors of residential schools"—details attempted rape, sexual abuse, and teenage pregnancy, maintaining the ethos that "[e]mpathy is for the privileged. Empathy is not for Nature" (61). There is an account of sexual abuse in Chrissie Hynde's 2015 autobiography, *Reckless*, perhaps made more distressing by the facetiousness of "your hapless narrator," recounting what she calls elsewhere "another event that should have been enacted only onstage in the theatre of the absurd," for which she blames herself and drug use (117, 305). Chapter 14 details Quaalude-fueled sexual violence at the hands of members of a white supremacist biker gang for whom "[c]hicks were a commodity to be exploited and 'disposed of' .... They lent a whole new meaning to the expression 'dumped'—but I didn't know that yet" (123).

The sex work which made Tutti's art projects so controversial might appear to be a traumatized reaction to an abusive father, who beat her and threatened to chop off her fingers or murder her pet rabbit (14), disappointed at not having a son, though he did teach her to fight for self-protection, a skill useful later. Her father also might appear to re-emerge in her relationship with P-Orridge. She protests, however, that she alone decided to engage in sex work and that this work enabled her sense of empowerment and personal agency. In some respects, handling this controversial material, the autobiography reads like an antagonistic "memoir of an undutiful" or "outcast daughter" as she says later, almost the antithesis of de Beauvoir's feminist classic (346), though it is clearly not an Augustinian-style *Confessions*, a title Tutti used for a limited edition book project on nude modeling (352, 377). In a strange quasi-feminist but ostensibly anti-feminist stance, Tutti stresses that she chose porn and took back its erotic power and defeated the objectifiers of women at their own game. In these explanations, the autobiography shifts into somewhat generic grant application language. Tutti, for example, styles herself an artist activist in a guerrilla art intervention transgressively "infiltrating" and "exploiting the sex industry for my own purposes, to subvert and use it to create my own art" (169, 171–2). She claims that by framing her nude modeling as her own work she was "subverting the 'male gaze'" and producing a "rich visual time capsule of the blatant 1970s sexism" (198, 340). This strategy resembles but departs significantly from that of another well-known intervention in the sex industry: Gloria Steinem's work at New York's Playboy Club in 1963, designed from its outset to research an exposé. Tutti's quasi-Fluxus and apparently autobiographical artistic manifesto is that "My Life Is My Art. My Art Is My Life" (116). It is sometimes unclear whether the sex work, either as magazine model (a so-called "glamour" model, a phrase achieving international recognition with the controversy surrounding the end of Paul McCartney's marriage to Heather Mills) or actor in pornographic films like 1975's *Pussy's Galore*, or stripper[28] was performed mainly to supply more "honest" images for collages (one of Robert Mapplethorpe's motives for entering photography), or as a way to enjoy the "process of co-creating" sexualized images, or mainly to make money to do art (171). Another "justification" for the sex work is her embrace of presumably porn-friendly gay liberation—as opposed to what she sees as rule-based, censorious feminist liberation (115)—the demonstration of art as life and hence by extension a celebration of all experience and the body, and also the representation of conventional art itself as a type of prostitution. There's also a sense that the porn work is Duchampian ready-made art, in that as performed by an artist and so designated, it is art.

After communicating via "hand grenade" emails and then media interviews, and later through lawyers, and perhaps finally through autobiographies,[29] Tutti and P-Orridge and the rest of TG reunited in 2004 due to fan and art establishment interest, and in order to generate revenue (398). P-Orridge would claim in 2008 that the other members of Throbbing Gristle "were hoping that I'd die on stage" so that "they'd be on a gravy train forever" (*Sacred* 204), and in 2012 s/he accused Tutti and Carter—the last two remaining members of the band, Sleazy having died in 2010—of attempting to "appropriate the mythological aspect of TG" (*Sacred* 213). As Tutti anticipated, the 2004 reunion exacerbated the interpersonal antagonism within the band from its genesis as well as the controversy surrounding Tutti's porn industry work. Any visual reference to her sex work projects attracted anti-pornography authorities and also sometimes those expecting some version of a rock 'n' roll striptease, as when at the band's initial launch in 1976, Tutti removed her leather biker jacket to reveal herself naked underneath with one breast cosmetically altered to resemble a bleeding gash (204). Just prior to COUM Transmissions' invitation to the prestigious 9th Paris Biennale in 1975, she had hired a photographer who was presumably too shocked to document an art action concluding with "dildos" on the ends of a five foot pole inserted "into my vagina and [P-Orridge's] … anus" (176). Over and above this range of audience expectations, problems with printers refusing to print and exhibitions refusing to exhibit on moral grounds persisted after the reunion.

The major challenge for TG and its possibly revived fortunes in 2004 in Tutti's assessment was P-Orridge's acting like a rogue agent and becoming a self-mythologizing rip-off artist and wanna-be rock star rather than a collaborator committed to the band's legacy. Even Sleazy, with whom s/he shared an accelerating appetite for drugs and alcohol, became exasperated, saying the rest of TG should "treat Gen like a Prague rent boy—make him earn his money and don't trust him an inch" (364). P-Orridge initially made extravagant demands for participating in reunion recordings and gigs, and styled him/herself the band's leader in interviews, personally licensing and profiting from TG bootlegs, while continuing to perform their material with his/her own band, and violated agreements about making and selling TG merchandise, as well as misappropriated and mixed-up TG song lyrics in live performance. According to Tutti, s/he also forged letters in Tutti's name, stole some of the band's gear, and undermined the band's unified response to Tate Britain's request to acquire TG material by making a clandestine solo deal. Tutti offers an extended account of the final days of the band's reunion and its resistance to becoming an iconoclastic— "entertainment through pain" as their *Greatest Hits* was sub-titled—version of a golden oldies band amid increasing medical challenges and the creep of later middle age. Tutti and Carter would eventually became the ABBA- and Eurythmics-friendly Chris & Cosey and then Carter Tutti, and undertake the frantic cottage industry of creating and manufacturing recordings and other types of merchandise. P-Orridge with Sleazy would establish the dysfunctional Psychic TV, which had a cult offshoot.[30] *Art Sex Music* logs the more recent requests that have come to her for performances, lectures, and appearances, and documents the author's attempt to secure credit for her work, after career-long obstructions from P-Orridge and the porn-averse institutions of higher art. Tutti and P-Orridge, despite their years of rancour and their shared belief in art's impermanence and the creative process itself being of greater importance than the final product—central to the notion of performance art—were delighted and felt vindicated seeing their work gaining recognition by being housed and thereby institutionalized in major national and international art galleries.

Brett Anderson

Brett Anderson's *Coal Black Mornings* is a self-consciously conventional and intentionally didactic autobiography written in an oddly old-fashioned register, aiming, so it claims, to provoke self-understanding and to provide a genealogical narrative for the author's children as well as a genealogical caution for himself. He seeks to repair the broken genealogy in his parents' relationships with their own parents and knowledge of forebears, and—in an inverted Oedipal twist—to resist becoming his father. Hence, it avoids being a sex, drugs, and rock 'n' roll bacchanalia or what he calls a "'coke and gold discs' memoir" or even "a predictable avalanche of dropped names," as he maintains in the autobiography's second volume, *Afternoons with the Blinds Drawn*, "the book I said I wouldn't write" (*Mornings* ix; *Afternoons* 5, 158).[31] Both texts focus on the creation and performance of Anderson's own image as the frontman of the late-glam rock, anticipatory Britpop band Suede, and confront fan and media misinterpretations of this image.[32] He offers a somewhat incongruously formal account of a pop career within a kaleidoscope of shifting self-created and imposed performative personas from the androgynous poser and genteel tourist or anthropologist exploring the gutter to the media-created simulacra. Suede was identified with the "new generation" of the Britpop scene but Anderson claims to have anticipated that scene and to be, instead, a kind of spokesperson for the pre-Cool Britannia generation and later for distancing Suede from the excesses of Britpop stars like Oasis and Blur. Significantly, for such a visual pop artist, the autobiographical volumes lack photographs. *Coal Black Mornings* is also a detailed, almost Dickensian narrative of an eccentric and tragic father, who might be another notional implied reader of the autobiography, in addition to the writer himself, his sons, his critics, and his fans.

Another ghostly implied presence is that of the major influence on Suede, the Smiths, whose music in the mid-1980s had been for their devotees an anti-suicide prophylaxis despite their songs' preoccupation with misery,[33] and perhaps particularly their principle lyricist and singer, Morrissey.[34] Yet another implied specter is that of Morrissey's celebrated *Autobiography* (2013) as we shall see, though Anderson's quintessentially English self-deprecating reticence is almost the opposite of Morrissey's self-important bombast. While Morrissey does declare "[t]here will be no secrets of flesh or fantasy" (277)—though he is more forthcoming about his disinterest in girls' bodies (75–6)—his tales of creativity, romance, and finance seem predicated on the assumption of his insufficiently celebrated genius. *Coal Black Mornings* quotes Morrissey's remark that Anderson is a "deeply boring young man" (25). Morrissey's autobiography makes no mention of Anderson or Suede, and his partner in the Smiths, Johnny Marr, only briefly refers to Suede's original guitarist Bernard Butler in his autobiography *Set the Boy Free* (2016) (347–8). Anderson stresses his credentials as someone raised in relative poverty to authorize his unsentimental portrait of the non-psychedelic, non-swinging 1960s.[35] He also describes himself as the one-time boyfriend of the muse of Britpop and original member of Suede, the "urbane and worldly" artist and descendant of Holocaust survivors Justine Frischmann (*Mornings* 111). She assisted with creating his image as an androgynous latter-day glam popster who notoriously said he was a "bisexual man who's never had a homosexual experience," and he makes it clear that, in fact, he did inhale (*Afternoons* 46).

While self-identifying as a representative of the disenfranchised, post-punk, slacker generation of the 1980s and early 1990s, Anderson resists inclusion in the retro-psychedelic scene later in the period when Britpop emerged. His references to the first summer of love in 1967, when he was born, and "the second Summer of Love" are bitterly ironic (*Mornings* 134). He does, however, want to acknowledge the influence of key figures such as David Bowie and bands such as the Sex Pistols as well as the Smiths. Part of his very English self-deprecation and reticence is his unwillingness to say too much about Justine Frischmann and as a result he sometimes refers to her bizarrely as "the previously mentioned artist" (*Afternoons* 113).[36] A neo-abstract expressionist painter, Frischmann was a founding member of Suede and later Elastica, and also a kind of Britpop muse, an accomplished artist with establishment ancestry like Marianne Faithfull and Yoko Ono. Just as Anderson's mother introduced him to a DIY aesthetic in making art, Frischmann educated him about contemporary art. He studies architecture with her, after abandoning town planning, a secondary focus in the two volumes being the transformation of England's rural and urban geography over the past three decades, though the nation's entrenched class structures persist. His remark by way of explanation for the split—"I suppose she had glimpsed what she thought was a better life for herself"—may be the closest he comes to resentment at being dumped for Damon Albarn of Blur, the soon-to-be international supernova (*Mornings* 159). Given the autobiography's decidedly retrospective cast, it sometimes negotiates awkwardly between Anderson's self-perception as an outsider and his institution as part of the popular music establishment whose career trajectory demonstrates that rock 'n' roll remains one of the few ways to change one's class.

The relative merits of acquired vs inherited gentility was an obsession of Charles Dickens, and Anderson presents class envy metaphorically by describing the members of Suede initially as children pressed against the window of a sweet shop. While perceived by the media "as members of some closed circle of the urbane metropolitan elite," "all of us [in Suede] felt utterly excluded .... We were like grubby-cheeked urchins with our faces pressed up against the window of a sweet shop: unlikely, unconnected and adrift" (*Mornings* 144). Even after they achieve "some sort of nascent, stuttering momentum," they continue searching for "the keys to a secret garden" constructed from "our own private rock fantasies" (*Mornings* 201, 150). This Dickensian or Burnett-like tableau is of a piece with the literary or writerly style, in an old-fashioned register, of much of *Coal Black Mornings*. His title reappears throughout as a literary motif, and the titular mornings and afternoons of childhood and young manhood anticipate a final "evening" volume. Allusions to great authors abound such as in the early reference to his son eventually reading the book and learning what "his father loved and lost" (xiii), which as Alfred Tennyson put it regarding his deceased friend, is better "[t]han never to have loved at all" (222, line 16).

This style may be in keeping with his father's Victorian great manism or devotion to heroes such as Churchill, Liszt, Nelson, and T.E. Lawrence, and it reinforces the sense that "the point of this book" is to be instructional for his children (*Mornings* 149). It may also be an act of homage to his father and hence written in a fashion he would have appreciated. There is often quite an old-timey or even archaic register as when "I digress" or we are asked, "let's sup with that problem later" (*Mornings* 63; *Afternoons* 221). There is also a fondness for somewhat incongruously pompous expressions as in the pious homily: "I think it's important to realise that art generally is just a process of documenting and interpreting and channelling one's experiences and turning them into something that lives in a place beyond reality" because, after all, "sometimes, in music and in life, that's all that really counts" (*Mornings* 34, 137–8). There's also a tendency—initially somewhat charming, if otherworldly—toward stuffy or crusty expressions as from someone born old or delivering an after-dinner speech at a town planning association meeting as we see in the following mashed together examples: "As the years march on" and "we soldiered clumsily on" searching for "the jigsaw's missing piece," if we are "honest" or "frank," and "I hope he wouldn't think it unfair of me to say that looking back" or that "she would be the first to agree" that "despite a few pockets of unpleasantness, I can't pretend that my time there [at school] wasn't relatively carefree" (*Mornings* 135, 147, 156, 192, 158, 189, 38). While a regard for what must be his father's values of decency and fair play predominates, there is sometimes a slide into expressions of cod-universal wisdom or New Age recovery speak: "You can find yourself projecting frustrations on to others ... until you gently tap yourself on the shoulder and remind yourself that failure and inertia are points on the path, and that the challenge is always, always actually a challenge within yourself" (*Mornings* 172). This tendency may derive from the therapeutic language of self-encouragement and non-judgemental catharsis emerging from recovery treatment. With a desire to acknowledge debts and influences in his success with Suede, he is highly reticent about making claims that might appear to impinge on others, and there might be just a shadow here of his father's final paranoia about people observing him, though Anderson speaks as his father's son in somewhat curmudgeonly pronouncements such as that "[t]he implications [of shifts in technology] for the future of creativity in music are bleak indeed" (*Mornings* 147). At moments, a more naturalistic, scatological register enters, as when, after Frischmann leaves him, he "trudged back on to the familiar, dog shit-strewn pavements of my single life" (*Mornings* 161).

However, the first third of *Coal Black Mornings* is an accomplished, disarming tour de force in which Anderson's eccentric parents emerge, and, in this respect, it is a dual auto/biography. Raised by an abusive, alcoholic father until he abandoned the family and was reported dead twice, Anderson's father is brought up to fit into a class position ensuring little more than economic survival. His series of dead-end jobs barely provide his own family's meagre subsistence. Amazingly, he celebrates the high culture of classical music and museum exhibitions of the class positioned above him. He purchases a cheap piano which no one plays, works as a swimming pool attendant when he can't swim, and assumes his wanna-be pop star son will be the next Liszt. He sometimes parades around their tiny council house dressed like Lawrence of Arabia, hoists a flag on Liszt's birthday, and wears a phial around his neck with soil from Liszt's birthplace, and when called for jury duty, requests to swear on a Liszt biography rather than the Bible. Anderson's mother sews most of her family's clothes, washes the family laundry by hand, reads *Beowulf* to her son, and sunbathes nude in the garden. Anderson shows his own inheritance of shame, however, in his regret at not attending his mother's funeral, his humiliation at the public consumption of subsidized school lunches, his embarrassment at the exposure of his list of punishments for his teachers, and his mortification when he witnesses his father shout "rubbish" at the end of a Bartók performance at the Royal Albert Hall (*Mornings* 69). He sees his father as having been permanently damaged by the unfairness of his bleak circumstances, and Anderson interprets his father's occasional displays of affection as if he were "passing on kindness to a childhood spectre of himself" (*Mornings* 55). Anderson protests his father's lifelong diet of humble pie when his songs incorporate some of his father's bawdy working-class slang and when he embraces the graffiti slogan "Modern Life is Rubbish," also the title of Blur's 1992 album (*Mornings* 114).

Anderson claims that his famously androgynous persona and his stage shows ending with an audience-assisted striptease originated in grappling with his inner anima.[37] This persona was a traumatized reaction to the death of his mother who encouraged his music. It also resulted from the termination of his relationship with Frischmann around the same time. Hence, adopting "an overt femininity that I explored as a style" was "an expression of grief," but it immediately provoked misinterpretation as if it were a "fake gay thing or a nod to seventies glam, or something similarly dreary, but looking back I'm convinced I was trying to replace the feminine absence in my life with an ersatz one of my own making" (*Mornings* 162). What he considers his later attempts at LGBTQ2 inclusion similarly led to charges of being phony and "opportunistic" (*Mornings* 196). However, a desire to rewire his neurology and play "around with the idea of becoming someone else" had been with him much earlier (*Mornings* 79). Whatever the roots of Anderson's flirtation with gendered transformation later, the androgynous iconography of Suede in its publicity photographs and album covers does conjure early David Bowie if not the fey provocation associated with Blur's "Girls & Boys" hit single of 1994, as well as the Smiths' playing of the gay card to garner attention (Marr 132–3, 146). Anderson does not consider, however, how his own under-explained encounters with male street prostitution, including interpreting "thinly disguised" job ads for "positions as sex workers" at the local job center or visits to the gay club Heaven "to mingle with the lovely wide-eyed boys," may have influenced this image (*Mornings* 101, 118). He briefly refers, for example, to hanging out "with a gang of rent boys" who "were a hilarious and strangely inspiring bunch—flamboyant and funny and utterly inclusive"; together they went "parading in altered states around the plush and moneyed streets, giggling uncontrollably and pirouetting on bins and swinging like scruffy Gene Kellys" (*Mornings* 99–100). More generally, Anderson does not elaborate on his personality-challenging walks on the wild side, "my fascination with the murkier corners of life" (*Mornings* 72), as when at the dawn of Suede's success, "my private life" became merely a

> vehicle to generate songs as I willingly exposed myself to increasingly bizarre and frictional personal dramas and extreme situations …. It was almost as if my life was starting to belong to someone else as I began to see it as some curious experiment in songwriting. Slowly a persona was taking grip of me, and it would only be many years later that I would be able to begin the quiet, private process of redressing that.
>
> (*Mornings* 204–5)

Given what he has said earlier about his father's final slide into paranoid delusion, Anderson is not forthcoming about what may have been his own mental health challenges.

Anderson details the development of Suede's music through his lyrical response to guitarist Bernard Butler's musical virtuosity. It was also a response to listening to the distortion of a broken record player played at the wrong speed, his father's admiration for melody and bombast, and the sometimes vicious and erotic innuendo of his father's speech. Suede's music created a portrait, celebration, and critique of Anderson's parents' social and economic circumstances. He credits Bowie and the Smiths, and mid-1980s "[s]ongs about weakness and failure and the drudgery of real life" as major influences, but eventually this acknowledgement in interviews would become a "strait jacket" (*Mornings* 85, 175). He regards Suede in retrospect as groundbreaking in its songs' combination of "overt Englishness … quirky realism and … fumbling, scruffy sexuality"; the band's members in colonial guise, were "like explorers cutting a path through the forest with machetes and pith helmets" (*Mornings* 205, 194). Before retro culture was popular and accessible, he listened to 1960s music with "a kind of breathless, archaeological thrill" and even busks Dylan's "With God On Our Side" (*Mornings* 59, 83), and later he came to love Nic Roeg's *Performance*, starring Mick Jagger. He claims paradoxically to have been both terminally lacking in ambition, embracing a "ridiculous idealisation of the romance of idling," convinced that "success was something that happened to other people," but also possessed with an assurance that success was his birthright, "the accolades and the status I thought the world owed me" (*Mornings* 159, 144, 130). Anderson's songs ultimately would reject "documenting a kind of romanticised 'beautiful loser' sort of lifestyle" that "idealised dole life and inaction" (*Mornings* 176), but learning to write and perform effectively was an agonizing process. He laments his early "weak, derivative, misshapen songs" which lacked coherent storytelling (*Mornings* 135), and he struggles to revise wordy drafts, to introduce form, melody, and hooks, and to improve his singing: "It took a while for me to develop any power in my voice and for me to overcome my self-consciousness and inhibitions, and to embrace the violence and the madness and the river of feeling that one must in order really to be able to sing" (*Mornings* 133). Early songs and performances were "masterclass[es] in ineptitude" (*Mornings* 139). He studied other bands and worked to improve his stagecraft, but the band's real breakthrough came after discarding a faulty drum machine and hiring a real drummer, Simon Gilbert in a period when it seemed that electronic dance music might be rendering rock music obsolete. Gilbert "made us veer away from … 'groove,' and teased out all of the punk and post-punk elements that were lying dormant in the band" (*Mornings* 154).

Afternoons with the Blinds Drawn tackles Anderson's descent into addiction to "narcotics" and Suede's parallel downward spiral (160), but it lacks the detail of memoirs like Mark Lanegan's harrowing *Sing Backwards and Weep* or Richard Lloyd's *Everything is Combustable*. We're not going to learn about Anderson injecting heroin into his penis or contracting endocarditis (Lanegan 216; Lloyd 285-7, 302-5), and in fact there are no references to specific drugs, methods of ingestion, or body parts engaged. The detritus of "burnt tin foil" and "coke promises" probably points to smoking heroin or crack, however (*Afternoons* 220, 150). The majority of Anderson's second volume, moreover, is a somewhat laborious, song by song dissection of the subjects and circumstances of Suede's records, somewhat similar to George Harrison's impersonal "autobiography" *I, Me, Mine*, and it appears to be for die-hard fans only. It is also an itinerary of how to sabotage a career in the music industry. By the end, we are grateful for the band's "graceful closing act," and perhaps hopeful that there will not be a third, "evening" volume about the band's rebirth a decade later (*Afternoons* 278). A certain whiney, hand-wringing quality predominates in the laments regarding career-hampering decisions such as the relegation of "criminally underrated tracks" to B-sides, Anderson's dangerous delusion "that there was very little I could do to avoid success," and his ignorance of or complicity in the fabrication of his persona and the band's character in the media (*Afternoons* 168,

221). This is the pop cartoon, soap opera, or theatrical piece, variously defined, that shifts into the dismissal of Anderson and Suede in the media as inauthentic and soon-to-be-redundant, hype-driven posers. Such predictions accelerate after Anderson and his co-writer Butler begin to communicate only in press interviews one of which fatally dismisses Anderson as being "unmusical and slow, a slightly inept, shallow inversion of the purity and brilliance of Bernard's musicianship" (*Afternoons* 123).

Like *Coal Black Mornings* and also Keith Richards' *Life*, Morrissey's *Autobiography* begins with a remarkable account of growing up in post-war England. Morrissey's opening has something aspiring to a Joycean vision of hard-bitten, violent, intolerant Manchester with places presented like characters and characters who think of Ireland as home and of celluloid America as paradise: "Birds abstain from song in post-war industrial Manchester, where the 1960s will not swing," where the parks on Sundays are full of "dingy, dreary, unkillable families," and, indirectly, where "sadness is habit-forming" (4, 51, 11). Morrissey's schools offer specters of hell with predatory teachers specialized in humiliation, prurience, and corporal punishment. Music and especially singing allow the prospect of escape and the assertion of identity, more than a career in the Church or the other local religion, football. His first record purchase is a disc by Marianne Faithfull, and he loves divas who perform with "the Maria Callas history-of-human-torture facial expressions," but he recognizes that singers like Buffy Sainte-Marie—and not Elvis—write their own songs; for Morrissey, the solitary singer is a "physical autobiography" (45). He is transfixed by the "glamorous, fearless" David Bowie singing on television, "a Wildean visionary about to re-mold England," a figure who "transcends our gloomy coal-fire existence" (66, 62). Morrissey's reactions to influential poets, sports stars, and musicians are similarly grandiose and diva-like. Watching the handsome George Best play soccer, "I faint," seeing Bowie on TV "the child [within me] dies," hearing Lou Reed in performance "my senses never return," and witnessing the New York Dolls makes him confess, "[a]t last I am someone!" (28, 62, 67, 71). He admires writers like Oscar Wilde, who appears to be the first pop star, "destroyed in order to save the world from homosexuality" (98, 99), though, perhaps significantly in terms of Morrissey's own later actions, he ignores Wilde's virtual courtship of his doom. Morrissey decides to be a writer and singer of songs with the mantra "[b]lend noise and words and save the world" (92). The Smiths (1982–7) form in short order once Morrissey meets Johnny Marr, whom he will later characterize as duplicitous, and in Morrissey's telling the band is quickly successful, though very quickly, too, his recollection is engulfed in a tide of retrospective recrimination. He has blame for his record label's ineptitude, the band's badly produced first record, radio hosts unfairly credited with supporting the band, lack of tour support or promotion from their American label, ingratitude from those covering the band's songs, a failed coup attempt against him within the band, and general exploitation by the music industry and the courts where "[t]he artist is the enemy" (186). The signing of the Smiths, comprising Morrissey and Johnny Marr and not the band's bassist or drummer, will eventually fuel lawsuits and give Morrissey membership in what he describes as the "indignation generation" (35).

Unlike Anderson's work, in its pacing, Morrissey's *Autobiography* is very uneven. The persona that emerges is of a highly successful, imaginative, and somewhat self-aware narcissist, self-styled a Wildean social critic and dandy, with a deeply ingrained persecution and martyr complex, perpetually anguished by the ingratitude of others and never forgotten slights from "the unhappy past" (225). Much of the *Autobiography* is an obsessive tracking of the chart positions of albums and singles or a detailed, stream of consciousness road diary or tour itinerary with minutely accounted records of ticket sales, designed to shout down those who predicted his failure. He is perpetually embittered about "zero airplay," "knife-wielding reviews," and especially deliberate misrepresentation in interviews, but more generally the vitriol of the British tabloid and music press (424). He is at pains to demonstrate that financially and in terms of fans' fanaticism—"a Beatlemania that dare not speak its name" (243)—the Morrissey brand bests the Smiths'. There are also shrill rants against British Prime Minister Margaret Thatcher or the "Holocaust carnage" of the meat industry (182); a stand-alone digression on a ghostly trip to Saddleworth Moor; and especially the details of a number of court actions, littered with what in a different context he calls his signature "over-reaching squeaks of tourette's"-style personal attacks (444). The autobiography is loaded, too, with usually disillusioning close encounters with the famous from stage and screen such as Dirk Bogarde, the New York Dolls, and even Bowie, though Kirk Douglas, Patti Smith, Chrissie Hynde, and Nancy Sinatra retain their allure. Perhaps the most powerful embedded narrative is the account of Jake Walters which might have afforded a heartfelt, unsentimental autofiction.[38] He sees Walters in a restaurant, Morrissey leaves, and "the doorbell rings. It is Jake. ... He steps inside and he stays for two years. Conversation is the bond of companionship (according to the Wildean scripture) ... and for the first time in my life the eternal 'I' becomes 'we'" (274). Morrissey's generally breathless if also long-winded sprint through the selective details of much of his career is punctuated with somewhat incongruous if characteristic aphorisms about life's suffering, people's isolation, and death's inevitability. He appears to aspire to an epigrammatic Wildean wit, and portrays a self-perception of entrapment in a Wildean martyrdom, as when in his account of the court action against him and Marr, he alludes to Wilde's "The Ballad of Reading Gaol" (349).

For Johnny Marr in *Set the Boy Free*, perhaps significantly given his later break with Morrissey after which only "disaffection and distrust" remain (409), Wilde was someone whose "talent was spoiled by his smug self-regard and pomposity" (204). Marr's account of the Smiths' fortunes focuses on the dynamics of writing, arranging, recording, and later remastering songs while developing his "Guitarchestra" sound (182). While its music was heavily influenced by 1960s British bands and also Motown girl groups, and its style by early 1960s films and the fashion and haircuts of figures like the Beatles' Stu Sutcliffe, Marr insists that the "Smiths aesthetic" was designed "for my own generation" (83, 203). His generation, however, is very much that of Margaret Thatcher, and he comes to regard most politicians, including David Cameron later, as "fame hounds" (243). He becomes similarly disillusioned at the ways 1990s Britpop would embody the jingoistic, macho culture of jock rock and at how the rave scene, with its appetite for ecstasy (MDMA), would enable organized crime. Writing as a non-smoking, teetotal, vegan marathon runner, a professor of popular music at Manchester's Salford University, who was invited for an audience with the Dalai Lama, Marr offers a poignant description of the impoverishment of Irish immigrants in the northern English, industrial city of Manchester, including his large extended family, and also a chastening portrait of virtually omnipresent violence in "Madchester."[39] Marr delivers a somewhat more straightforward account of the band's demise, resulting from ill-informed, naive, and romantic decisions or non-decisions regarding labels and label support, managers, lawyers, and accountants, most of whom he estimates are "anti-music" in orientation (240). Sharing the band's profits perhaps ironically was based on an oral gentleman's agreement that ran afoul a late Victorian law demanding equal division or written exceptions. Marr's version of events contradicts Morrissey's autobiography on a myriad of details from the radio support of John Peel, satisfaction with the Rough Trade label, and Morrissey's own actions as the band dissolved. As a member of a band that forged a template for greatness in 1960s popular music as well as for the miseries of recrimination and vindictiveness post-breakup, Paul McCartney commented sagely to Marr on the Smiths' ultimate collapse into long-running lawsuits: "That's bands for ya" (279).

Moby

Moby (Richard Melville Hall) tells a riotous whale of a tale in his two volumes of life writing, with a third possibly forthcoming (Danis). His first memoir *Porcelain* may be an anti-popular music autobiography. It dispenses in short order with rock star grandiosity, fixing instead on the creation of a persona, a performative identity, often through the memoir's use of language, amid the comedy and absurdity of his rise and fall in the electronic dance music pantheon as fortune's wheel turns. *Porcelain*, however, does run the gamut of rock 'n' roll narrative clichés such as drug-addled record mixers, promoters, and announcers; inept travel arrangements, bad hotels, worse venues; and threatened plagiarism suits and contract disputes, but they are all measured against the potential for communal ecstasy, star gazing, and delight at *This is Spinal Tap*-worthy outrageousness (357). *Then It Fell Apart*—as befitting a self-styled "traditional autobiography," as its Preface puts it, beginning with a suicide attempt and ending with entry into AA—is considerably darker. It sets out to explain how and why copious consumption of alcohol, drugs, sex, and fame does not alleviate panic attacks or feelings of being an imposter (and not just for promoting an interpretation of the unread *Moby-Dick; or, The Whale*). It claims to offer Moby's plateau panic disorder's "origin story" in childhood trauma (43, 352). As a result, *Then It Fell Apart* is closer to the disability-type rock 'n' recovery autobiographies examined earlier in Chapter 1, though Moby doesn't seek drugs to medicate the rigors of fame; instead, he initially at least regards fame as the "fix" for his brokenness (29). However, what becomes his fame addiction and alcoholism will pressure him to compromise his music in the aftermath of the mammoth success of *Play*.

As a descendant of the settler colonizers on the *Mayflower* as well as the literary giant Herman Melville, Moby faced his agent's refusal to hire a ghostwriter for *Porcelain*. Moby's literary ancestor, writes Salman Rushdie in his blurb, "would, I think, be simultaneously revolted and proud" of the result. Rushdie, the literary rock star, makes a brief appearance in *Then It Fell Apart* (76), showing the overlap of the celebrity cultures of literature, movies, art, fashion, and music. Conscious of belonging to the lineage of the Great American novelist, Moby carefully crafted his memoir, though he took the *Journals* of John Cheever—a writer of whom he had been a fan since high school—as one of his main models, admiring their "level of unflinching honesty" (Moby qtd. in Danis), and sharing with

Cheever a far from Platonic enthusiasm for alcohol. Both Melville and Cheever are highly respected, but there are significant differences between the writer of mythic epics and the chronicler of suburban ennui. Cheever and Melville both in different ways, however, shadow boxed with the secret of their same-sex desires and relationships, but Moby also has a secret revealed most fully in *Then It Fell Apart*. His revelation is the legacy of his own child sexual abuse, presented as one consequence of the negligent freedom of his hippy upbringing (*Porcelain* 402–3). A somewhat unlikely wunderkind of electonica, dancing above complicated set-ups at some of New York's and then the world's top clubs and festivals, Moby was a bald, somewhat nerdy, Christian vegan who became an alcoholic and possibly sex addict, a catalog of outsider traits he rehearses often. In *Porcelain* and *Then It Fell Apart*, he exposes his public performance of confidence, self-assurance, and expertise as a successful electronic musician and then rock star when he always felt like an imposter. He presents his chronic insecurity, history of self harm, panic attacks, post-LSD trip disorientation, commitment phobia, and feelings of being an imposter in relation to his role in the electronic music scene and also his methods of composition, which often layer and recombine elements of others' musical ideas, as if they motivated the picaresque adventures of a modern-day Candide.

Moby claims to have modeled his memoir on Cheever's *Journals* (Danis), partly to distance it from popular music autobiographies and presumably his perception of their self-serving smorgasbord of sex, drugs, and rock 'n' roll. He may have had Mötley Crüe's *The Dirt* in mind (*Porcelain* 405). Moby does not model his work on that of the confessional, suicidal Sylvia Plath, whom he refers to briefly, though he contemplated suicide as an adolescent, regarding it as a "Swiss Army Knife" ever ready to solve all of his problems; instead, he maintains his "nauseous lifeline" with "my drunken literary heroes" (286, 392). While Cheever's literary fortunes have shifted, at the end of his career he was a pillar of the American literary establishment with Saul Bellow, Philip Roth, and John Updike, among whom he detected a "rivalry … quite as intense as that among sopranos" (*Journals* 330). As he recognized, "I'm a brandname … like cornflakes" (qtd. in Benjamin Cheever ix). Combining incidental notebooks, diaries, confessions, and a type of "crypto-autobiography," though never "my sexual autobiography," Cheever's *Journals* were a startling revelation for his admirers in exposing a profoundly unhappy man, wracked by anxieties about alcoholism, homosexuality, hatred and even contempt for his "peevish" wife, and his literary reputation (*Journals* 319, 65, 323). Cheever's published *Journals* present only about 20 percent of the original and the entries are undated and fragmentary (Gottlieb 397), whereas Moby's chapters in *Porcelain* are very carefully crafted. The Moby of the memoir shares with the Cheever of the *Journals* a sense of his own bodily ugliness and a more general alienation from society. Moby replaces Cheever's often mean, self-pitying, whiney tone with self-deprecating comedy as he recounts his success in a world of unabashed hedonism.

Cheever's *Journals*, as befitting a work at least initially not intended for publication, focus on Cheever's sense of inadequacy and his homoerotic desires, and the publication of the journals, to which he consented before his death, was a type of posthumous coming out of the closet. Cheever's own model may have been, at least in part, J.R. Ackerley's posthumously published *My Father and Myself* (1968), which Cheever admired (Bailey 480), a dual autobiography of himself and biography of his father, containing Ackerley's own detailed reminiscences of affairs with lower-class men who met his exacting standards and his later engagements with prostitutes. Ackerley is unable to establish a satisfactory long-term same-sex relationship—a difficulty he also has in India, where he goes in 1923 at the suggestion of E.M. Forster, after surviving the Somme in the First World War, to be the private secretary of a gay maharajah, recounted in his memoir *Hindoo Holiday* (1932). Later, he somewhat bizarrely sublimates his sexual desires in the care of his dog, the subject of his autobiographical novel *We Think the World of You* (1960). Ackerley was thrilled that 1960s pop heart-throb Cliff Richard was keen on a possible film adaptation (Parker 399). While Cheever attempts to explain his search for manly, sporting, Whitmanesque comradeship, with hand-jobs on the side, as perfectly ordinary (Bailey 675), he also regards homosexuality as pathological.[40]

Looking into Cheever's conflicted homophobia may be useful for understanding Moby's differently conflicted sense of shame and his work in popular music as well as for the sense it offers of the atmosphere in which figures like Robert Mapplethorpe and David Wojnarowicz, whom we shall consider in the next chapter, were raised. Cheever finds the roots of his gay desires in his Freudian narcissism, his displaced love for his brother, and parental disapproval as well as a reaction to his own attempts at suppression (226, 312, 324). Hence, his own homophobia, he believes, has intensified his gay desires, which otherwise would have been part of a normal—if epicurean—sexual appetite. Repressing his gay desires has enflamed them. His conflicted attitude appears in the swing from occasionally acknowledging that he is gay or queer, a "sexual expatriate" (344), whose predilections are part of the chemistry of a man who was not "invented by an advertising agency" (312), on the one hand, to his conviction that homosexuality is wicked, on the other. In this stance, Cheever resembles Oscar Wilde, who has become almost more famous as the quintessential gay martyr than as a playwright.[41] Blake Bailey's biography details Cheever's relationships with specific men, often associated with the Yaddo artists' colony, such as composer and diarist Ned Rorem (Bailey 395–6), and the fact that Cheever sometimes traded mentorship and assistance with publication for sexual favors. Cheever was well aware of the dangers he courted, given the disgrace and career devastation that came with the charge against Newton Arvin of Yaddo and Smith College—the esteemed biographer of gay writers such as Walt Whitman and Moby's ancestor Melville, as well as the lover and mentor of Truman Capote—for possession of gay pornography.[42] The *Journals* reveal Cheever's disdain for gay men and signs of effeminacy, and his belief that a lasting, loving relationship between men was "impossible" (191, 364). Homosexuality, he maintains, has "a caul of darkness," from which "I mean to cure myself" (331, 215). In comparison, Cheever's remarks about his alcoholism are unambiguous and almost wholesome, in their unconflicted honesty. He refers to drinking from a flask in public toilet stalls, the siren call of gin bottles in the pantry, resolutions not to drink before 11:30 am, and of partaking in "[v]odka for breakfast" (290); he even notes with a dry wit that the boredom of testimonials at AA meetings drives him to drink (308). The only equivalent levity in the documenting of his gay anxieties appears in recounting a nightmare of "having a homosexual escapade, unconsummated with Ronald Reagan" (224).

Porcelain has a carefully crafted persona at its center, the impossibly naive, impossibly innocent, childlike, virtuous, intelligent or at least nerdy, pop culture loving, vulnerable and self-deprecating man child.[43] In light of the revelations in *Then It Fell Apart*, it's possible to interpret *Porcelain*'s persona as the self-deprecating song and dance man's cover for the traumas that have made him a "suicidal addict" (*Then* 393). *Porcelain* is less the *bildungs* narrative of chronological autobiography and more a type of cautionary, Hogarthian rake's or "rave's progress" (365). As in most popular music autobiographies, however, there is a specter in the room: the image of the star Moby would become and hence the reader's foreknowledge of—if not endings, then—climaxes and crises. As a whole, the memoir neatly builds tension in its account of Moby's rise to relative fame and fortune, which arrives with his creation of "Go"; braces for the crisis of commitment phobia just as darkness begins to descend on the electronic music scene; and reaches a negative climax with Moby's fateful return to alcohol, first encountered at age ten, after eight years of sobriety. The memoir's progress then descends to Moby's relationships with sex workers, his anguish over his mother's death from cancer, and the increase in his panic attacks relating to his calculated attempt at career suicide with his speed metal punk rock album *Animal Rights*, the mortification of hair loss, and the closest thing to a near-death experience in the memoir when he contemplates a future teaching philosophy at a community college. There are also occasional interludes such as chapter 39's meditation on ants and God, and the following chapter's account of Moby as a professional dominatrix to show he hasn't lost his taste for tawdry fun. As in *How It Fell Apart*, we learn in *Porcelain* of Moby's upbringing in poverty while incongruously surrounded by wealthy friends, but *Porcelain* gives much more attention to Moby's quest to succeed in the racially and in other ways diverse worlds of electronic music in the late 1980s and early 1990s, amid the squalor, crack-addition, gang warfare, and poverty of AIDS-ravaged New York. He is a Bible-reading teetotal vegan in this period with perhaps an equally improbable knowledge of music theory and technology. He and his girlfriend make a virtue of abstaining from sex with every fall succeeded by prayers of repentance. However, he is sufficiently self-aware to admit his critical, judgemental nature ("I was Christian, but I was also a dick" 23), and the glamorous appeal of the gilded palace of sin, which keeps *Porcelain* from being a temperance tract: "I wanted to be a good Christian in a loving relationship, not someone who deep down was turned on by emaciated prostitutes hanging out at the entrance to the Lincoln Tunnel, hustling for enough money to score some crack" (68).

Moby in *Porcelain* trespasses and become a voyeur, whether in Bible-study groups of the children of the rich in Martha's Vineyard, abandoned factories in the meatpacking district of New York, at turkey dinners with grandparents in rural Connecticut, or at piss-drinking, sex party clubs in the wastelands of New Jersey. He is ever a self-conscious interloper in alien worlds, an outsider who just passes sufficiently or seems too inconsequential to be denied insider access. He allows the reader to slip through normally closed doors as a type of contemporary anthropologist or a child adrift among adults. He assumes, for example, "there were codes of behavior at sex parties, but I had no idea what any of them were. Could I look? ... Was I allowed to be straight?" (52). Unusually for a memoir, each chapter is named and crafted in order to give a different perspective on the self-portrait. There is a controlling intelligence at work, setting out and emphasizing the very impossibility of the progress, conveyed in summary statements about the utter improbability of his situation, which display his own sense of the apparently magical nature of his experience and his desire to remember events even while living through them. He says, for example, "there was something odd about a twenty-five-year-old man eating baby food as he flew over the Atlantic Ocean en route to play at drug-fueled raves in London" (140). A little later with a friend of infamous Hollywood madam Heidi Fleiss, he recalls that "[a] few years ago I'd been sober and teaching Bible study. Now I was drinking postcoital beer in Los Angeles with a woman telling me that she was a high-priced hooker" (283).

Comedy is a large part of the construction of *Porcelain*'s persona, and its writing style embodies a hilarious, sometimes jarring mash-up of different discursive levels from street slang to pop culture reference or literary allusion. He moves from references to reading *Dune* or watching *Twin Peaks* or *Star Trek* to allusions to Marcel Proust's memory-triggering madeleine, to waiting for Madonna as if she were Samuel Beckett's Godot, and calling August, not April, the cruellest month in New York, as in T.S. Eliot's *The Waste Land*. This discursive heteroglossia is accompanied by a certain linguistic self-consciousness as in his fecal expletive when he encounters a deluge of canine poop "without intending any wordplay," or in his account of learning to pronounce "vegan," or his reference to the "alphabet of hepatitis in the toilets" (238, 269, 259). He juxtaposes matter-of-fact statements, clichés, and startling bon mots. This knowing, writerly style also appears in lists or strings of nouns or phrases ending periodically with the verbal equivalent of a punchline as in the description of "a perfect New York autumn evening, the sort of night where people held hands and fell in love while walking in the park and stepping over homeless people" (46). He also juxtaposes or mashes together the formal, matter-of-fact, slightly self-important phrasing of a polite child with raw specifics. The remarks about behavior in keeping with his values, the quality of mercy, or the universal gesture in the following, most of which also use litotes or understatement, demonstrate this juxtaposition: "In 1987 I became a vegan, started teaching Bible study, and decided that crashing cars and waking up covered in vomit wasn't in keeping with my values" (32); "The quality of mercy is especially strained when people are trying to sleep, even if a human being is dying in the garbage a few feet away from them" (44); or, when encountering a belligerent homeless person, "I'd back away, hands raised in the universal gesture of 'I mean you no harm, crazy person, please don't stab me'" (87).

A similar device is the use of almost childish neologisms and hyperbole. He refers, for example, to trying when on the New York subway to stay "anonymous and unstabbed," or to responding to drug-induced rants with "something equally Tourette's-y," or imagining that well-paid sex workers lived "in apartments that were more, well, prostitutey" (37, 134, 285). A related device appears when, while wishing facetiously to be "vegan without being blatantly vegan," he asks using something resembling synesthesia whether turkey "taste[s] like suffering" (89, 112). *Porcelain* also uses a kind of companion device to litotes, hyperbole, or exaggeration. Moby's is a scatological or sperm-atological vision, and returns to alcohol in a reaction to hearing a man's voice when phoning his ex-girlfriend, and imagining "his semen is drying on her breasts" (254). He earlier accused her of inhumanity in her antipathy to illness: "she'd acted like Leni Riefenstahl, cold and clinical and disappointed in my exhibition of human frailty" (248). His return to alcohol and his release of a speed metal punk rock record when electronic dance music is in demand precipitate what he reads as the end of his career in music, a reality he accepts in hyperbolic fashion as if he "was at the end of Elisabeth Kübler-Ross's stages of grief" (394).

Porcelain's elaborate wordplay also alludes to the tradition of the picaresque novel, emphasizing his performative persona's resemblance to the picaroon. DJing at a makeshift sex party, Moby rhapsodizes about his "semen-covered Nordic Dulcinea," conjuring with raw, naturalistic detail the delusional idealization of the virginal beloved by Don Quixote in Cervantes's picaresque Spanish novel, but he then mashes this allusion together with a reference to wanting to be her Holden Caulfield of *The Catcher in the Rye* fame (54). He observes the intercourse of "my Nordic goddess" and "two overweight guys who looked like they worked in a deli when they weren't befouling the love of my life" (54). He shows his panic at skipping a record while a hip-hop legend is rapping using comic circumlocution worthy of Cervantes or his English successor in the comic heroic epic, Henry Fielding. To convey this, he introduces a delay in the text for effect: "There's a word missing from the English language. Maybe it exists in other languages. It describes the unspeakable, incomprehensible panic that comes from standing onstage to play your second-ever solo show in front of thousands of hostile fans who've just found out the headliner canceled and then hitting 'start' on your sequencer with absolutely no result" (103). A few chapters later, he meets a homeless man who calls himself Sancho Panza, Don Quixote's sidekick in Cervantes' novel (118). Moby also employs a downmarket version of the mock heroic allusion and his own comic deflation by introducing an apostrophe to the disembodied figure of the goddess or god of love, when, expressed with deliberate laboriousness, wracked with jealousy over his ex-girlfriend's new love affair, he attempts to upgrade his appearance: "I wanted the cashier to notice the [Agnostic Front] T-shirt and fall in love with me, but ... she was not my soul mate. Love had stood before her, openhearted, balding, and well intentioned, and she had ignored it, checking out a Cro-Mags poster on the wall" (269).

Another aspect of Moby's comic persona in *Porcelain* is his improbable encounters with celebrities, and *Then It Fell Apart*'s notoriety was enhanced when Natalie Portman denied having a relationship with Moby, a claim he had attempted to authenticate in that book's goofy photograph of him with the actress. He has a brief encounter with Miles Davis looking "predatory" in a "silk suit that looked like it cost more money than I had made in the previous ten years" (101). He details interactions with members of New Order and the Butthole Surfers, Iggy Pop, David Bowie, and Trent Reznor, and an aborted bid to have sex in Sonic Youth's dressing room at CBGB and an interaction with Flea and Anthony Kiedis of the Red Hot Chili Peppers. He agrees to DJ a "rare groove" night at Mars without knowing what "rare groove" means, and discovers that even the famous Flea also doesn't know it (78). Inadvertently, he introduces the pressure on some of the stars he worships who are driven to investigate emerging music scenes in dodgy locations to find inspiration and check on the competition, as well as the mania for ever new monikers within sub-cultural scenes to camouflage the latest cool development from the uninitiated. Moby tells of going to see soon-to-be alternative star Jeff Buckley at the tiny Irish folk club Sin-é when Buckley was trying to distance himself from the weight of inherited fame and notoriety, as the son of Tim Buckley who died of a heroin overdose in 1975. As his own fame and record company pressure grew after the release of *Grace*, Buckley would confront his father's legacy and that of other 1960s heroes by performing celebrity overdose scenes onstage (Lovesey, "Anti-Orpheus" 343). The performance savvy Moby recognizes the awkwardness of Buckley's pre-fame show, but he appreciates Buckley's ethereal voice and "compelling" "strangeness" as well as Buckley's power to render his female fans "rapt and transfixed" (126–7).

Porcelain offers a type of sociological classification of various cultural groups and sub-groups in 1980s and 90s America from "postapocalyptic" Hollywood and the different districts of New York before the city was sanitized and yuppified, to New England where "happiness" is "suspect unless football or alcohol or money was involved" or the "ravaged war zone" of parts of New Jersey (281, 190, 67). Moby is raised by a single mother, sometimes surviving on food stamps and welfare, both materially deprived and psychologically embarrassed in his peer group, and he considers himself a type of refugee in the mansions and summer homes of his wealthy friends. Well before the Black Lives Matter movement, he is aware of being an outsider in the electronic dance music scene but rarely of his innate privilege as a white man. Whether in the African American neighborhoods surrounding the derelict buildings where he lives or in the emerging African American and Latino music clubs, he is perceived as a white suburban tourist in search of drugs. He is apologetic for being "too white" and ever hopeful of an interracial affair that might transform him into someone more "confident and less white" (39, 69, 71). As a knowing outsider, he offers the reader insider knowledge of the race, clothes, hairstyles, and sexual orientations of various almost "tribal" communities and sub-cultures, from club kids, ravers, goths, or those with a fondness for house, techno, jungle, hip-hop, or straight edge. Membership in the different musical scenes is denoted as much by the artists depicted on T-shirts as by particular drugs, though over time the predominance of drugs in certain scenes changes. He refers to a nightclub game, "What Drug Is He On":

> If someone in a nightclub touches your face and tells you that you're beautiful, it's a safe bet they're on ecstasy. If someone is dancing slowly and staring at the lights shining through their hands, they're probably on acid. If someone is sitting on the floor staring at their shoes, they're likely on ketamine. If a white person tells you how much they love Haile Selassie, they've almost certainly been smoking too much pot. And if someone … is asleep on a thumping speaker box at two a.m., it's safe to conclude that they're a junkie.
>
> (174)

A large part of Moby's authority in the memoir comes from his genuine appreciation for the spiritual ambiance of electronic dance music and for how its scene provides him a sense of community, and also from his detailed descriptions of creating songs using an array of sequencers, samplers, keyboards, drum machines, and mixers, beginning with a return to a draft of "Go" and ending with pressing "Play." In this respect, Moby's work resembles the recent, tech-savvy memoirs by members of some of the 1970s' best-known prog rockers such as Yes, as well as in this respect at least and somewhat unusually Dylan's *Chronicles*. While he recognizes the bafflement of some club DJs at the complexity of electronic music composition; the disdain of guitar, piano, bass, and drums musicians like Phil Collins (160); and even the indifference of artists who merely sing in concert over pre-recorded tapes, Moby rhapsodizes that German literary and scientific giant Goethe's last words, "more light," mark him as "a prescient raver" (192). This music has enlightened Moby and led to his rebirth from being "an uptight WASP from Connecticut" to participating in the invention of "new musical forms: joyful, futuristic music that was the soundtrack to this new world we'd created" (190, 182). The music and its community offer him a sense of belonging until he is unseated briefly "like the rave equivalent of Comrade Trotsky" when his joyous sounds begin to seem old-fashioned (218).

Moby explains his set-up at an early club gig to a DJ: "The sequencer controls the synths and the samplers. The keyboards make MIDI and audio. The audio from the synths and samplers runs through the mixer, and the QuadraVerb gives reverb and delay" (119). He explains the creation of his break-out song "Go" from its beginning as a minimal techno track. He experiments with stripped down and then "tribal" remixes before sampling and accelerating a breakbeat taken from a compilation album, and then he adds three notes of "Laura Palmer's Theme" from *Twin Peaks* in string sounds on his keyboard (132-6). He finally superimposes disco piano and makes other tweaks before arranging the track. Soon "Go"'s popularity has gone bonkers in England, his career accelerates, and phrases like "my contractor" enter his lexicon. Seeking permission to sample an obscure 1970s disco song on what he hopes will be a rave anthem to propel the dance scene out of the darkness induced by the animal tranquilizer Special-K, he encounters the inflated demands of the recording's owner. The track has "the lunatic and propulsive breakbeats and the giant strings and the huge sawtooth synth parts ... the Juno-106 sub-bass ... the insistent 4/4 Roland TR-909 kick," but without the sampled vocal it is unspectacular. He records a singer modifying the three notes and adjusting the lyrics, and the result is his rhapsodic "Feeling So Real" (241-44). Moby also describes the creation of a classical piece. "I overlaid a second piano part in C major, adding a hopeful counterpoint to the plaintive A-minor arpeggio," and he then adds a cello part, "filigreed violins," "orchestral cords," and reverb-softened drums to represent sonically the world's creation (256):

> I thought about God moving over the face of the waters, when the Earth was new, before there was land and before anything was alive. The spirit of God, full of prescience and omniscience, seeing the emptiness and expanse of the

new world, aware of all that's there and all that's going to follow. The life that will come, and the death that will end each life. The trillions of creatures who will come out of this ocean, all wanting to live as long and as well as possible, resisting death until the end. All the life and death and longing and heartbreak and hope.

(257)

His return to electronic music resulting in the mammoth success of *Play* follows from his resolution to press pause on the speed metal punk rock of *Animal Rights* and create something "melodic and emotional" to offer listeners "happiness, or at least a beautiful sadness that offered consolation" (355).

Then It Fell Apart while inevitably revisiting some of *Porcelain*'s material resembles a more conventional or stereotypical entertainment celebrity biography in locating the drive to perform at least partly in childhood trauma. It departs from this narrative, however, in various ways including its focus on alcoholism. Alcohol is "my best friend, lover, godhead, and muse," and when it is working its magic, he wonders "why doesn't God let us feel like this all the time?" (172, 75). Over time, Moby devises a "rock star cocktail," combining hits of ecstasy with champagne and vodka, and eventually he considers having fifteen to twenty drinks without cocaine a "horrible compromise" (74, 347). His hangovers worsen till he feels "like I had poisoned my DNA" (390). *Then It Fell Apart*'s bifurcated shuffling of present excess and past trauma is also unusual, and Moby's Preface locates its precedent in Kurt Vonnegut's novel *Slaughterhouse-Five*, but it may also owe something to his experience DJing. While detailing his pursuit of alcohol and drugs, he generally offers few specifics of his sexual debauchery unless sex-workers or groupies are involved; there is a threat of violence; or blood, vomit, or feces make an appearance. *Then It Fell Apart* somewhat obsessively quantifies the accelerating number of drinks consumed; the quantity of pills (ecstasy, Xanax, Vicodin) swallowed or lines of coke or horse tranquilizer sniffed; and also, in round numbers, the amount of money earned and spent on expensive real estate. As a poor boy growing up in a wealthy enclave, Moby may come by this concern for accounting legitimately. It also enables entry for a non-insider audience, who may want to know the price of a "sky castle" in the El Dorado beside Central Park ($7 million) or a 60-acre estate an hour from the city ($1,250,000) as much as the limpness of Mick Jagger's handshake (221, 259, 264). While raised in relative material hardship,

Moby perceives that his upbringing gives him a certain "street cred" but also that he has profited from his access to the trappings of white privilege (263). He grows up near his wealthy grandparents in Darien, Connecticut, "a town of fifteen thousand millionaires," "an endless sea of blond, wealthy parents and their blond, beautiful children. They played tennis. They skied. They were good at lacrosse and field hockey. ... They went to Switzerland for holidays" (321, 50). He has access to well-funded, white schools whose teachers were "progressive academics" (321) and who can assume their students will enter Ivy League universities and go on to plush careers.

Moby's alcoholic father committed suicide when Moby was two, and his mother is a single parent whose crushed ambitions to be a beatnik artist were subsumed in a devotion to the trappings of 1960s hippydom: "When my mom and her friends got drunk and high they stopped being adults. When my mom got high, which was almost every day, she stopped being my mom" (39). Moby's own excess and dysfunction eventually mimic and surpass hers. *Then It Fell Apart* suggests that Moby's general disdain for 1960s music, other than that of Led Zeppelin, Creedence Clearwater Revival, Neil Young, and soul divas like Diana Ross, results from its being the soundtrack to his mother's and her friends' narcissism and neglect. Much later he will spin Led Zeppelin's folky "Going to California," from their fourth 1971 album, DJing when he's feeling both sad for himself and disgusted at his manic audience, and this choice represents the nadir of his popularity, discounting the times he's thrown a knife or a punch or sniffed cocaine while DJing or grabbed the headliner's mike to canvass the crowd for cocaine. Nailing his punk rock credentials to the wall with heavy metal lite, however, after "Going to California" nearly kills the party mood, he plays the song again (374–5). Moby was sexually abused by a worker at a makeshift hippy day care in California when his mother and her friends went off to take LSD for the day. His mother is a sad, defeated woman, and he learns early that he is an encumbrance to her reckless pursuit of independence which entails a string of abusive boyfriends with gang associations and pot- or possibly Quaalude-fueled outings. His regard for the anger and aggression of punk rock and the angst of Joy Division, his "favorite band of all time" whose singer Ian Curtis killed himself aged twenty-three on the eve of their first US tour in 1980, is unsurprising if for nothing else than the distance it represents from what he has experienced as the selfish hypocrisy of the peace and love generation (305). In the clubs and raves of the electronic dance scene, he discovers a tangible sense of homecoming so that when he parties at Danceteria, where Wojnarowicz will work in a few years, Moby says to his friends that he hopes to "find its DNA, and weave it into our own chromosomes" (307).

Fame would appear, as in the title of his song "Feeling So Real," to make Moby feel real, or at least as less of an imposter, a religious hypocrite, "a bald novelty musician with a hit record," prepared to prostitute himself in its "obsequious running-dog pursuit" (73, 34). He sees that rock culture's validation comes partly from peer recognition, within a rigid but ever-shifting hierarchy, and that those embraced as "stratospherically famous" at one moment are in the next avoided as if they carried the contagious virus of the has-been or "obscure *Jeopardy!* question" star (164, 343). Being a rock star has made him feel like "a new god" or "a king" and "[f]ame and wealth were supposed to have protected me and given my life meaning" (163, 393), but his elegiac reflections recall those of Oscar Wilde who experienced a far more devastating fall from grace.[44] *Then It Fell Apart* ratchets up *Porcelain*'s rock celebrity encounters due to Moby's enhanced reputation after issuing the ten-million seller *Play*, though these rock 'n' roll walk-ons increasingly drift into the orbits of politics, philanthropy, and organized crime. He encounters gangsters while on tour in Eastern Europe and in New York, and once at a party attended by Vladimir Putin's daughter. He dates famous actresses, feuds with Eminem, despite their similar underprivileged backgrounds, and socializes with Lou Reed and David Bowie sharing small dinner parties, new songs, and advice about home recording studio construction. Although he autographs genitals, Bibles, and even copies of *Moby-Dick*, and models for a Calvin Klein ad, because Sonic Youth's Kim Gordon has done it, Moby is a *New Yorker*- and John Cheever's *Journals*-reading electronic musician, and he frequently feels he is an illegitimate rock star and a phony representative of the youth vote at political gatherings such as one attended by Hillary Clinton. He notably encounters Donald Trump at a party, describing him soberly in ways that the man himself as well as his supporters in Trump nation would hardly recognize as "a mid-level real-estate developer and tabloid-newspaper staple whose career had recently been resuscitated by a reality-TV show" (117). Moby is challenged by his friends to perform a "knob touch," and "I drank a shot of vodka to brace myself, pulled my flaccid penis out of my pants, and casually walked past Trump, trying to brush the edge of his jacket with my penis" (117). For legions of "never Trumpers," this may be worth the price of admission to the autobiography or go a long way towards forgiving Moby's acts of alcoholic selfishness, though Moby is careful not to overplay the incident.

Notes

1. See Frith and Horne's *Art Into Pop*.
2. Frith cautions that "windy phrases" such as the "Woodstock generation" convey a distorted sense of collective identity ("The Magic" 164). As the Woodstock festival's talent coordinator Bill Belmont remembers, the crowd at Woodstock in 1969 was remarkably homogeneous and it's a stretch to regard them as epitomizing a counterculture: Woodstock's "audience came from every college within 100+ miles of the site, by word of mouth" (personal communication).
3. See Andy Bennett's discussion of "subcultures" and "neotribalism" in popular music contexts ("Subcultures" 106–13). In addition, see Chris Rojek's *Pop Music* (78–89).
4. Glam rock is significant in this development because it advanced an idea of "identity as something entirely malleable and open to radical re-definition," as Philip Auslander argues ("Watch" 71). In so doing and in emphasizing "style and pose over authenticity," glam performers challenged the convention in rock culture that "the musician's performance persona and true self … [were] identical" (72).
5. See Elizabeth Bruss's *Autobiographical Acts*, Sidonie Smith's "Performativity, Autobiographical Practice, Resistance," and Smith and Watson's *Reading Autobiography* (214–15).
6. The term was coined by Allan Kaprow, partly influenced by his mentor John Cage (Gefter 72–3), and Kaprow developed strict demarcations for happenings (Sell 177).
7. For Carroll, "performance artists" were "the same folks who did 'Happenings' in the sixties" (59). However, "many of them are wrapped in so many layers of pretense that it would be a performance piece in itself to strip them all away. They are boundless in their energy to bore, and they are so smug you want to go after their most sensitive bodily parts with rusty tweezers" (59–60).
8. In his "confession of a Motherfucker," Osha Neumann asserts that Up Against the Wall Motherfuckers was "inventing a new way to be white revolutionaries in America," by moving from "war on cultural institutions [such as art galleries] to total war on The System," a megalith denoting "presidents and penises, the Pentagon and our parents, desires and disaffections, torturers and toothpaste" (9, 73, 66): "[w]e saw ourselves as urban guerrillas swimming in the countercultural sea" adhering to a belief in the "propaganda of the deed" (7).
9. Warhol wanted to grow his empire into virtually all forms from films to magazines to books, and place his name brand on all of them. His claims to be the creator of the Velvet Underground and the producer of its first album, which his iconic cover art may have financed, would perpetually annoy Lou Reed. Warhol exchanged art to cover the band's expenses, including instruments, recognizing the imperative of

10. Tutti addresses the vexed term "industrial" as a popular music genre (236–40), which developed just when England was becoming post-industrial (Ford 7.16). While Throbbing Gristle is often credited as the genre's founder, there are other contenders such as Monte Cazazza, a sound musician who worked closely with Throbbing Gristle (Reynolds, *Rip* 237), and also Cabaret Voltaire, with Nine Inch Nails probably its most successful successor. Lou Reed's feedback fest *Metal Machine Music* appeared in 1975. See Stephen Mallinder insider's examination of the genre (ix–xiv), David Keenan's view of it as ritualistic and "redemptive" (xvi), and Simon Reynolds' account of possible American precursors (*Rip* 30–1).
11. See Florian Zappe's study of the "abject unpopular" in P-Orridge's work.
12. Reed styles Tutti the band's "face," her contributions motivated by instinct; for Reed, Chris Carter is the technical brain, Sleazy is "the emotional (if pervy) heart," and P-Orridge is the head and voice (74).
13. P-Orridge said similarly that s/he preferred reading John Cage's books over listening to his music and also preferred contemplating Andy Warhol's artistic strategies to looking at his pictures (P-Orridge, *Sacred* 87).
14. See Simon Ford's groundbreaking study of the band in *Wreckers of Civilisation*, which may be Tutti's first account of TG, including "revisiting my past" though consultation with her diaries, in that she contributed to it by "reading through drafts as he progressed" and correcting, not always successfully in terms of her opinion of the final product, "Gen's fantasies and inaccuracies" (Tutti 324–6). She may refer to Ford's account of P-Orridge claiming to have originated tampon art, for example (3.7). Ford refers to Tutti's and P-Orridge's relationship having "deteriorated significantly" when the band was breaking up, but there's no mention of violence (8.5).
15. Among discussions of the cut-up, the Dreamachine, and Control, Gysin details the threatening environs of gay New York and gay Paris as well as his encounters with the Rolling Stones in Tangier (P-Orridge, *Brion* 351–4, 69–73).
16. S/he was given a one-year suspended sentence with the ominous warning "that if they found anything else that was offensive … in my art, I would automatically go to jail for a year" (P-Orridge qtd. in Daniel 84; see, too, Ford 6.11–6.13).
17. P-Orridge grew up in Manchester and claimed in 2008 that Joy Division's Ian Curtis wanted to start a band with him/her which would be announced after a joint Joy Division/TG concert in Paris, and that Curtis committed suicide because he said "categorically that he'd rather be dead than go to America" (P-Orridge, *Sacred* 204–5).
18. She is highly intelligent and sexually precocious and whistles at male teachers, gets ejected from the Girl Guides for cavorting with Boy Scouts, and as a girl discovers

that "[p]laying sex games with boys had become my favourite pastime." Thus, when asked what she would do on the eve of nuclear armageddon, she remembers, "I said I'd be a boy for the day so I could have sex and see what it was like without the fear of getting pregnant" (26).

19 TG's music "resists analysis" because of the band's antagonism to conventional ideas about music and the "kink and mayhem" surrounding them, writes TG fan, "former go-go dancer in gay bars," and English professor Drew Daniel in his meticulous song-by-song analysis of TG's self-consciously kitsch, fan-expectations defeating release *20 Jazz Funk Greats* (1, 159, 99).

20 TG's insistence on artistic integrity and rejection of the profit motive terminated an approach from Virgin Records, P-Orridge claiming the band sent the label a smashed demo tape in response to their inquiry (P-Orridge, *Sacred* 300, 311–12). Their reputation for creating chaotic/erotic disturbia may have doomed their request for an endorsement deal from Roland equipment. Expanding their music's reach into film work, they had a soundtrack commissioned by experimental gay filmmaker Derek Jarman but not Disney, despite some locational proximity in art actions to that empire. When the band did become more commercially successful and were also met with fan adulation, the writing was on the wall for its termination.

21 See Ford's extended description of the action (6.19–6.30).

22 Tutti's website mentions her own forthcoming study of Kempe.

23 One such example is when a transsexual seeking to fund gender reassignment surgery performs with a young man: "Him buggering Daisy was a sad sight …. Neither of them wanted to do it and Daisy was self-conscious about her small, atrophying penis, which was cruelly made the main focus, to drive home that she was transsexual" (173).

24 Tutti complains, for example, that "much of what he presented as 'his' concept and the whole ethos of his new project, COUM Transmissions, came from that of the Exploding Galaxy and Transmedia Explorations: 'Life Is Art,' communal creativity, everyone is an artist, costumes, rituals, play, artworks, scavenging for art materials, street theatre, rejection of conventions, and the advocation of sexual liberation" (59).

25 See Virginia Nicholson's analysis of misogynistic attitudes a decade earlier in the 1960s radical underground in *How Was It For You*.

26 Ballad singer Carolyn Hester, similarly, in the early 1960s, according to David Hajdu, resented her husband Richard Fariña's attempts "to turn over her career to him," and his insulting behavior and pursuit of the seventeen-year-old Mimi Baez, possibly as a way to romance Joan Baez, led Hester to consider shooting Fariña in Paris with the gun he'd persuaded her to carry across international borders, till she realized he would relish such a dramatic demise (114).

27 Talking Heads' drummer Chris Frantz in his 2020 autobiography *Remain in Love* writes of having witnessed Martyn later on honeymoon with his wife Annie Furlong: "he was holding his naked wife's head underwater in the kitchen sink while beating her neck and shoulders with his free hand"; tellingly, when she is escorted back to Ireland, her brothers tell the escort to "mind her own business" (303, 304).

28 She writes of enjoying the "power trip" of stripping and walking the "fine line between teasing for pleasure and teasing to belittle and insult the guys" (288, 289).

29 P-Orridge's autobiography appeared in 2021, though s/he claimed to have begun it as early as 2012. S/he blamed the delay on the project's seeming to be too "egocentric," the difficulty of handling the volume of material, and because "we're not a nostalgic person" (P-Orridge, *Sacred* 316, 225, 203, 306). P-Orridge's 2002 collation, *Painful But Fabulous*, anticipates an autobiography. In *Nonbinary, A Memoir* (2021), P-Orridge and variously designated cowriter, collaborator, and editor Tim Mohr do not refer to Tutti's autobiography or its allegations of abuse, but they are generally dismissive of Tutti and other members of TG, while conceding that the band's creativity emerged "through discussion" (241). P-Orridge is self-styled as the genius generator of TG's concept, ideas, performance, sound, DIY and anti-art aesthetic, and even the instigator of Tutti's relationship with Chris Carter. *Nonbinary* refers to Tutti as very conventional, and P-Orridge is mostly indifferent and contemptuous if a little disappointed she wasn't more "honest" in her accounts of the band's history (223).

30 The cult development "unnerved" David Tibet (qtd. in Keenan 61), and led Sleazy and John Balance to leave Psychic TV (Keenan 64, 151), in turn inaugurating the creation of the gay-positive "drug group" Coil (Keenan 281), named as a favorite band by Karlheinz Stockhausen (Reed 145), who may have accepted a facetious offer to join them (Keenan 409–11). Coil was committed to "a systematic investigation of the extremes, to going as far as they could, into altered states, into new ways of framing reality, and reporting back with their findings" (Keenan 429); sadly, according to Tutti, Balance's terminal excess was pursued because "our fans expect it of me now" (qtd. in Keenan 428).

31 *Mornings* does refer to Ricky Gervais (157–8), to Morrissey's attending an early concert (207), and to living in a flat below "the pre-success Anish Kapoor" (165).

32 He especially resents interpretations of his songs as detailing conflicts with co-writer Bernard Butler. Revisiting the past is a "wrenching experience," not least because he dreads the wilful misreading of those who have not read his book (*Mornings* xi, xii).

33 Jeff Buckley gave a poignant reading of their "I Know It's Over" from 1986's *The Queen is Dead* which begins "O Mother, I can feel the soil falling over my head" on his *So Real* compilation, 2007.

34 The Smiths' drummer Mike Joyce would later audition for Suede (*Mornings* 151–3).
35 Anderson's 1980s anxiety about nuclear war (*Mornings* 23) recalls Jeff Nuttall's emphasis on the importance of the threat of annihilation in the countercultural underground of the 1960s (16–18, 173). See, too, Dylan's *Chronicles* (29, 270–2).
36 In *Mornings*, he writes, "[t]here were never any limits with Justine—she was always fascinated and fascinating, wise yet humble, intellectual yet earthy, murky and thoughtful, yet silly and joyous and wonderfully playful" (112).
37 Morrissey details a similar ritual of fans ripping off his shirt (252).
38 Morrissey's 2015 novel *List of the Lost*, however, lacks the qualities of the best parts of the autobiography.
39 "Madchester" is a rock sub-genre but more commonly a description of Manchester's volatile social and cultural scene. In his memoir *Unknown Pleasures*, Joy Division's Peter Hook refers to the Sex Pistols' notorious 1976 concert in Manchester as inspiring the city's distinctive musical evolution (35–8). Joy Division's Ian Curtis and Bernard Sumner—his name earlier changed from Dickin to Albrecht in conformity with "Nazi chic" according to early manager Terry Mason (qtd. in Nolan 47)—also attended, and in his autobiography *Chapter and Verse*, Sumner disputes some of Hook's versions of events, though his writing is clearly motivated by a kind of survivor's guilt at having been unable to prevent Curtis's suicide, though he even attempted his own cures for Curtis with "past-life regression therapy" using hypnosis (131, 301–20). Sumner eventually started a band with Marr, though he claims his interest in electronic music began with Joy Division (150–1). Hook credits Oasis with broadcasting the Madchester scene internationally by being "working class thieves" of everything, including music (12). Oasis's Manchester vs London tabloid media feud with Blur hinged partly on a perception of the more middle- or upper-middle class background of Blur, the notion of "posh rock" being oxymoronic.
40 Cheever writes, for example: "Homosexuality seemed to me a lingering death. If I followed my instincts I would be strangled by some hairy sailor in a public urinal. Every comely man, every bank clerk and delivery boy, was aimed at my life like a loaded pistol. In order to prove my maleness, I resorted to such absurd strategies as not letting my eye rest on the woman's page in the morning *Times*. But now I seem to see it clearly. Homosexuality is not, as I live, an evil. The evil is anxiety, an anxiety that can take on all the shapes and colors of hopeless passion" (219).
41 In his autobiographical prison letter *De Profundis*, Wilde refers to same-sex desires as the consequence of professional curiosity about all experience and an artistic embrace of the paradox (Wilde, *De Profundis* 101). Wilde would rehearse more conventional late Victorian explanations in his letter to the Home Secretary seeking early release where he refers to his desires as a species of mental illness, "sexual

madness," or "erotomania" (Wilde, "Letter" 16). Unlike Wilde, however, Cheever says he "find[s] a double life loathsome, morbid, and anyhow impossible" (172).

42 See Barry Werth's *The Scarlet Professor*.

43 A different, less obviously stylized version of the innocent abroad appears in Chris Frantz's autobiography, *Remain in Light*. We have a preppy college student from a Southern patrician family wearing Brooks Brothers clothes bought by his mother meeting Lou Reed's transgender lover Rachel and listening to Reed's monologue on favorite drugs. Warhol advises him to watch his figure, and most people say he's too nice to be in the punk scene. The autobiography, which sometimes has the momentum of watching a neighbor's holiday slides and oddly, for a member of a new wave band dedicated to producing anything other than yacht rock, ends with tales of wintering in France and yachting with the family.

44 Wilde wrote, "The gods had given me almost everything. I had genius, a distinguished name, high social position, brilliancy, intellectual daring: I made art a philosophy, and philosophy an art: I altered the minds of men and the colours of things: there was nothing I said or did that did not make people wonder … whatever I touched I made beautiful in a new mode of beauty: to truth itself I gave what is false no less than what is true as its rightful province …. I treated Art as the supreme reality, and life as a mere mode of fiction" (*De Profundis* 100).

4

Performative Identity: Patti Smith, David Wojnarowicz

The performative identity in the life writing of Patti Smith and David Wojnarowicz emerged in work produced in the music and art renaissance in New York's Lower East Side in the 1970s and 1980s. It was a very different area from the one in which a decade later Moby discovered his sky palace and somewhat closer to the gritty environs of Hull and Manchester, which appear in the works of Cosey Fanni Tutti and Brett Anderson, on the other side of the Black Atlantic. Smith and Wojnarowicz both embraced a DIY aesthetic and were associated in different ways with Arthur Rimbaud and William Burroughs, as well as with the discipline of photography which was gaining recognition as an art form in this period. Each was a practitioner of the art and also a subject of one of the two finest, most famous, and even infamous American photographers, Robert Mapplethorpe and Peter Hujar, both of whom died during the AIDS plague of the 1980s and 1990s. Smith's punk rock and Wojnarowicz's no wave[1] experimentation embodied aspects of their emerging performative selves that would find expression in their multiple works of autobiographical writing.

Patti Smith

At the Nobel Prize ceremony honoring Bob Dylan as the winner of the Nobel Prize for Literature, Patti Smith, iconic punk rock performance poet, sang the funereal "A Hard Rain's A-Gonna Fall," written when Dylan was twenty-one, with an orchestra in the palatial concert hall before the King of Sweden, and her performance has become one of her most famous due to its false starts.[2] The "godmother of punk" as Smith is often called, has always been both a writer and a fan, as well as a musician. Smith wears her fandom easily, acknowledging Dylan and Keith Richards as influences, in image and attitude[3]—their personas sometimes adopted onstage—as well as Arthur Rimbaud, Antonin Artaud, and Jean Genet, and constructing her most famous music, 1975's *Horses*, as homage to 1960s rock. The Patti Smith Group was "the last of the sixties bands," recalls guitarist Lenny Kaye, fusing that period's "revolutionary ... fervor" with "urban noire music" (qtd. in McNeil and McCain 411). Her reverence for legendary figures from the 1960s and Francophilia in her devotion to these figures from French culture may be one of her most American qualities. This performance of fandom, the open acknowledgment of sources and influences, operates in different registers in her three volumes of memoir, *Just Kids* (2010), *M Train* (2015), and *Year of the Monkey* (2019). She had written music reviews—because French symbolist poet Charles Baudelaire wrote them—for *Rolling Stone* and *Crawdaddy* and other rock journals before she ever recorded a song. In addition, for a physically striking woman, Smith has been adept at modeling androgyny, as in Robert Mapplethorpe's famous cover image for *Horses*, its louche elegance a striking contrast to the recording's self-consciously amateurish rawness that became a template for much alternative rock. A central focus of her first autobiographical work, for which she is increasingly best known, is her intimate relationship with the famous photographer of the homoerotic. She lived with Mapplethorpe in and around New York's Chelsea Hotel in turbulent times when she was an astute observer and one of the period's designated drivers, as it were, a famously sober presence amid rampant chemical excess.[4] The memory palace of Patti Smith is no doubt enhanced by her abstemiousness as much as by her focus on "nostalgia" and "humor" rather than what might be a very understandable vindictiveness or desire to settle scores (*Just Kids* 167). Smith writes as one who has breached the divide between the avant-garde and the popular, or the street, without the loss of her punk rock and punk poet credibility, and become a respected, if still somewhat charmingly outré, member of the American literary establishment. In a recent interview, she remarks on her artistic vocation: "I was a flawed singer. I was not particularly gifted, but I did have guts. It's ridiculous to judge your young self. I know that everything I did, no matter how questionable it was or how many people I might have offended along the way, it was to try to open territory, to open things up for new generations" (Long 57).[5]

The third of Smith's volumes of memoir, *Year of the Monkey*, has an epigraph from Antonin Artaud, the theorist of performance, poet, and artist, which informs her work as a punk rock performance artist. She also carries his work on her travels in *M Train*. In 2019, Smith released a performance of Artaud's *The Peyote Dance* in readings, adaptations, and original work with sound artists

Soundwalk Collective in their *Perfect Vision* triptych. Smith acknowledges that her interpretation of the unorthodox Artaud, creator of the "theatre of cruelty," is itself unorthodox and non-doctrinaire, and that her devotion to his revolutionary ideas began with her being mesmerized by photographs of Artaud (Rowell, "A Conversation" 141).[6] Moreover, she was first moved by his drawings, though his example encouraged her not to specialize in a single art form but to move in different areas (142). Interestingly, Smith regards Artaud's failing as his drug addiction (143), which is somewhat surprising given that his advocacy of opiates resembled that of another of Smith's mentor figures, William Burroughs.[7] Punk rock, at least for Smith and her fellow punk rocker turned diarist and former heroin addict Richard Hell, has claimed kinship with Artaud, though as David Shafter puts it, "punk might contain Artaud's DNA without necessarily being Artaud's offspring" (216). The Sex Pistols' John Lydon, however, rejected any influence, possibly due to the more class-based grounding of British punk (215–18). Punk, however conflicted its origin story, always had a relationship with fashion.[8] While many aspects of Artaud's work are in line with 1960s and 1970s rock and punk cultures, he was terrified of sexuality, believing, for example, that he had been defiled by the mingling of "sperm and excrement" at his conception (Shafer 165). His writings also suggest that he was at times misogynistic, anti-Semitic, pro-fascist, and messianic. Artaud has been fetishized as representing a broad range of rebellious, anti-rational, anti-authoritarian positions relating to performance, and even as a proto-theorist of the 1960s cultural revolution in popular music.[9] This association has been facilitated by the breadth of Artaud's positions on different subjects, the disconnect between his theories and their application, and the unevenness and sometimes contradictory nature of his writing, resulting, partly at least, from his mental instability, drug addiction, and the effects of electroshock therapy.[10] These factors render some of Artaud's writings highly ambiguous, though he has been embraced with proprietary zeal by a range of French philosophers from Derrida to Kristeva and Foucault. Susan Sontag notes that some of Artaud's writings are "morally monstrous or terribly painful" and even designed to be indecipherable or unintelligible and instead "to be directly apprehended as sound" ("Approaching" 53, 47).

Certain tenets from Artaud's manifestos regarding the revolutionary nature of the "theatre of cruelty" have been enormously influential.[11] Performance, which for Artaud must be interactive and hence require a new type of architecture, should provoke an extreme reaction, a violent, alchemical gestalt and not merely a type of healing, restorative catharsis. He refers to the theatre of cruelty, not as entertainment or diversion, but as "unforgettable soul therapy" ("Theatre" 64). For Smith, raised a Jehovah's Witness, too, the punk performance was a blasphemously spiritual experience. Her provocation in "Gloria": "Jesus died for somebody's sins but not mine" belies her persistent focus on the sacred and profane (qtd. in Shaw 2–3).[12] Novelist and briefly Smith's partner Jim Carroll noted revealingly that "[i]n her own way, Patti is extremely old-fashioned"; "I always found Patti to be very Christian" (qtd. in McNeil and McCain 115, 327). The experience for Artaud should amount to an almost therapeutic confrontation of the "whole anatomy" of the spectator with primordial psychic terrors ("Theatre" 66). The theatre of cruelty must provide "the audience with truthful distillations of dreams where its taste for crime, its erotic obsessions, its savageness, its fantasies, its utopian sense of life and objects, even its cannibalism, do not gush out on an illusory make-believe, but on an inner level" ("The Theatre" 70). Artaud's views were based in part on a romantic, utopian, and exoticist view of non-European performance traditions such as those of the Indigenous cultures of Bali or Mexico and partook of magical, miraculous, and ritualized elements. He also traveled to Ireland in 1937 to connect with a lost, magical culture, but he would return to France in a straightjacket. Artaud's multimedia, "total theatre" would be largely post-linguistic or at least would foreground bodily gestures and movement ("Theatre" 66), incorporating the potential of cinema, circus, music hall, and dance. To achieve this aim, he rejected the staging of "masterpieces" from the past ("No More" 56), seeking instead for new forms that would emerge naturally from the locale of the performance. It would replace Western theatre's over-reliance on text with noise or glossolalia, speaking in tongues, or the sonic equivalent of hieroglyphics. In this development, he was partly responding to what he saw as the masses' exclusion from a cultural expression favoring the elite. Instead, he advocated visceral performance or spectacle.[13]

Artaud's ambitious manifesto for a new theatre of the future in some respects sounds like an aspirational manifesto for a somewhat terrifying rock concert. "In Europe no one knows how to scream any more," he lamented, stressing the imperative for performers to flex their vocal muscles ("Affective" 106). While the performer has an anatomy of emotions corresponding to the structure of the body which can be tapped into by regulating the breath or manipulating the body's pressure points, Artaud emphasizes that the "soul's athleticism" can also be unleashed and its effects can be "achieved by screams" ("Affective" 107). He stresses the need for discordant, pulsating rhythms. Artaud's theatre of cruelty "pile-drives sounds," "expands the voice," and via "the wild pounding of rhythms and sound" will enact its liberating exorcism ("The Theatre" 69, 72). He calls, moreover, for new instruments, perhaps like electric guitars and synthesizers, which will

> [n]eed to act deeply and directly on our sensibility through the senses, and from the point of view of sound they invite research into utterly unusual sound properties and vibrations which present-day musical instruments do not possess, urging us to use ancient or forgotten instruments or to invent new ones. Apart from music, research is also needed into instruments and appliances based on special refining and new alloys which can reach a new scale in the octave and produce an unbearably piercing sound or noise.
>
> ("The Theatre" 73)

Artaud's conception of performance resembles a psychedelic experience with equal elements ordeal, therapy, ritual, and transcendence, during which the spectator's mind and body become a type of laboratory. While Artaud's spectacle taken together may be an "instrument of revolution," as Sontag suggests, it is stridently apolitical, and while it suggests the creation of a unified mind and body, "the terms of … [Artaud's] thinking imply the annihilation of consciousness" (Sontag, "Approaching" 35, 47).

Just Kids is a dual auto/biography like Edmund Gosse's *Father and Son* and J.R. Ackerley's *My Father and Myself*, though it is also an AIDS memoir, like some of the work of David Wojnarowicz as we shall see, in that it begins and ends with Robert Mapplethorpe's death. It fulfills her promise to Mapplethorpe who shared Smith's life for a number of tumultuous years marked by Smith's interpretation of omens and talismans showing the predestination of their future success in different fields and even his demise.[14] It is memoir as prophecy.[15] They are childlike sibling twins, lovers, and self-described "interchangeable" artists and muses (252). Smith traces the still, quiet center from which her own art emerged as well as the religious and ethical devotion to beauty which inspired Mapplethorpe's work. While a commitment to equality ostensibly governs their union, at times it's also as if he has created her and was "the artist of my life" (157). Mapplethorpe and the development of his aesthetic aims receive greater attention in *Just Kids*, as in their lives together, and Smith even wonders if she'll be merely a footnote in his story (120). Other than occasional references to a lack of inspiration when writing—the impasse at which *M Train* begins—or an inability to complete poems or laments about writing's lack of physicality (177), one exception to Smith's reticence about exploring the roots of her artistic vocation is her reference to a childhood memory of outrage, presumably the "submerged arrogance" that Mapplethorpe's "censorious eye" warns her to suppress (182, 199). Unusually for one who would become so devoted to older poets, she recalls feeling angry as a child that "we are born into a world where everything was mapped out by those before us. I struggled to suppress destructive impulses and worked instead on creative ones" (174). Apparently, from this sense of dispossession comes her manifesto, articulated before her break-out performance opening for Gerard Malanga at the Poetry Project, attended by the famous and emerging from Lou Reed and Andy Warhol to John Giorno and Joe Brainard, after which her career takes off: "I wanted to infuse the written word with the immediacy and frontal attack of rock and roll" (180). She will suspect, of course, that her success is both far too sudden and undeserved, though its auspiciousness is enhanced by coinciding with Bertolt Brecht's birthday.[16] Smith presents herself as the ideal bride of Rimbaud and Mapplethorpe as the image of her "rock 'n' roll Jesus" (186) and she stridently sets out to counter dismissals of Mapplethorpe as a pornographer. For Smith, Mapplethorpe's background as an altar boy had led him to explore the fascination of Lucifer and make a "Faustian pact" whereby "Satan would grant him fame and fortune," though he is also a playful kid who loves the Stones' "Sympathy for the Devil" (188, 63, 79).

The determinations of gender roles in this period also mandated aspects of their union. The self-deprecating Smith, for example, had aspired to be "an artist's mistress"—not an artist—as a child (12), and she would assume a 1950s "wifely" role, working 9 to 5 to support Mapplethorpe's ambitions. Before she met Mapplethorpe, she gave up a child for adoption—the nurses berating her as "Dracula's daughter"—just as the libertine Mapplethorpe was taking LSD (19–20). Mapplethorpe places her in awkward positions later, and she is very accommodating, even motherly, tolerating his taking LSD before first meeting her parents, getting tested for gonorrhea after his gay sex work and desire for intimacy expose her to infection, and agonizing with Mapplethorpe's patron John McKendry, the married curator of photography at the Metropolitan Museum of Art, over his unrequited sexual obsession with Mapplethorpe. Smith is a remarkably compliant partner, in other relationships, too, so long as art is part of the equation. She describes her affair with autobiographer, novelist, and sometime musician Jim Carroll who has a "modest heroin habit" and works as a gay prostitute, sometimes with Mapplethorpe, though only for money: "He was unreliable, evasive, and sometimes too stoned to speak, but he was also kind, ingenuous, and a true poet. I knew he didn't love me but I adored him anyway"

(163, 167).[17] Smith and Mapplethorpe's relationship survived, however, partly because both were committed to being successful artists though Mapplethorpe's drive was more frantic, and he tried to emulate Warhol just when the pop artist was moving into business art including society portraits of dictators. There was at least one other third party in Smith's relationship with Mapplethorpe: the nineteenth-century French symbolist poet Arthur Rimbaud who is her inspiration. She romanticizes her relationship with Mapplethorpe and his lovers David Croland and Sam Wagstaff in terms of Rimbaud's tumultuous affair with his married lover and mentor Paul Verlaine.[18] Smith dreams "about the dead and their vanished centuries" until she comes to wish she could "write something that would awake the dead"; later, she will mourn her inability to resurrect Mapplethorpe after his agonized passing from complications due to AIDS (64, 279).

Smith does not present herself as the voice of a generation or even a particular scene, and she narrates her course within the New York punk explosion as if her moves were fated and followed in the footsteps of European artistic giants. The geography of her New York is marked less by soon-to-be famous punk clubs[19] than by the site where Picasso's *Guernica* is hanging, the junkies' hotel whose lice reminds her of Rimbaud's world, and even the coordinates of her and Mapplethorpe's thefts, including a Blake drawing, sanctified by association with the criminal career of French novelist Jean Genet. However, the iconic Chelsea Hotel is her "university," with its ghosts of Dylan Thomas and Bob Dylan, and it is here that she meets William Burroughs and Allen Ginsberg—who assumes she is a beautiful boy and tries to pick her up—and where even a bad LSD trip conjures Thomas de Quincey (138, 134). It is less prominent Beat poet Gregory Corso who inspires her aggressive stage performance, however. At the Chelsea she also seeks out Harry Smith, the eccentric anthropologist and filmmaker, most famous as the creator of *The Anthology of American Folk Music* (1952), the bible of the 1960s folk scene. Smith doesn't mention his same-sex interests other than noting "Harry was taken with Robert but wound up with me" (113).[20] She shares his interests in alchemy and magic, Kiowa peyote rituals, and the archiving of Ukrainian eggs, magic wands, and string figures (113–16). Smith also shares his fondness for the music of Charlie Patton, who embodied the historic linkages between Indigenous North American music and the blues. At Max's Kansas City, the watering hole of Warhol's Factory, Mapplethorpe makes a bid to enter Warhol's circle and Smith hears the Velvet Underground, whose John Cale, alumnus of La Monte Young's avant-garde Dream Syndicate, will produce her first album. She also begins a creative liaison with the playwright Sam Shephard, first encountered playing "an Arabian hoedown with a band of psychedelic hillbillies" (171).

Just Kids is partly a work of homage, and it credits the influence of various rock musicians and fellow travelers. From certain rock legends, Smith learns about performance and the projection of a persona onstage, the language of music, and artistic integrity. She exults with a fan's adoration, but she also feels a sense of "kinship" and also one of "prescience" as if she were fulfilling an inevitable destiny and "the vibrating patterns … were sliding into place" (106). She cuts her hair to resemble Keith Richards' and "miraculously turned androgynous overnight" making clear that at least some of her appeal on the New York punk scene related to image or fashion that would be of such importance in the British punk scene (140). She also at least partly venerates Dylan for his image and album covers which influence her work as a rock reviewer, model, and poet; however, when she performs with Dylan in the audience, she feels that she "become[s] fully myself in the presence of the one I had modeled myself after" (248). She also venerates those now mythic figures who died young at the end of the 1960s. Sharing Mapplethorpe's fondness for shrines or altars, she keeps Brian Jones' image over her bed and dreams of him, finding inspiration in his Moroccan recording, *The Pipes of Pan at Joujouka*, and writing her first rock 'n' roll poetry to him, though she also credits Jim Morrison and Lou Reed with inspiring her hybrid rock performance poetry.[21] She acknowledges her debt in discovering her vocation to Bob Neuwirth and Todd Rundgren, and also Matthew Reich, Lenny Kaye, Allen Lanier of Blue Öyster Cult, as well as Lee Crabtree who puts music to her words just before his suicide (197–8), but her greatest debt is to Janis Joplin, Jimi Hendrix, and Jim Morrison. Neuwirth introduces Smith to Joplin as "the poet" and it appears she gives Joplin the name and persona of Pearl (158, 166). She meets Hendrix at Electric Lady Studios, where she will later record *Horses*, and he tells her of his universal musical language, "the language of peace" (169). Smith was transformed, however, by witnessing Jim Morrison's performance at the Fillmore East, identifying with his physicality and his vulnerable projected persona more than his singing or the Doors' music. She observes his movements "in a state of cold hyperawareness," feeling "I could do that": "I felt both kinship and contempt for him. I could feel his self-consciousness as well as his supreme confidence. He exuded a mixture of beauty and self-loathing, and mystic pain, like a West Coast Saint Sebastian" (59).

Smith eventually embraces what she reads as her predestined emergence as a rock 'n' roll performance punk poet, crediting Tom Verlaine, the virtuosic guitarist and leader of Television, and, in her early recording, the inspiration of revolutionary 1960s music. She watches Television with Richard Hell perform at CBGB, appreciating "their spasmodic movements, the drummer's jazz flourishes, their disjointed, orgasmic musical structures" (240). She senses "a scene emerging," and, conjuring the words of *Jane Eyre* when Jane hears Mr. Rochester's telepathic, apocalyptic call in Brontë's novel—referred to directly in *M Train*—Smith exults that "the stars were aligning, the angels were calling" (240). This new direction represented a significant shift because earlier Smith had been committed to a far more eclectic approach, though still committed to moving poetry reading from the recitation of dead letters towards performance.[22] Her DIY sensibility or disdain for expertise was part of her onstage musicianship as she noted in an interview: "I never learned [guitar] chords, I didn't learn notes, I dealt with sound. I was really interested to see how you could push it further and get past the skeleton, into the entrails of the instrument" (qtd. in Rowell, "Conversation" 142). *Just Kids* tells of her purchase of a heritage Martin acoustic, funded by Sam Shepard, though some time elapsed before she realized that "you had to tune a guitar" (164), a fortuitous revelation that led her to seek out tuners who become accompanists, co-writers, and bandmates, like Lenny Kaye. She asked Kaye to accompany her poetry reading by imitating the sound of cars crashing on his guitar. While many male musicians refused to work for a female band leader, eventually her band is complete with the addition of accomplished Czechoslovakian musician Ivan Král. However, her band begins in more conventional fashion by doing covers of songs like "Hey Joe," "Gloria," and "My Generation."[23]

Rock 'n' roll moves Smith beyond her devotion to sonic landscapes as backgrounds for her poetry readings and suggests the radical performance style modeled on Artaud's work that drove her aggressive onstage connection with her audience. In his autobiography, Richard Hell recalls that "[s]he was the most accomplished, talented sheer performer [on the scene], though her band was generic and undistinguished, and her songs became more and more ordinary too" (148).[24] In fact, performance may have superseded music for Smith, as it did in her appreciation for Mick Jagger's "naked performance" (qtd. in McNeil and McCain 173). Her own "performance poetry," she said elsewhere, "can seduce people into mass consciousness" and similarly transform the performer:

through performance, I reach such states, in which my brain feels so open—so full of light, it feels huge, it feels as big as the Empire State Building—and if I can develop a communication with an audience, a bunch of people, when my brain is that big and receptive, imagine the energy and the intelligence and all the things I can steal from them.

(qtd. in McNeil and McCain 175)

When she does finally assemble a band, it can explore "what rock and roll could be" through their "mission to preserve, protect, and project the revolutionary spirit of rock and roll" and save it from "spiritual starvation" via "spectacle, finance, and vapid technical complexity" (*Just Kids* 244, 245). In effect, pushing forward the needle on rock 'n' roll ensures its conservation. On *Horses*, a deeply personal if not exactly autobiographical work,[25] she tries to realize Hendrix's "hopes for the future of our cultural voice," and to celebrate rock 'n' roll as a survival mechanism for adolescents, a bringer of joy through dancing, and an expression of its musicians' moral integrity: "These things were encoded in *Horses* as well as a salute to those who paved the way" (249). Its individual songs would merge mythic imaginings with laments for the fate of 1960s rock legends:

> In "Break It Up," Tom Verlaine and I wrote of a dream in which Jim Morrison, bound like Prometheus, suddenly broke free. In "Land," wild-boy imagery fused with the stages of Hendrix's death. In "Elegie," remembering them all, past, present, and future, those we had lost, were losing, and would ultimately lose.
>
> (249)

Just Kids is partly a work of musical homage, but *M Train* draws closer to literary homage. Like Joni Mitchell, the great folk and jazz musician who considers herself primarily a painter, and even Allen Ginsberg who would like to have been a rock star with the accompanying mass influence, Smith in *M Train* thinks of herself as a performance punk poet and visual artist and only then as a musician. In many ways, *M Train* is her *Hejira*, a paean to pilgrimage and leave taking and dark, cafe days. Like *Just Kids*, *M Train* has elegiac qualities, as Fred "Sonic" Smith, founding member of MC5 and her beloved husband, "a king among men" as she says in *Just Kids* (263), who shared in her romantic obsessions, is a mostly absent presence throughout. *M Train* is a memoir imbued with magical thinking which generally avoids agonized laments for the departed, despite addressing objects, rooms, and sometimes the wraiths of the vanished as when she begins weeping on a long flight from Japan and pleads "[j]ust come back .... You've been gone long enough" (171). *M Train* is the memoir of a *flâneur*, if that notion of meditative meandering on foot can extend to taking trains and boats and planes, and also binge-watching TV crime dramas. It's very much about writing or not writing, and the importance of reflection, rumination, and mental wandering when staring down writer's block. *M Train*'s refrain is "[i]t's not so easy writing about nothing" (7), and as such it is a memoir of a mind in motion, of consciousness caught or observed on the wing, with all its false starts, incompletions, and free associations. The memoir's major preoccupation is the writer's attempt to divine—sometimes with tarot cards—the meaning of signs, coincidences, dreams, and disappearances confronted on quixotic journeys. *M Train* is Smith's diary as a writer, often set in myriad cafes or amid her quest for a headache-curing or awareness-expanding perfect cup of coffee, a quest narrative which she once considered writing—one of a number of abandoned writing projects referred to—in post-Beat form to be entitled *Java Head*. Smith's reading of a heterogeneous variety of world literature classics in this memoir is often biographical, if that designation can encompass reading that sparks compulsions to visit writers' houses or more commonly tombs or to write living writers asking them about seemingly missing or unresolved plot points. Visits to writers' tombs are usually grave, reverent occasions, accompanied by delivering totems and taking away mementos, though not on one visit to Sylvia Plath's grave in the remorselessly cold Yorkshire winter. Avoiding the saga of the Plath–Hughes' war over Plath's legacy and hence her resting place, Smith, nevertheless, with true punk rock outrage, restrains a desire to urinate on the grave (200).

While it begins with references to performing at the Fillmore in San Francisco—"three nights of feedback, poetry, improvisational rants, politics, and rock 'n' roll"—*Year of the Monkey* is a hybrid textual and photographic meditation on death and impermanence written in a kind of autobiographical magic realism (9). It sees Smith marking the days of the passing year with commemorations for the departed, and assuming, however reluctantly, the role of archivist of some of the great hearts, minds, and voices of her generation. Even more than in *M Train*, Smith wears her avant-garde punk rock sensibility on her sleeve, freely performing a mash-up of references to popular culture and high art. While touching on Roman emperor Marcus Aurelius's meditations on fame, *Alice in Wonderland*, and also being indebted to the work of Chilean poet, novelist, and fabulist Roberto Bolaño, the memoir's main focus is the lingering demise of producer and music professor Sandy Pearlman, who loved opera as much as rock, and the final months of Sam Shepard, though it also attends to the memory of her beloved younger brother and to Smith's own approach to seventy and the election of Donald Trump. A series of interconnected but fragmentary scenes or mini-narratives, much of *Year of the Monkey* is suspended over the hospitalization of Pearlman, who importantly suggested after hearing Smith's break-out poetry performance with Lenny Kaye, covered in *Just Kids*, that she "should front a rock band" (*Year* 24). Smith or her "dual-self" is on a mysterious voyage throughout in which there are incidental references to songs, but, as in *M Train*, a unifying focus remains on the interpretation of premonitions, signs, impulses, and "[a]n ardent Artaud type of spell" (*Year* 11, 113) as well as detecting portals or channels to dream worlds while always more or less successfully resisting the seduction of detective fiction. The possibility of Smith's pilgrimage to Ayers Rock in Australia, the idea of a spiritual journey she has shared with Shepard, tantalizes throughout but ends up being a false lead or dropped clue. In a kind of metafictional gesture, Smith assists in editing Shepard's fragmentary, impressionistic memoir *The One Inside*, mostly focused on a passionate but traumatic affair when he was thirteen with his father's young mistress who commits suicide, written as he faces the end of his life. It blends fact and fiction, though, as Smith writes in her "Foreword," "[r]eality is overrated" (xii). The famous playwright and collaborator with Smith and with Dylan on *Renaldo and Clara* (1978), and the subject of Joni Mitchell's song "Coyote," Shepard accepts his mortality because "I've lived my life the way I wanted," though Smith "still harbored the hope that I would not be destined to grow old without him" (*Year* 88, 146). What does appear to be the crime or the nightmare from which one cannot awaken in the memoir is not the various references to the missing and the disappeared or to psychic doubles appearing and vanishing, but the American election of 2016, "an avalanche of toxicity" (126). An election "decided by … those who do not vote" due to "our American apathy" and "the twisted wisdom of the Electoral College" is won by someone who "builds empty edifices in his own name, another kind of immoral waste" (137–8). Smith makes it quite clear that she was not one of the majority of white women in America who did not vote for Hillary Clinton. The consequence is that the poor will pay for "that damn wall," "[p]esticides will be a food group," and "the rich" will prepare "to board a ship for a night on the moon" (159).

In light of a toxic, cartoonish reality which bests fiction and perhaps also/if not fabulist autobiography/self writing in the era of Trump, this memoir is witness to Smith's move away from punk poet stardom. This move had began much earlier because, as Philip Gefter suggests, "Smith had reached a level of fame in the world of rock 'n' roll that had begun to take a psychic toll" (323), and as Lenny Kaye recalled "[s]he didn't wanna become her own oldies act," attempting to replicate transformative punk rock performance slams in stadiums (qtd. in McNeil and McCain 411). Moreover, she had confronted her own mortality after a fall from the stage in Florida and perhaps began to reconsider her commitment to making "every performance … a life-and-death encounter with ecstasy" by putting "herself into a trance" and even "masturbat[ing] onstage," as William Burroughs' secretary James Grauerholz recalled Smith telling him about her performance philosophy (qtd. in McNeil and McCain 326). As Grauerholz recognized, noting Smith's inspiration in the departed legends of the late 1960s, her retirement from the stage allowed her to realize with a sleight of hand the greatest performance of all: "She managed to be a rock & roll death without having to die" (qtd. in McNeil and McCain 412). Moreover, she had briefly entered a certain type of rock 'n' roll nirvana by having a hit single with "Because the Night." Increasingly, Smith's concerts compete with other work assignments such as lectures, work she accepts partly in order to fund her travels all the while recording in her notebooks and recognizing the impossibility of recording time passing. Her three memoirs are increasingly impressionistic with a frequent reference to wanting to but not writing. As she says in *Just Kids*, "I've always worked in spurts" (256), perhaps inadvertently conjuring Richard Hell's immortal "Love Comes In Spurts," and the still lingering heritage of punk from times past. She addresses the conundrum of memoir in which "you write in time then time is gone and in trying to catch up you're writing a whole other book" (167–8). Increasingly assuming the position of memoirist or archivist of those of her generation who have moved her, Smith is typically self-effacing and humorous regarding the final self-effacement. As she writes, getting to seventy years of age is not important because it is "[m]erely a number but one indicating the passing of a significant percentage of the allotted sand in an egg timer, with oneself the darn egg" (*Year* 78–9).

David Wojnarowicz

David Wojnarowicz[26] (1954–92) was a multimedia artist, memoirist, and musician, but his predominant aesthetic modes were collage and autobiographical narrative. His work encompassed painting, sculpture, folk art, anthology, photography, graffiti, installations, performance art, film, and music. Wojnarowicz's short film *Beautiful People*, available on YouTube, features a cross-dressing Jesse Hultberg from the post-punk no wave band they founded, 3 Teens Kill 4 (3TK4).[27] Wojnarowicz had a peripheral involvement as an actor with the so-called Cinema of Transgression associated with Richard Kern, who would later make videos for Sonic Youth's "Death Valley '69" and King Missile's "Detachable Penis." Wojnarowicz was also involved in guerrilla street art activism, action installations, or trickster vandalism sometimes including deposits of cows' blood and bones or the release of artistically altered cockroaches (his *Roach Bunnies* installation). He impersonated Lou Reed and sang "Heroin" for an installation/performance piece in which Mike Bidlo "recreated" Warhol's Factory scene for one night in 1984 (Bidlo 31). One of Wojnarowicz's last artistic projects before his death from complications due to AIDS at age thirty-seven was the multimedia performance with music *ITSOFOMO: In the Shadow of Forward Motion*, made in collaboration with Ben Neill and including Wojnarowicz's videotapes and recordings of found sounds.[28]

Wojnarowicz would become for some of his admirers an American Rimbaud—Rimbaud being one of his pantheon of outsider heroes, including Jean Genet, William Burroughs, and Peter Hujar—but later others would see Wojnarowicz as an American Jesus, with disciples, but also groupies. Some of his most famous work was fueled by righteous rage, confronting the norms of what he called the inherited or "pre-invented world" (Carr 66) and a "diseased society" (*Close* 114), but he is most widely remembered for his work in the agitprop aesthetic wing of ACT UP. Some of his extensive autobiographical writing belongs in the AIDS memoir sub-genre of life writing. Taken together, his work in multiple genres may encompass a synthesis of diverse artistic forms, as in the *gesamtkunstwerk* of Richard Wagner.[29] A number of these diverse elements appear in his least well-known work with the no wave band 3 Teens Kill 4 (3TK4) which he co-founded in 1980. Their totalized audiovisual gestalt integrated all aspects of the band, including its music, into a single performative art object. An earlier version of this concept appears in the 1970s German industrial avatars Kraftwerk with its debts to the Fluxus movement and Joseph Beuys, with whom Kraftwerk's collaborator and designer Emil Schult studied. Present in all of Wojnarowicz's work is a powerful, confrontational autobiographical mythology of the artist as abused child, street hustler, and furious ACT UP activist, an uncompromising stance which, as Felix Guattari recognized in 1989, "reinvents … the inspiration of the great 60's movements."

Wojnarowicz's first recognition, however, came through photography, which shaped his self-construction throughout his short career, and even very briefly as a vampirishly glam rock star. He would later embrace photographer Peter Hujar as mentor, lover, and father figure. Hujar enabled Wojnarowicz to move away from "all the shit I brought in from the streets," as Wojnarowicz put it, and to "break free from the more puerile received ideas of his generation" in the assessment of Stephen Koch.[30] Prior to following his own austere artistic vision, Hujar had been an outlier at Warhol's Factory who sat for a Screen Test,[31] before taking a master class with Richard Avedon and working in fashion and rock 'n' roll photography. He shot the Fugs and Janis Joplin, for example, and made some of the best portraits of Iggy Pop, and he photographed at the Filmore East and attended at least the first day of Woodstock (Smith and Burton 232). However, Wojnarowicz's mentor's own taste in music ran more to Motown or opera, though he also admired drag performance artists like Ethyl Eichelberger, and Hujar's interest in music and perhaps also sex may have been distinctly performative and focused on spectacle (Aletti "No Part"). Hujar was also a musician, albeit briefly, a career direction that ended when he smashed his harpsichord with a hammer—offstage—in one of his ungovernable rages, a trait he shared with Wojnarowicz, that terminated his relationship with Twyla Tharp dancer and later psychotherapist Robert Levithan (J. Smith, "Gorgeous" 28).[32] Hujar and Wojnarowicz were also good friends of underground music writer and later art critic Vince Aletti who had a major role as a scholar of disco.[33] Hujar's hugely sympathetic, soulful images of Wojnarowicz, which transform him into a boyish man of sorrows or "a serene young god" as Stephen Koch puts it ("The Pictures") are part of his mythology.

Wojnarowicz's own *Arthur Rimbaud in New York* series, 1978–9, parts of it published in the *SoHo News* in 1980, however, was his first success. These photographs show individuals in various gritty sites in New York wearing a crude, photocopied reproduction of a famous, mournful photograph of the youthful Rimbaud. The great symbolist poet and *enfant terrible* supreme, a nineteenth-century teenage rebel with a cause,[34] with whom Wojnarowicz identified, was an inspiration for Patti Smith, Jim Morrison,[35] and Bob Dylan, and Rimbaud had a openly gay relationship with Decadent poet Paul Verlaine (homosexual relations had been legal in France since the French Revolution) and abandoned poetry in France to become a gun runner in Abyssinia. Wojnarowicz's photographs show the ghost or wraith of the poet in contemporary New York, with the photocopied mask of Rimbaud's face modeled by Wojnarowicz's lovers—

including 3TK4's Brian Butterick—who often resemble him physically, in spaces which Wojnarowicz knew well such as the subway or the piers and abandoned buildings of the East Village, engaged in eating or sitting, urinating, injecting heroin, and masturbating. The concept is as preposterously naive and ephemeral as it is powerfully effective, unselfconsciously announcing its playful folk art and DIY limitations while conjuring a projection of Wojnarowicz as Rimbaud embodying the spirit of the genius outcast in a decaying city, and perhaps inadvertently the Wildean truth of masks. Wojnarowicz would later incorporate actual photographic self-portraits into his collage paintings, such as *Fuck You Faggot Fucker*, 1984, its central image his stencil of two all-American young men kissing.

A number of Wojnarowicz's images, like his autobiographical writing, engage with ephemerality and mortality. Wojnarowicz's debt to Hujar and his serious artistic vocation are conveyed in his iconic photographs of Hujar's head, feet, and hands taken just after his death in 1987, as recounted in *Close to the Knives* (102–3). This was a project Hujar may have inspired years earlier in his somber photographs of the Catacombs at Palermo, which Susan Sontag referred to in her 1967 novel *Death Kit*, or in Hujar's 1974 photograph of Warhol's Factory superstar Candy Darling on her deathbed. Richard Avedon's controversial 1974 photographs of his dying father may be another inspiration (Stevens and Aronson 26–30). Sontag objected to Avedon's photographs and his therapist considered them a form of symbolic "patricide," perhaps exposing the root of Avedon's nearly pathological internalized homophobia and dread of being outed (29, 261–74). Annie Leibovitz's debt to Hujar is apparent in her own photographs of the dying and deceased Sontag. In her introductory essay to Hujar's book of photography, *Portraits in Life and Death*, first published in *Vogue* magazine, Sontag wrote that "[p]hotography ... converts the whole world into a cemetery. Photographers, connoisseurs of beauty, are also ... the recording-angels of death. The photograph-as-photograph shows death. More than that, it shows the sex-appeal of death" ("Photographic" 349). She interprets Hujar's portraits of the living as "portraits in death," as if his subjects "appear to meditate on their own mortality" (349). Wojnarowicz refers to these remarks by "Susan Whatsername" either to show his punk sensibility, his failing memory, or his awareness of Hujar's resentment at having his photographs frozen out of the frame of Sontag's learned discussion of the field in *On Photography* (*Close* 143–4). Near the end of his life, Wojnarowicz modeled for two of his most famous photographic meditations on mortality, collaborations showing his mouth wired shut or his face half buried underground: "*Silence=Death*," 1989, and *Untitled (Face in Dirt)*, 1991, by Marion Scemama.

Wojnarowicz's first published writing project assembled autobiographical accounts with reconstructions of monologues by destitute, often gay members of America's underclass. Titled *Sounds in the Distance* when it appeared in 1982 and reissued posthumously as *The Waterfront Journals*, this project resembles the "routines" of William Burroughs—who wrote a cover blurb for Wojnarowicz's *Close to the Knives*—the oral histories of Studs Terkel or the work of anthropologist and musicologist Harry Smith. Smith recorded the last words and even dying groans of the homeless, an attempt to give voice to the lost in their last moments. Wojnarowicz's transcriptions of remembered monologues pioneered the somewhat fragmentary, anecdotal, montage-like form of his later autobiographical work. A number of *The Waterfront Journals*'s narratives are autobiographical (Carr 99; Wojnarowicz and Lotringer 170, 179), however, and some were used again in later writing, such as the account of rape (99-101) which reappears in *Memories That Smell Like Gasoline* (15-26). Another autobiographical narrative, "Young Boy in Times Square 4:00 A.M. New York City," details Wojnarowicz's particularly distressing encounter as a child prostitute, and he reproduces this incident with images by James Romberger in their co-created comic book of Wojnarowicz's life, *Seven Miles a Second* (4-13), a kind of graphic autobiography or auto-cartoon in which finally, however, the artist morphs into a super hero (McCormick 64). The child prostitute in this incident is picked up by an older man who insists the boy watch through a hotel wall's peephole another man and a female sex worker having sex in an adjoining room. The woman has fresh scars on her body, a sight which sickens the boy and causes the older man to give him more money. This sort of traumatic incident, as we shall see more fully a little later, recurs in Wojnarowicz's writing, where the dangerous, distressing sexual scene reinforces a sense of alienation and a desire for escape but also sometimes evokes an aura of romance. In *The Waterfront Journals*, he refers to himself as an alien living in a "fucking schizo-culture" that resembles his stance in "From the Diaries of a Wolf Boy" where sexual desire has an untroubled purity which enables a fantasy of ecstatic escape: "all I really want is the rude perfume of some guy's furry underarms and crotch to lean into. I'll make guttural sounds and stop eating and drinking and I'll be dead within the year. My eyes have always been advertisements for an early death" (*Waterfront* 170).

Despite his suspicion of its origins in the pre-existing world, language, even of a visual if not musical nature, permeates Wojnarowicz's work. He referred to words as "preformed gestures on the tip of my tongue," claiming they would allow him to "write my way out" of entrapment by his past, society, or artistic conventions (*Weight* 148, 94). His paintings assemble a personal iconography of images (burning men, houses in flames, ants, laughing or screaming cows). These aggressive images, from some of which he made stencils, originated in European commercial and industrial design, as his 3TK4 bandmate Julie Hair remembered (23), in the graffiti tags of street art, and in comic book graphics such as those from Krazy Kat comics (Rauffenbart, "Introduction" 2). As a child, Wojnarowicz had manipulated figures from Archie comics into sexual configurations using a detached Jughead nose as a penis in a diversified sexualized universe (*Close* 157). He arranged the elements of this personal iconography as if they were hieroglyphs, their syntax suggesting a narrative visual language. In some ways, Wojnarowicz painted or used collage as a writer would, and at least some critics suggest that he was first and foremost a writer (Blinderman 92). He referred to his paintings as "diaries" and his work in photography as a "journal" (Wojnarowicz and Lotringer 163). *Rimbaud in New York* may have originated as an autofictional graphic novel. Reading his visual sentences or interpreting their narrative semantics in more precise ways than as a generalized expression of personal alienation, however, is difficult. Post-structuralist philosopher of psychology Felix Guattari, who stresses the heterogeneity of individual subjectivity, located the authority, power, "authenticity," and "extraordinary vigor" of Wojnarowicz's creative work in its being rooted in "his whole life" and his systematic archiving of his fantasies and dreams. Writing, often recycled, is prominent in many of Wojnarowicz's paintings and particularly some of his most famous such as *Untitled (One Day This Kid ...)* 1990, the text surrounding a photograph of Wojnarowicz as a child; *Untitled (Sometimes I Come to Hate People)* 1992, the text laid over a photograph of bandaged hands; and his rhapsodic *When I Put My Hands on Your Body* 1990, its text superimposed over his photograph of skeletons in an Indigenous burial ground at Normal, Illinois.[36] These pieces suggest that Wojnarowicz was a writer of powerful poetic lines and passages, against which the fragmentary nature of his larger works, which are assembled montages, inevitably have less force or momentum.

Wojnarowicz has come to epitomize various scenes and movements: the East Village cultural renaissance of the early 1980s and the plague years of the AIDS epidemic in the 1980s and 1990s. Cynthia Carr's biography is a remarkably thorough document written by someone who befriended Wojnarowicz and who tackled her subject while the memories of friends and associates were still clear. Her biography is a parallel account of Wojnarowicz's abusive upbringing, self-created mythology, and later career, and at the same time a story of the rise and fall of New York's East Village art and music scene and a history of the AIDS epidemic, which at its worst lasted from 1981 until 1996, when the antiretroviral cocktail of drugs allowed some management of the illness. A stark contrast emerges between the unbridled sexual and creative hedonism of the post-Stonewall gay 70s—intensified by the preceding decades' repression—and the agonies of so many primarily young men suffering and dying in the 80s and 90s. This linkage of hedonism and catastrophe drove the official response or non-response to the AIDS crisis and has informed the lingering stereotype that the "gay lifestyle" = death. Wojnarowicz is represented in Steve McLean's 2001 film *Postcards from America*, based on Wojnarowicz's writings, and in Jim Hubbard's 2014 documentary *United in Anger: A History of ACT UP*. One of the actors portraying Wojnarowicz in McLean's film is the actor/guitarist Michael Tighe, who would become prominent as musician and co-writer in Jeff Buckley's band. Tighe features in a scene taken from *Close to the Knives* where Wojnarowicz as a teenaged prostitute imagines murdering a client with a stone statue (32–3) and also in the violent rape scene in the back of a van from *Memories That Smell Like Gasoline* (15–26). Here, as in other explicit scenes, the filmmakers' reticence comes across clearly in the use of shadows or absolute darkness to cloak representation. Wojnarowicz appears briefly in the documentary *United in Anger* at the Die-In protest at St Patrick's Cathedral in New York against the Roman Catholic Church's and Cardinal John O'Connor's complicity in restricting access to safe sex information during the crisis.

Wojnarowicz was a prominent AIDS activist, and some of his autobiographical work, such as *Close to the Knives*, belongs in the category of AIDS memoirs of different types like Paul Monette's *Borrowed Time* (1988), Tom Gunn's *The Man with Night Sweats* (1992), or the poignant biographical/autobiographical memoir about Howard Brookner, *Smash Cut* (2015) by Brad Gooch. Wojnarowicz details his own agonizing decline from AIDS-related illnesses, when a kind of sexual self-censorship even entered his dreams, as well as the desire of Hujar who made quixotic trips to quack doctors peddling injections of human feces and even typhoid as AIDS cures (*Close* 111–23, 94–6), though Hujar had always been attracted to spiritual charlatans. Wojnarowicz's furious responses to the injustices of government inaction on AIDS due to homophobia have become legendary: he "daydreams of tipping amazonian blowdarts in 'infected blood' and spitting them at the exposed necklines of certain politicians or nazi-preachers" and notoriously of dumping the bodies of the dead at the White House (*Close* 104, 122).[37] Wojnarowicz's inflammatory remarks about Cardinal O'Connor and Senator Jesse Helms in the catalog essay for Nan Goldin's curated show *Witnesses: Against Our Vanishing*, as well as some of his work's sexual images, elicited a virulent reaction. He rejected distinctions between erotica and pornography in his insistence that for heterosexuals any form of gay representation is regarded as provocation (*Close* 144). Sick with complications from AIDS, Wojnarowicz was caught up in the atmosphere of homophobic intolerance following the attacks by the American Family Association on the National Endowment for the Arts' funding of shows featuring Andres Serrano's *Piss Christ* and Robert Mapplethorpe classically stylized dick pics.[38]

In the time of the Covid-19 pandemic, it's worth remembering that some welcomed AIDS as a gay genocide. "AIDS KILLS FAGS DEAD" went one slogan of the time, adapting a phrase from an ad for insecticide (Wojnarowicz and Lotringer 191). Somewhat similarly, at least initially, some welcomed Covid-19 as a baby "boomer remover." Homosexuality, of course, was only removed from the American Psychiatric Association's list of mental illnesses in 1973,[39] and firing employees due to their sexual orientation was only made illegal at the national level in America in 2020. Moreover, the philosopher Michel Foucault greeted the first news about AIDS in the early 1980s with laughter: he couldn't believe the apparent perfection of a deadly disease targeting only gay people, the ideal solution in the public mind to the virus of homosexuality (White, "Q&A" 185; White, *My Lives* 203). In the "Art Arm" of ACT UP—Wojnarowicz belonged to New York's ACT UP affinity group Art+Positive—Wojnarowicz created posters and designed militant performance art. ACT UP may have forced the medical establishment to revise traditional drug testing procedures leading to the creation of the antiretroviral drug therapy of 1996. After this, AIDS became a treatable, chronic disease though one with no vaccine. Despite these efforts, however, the virus had spread exponentially from approximately fifty cases in New York in 1981 to over seventy million cases globally three decades later. Wojnarowicz didn't live to see ACT UP's protest against government indifference devolve into internal divisions between those seeking universal health care and those still targeting AIDS treatments. After his death from complications related to AIDS, Wojnarowicz's embodiment of the figure of the activist artist would lead some to refer to him as "kind of the moral conscience of our time" (Nan Goldin qtd. in

Breslin and Kiehl, "Acknowledgments" 10) or "Saint Wojnarowicz" (Burgher 15; Kathy Acker qtd. in Carr 551).[40]

Wojnarowicz's 3 Teens Kill 4 (3TK4) deployed at least some of his uncompromising artistic militancy. 3TK4—its name taken from a *New York Post* headline—was a performing post-punk or no wave band of a distinctly Dada-esque variety. It was an experimental, progressive, art rock ensemble, of which Wojnarowicz was a member until 1983, made up of individuals who worked together at the New York club Danceteria, though not including another well-known busboy there, Keith Haring. Its genesis was a work of musical performance art following Danceteria's closing for a liquor license violation after a police raid on October 4, 1980 (Hultberg; Carr 163). Max Blagg "remembered the band beginning as more of a performance group" (qtd. in Carr 163). One might say that 3TK4 performed being a band onstage, given that a number of its members had no musical training and could not play any instruments. 3TK4 may also have been a performance of camp, with three of its original members being gay and one, Brian Butterick (aka Hattie Hathaway), being a drag performer and later a founder of Wigstock, where Jesse Hultberg also would perform. While Wojnarowicz was devoted to Patti Smith's punk/new wave *Horses* (Carr 84) and noise meisters Sonic Youth, 3TK4 had a distinctly esoteric, DIY aesthetic grounded in the arts scene. As band member Julie Hair recalled in 2017, a friend "convinced me that even though I had no musical training—I could make music because I was an artist and it's the same sensibility" ("3 Teens"). As band member Doug Bressler remembered, 3TK4 sought a sound in which the listener was "supposed to hear the white of the canvas" (qtd. in Carr 170).

The band utilized guitars, synthesizers, and drum machines, but also recorded tapes of found sounds including newscasts, children's toy instruments, and objects such as cans of beans. Brian Butterick remembered that everyone in 3TK4 would play all instruments, whether with any ability or not, and everyone sang; their layered sound was "[a] sort of sonic Duchamp" ("3 Teens"). Their poise of expertise-free, anti-professional, success-be-damned bravado was of a kind that earned the contempt of Talking Heads' Tina Weymouth, herself an art college graduate who could barely play bass when her fiancé, fellow Rhode Island School of Design graduate Chris Frantz encouraged her to join his and David Byrne's new wave band in 1973. She noted in 1980 the number of new groups "who are afraid of success or afraid of learning to play their instruments, or afraid of becoming heroes" (Weymouth qtd. in L. Goldsmith 105). Wojnarowicz "played" the Sony portable tape recorder, a new technology of the time,[41] sang, chanted, wrote songs, and composed promotional graphics. One band photo shows Wojnarowicz with mock lascivious gaze sliding his hand down the front of Jesse Hultberg's pants. His inserted print in *No Motive*, entitled "Escape Diptych," shows a man below the surface of the water breathing with a straw. It illustrates the concern with nightmares of entrapment and torture in the album's songs, which mostly carry a doomed, end-of-the-world vibe, in keeping with no wave nihilism. The band's live performances emphasized a tone of ominous foreboding with projected images of planes on Cold War bombing missions.

3TK4's *No Motive*, however, is a much more polished production than one might expect from the band's unorthodox origins and methods. It credits all songs to the band as a whole, perhaps to avoid one of the reasons for many bands' implosion, and its 2017 remastered reissue includes extra tracks and a commemorative booklet. In places, the music resembles a combination of the parodic disco/funk-driven work of Talking Heads with a post-punk version of the jazz ambiance created behind some of Jack Kerouac's spoken word performances or those of William Burroughs with Kurt Cobain on distorted guitar. On "Tell me Something Good," Wojnarowicz incorporates an audio newsreel of Ronald Reagan's assassination attempt. In a few years, in his autobiographical writing, Wojnarowicz would be targeting Reagan's active indifference to funding AIDS research, and be outraged by media fascination with "the polyps in Ronald Reagan's asshole" or George Bush's aversion to broccoli when thousands were dying in agony (*Close* 144, 237). "I've Chosen to Stay and Fight" resembles Wojnarowicz's stance in his later autobiographical writings, and this song and "Desire" were added to the remastered 2017 reissue. "Desire" is one of Wojnarowicz's cruising tales, when a casual pick up develops—unusually, he says—into an extended conversation and an actual exchange of phone numbers after the radio-unfriendly remarks that though "[i]t was sort of one sided … [a]fter I came I asked him [for his number]" and the speaker departs so his companion who "had been doing mescaline … [can] get to sleep and get up at 7 for work." It is a spoken word performance, a fragment of which appears on YouTube, and it sounds as if a musical soundscape were imposed over Wojnarowicz's remarkably deep bass voice. His lyrics for other songs, such as "I GOT LIVIN' ON MY SIDE" included in *In the Shadow of the American Dream* (97–8), are far closer to conventional pop forms. "Hole Up," mixed by Ivan Ivan, is clearly designed to be *No Motive*'s single, sounding a little like Talking Heads' "Psycho Killer" with a tight bass line and equal parts funk and rhythm and blues. It has the crafted lyrics, choruses, and hooks lacking in the other songs. "Bean Song" is a progressive, no wave art band's version of a campy novelty song, accompanied by hiccups and other arbitrary mouth noises over a layer of atmospheric sounds and a four-note bass line, with a drag show-worthy chorus: "We must / We must increase our bust / The bigger the better / The tighter the sweater / You know those boys depend on us."

As in his writing and art work, with music Wojnarowicz sought a medium that didn't simply reproduce the genres of the "pre-existing world" with all the ideological baggage they carried. When he was a member of an actual band, however unorthodox, Wojnarowicz's assurance in his own artistic voice may have empowered him to abandon songwriting conventions and ultimately hastened his exit. He also mainly seems to have resisted the temptations of wanna-be alt rock stardom, though he was photographed by Nan Goldin in make-up with elegantly wasted rock star insouciance in *David Wojnarowicz at Home, NYC*, 1990. He was clearly disillusioned with aspects of the music scene due to his disgust as a busboy cleaning up the detritus of the punk crowd, his perception of new wave music as "boring and repetitive and predictable" as well as his contempt for its much-vaunted but toothless, self-congratulatory political radicalism (*In the Shadow* 162). He was also disdainful of the posturing of rising punk stars like Richard Hell and the Voidoids whose performance he found "awful. I mean, it was pure image. Responding to image, to fame, to stardom" (*Weight* 37). There was a growing tension within 3TK4 between those who valued instrumental expertise, well-crafted, radio-ready songs, and commercial success, on the one hand, and those who saw the band as a performative extension of their art projects, on the other. This internal tension intensified when the band's Jesse Hultberg had a brief affair with Wojnarowicz's long-distance boyfriend Jean-Pierre Delage, inciting one of Wojnarowicz's incendiary rages. Moreover, the danger that Wojnarowicz's use of heroin with some band members threatened his precious mentoring relationship with Hujar may also have been a factor (Kern 66; *Close* 206), though Wojnarowicz's painting was increasingly in demand and he was also growing more committed to writing (Bidlo 31). After Wojnarowicz left, 3TK4 would play in Seattle on December 21, 1984, a show opened by an early version of Soundgarden, with its shirtless singing drummer Chris Cornell, the "total fucking godhead" of the emerging grunge scene, who, like Wojnarowicz, had a physically abusive alcoholic father (Reiff 31, 44).

In his multimedia artistic production, including his work with 3TK4, but particularly in his autobiographical writing, Wojnarowicz was committed to the idea of "self-truth." He wrote,

> I feel that in my work I can only declare myself, I can only declare my allegiance, or my ideas, in a search for some kind of self-truth. And although maybe my ideas and my views of things come from years of living inside a pre-invented existence, I think through the imagination the messages I learned growing up can be turned upside down or can be bent or can be broken. And at least there one can stretch until there are no longer countries, no longer borders, no longer governments or wars.
>
> (*Weight* 120–1)

Wojnarowicz's self-construction in his autobiographical writing is thus characterized by a double consciousness, and also as we shall see a dual voice and a divided self, recalling Simon Frith's evocation of the notion of "double enactment" (*Performing* 212). Thus, Wojnarowicz's work represented in his own words "a particular moment in the history of my body on this planet, in america [*sic*] ... given that I have always felt alienated in this country, and thus have lived with the sensation of being an observer of my own life as it occurs" (*Close* 149). This sense of a double consciousness, of being divided between participation and observation, Wojnarowicz conveys as a division between the visible world and "this movie that plays in your head ... 'the film behind the eyeball'" (John Ensslin qtd. in Carr 66), an image familiar from William Burroughs' *Nova Express*.

Wojnarowicz's performative identity or self-presentation as participant observer, as a kind of anthropologist of the self, may enhance a perception of him as a knowing and willing promoter of his own mythology. This mythology is focused on his dark past, and he used it knowingly to market himself in the highly competitive art world. He also attempted to eliminate inconvenient elements from this story. He obsessively revisits the credentials of his outsider status as an abuse survivor, gay hustler, and embodiment of societal loathing as a homosexual and carrier of the AIDS virus. As Wojnarowicz put it, "I've created myth in my identity and what I project to people, my memories mixed with my fantasies" (Wojnarowicz and Lotringer 163). However, Wojnarowicz's recall of dates and geography is sometimes blurred, as Carr points out (Wojnarowicz and Carr, "Biographical" 285–308), and his self-writing, in works like *In the Shadow of the American Dream* and *Close to the Knives*, at times overlaps uneasily with fiction and dream diaries. The Wojnarowicz mythology, as his friend and sometime artistic collaborator Steve Doughton remembered, was very much part of his cache as an artist (Doughton 52–3). A little like the consummate self-promoter Warhol and totally unlike artistic self-saboteur Hujar (Lebowitz), Wojnarowicz was sufficiently savvy to brand himself.[42] Moreover, his outsider position and his "fuck you to the art world" stance were utterly irresistible to the art world (McCormick "Collaborators" 16). The market for contemporary art had exploded in Wojnarowicz's most creative period and buyers were after the next hot commodity after the Scull Auction at Sotheby's on October 18, 1973 made fine art, along with stocks and real estate, part of a well-balanced portfolio for the super rich and soon-to-be trillionaires. Moreover, as it turned out, Wojnarowicz's back story was priceless to the art world of wealthy dealers and collectors when marketing his aggressive, unsettling imagery. "People ate it up," Doughton remembered (53).

Another part of the Wojnarowicz mythology was that he was a self-taught genius who had emerged fully formed from an abusive upbringing without education, initiation, or apprenticeship. However, as Carr's biography details, he had been heavily involved in poetry scenes in the mid-1970s—in the period when Patti Smith was galvanizing attention—and he later attempted to suppress this early experimentation (Carr 54–76), though he first met his future lover and 3TK4 bandmate Brian Butterick at a poetry reading. As Carr points out, in addition, Wojnarowicz was something of a magpie in collecting images and ideas, and not always forthcoming in acknowledging influences and sources. His *Rimbaud in New York* series, for example, was perhaps inspired by Ernest Pignon-Ernest's images of a contemporary Rimbaud; Wojnarowicz's burning house stencil was created through an exchange with Saul Ostrow; Wojnarowicz's *Sex Series (for Marion Scemama)* 1988–9 was influenced by the performative, homoerotic surrealism in the photographs of Arthur Tress with whom he had a brief affair; and Wojnarowicz's images of sewn bread and his self-portrait with sewn mouth, used for the poster advertising the 1989 film *Silence=Death*, may have originated in Catalina Parra's *Diariamente* (Carr 133, 123, 137–8, 96). In addition to recycling his stencils, Wojnarowicz also frequently used "found" or scavenged images such as the scenes taken from Hujar's personal pornography stash in the *Sex Series* which would generate such controversy, and famously his enlargement of a detail from a museum exhibition in his falling buffalo image, used for the cover of U2's vinyl single "One" from 1991's *Achtung Baby*. He briefly met the band but declined Bono's offer to join a group prayer, shortly before his death.

Wojnarowicz's life writing is characterized by its apparently paradoxical dual voice, that of passive victim of oppression and that of active agent and provocateur, complications that say much about the difficulty of giving utterance to a legacy of child sexual abuse. The dynamic of these sometimes competing voices also plays out in a disjunction between what appears to be Wojnarowicz's motive in writing and its reception. His work has been interpreted as that of an abject survivor of pedophilia, and one who may have suffered incest at the hands of his father who regularly beat his son, and even fed his children their own pets (*Close* 266–7; Wojnarowicz and Goldin 202). However, Wojnarowicz's writing is driven by a desire to portray the romance and ecstatic fantasy embedded in exploitative sexual encounters, which always carry an element of danger. His self-representation as active agent, not victim, voicing the position of survivors of sexual abuse and also of all homosexuals in a repressive, hypocritical, heterosexist society gives him agency and affords his writing a frank, unsentimental quality light years from his image as an exploited, abandoned child man. Moreover, sometimes in their fleeting encounters, he ministers to the internalized homophobia of his anonymous partners, and his stance as ministering angel, full of tolerance and generosity, also transforms his narratives. *Memories That Smell Like Gasoline*, for example, illustrated with Wojnarowicz's ink paintings of sexual encounters in the hell and homotopia of the porn theaters on New York's 3rd Avenue, recounts anonymous interactions that carry the disturbing aphrodisiac of potential violence. There is an electric thrill, he writes, "when violence hangs above the road to the sexual act" (28). These encounters, in addition, appear to have the potential to transform memories of pain into tenderness as if they might constitute a form of self-therapy mending past wounds. They evoke *Close to the Knives*'s account of the moment when Wojnarowicz's father's assaults intensified after his son is caught in a compromised position with an older boy, and his father attempts to initiate sexual touching with his son. In a psychically fraught and disturbing way, the abused child appears to crave the conversion of physical cruelty into emotional tenderness through sexual arousal. As he writes in *Close to the Knives*, "I have always been attracted to dangerous men, men whose gestures intimated the possibilities of violence, and I have always seduced them into states of gentle grace with my hands and lips" (271).

Wojnarowicz's diaries published as *In the Shadow of the American Dream* as well as his other life writing reveal a deeply divided attitude towards committed, loving relationships and towards received literary conventions. As Carr points out, "[t]he men he loved the most got the least ink, at least in the journals" (89). He is suspicious of personal commitment as if it were a threat to his role as a witness whose identity and artistic vocation are tied to the radical freedom of erotic adventure. Thus, any sustained compromise with apparently heteronormative styles of coupling from the "pre-existing world" would threaten his self-identity, and sense of personal and artistic integrity. This may lie behind his "fear that loving someone and living with them will ruin me" (*Weight* 63). He also insists on maintaining a distance from and being "a stranger to all events so that I can witness them without complicated emotional connections," and, similarly, he rejects "creating literature" or utilizing a conventional "literary form" because "a strict form, just bleeds the life from an experience" (*In the Shadow* 227, 235). He does suspect later in his life, however, that his abusive background and his position as a person who never really had a childhood, has left him unable to care for himself or trust another person. He has "thirty-four-year-old eyes staring out of a six-year-old's skull" (*Weight* 116). Hence, while he is moved by the care and commitment of a man he meets in Paris where he had gone partly to learn guitar and write songs, Jean-Pierre Delage, a relationship which would last till the end of his life, he deliberately attempts to sabotage or challenge it by seeking out a casual hook-up (*In the Shadow* 71–111). He writes of feeling impelled to pursue this possibility while agonizing over the genuine love of Delage who waits for him and is clearly wounded by his behavior. Simultaneously, he invites his American lover and future 3TK4 bandmate Brian Butterick to visit him in Paris without informing him of his relationship with Delage. Even when later he is in a secure partnership with the passionate and pragmatic Tom Rauffenbart, whom he will eventually entrust with his estate and who threw some of Wojnarowicz's ashes on the White House lawn in 1996 (Carr 578), Wojnarowicz enters a terrifying master–slave relationship at "the hands of a sadist I met in a movie house" in the traumatic aftermath of Hujar's death (*In the Shadow* 266; Rauffenbart, "Collaborators" 152). He attempts to explain this apparently self-destructive drive for radical freedom in a somewhat unconvincing, hyperbolic fashion as part of an absolute commitment to "self-searching in the face of a world that kills people with bombs" (*In the Shadow* 104). Wojnarowicz appears in his autobiographical writing to be debating with himself about his choices. Moreover, it is worth remembering that he would meet two of the most meaningful loves of his life cruising in parks or porn theaters which may say as much about the constraints on acceptance of same-sex relations in the late twentieth century as it does about Wojnarowicz's unorthodox romanticism. Dying at age thirty-seven, he would not have the opportunity to revisit his past and make amends and reparations as would the venerable Bob Dylan as we shall see in the next chapter.

Notes

1. No wave began in New York in the late 1970s and early 1980s. It denotes a range of experimental art rock music, highly rhythmic and often atonal, based on a rejection of rock, punk, new wave, and celebrity culture clichés. The best-known exemplar is Sonic Youth. See Gordon (101–2, 118–19).
2. Smith recounts her experience, and justifies the problems as a projection of some of the song's lyrics, in an essay in *The New Yorker*, "How Does It Feel." A somewhat similar instance appears in *M Train*, when she lectures to the Continental Drift Society in Berlin, her notes just written on napkins at the nearby Pasternak Café, which are smeared and largely illegible due to her nervousness, though even then she "hadn't wholly mapped out my talk, leaving a section open for improvisation and the whims of fate" (48).
3. Smith's friend, Warhol superstar Penny Arcade, noted Smith's romantic identification with an "incredible pantheon of icons" as bordering on the pathological: "Patti lived her whole life pretending to be John Lennon or Paul McCartney or Brian Jones or some other rock star. ... It was like she was involved with these people, but it was all in her head. Other people have imaginary playmates, but Patti had imaginary playmates who were Keith Richards and people like that" (qtd. in McNeil and McCain 111, 109).
4. Smith remarks that rumors of her drug-taking excess are greatly exaggerated. She experimented with drugs occasionally when creating art, though she was devoted to pot between 1977 and 1979, but renounced all drugs in 1980 (Rowell, "Conversation" 142–3).
5. As she concludes her Windham-Campbell lecture in 2016, Smith writes "[b]ecause we cannot simply live" (*Devotion* 93). This may be Smith's response to the opening of Joan Didion's *The White Album*: "We tell ourselves stories in order to live" (11).
6. In his autobiography, Richard Hell denies that his famous 70s haircut and look were based on Artaud's or Rimbaud's, though he recognizes the importance of clothes and hair in rock 'n' roll (120, 117).
7. Both men were virtually lifelong addicts. While Artaud suffered the torments of addiction, he regarded opiates as necessary for dealing with the natural pain of being alive. He saw addiction, entry into the "culture of nothingness," as an essential part of his identity, a manifestation of the addict's version of Descartes' *cogito, ergo sum*: "I take opium in the same way that I am myself, without recovering from myself" ("Appeal" 339, 338).

8   Jon Savage suggests that British punk "style" owed much to Richard Hell's "visual package" (*England's Dreaming* 89), which greatly impressed Malcolm McLaren in particular. Hell discusses his deliberations on his style and haircut in his autobiography (116–20), and in an essay on fashion in British and American punk ("'Punk' Couture" 118–19).

9   In 1973, Susan Sontag noted that "[m]ost of the once exotic themes of Artaud's work have within the last decade become loudly topical.... Artaud in the nineteen-twenties had just about every taste ... prominent in the American counterculture of the nineteen-sixties.... [However, his work which] the culture attempts to assimilate ... remains profoundly indigestible" ("Approaching" 52).

10 Electroshock treatment was a new procedure when it was administered against his will at a state asylum in the early 1940s, when Artaud was confined in Nazi-occupied France, a terrifying prospect given the Nazis' practices regarding the disabled, in a period when theorist Jacques Lacan was briefly his psychiatrist. Artaud believed that massive doses of high-quality opium—he was convinced that only low-grade heroin caused addiction—would cure his mental illness. Electroshock in the 1950s and 1960s was also used in so-called gay conversion therapy as suffered by Lou Reed (McNeil and McCain 3–4).

11 "Cruelty" for Artaud doesn't mean torture or bloodshed, but "strictness, diligence, unrelenting decisiveness, irreversible and absolute determination" ("The Theatre" 77).

12 See Richard Middleton's cogent analysis of this song in light of a brief consideration of Smith's biography (*Voicing* 98–116).

13 One difficulty of understanding what these new types of performance would look like is suggested by contemporaries' reactions to Artaud's own acting onstage as exaggerated and even clownish. When he lectured, almost anything could happen, suggesting his propensity to transform all manner of public events, and as Anaïs Nin recalled after hearing his lecture at the Sorbonne, Artaud began "screaming. He was delirious. He was enacting his own death, his own crucifixion" (qtd. in Shafer 117).

14 Smith's first response to Mapplethorpe's dying request was *The Coral Sea* (1996), a collection of prose poems. They trace his mythic voyage as one who is "destined to be ill" but who resolves "to set right destiny" until he becomes destiny's "slave" only finally to escape its grasp (41, 43, 74, 89). Edmund White rhapsodizes in the 2012 paperback jacket's blurb: "Patti Smith ... was once our savage Rimbaud, but suffering has turned her into our St. John of the Cross, a mystic full of compassion." On *Just Kids*'s relationality, see Julia Watson's "Patti Smith Kicks In the Walls of Memoir" (131–51).

15 A tarot card reader, Smith is attuned to the workings of destiny or at least auspicious coincidence. For example, she and Mapplethorpe move house on Rimbaud's birthday, facilitating his "seemingly predestined union" with Sam

16 Wagstaff (205); shortly afterwards, Smith plans a pilgrimage to Ethiopia because "I truly believed I was destined to find" Rimbaud's secret papers (216).
16 Other than modest success peddling his jewelry, prior to his similarly explosive rise to fame, Mapplethorpe attracted most interest from art dealers for his body. Smith encouraged his move to photography and she was his first model, assuming poses derived from the covers of Dylan's albums. Mapplethorpe would soon try to raise photography's status as art.
17 Smith's introductory "note" to Carroll's posthumously published novel *The Petting Zoo* refers to his "diamond mind" and also "the prison of his own infirmities" (v, vi). Approximating Smith's portrait of Carroll in *Just Kids*, the novel's Billy seeks to determine his sexual orientation via gay prostitution, until he balks at performing in lederhosen (145–6).
18 The complexities of Mapplethorpe's important relationship with Wagstaff amid the complications of the gay 1970s and early 1980s are addressed in Philip Gefter's revealing *Wagstaff*.
19 The sites of the folk scene of the 1960s and the punk scene of the 1970s, such as CBGB and the Mudd Club are disappearing; as Kim Gordon says soberly, "these days the Mudd Club is just a throwaway line in an old Talking Heads song" (118). See Richard Lloyd's account of the development of CBGBs as a music venue where Television, Talking Heads, and Smith performed (178–205), as well as Richard Hell's "CBGB" (154–7).
20 While he had a "spiritual wife," Rosebud Feliu-Pettet, it appears Harry Smith was mainly celibate though he had an abiding sexual interest in young men as well as a predeliction for S&M (Rosebud 97–105). In a 1972 interview with Mary Hill, he says that though preparation for death is his "true vocation" (169), "I'll fool with the Devil. ... I like the Devil better [than God], because he has nicer muscles. ... At least I'd rather be in bed with the Devil than with God. He's more handsome. ... Naturally, God allows Lucifer to be beautiful and handsome and brutal and sadistic and all the things that I like" (Hill 169–70).
21 *M Train* gives a moving account of Reed's passing and of what Smith considers his masterpiece, "Heroin" (257–9).
22 Beat poet John Giorno, in his memoir, writes that in the mid-1960s, "poetry was dead" and nearly a century "behind painting, sculpture, music, and dance," and that sound poetry (*poésie sonore*) was just beginning; the golden future lay in performance poetry through the use of new electronic technology (116, 128).
23 Smith's early version of the Who's classic, propelled by Král's bass, was added to the 1996 CD reissue of *Horses*.
24 Earlier, however, he had admired her provocative physicality and her dynamic performances as being "frighteningly new and good": "she would improvise and

riff extensions [of her poems] as she read, like a bebop soloist or an action painter" (109). He resented that her affair with Verlaine edged Hell out of their band Television (145–6), an exit possibly accelerated by his limited musicianship and worsening heroin addiction.

25 Philip Shaw calls *Horses* a "memento mori" in which Smith proclaims her affinity with doomed heroes like Morrison and Hendrix (121, 127), though it also has elements of "autobiography" (29). *Horses*' use of "the mixing desk as a tool to create a multileveled sound collage" produced a "sense of disjunction [which] resembles, in many ways, the asymmetrical structure of the self" (131, 132).

26 Pronounced "Voyna-ROW-vich" (Carr 1).

27 Hultberg also performed in Wojnarowicz's unfinished short film *Heroin* of 1981, also available on YouTube, and he makes a brief appearance in the film *Longtime Companion* (1989).

28 The music integrated Wojnarowicz's aural contributions with Neill's "mutantrumpet [*sic*] and an interactive electronics computer setup. There's a live orchestral percussion setup with timpani, vibraphone, and a full drum battery, all processed electronically as well. ... David is reading with different processing done with his voice. I set it up so he could control it himself with volume pedals and really play his voice as an instrument" (Neill 114).

29 Elijah Burgher refers to a similar totality in Wojnarowicz's work as if it were a book of magic or *grimoire* and also a survival guide (19).

30 Stephen Koch (personal communication).

31 Hujar's involvement, like that of Paul Thek, is omitted from Blake Gopnik's account of the Screen Tests (355–9), which is odd given their later prominence and their images' use in Warhol's *Thirteen Most Beautiful Boys* series.

32 See Koch's account of this incident ("The Pictures"); Hujar told Koch he'd had "at least 6000" lovers ("If You're Vincent"). Levithan later wrote a sincere if slightly vacuous inspirational self-help memoir about how to be gay, HIV positive, and fabulous at sixty. He refers to Hujar as his "beloved once-upon-a-time lover," "a particularly insightful mentor," "strong and vulnerable" (66, 28, 61). Testing positive in 1984, he won a lottery in 1995 to enter an antiretroviral drug cocktail trial and survived until 2015 (53). For a long life, he advises fighting "internalized ageism" (3), keeping one's hair, staying optimistic and in shape, and having lots of sex with much younger men.

33 Aletti's *The Disco Files 1973–78* is mostly a collection of his record reviews though the cover blurb describes it as Aletti's "personal memoir"—measuring out his life with new releases—and it does offer a subtle analysis of the music, usually leaving the ultimate judgement on quality to its success on the dance floor, but it also conjures disco's distinctly urban, gay milieu and reception.

34 See Edmund White's account of Rimbaud's lasting, intergenerational renown (*Rimbaud* 180–5).
35 See Wallace Fowlie's autobiographical reflection on Rimbaud's influence on Morrison (1–34).
36 The *When I Put My Hands on Your Body* text, originally in draft diary form in *In the Shadow* (265–6), was also used in *Untitled (map installation)* 1990 where it is superimposed over a world map, and it was used again in *Seven Miles a Second*.
37 Wojnarowicz's enraged response was very different from the stance of Howard Brookner, director of an acclaimed documentary on Burroughs and the feature *Bloodhounds of Broadway* starring Madonna. He died of complications from AIDS at age thirty-five in 1989. At least in a letter to his parents, included at the end of his nephew Aaron Brookner's documentary, he writes: "The worst part of all this for me was knowing what my death would do to you. Death is not so bad for the dying—it [is] much worse for the living. So please do not be too sad. Do not let this ruin your lives, for if I continue to live, I live in memories and your hearts and also in the films I made. You know it isn't so bad to live a short life as long as you do what you want with it—and I did. This is what is important in life: DO WHAT YOU WANT TO DO. USE YOUR LIFE TO FULFILL YOURSELF. GO AS FAR AS YOU CAN, REGARDLESS OF THE RISKS. This is what I did, and so I am content in the end."
38 Hujar regarded Mapplethorpe as a plagiarist of his own work with the male nude (Koch "If You're Vincent"), and he disliked Mapplethorpe's work's highly stylized, artsy coolness and the fact that he let others develop his prints. Stephen Koch writes that "Robert [Mapplethorpe] first attached himself with Patti Smith to Peter as sort of a senior person. He got the idea of doing something radical with the male nude from Peter. Robert was by far the most skilful opportunist and careerist I had ever met. He was brilliant at creating a reputation" ("If You're Vincent"). Diane Arbus saw Hujar as a plagiarist of her own work chronicling society's outsiders (J. Smith, "Gorgeous" 20).
39 For the period's homophobia, see the publication history of the gay men's sex and health "lifestyle" guide, *The Joy of Gay Sex* (Silverstein and Picano xv–xx). The original coauthor, Edmund White, remarks that the publication entailed his professional coming out (White, "*Publishers*" 5–6). In 2011, White noted, "[p]eople made fun of me for writing it, but Americans love money and anything that makes money they end up respecting" (White, "An Interview" 166).
40 Steve Brown who was present when Wojnarowicz died in hospital recalled earlier joking with him that in future Wojnarowicz would be labeled a "messiah" (40). Nan Goldin asked Wojnarowicz about such comparisons, and he replied "I ain't no Jesus" (Wojnarowicz and Goldin 210).

41 Warhol referred to his Sony as his "wife" (qtd. in Colacello 7).
42 Vince Aletti notes that Hujar was rarely happy in his emotional life or career, partly because "[h]e could never sell himself" (Aletti, "Interview" 40). Hujar was so impoverished that he washed his own clothes by hand (Lebowitz), perhaps including the jock strap that looks the worse for wear or rewashing in his nearly nude "Self-Portrait Standing" (1980), used for the cover of *Peter Hujar: Love and Lust*. It is vastly different from another portrait in the collection, "Keith Cameron (II)" (1981), plate 17, in which the subject sports a more portrait-ready athletic support. This detail gives a certain pathetic insight into what might otherwise be a self-portrait of the middle-aged artist as master of physical fitness, and an understanding of a photographer who must have been a brilliant but deeply wounded man. Along the same lines, Joe Orton's maintenance of his physique had led him to remark to his agent: "I shall be the most perfectly developed of modern playrights if nothing else" (qtd. in Lahr, "Introduction" 15).

5

The Invention of Bob Dylan and the Archival Autograph

The invention of "Bob Dylan" may be the greatest creation of Robert Allen Zimmerman, and this legacy has also been one of his heaviest burdens over six decades when he has become increasingly a "Dylanologist." Alternately a self-made and self-denying creation, "Bob Dylan" was forged in part by ignoring Russian Jewish ancestors, parents, race, and religion, and embracing an all- and alt-American, assimilationist ethic, and performing a type of identity theft. He would protest his role in celebrity culture, his function as entertainer, and his elevation as the voice of a generation, while, via a carefully fabricated and fetishized identity, simultaneously styling himself a kind of "song and dance" Shakespeare.[1] His most famous songs' construction of a private mythology has partly enabled them to be a generation's Rorschach test, resonating widely and provoking remarkably desperate interpretations.[2] His work as a catalyst for transferring literary into popular culture by opening a space for poetry in popular song was recognized in 2016 by the Nobel Committee. This chapter examines the autobiographical emphasis in much of Dylan's work, from his artistic impetus in Woody Guthrie's autobiography, *Bound for Glory* (its writing encouraged by Black Mountain poet Charles Olsen), his memoir *Chronicles*, his autofictional *Tarantula*, some of his art songs, and his archival self-construction in the Bob Dylan Archive and proposed Bob Dylan Center in Tulsa, Oklahoma, site of the Woody Guthrie Center. This archival autograph embodies something of a late career shift in self-fashioning. It emphasizes proximity to both the Beat writers, with their own archival ethos, and the roots of American folklore, and it suggests a more inclusive relational identity via a recognition of sources and influences, and acknowledgment of debts.

In his eighth decade, Dylan is making anything other than yacht rock—though he mentions his yacht in *Chronicles* (162–3)—and, once again, he is reflecting on American history. His 2020 *Rough and Rowdy Ways* was *Uncut* magazine's Album of the Year as well as achieving other honors, mostly for its 17-minute opus "Murder Most Foul," about John F. Kennedy's assassination, which happened on the day of Aldous Huxley's exit through the doors of perception.[3] As the *Guardian*'s review puts it, "[g]rouchily informing the world that everything is turning to shit has been one of Dylan's prevalent songwriting modes," "but you don't need a PhD in Dylanology to appreciate its singular quality and power" (Petridis, "Music" 56). *Chronicles* makes clear that Dylan's classic songs' apocalyptic foreboding was rooted in his readings about the—perhaps still unresolved—American Civil War, "when America was put on the cross, died and was resurrected" (86). In hindsight, Dylan's songwriting career demarcates a clear trajectory, but it was much less so at its origins, and as Robbie Robertson points out in a different context, Dylan was always hesitant about planning and making commitments (465). In her memoir *And a Voice to Sing With* (1987), Joan Baez refers to Dylan's intoxicating "charisma" in the early 1960s and his fans' obsessive adoration, rendering them and even herself "sycophants" (89–90, 97).[4] Suze Rotolo, Dylan's girlfriend in this period, also refers to his charisma, but adds that Dylan was a secretive, morbidly paranoid "black hole" with "an aura of darkness," and that those surrounding him garnered a kind of potentially dangerous "trickle-down-fame" (273, 276, 275).[5] Dylan's continuing success as a songwriter after half a century belies the swiftness of his ascent to fame in the early 1960s. His rise, in fact, was so sudden, especially in hindsight, and his apprenticeship was so public in New York's folk scene, that it left a broad wake among his mentors, friends, and contemporaries, like Joan Baez and Dave Van Ronk, and those who felt suddenly stranded and unable to catch up, like Phil Ochs, Peter La Farge, and Paul Clayton who are sometimes regarded as collateral damage for Dylan's success.[6]

Dylan might have been a footnote in the story of Paul Clayton (1931–67), for example, but instead Clayton gets brief attention in the multiple works of Dylanology, including Dylan's own. His tragic story encapsulates the diversity and complexity, factionalism and competitiveness of the Greenwich Village scene in which Dylan triumphed and which dominates in *Chronicles*. Clayton was a mentor for Dylan after he arrived in New York in January 1961, a living archive of vernacular song tradition, and a queer voice in folk music before Stonewall (June 28–9, 1969, a few months before Woodstock),[7] a figure "who recorded more LPs ... knew more of poetry ... of drugs ... of all sex" than his famous disciples as Izzy Young recalled (qtd. in Cohen 274–5). Clayton had a graduate English degree on musicology, and he had hits, though he didn't finesse these into a career. Dylan's *Chronicles* calls Clayton a "nonconformist," "unique—elegiac, very princely—part Yankee gentleman and part Southern rakish dandy" (261). When he met Dylan, the future Nobel laureate was a cover artist, first recorded as a harmonica accompanist.

The folk revival in which Dylan emerged had a "pedagogical" component, and over its duration, folklore studies—mixing English, anthropology, and music—became professionalized as ethnomusicology. Clayton's 1957 MA thesis examines nine Child ballads "recovered" from "oral tradition" (104), elevating the oral over the written and ignoring melodies in favor of textual variants. His field collecting in Virginia was of the sort that reinforced romantic notions of Appalachia as a landlocked El Dorado, the survival of an authentic, ancestral Anglo-Saxon Elizabethan culture, with its dialect and music. Interpreting Appalachia as being "unpolluted by … mixing [with African Americans and eastern Europeans]" reinforced a populist white immigrant origin for the nation (J. Becker 232). Appalachia and "Trumpalachia" continue to be contested terrain, as evidenced by the 2019 collection *Appalachian Reckoning* (Harkins and McCarroll 6). Clayton was generally uninterested in African American music,[8] and within the emerging field of ethnomusicology, his forensic classification of Child ballad survivals was somewhat old-fashioned, particularly as evolutionary and diffusionist as well as comparative approaches were giving way to functionalism (Filene 137). Moreover, performers were increasingly hostile to academics as paternalistic presenters of fossilized songs (Rosenberg 19), and some academics doubted the scholarship of performing scholars (Stekert 86). While Clayton tried to bridge these worlds, his professionalism in recording and his academic know-how, though respected, could be dismissed as antiquarian. In New York's coffee houses, Clayton introduced songs at length, detailing genealogy and lyrical variations, as in the liner notes for his Folkways' recordings, such as 1962's *Dulcimer Songs and Solos* (FG 3571), with its 3,500-word note about the dulcimer and its tuning. Clayton sang movingly with his melodic baritone on stage (Van Ronk 84–5), but his recordings highlight the song as a preserved still life. Clayton's approach to live performance suffered in competition with the emerging talents and ingenious "reverse-showmanship" of Dylan and others (Baez 91), and his gay advocacy from the stage was decidedly unwelcome.

Even Clayton's biggest hit, "Gotta Travel On," its melody taken from Ollis Martin's 1927 "Police and High Sheriff Come Ridin' Down" (Coltman 109–10), is now best known through Dylan's cover on *Self Portrait*. Clayton sings not in his neutral academic style, but in a sleepy version of the "arch coyness" favored by popular folk singers like Burl Ives (Shields). In the song's cod-traditional lyrics, the speaker has been six months on a chain gang, and he's unwelcome at home. Dylan's version cuts the incongruous chain gang, recasting the lyrics as the story of a train-riding prodigal son. Suze Rotolo's sister Carla's altercation with Dylan in March 1964, in which Clayton intervened, provoked Dylan's "Ballad in Plain D" (Shelton 159). Others saw Clayton's play for Carla as a way to draw near Dylan (Shelton 171), and their connection may exemplify what Eve Kosofsky Sedgwick terms a triangular relationship, an asymmetrical intersection of the bonds of rivalry and love in which women are symbolic "property for the ... purpose of cementing the bonds of men with men" (*Between Men* 26). Dylan's association with Clayton usually is remembered, however, for Dylan's possible plagiarism in "Don't Think Twice, It's All Right." While all folk songs almost "by definition ... [are] entirely a product of plagiarism," as musicologist Charles Seeger noted (qtd. in Shelton 125), and Clayton had little stomach for lawsuits against friends, Clayton's publisher took Dylan to court after "Don't Think Twice" was covered by Peter, Paul, and Mary, realizing that the answer blowing in the wind was money, my friend.[9] Dylan uses some of Clayton's words and his melody from "Who's Gonna Buy you Ribbons,"[10] itself derived from a 1870s Irish song, but Dylan's words and delivery are more pointed and acerbic than Clayton's sleepy, melancholic singing with autoharp accompaniment.

Legally, Dylan was right, but ungenerous, generosity not being his strong suit, according to Rotolo (158). A suddenly wealthy singer songwriter giving a poor former mentor a mere $500 out-of-court settlement outraged Dylan's friends (Scaduto 142), and it's become well established in the parlor game of tracing Dylan's influences, attributions, and possible thefts.[11] Dylan's driver and bodyguard Victor Maymudes notes that Clayton was "likely in love with Bob in a personal way" (70), and this has become another tainted legacy.[12] When Dylan and Clayton's February 1964 road trip, during which Dylan first heard the Beatles (McDougal 97–8), ended at Joan Baez's home in California, Richard Fariña, who played Clayton's beloved dulcimer like a rhythm guitar, remembered Clayton's playing and singing with "understated composure" (192). Fariña also noted Joan's plan for an album of Dylan's songs, a new direction by the best-known ballad popularizer, no doubt reinforcing Clayton's sense of being out of step with changing times. Maymudes reflects: "For a lot of other people ... [Dylan's] friendship wasn't such a good deal. He never really hurt people along the way other than denying people empathy" (122). In early 1964, Clayton often visited Dylan in Woodstock, "but he was gradually ostracized" (Shelton

184), as were many of Dylan's friends especially after the altercation with Carla Rotolo (Heylin, *Double* 251–2). Clayton would attempt a Dylanesque hybrid, "Gingerbreadd Mindd [sic]," recorded but not released until the custodian of Clayton's estate gave the master to Bandcamp in 2017.[13] Prior to his suicide on April 6, 1967 in New York (the plan for which he announced to friends and expressed in an autobiographical tape recording addressed to his lover John— included with his papers[14] but blocked to researchers at the request of the curator of Clayton's estate—even outlining his method of choice, electrocution), Clayton descended into psychosis. Clayton should probably have become a university professor, if not necessarily a professor of pop, gigging on weekends, though he openly expressed disinterest, and to Dylan he almost certainly represented an overly-idealistic professional dead end. Clayton would become a casualty burned by his proximity to the aura of rock star celebrity that would almost engulf Dylan.[15]

Chronicles

The fragmentary and circular straightforwardness of Dylan's memoir, *Chronicles: Volume One*, could not be anticipated by the snakes and ladders convolutions of *Tarantula*, a real self-consuming document, or Dylan's utterances about his life in his multiple early interviews, which really amount to "anti-interviews" (Shelton 15). These interviews combine an inarticulate humming and hawing, facetious and fictional asides, and an interrogation of the interrogator, but inadvertently they would enhance Dylan's reputation as a living enigma, rather than an artist unwilling or unable to elucidate origins and influences. In this way, Dylan offered an anti-entertainment industry performance of self-promotion, unlike the Beatles, for example, who inventively finessed the interview or press conference into an imitation *Goon Show* comedy fest (Bedford 24). An exasperated Dylan explains his modus operandi in *Chronicles*: "The press? I figured you lie to it" (123). Dylan's self-presentation in these interviews was a performance of "artifice" as "the new authenticity" (Petrus and Cohen 281). There has been much suspicion of the "highly idiosyncratic" (DeCurtis, "Bob Dylan" 45) or "fanciful" evasions or "hard-to-prove reminiscences" (McDougal 50, 51), self-justifications, and even plagiarism, according to Andy Greene ("Brief" 94– 5), of Dylan's autobiographical assertions, particularly in his memoir.[16] Andy McCarron refers to the borrowings or quotations in *Chronicles* and throughout

Dylan's work as a performance of "postmodern blackface" (25).[17] David Dalton's *Who Is That Man?* and Greil Marcus's *Bob Dylan* cite *Chronicles* as authentic if also a fabricated (Dalton 3, 31) self-interrogating "bildungsroman" (Marcus, *Bob Dylan* 340). More recently, Richard Thomas describes the memoir as "a play" rather than an "autobiography" (96). However, one of Dylan's best and earliest interpreters, Robert Shelton in *No Direction Home* noted that "self-made men" require "tailoring," and that over and above any devious or playful self-fabrication, Dylan is a great artist (15), and one, as Dylan says himself, who has always had "an extreme sense of destiny" (qtd. in Scott Marshall 171). Given Dylan's extensive cooperation, Shelton's work is almost a mediated autobiography.[18]

Fabricating an identity with "pure hokum" for Columbia Records promotional materials begins *Chronicles* after an expression of Dylan's amazement at being signed given folk music's lowly status in the very early 1960s (8). This reluctance to tell his life story continues more by omission as when he launches into an account of Auschwitz or explains not eating pork at Johnny Cash's dinner without mentioning his European Jewish roots or in his reluctance to tell Izzy Young about his life. He leaves out perhaps more emotionally or legally fraught terrain such as the charges of plagiarism over Clayton's song, Van Ronk's anger about Dylan's appropriation of his distinctive "House of the Rising Sun" arrangement (Rotolo 115–16), his firing of manager Albert Grossman, his rejection by folk labels before Columbia's offer, specifics of the writing of some of his most famous songs or *Tarantula*, Suze Rotolo's mother's suspicions and Suze's abortion (Rotolo 280), the folk community's dislike of his and Bobby Neuwirth's bullying attacks on others, his own divorce, and controversy over going electric or going gospel. The MS of *Chronicles* at the Dylan Archive, which might suggest more about what was covered, was unavailable to researchers during my visit in late 2018. Of course, *Chronicles'* enigmatic, "Dylanesque" subtitle "Volume One" teases that other stories may be forthcoming.

The early stages of *Chronicles* construct a relational identity, by naming sources and influences, including Clayton, Van Ronk, and Len Chandler. This inclusiveness suggests a Rimbaud-like (Dylan refers to "Je est un autre" [288]) or Martin Buber-like gesture as if Dylan is other people.[19] Such a constructed, other-oriented identity also has been suggested by Dylan more recently in "I Contain Multitudes" from *Rough and Rowdy Ways*; this song borrows a phrase from Walt Whitman's "Song of Myself" (123) with its echo of Legion from Mark 5:9 who says "we are many." However, as in his appreciation of folk songs, Dylan also appears to perceive other people as not simply constituents of his collective self but as quasi-fictional "archetypes" (236), as suggested by his hyperbolically heroic, spiritual, or romantic descriptions. Meeting Suze Rotolo, for example, he writes, was "like stepping into the tales of 1,001 Arabian nights" (265). John Hammond is a "true American aristocrat" (279), Van Ronk a "timeworn monument" (261), Bono "a closet philosopher" with "the soul of an ancient poet" (174), Robert Johnson "a guy who could have sprung from the head of Zeus in full armor" (282), and Mike Seeger "a duke, the knight errant .... He could push a stake through Dracula's black heart. He was the romantic, egalitarian and revolutionary type all at once—had chivalry in his blood. Like some figure from a restored monarchy, he had come to purify the church" (69–70). He describes voices as sacramental, and so Aaron Neville's voice "could almost redeem a lost soul" and Joan Baez's voice also "drove out bad spirits": "she looked like a religious icon, like somebody you'd sacrifice yourself for" (178, 254, 255). He also refers to fleeting encounters with superstars who appear to recognize his destiny in an instant. Elsewhere, he has noted receiving a type of transmission from Buddy Holly shortly before his death, when it appeared that Holly anoints him as his successor (Hudson 54; Thomas 120). Later, when blocked in performing or recording, similarly brief, magical encounters with an old jazz singer or Sun Pie in New Orleans miraculously re-awaken Dylan's creativity. Some of these individuals, however, represent dead ends for Dylan in his ambition to create something unique. Just as he notes Neuwirth's and Van Ronk's indifference to fame, so, too, Dylan sees that Guthrie's absolute integrity, Clayton's academic knowledge of the folk tradition, and Mike Seeger's instrumental and Van Ronk's performative virtuosity occupy pathways it would be impossible or pointless for Dylan to enter.

Much of *Chronicles* is engaged with Dylan's presentation of sometimes mystifying shadow boxing between a new sense of identity acquired through folk music and an identity imposed from without due to associations drawn between the song and the songwriter. Recognizing the religious power and philosophical depth of folk songs provides Dylan a sense of identity, he claims, when his identity previously had lacked "concrete" form (55). He has admired but distanced himself from those who had mastered the folk tradition or instrumental virtuosity. His contribution will be a fresh manner of songwriting, though presumably Dylan first will require a new "philosophical identity" (73). He had earlier experienced a kind of personal renaissance upon hearing Guthrie's recordings, and he read Guthrie's autobiography *Bound for Glory* "like a hurricane" (245).[20] While Dylan senses that he lacks those records' "compelling poise of self," they also allowed him to discover "some essence of self-command, that I was in the internal pocket of the system feeling more like myself than ever before" (252, 244). Thus, Guthrie had "pointed out the starting place for my identity," and Dylan will name himself Guthrie's heir (229, 246). Similarly, he claims that the blues, like the assured voice of Joan Baez, are "a counterpart of myself" (240, 255). Later, in the 1980s, due to circumstances upon which he doesn't elaborate, his performances become lackluster and he lacks inspiration to write songs, and he even contemplates changing jobs or retiring. At this impasse, he says "[t]here was a missing person inside of myself and I needed to find him": "I had closed the door on my own self" (147, 149). He recognizes the value of a creative rebirth, given that, despite the dead weight of his legacy and the often unrealistic expectations of audiences and those in the music industry, "[i]f I didn't exist, someone would have to have invented me" (153).

Dylan bitterly resents being styled a counterculture radical or bohemian rebel without a cause, adhering instead to the raw values embodied in Guthrie's work, the wisdom of the traditional songbook, and the Beats' social critique. He feels at best estranged from the "generation that I was supposed to be the voice of" (*Chronicles* 115), though this has accelerated more recently with "Dylan's embrace of capitalist culture" (Goss and Hoffman 4). He is infuriated in *Chronicles* particularly by fans invading his rural homelife in Woodstock, and, perhaps surprisingly, he styles himself an American patriot, who once wanted to attend West Point (41), and he is outraged that he cannot shoot or "set fire" to trespassers with impunity (117): "Being born and raised in America, the country of freedom and independence, I had always cherished the values and ideals of equality and liberty. I was determined to raise my children with those ideals" (115). While appearing to embody country music's heartland values, he wilfully violates the pose of meek "humility that all country performers were, and are, supposed to wear like a crown of thorns" (Escott 164). When people persist in regarding him as a prophet or seer, he is somewhat disingenuously baffled, given the portentous, apocalyptic warnings in some of his songs, his own reverence for and pilgrimage to see Guthrie and later Carl Sandburg (Shelton 172–3), his deliberately fabricated image, and listeners' propensity to identity the singer, particularly when he or she is also the songwriter, with the song. He responds by refashioning his image. He retreats from rural Woodstock for New York "in hopes to demolish my identity" or to "remodel the image of me, change the perception of it anyway. ... I'd have to send out deviating signals, crank up the wrecking train—create some different impressions" or at least make "[m]y outer image ... a bit more confusing, a bit more humdrum" (118, 120, 121). He begins a process of "freeze-framing my image ... learning how to suggest only shadows of my possible self" (140). This process, so he claims, includes being photographed in Jerusalem, releasing country rock records, and singing in "a different voice": "I would even record an entire album based on Chekhov short stories—critics thought it was autobiographical—that was fine" (122).

Chronicles details Dylan's songwriting education in New York's bohemian Greenwich Village, offering a clear perception of some of his major influences which belies his later difficulty articulating problems with recording and performance. He outlines readings in military history and literature, though especially biography. He appears to be searching to supply the absence in popular culture and particularly pop songs of the 1950s and early 1960s of a meaningful response to the present. In words redolent of Adorno's, he dismisses most pop songs for their enforcement of conformity or mind control, but also in hipster terms he rejects them as "strictly dullsville ... gutless and flabby" (33). He apparently seeks to create something between pop's catchiness and the cerebral and emotional heft of longer ballads, demonstrating his catholic musical tastes which have appeared over the past decade in Christmas and Sinatra covers albums. He reveres traditional folk songs, but he also appreciates Harold Arlen's show tunes and commercial work by folk entertainers like the Kingston Trio, anathema for the more-authentic-than-thou "folk police" (248). *Chronicles* does not address the vexed question of originality in folk music, though it offers many instances of musicians adapting traditional material and of songwriters, including Guthrie, fusing their own ideas into existing melodies or song structures. Dylan calls his lyrics "songs" even when they lack melodies, as in his account of his composing for the *Oh Mercy* project. He appears to prefer recording with a band of compatible players who presumably will conjure requisite melodies, changes, and riffs while he strums his guitar and recites lyrics; additionally, in the process, the producer, such as Daniel Lanois, may have "heard something" (185).[21]

Within the domain of popular song, Dylan seems to grasp an opening for the Beats' "street ideologies that were signaling a new type of human existence" (34). *On the Road*, "like a bible for me" (57), fueled his romantic quest to find Guthrie in New York (235), but, while the bravado of Kerouac's novel and its characters' appetite for "kicks" lose their appeal, Dylan still appreciates the Beats' denunciation of the trinity of "bourgeois conventionality, social artificiality and the man in the gray flannel suit" (247). Dylan also credits the influence of the urban landscapes of painter Red Grooms and the idiosyncratic country blues of Robert Johnson with its "[t]hrowaway lines," "free association," "sparkling allegories," and "big-ass truths wrapped in the hard shell of nonsensical abstraction" (284, 285). However, the major breakthrough for his songs remains the art songs of Bertolt Brecht and Kurt Weill and particularly "Pirate Jenny." He adopts these songs' creation of distinct characters from whose perspective the narrative can be presented; their deployment of direct, accusative address; a strong chorus; and an aura of mystery with an unresolved closure (272–4). *Chronicles'* straightforward account of influence gives way to an impressionistic account of Dylan's 1980s impasse in recording and performance, conveying how untrained musicians and singer songwriters communicate and how easily this sows frustration. For example, he describes a failed attempt at recording: "[e]very take [was] another ball of confusion. Takes that could almost make you question your own existence" (191). In 1987, with his performances becoming routine, he seeks reinvigoration to grow a new audience or simply to retire or take up another career. Audiences pay to see legends, he says revealingly, "but for most people, once is enough" (147). A chance encounter with a jazz singer who sees into his soul is inspirational, and Dylan determines to use the musician's "technique" to tap into his own power, but he doesn't name or explain the technique (151). Similarly and equally mysteriously, Dylan "conjured up some different type of mechanism to jump-start the other techniques that weren't working" (153). At this point, he finds liberation in recalling a method based on the number three, rather than two, as used in Link Wray's "Rumble" (160). He explains with an elliptical flourish, that he thus has tapped into "a new incantation code to infuse my vocals with manifest presence": "My playing was going to be an impellent in equanimity to my voice and I would use different algorithms that the ear is not accustomed to" (161).

Tarantula

Tarantula (1971) is Dylan's single "novel," if it is in fact a novel.[22] *Chronicles* cites *Ulysses* (1922) as a particularly unreadable novel, one of which he "couldn't make hide nor hair" (130), but in comparison with *Tarantula*, *Ulysses* is a straightforward, overnight stroll through a Dublin park or brightly-lit midtown

Manhattan. Dylan's publisher pumped *Tarantula* pre-release as being written by a "young James Joyce" and at least one reviewer called it bizarrely the *"Finnegans Wake* of the Pepsi generation" (qtd. in Shelton 166). While it may resemble William Burroughs' *Naked Lunch* (1959) or Richard Brautigan's *A Confederate General from Big Sur* (1965) and there may be a Beatles connection,[23] *Tarantula* bears a closer resemblance to the linguistic blizzard of Andy Warhol's novel *a* (1968) with the notable exception that Warhol almost certainly never wrote a word of his various books. However, in its recurring motifs and the relative uniformity of its breathless, run-on style as well as its manic allusiveness, *Tarantula* has a degree of overall unity, though it lacks a single coherent narrative or even a series of multiple plot lines. For our purposes, however, *Tarantula* is a type of autofiction in which the author, or at least a character named "bob dylan" in postmodern guise, does appear. That he is already dead should not overly concern us at this stage, however. As its disclaimer points out: "[a]ny resemblance to actual events or locales or persons, living or dead, is entirely coincidental" (x). *Tarantula* is a work of homage to American popular culture and its African American roots, and it begins with an extended apostrophe to the godlike voice of a gospel or soul singer, and Dylan had a romantic obsession with Mavis Staples, even proposing marriage (Sounes, *Down* 133–4).[24] The work also contains in elliptical form the more expected rehearsal of Dylan's exasperation at his songs' and his own image's misinterpretation.

Tarantula was written in a frantic, probably amphetamine-fueled, phase of Dylan's career just before his much-mythologized retreat from the public eye after his motorcycle accident in July 1966. When first published in 1971, it was regarded less as a novel than a mythic text or Ouija Board capable of conjuring up and justifying all manner of speculation. *Tarantula* has been a subject of controversy, contention, and contradiction, regarding its initial impetus, its method of composition, models and aims, as well as the question of whether the published "novel" remains unfinished. Dylan endlessly postponed submission of his MS: "I'd be so embarrassed at the nonsense I'd written I'd change the whole thing" (qtd. in Sounes, *Down* 223).[25] It has been suggested that there must be a handwritten draft of *Tarantula*, now long lost, resembling many of Dylan's songs in its style of composition.[26] However, there is no textual or documentary evidence for such a claim, however intriguing, and Dylan's other lengthy prose work, *Chronicles*, was typed and not handwritten. Moreover, as evidenced by documentary footage in *Dont Look Back*, Dylan was not only a formidable guitarist and harmonica player, but also a master, two-finger typist. This is not to suggest, however, that the work—as the presumed original of *Tarantula*'s character "truman peyote" or Truman Capote (38) once opined about *On the Road*—is not so much writing as type-writing. According to the *Tarantula* papers held by the Bob Dylan Archive, it appears that the novel was composed in four drafts, though these are not distinct versions of the novel but rather reworked sketches of an original *ur*-text. An initial investigation of these versions suggests that over time the earliest one became embellished as in the adaptive rhythms of Philip Glass's music, just as more abrupt slashes or virgules gave way to the slide of dashes which predominate in the published version. The first, briefest version shows—and particularly so in its handling of "aretha"—a somewhat more spiritually inclined and less adorned, complicated, and frantic narrative than appears in the published version.

Tarantula is experimental in its multi-vocal form. It begins and ends with the shifting, heroic apostrophe to "aretha," the speaker's muse and object of desire,[27] who may or may not be "Aretha Franklin." At least one edition of *Tarantula*—St. Martin's 1994's *Tarantula: Poems*, an otherwise exact replica of the original published by Macmillan—highlights its genre as a series of Baudelairean prose poems. Dylan's text is an episodic, picaresque, and epistolary series of letters and their elaborate, cartoon-like valedictions or complimentary closes. It is also a series of "routines," unified by a distinctly oral, bardic quality, rendering it an example of vernacular "litorature" (Ngũgĩ 3). The "routine" is Burroughs' term for experimental sketches or scenes showcasing a myriad of voices, resembling some of Dylan's Brechtian art songs, protest songs, and also his broadsides, as well as the parodic, trickster voices of his anti-interviews. In these early interviews, he deflected the pretentions of his interviewers' questions seeking to pin him down like an insect, perhaps a tarantula, in order to make him speak for postwar youth, and to elaborate his motivations.[28] *Tarantula* has the reckless, limit-testing drive of *On the Road* and its—as Kerouac's drafts indicate—hard-worked if not belabored "spontaneous prose" (Cunnell 26–32), as well as Kerouac's, Ginsberg's, and Whitman's very American long lines. These lines for the Beats were the exultations of tantric mantras, the breath-centric "Ahs" of Zen masters, and the ecstatic blows of inspired jazz solos. *Tarantula*'s lines make a mad dash—punctuated by slashes and ellipses and dashes and only very rarely periods or full stops—to the next sub-title, the next embedded aside, the next valedictory sign off. It isn't a latter-day Beat classic, like "Howl," though one of its carnivalesque characters is named "Moan." The profusion of voices and intertexts in *Tarantula* and its own indented asides or embedded contrapuntal narratives make the work in places resemble a folk or people's comic opera, as at least one sub-title suggests: "The Vandals Took the Handles (An Opera)" (115). Certainly some of the sub-sections resemble musical scores in rhythmic repetitions of nonce words such as "blam de lam" (12). There may be a connection between the use of transitional logic within *Tarantula* and the editing practices followed in Dylan's similarly disjointed films *Eat This Document* and *Renaldo and Clara*.

Tarantula has elements of autofiction or a type of anti-autobiography, perhaps the polar opposite of *Chronicles*. It may also be a posthumous autobiography in that its only direct reference to its author presumes he is dead. In keeping with the work's often valedictory tone, "bob dylan" appears in funeral eulogies or tombstone epitaphs. He has been destroyed in one instance by the force which claims to have created him: "here lies bob dylan / murdered / from behind / by trembling flesh ... here lies bob dylan / demolished by Vienna politeness- / which will now claim to have invented him ... bob dylan—killed by a discarded Oedipus / who turned / around / to investigate a ghost / & discovered that / the ghost too / was more than one person" (118–20). While not the artist formerly known as Bob Dylan—itself an invented name—this "bob dylan" is presumably the leader which "aretha," who has "no back" and no limitations, refuses to follow (1). However, her music is "diffused" in the speaker who has been "murdered / from behind" (1, 118–19). This "aretha," we learn, will be the speaker's "trump card" (135), though a different Trump than the one whom Woody Guthrie complained had made a "trump" out of him according to one of the displays at Tulsa's Woody Guthrie Center. *Tarantula*'s murdered "bob dylan" may signal the culmination and also the termination of a manic, self-destructive career of amazing creativity. In this respect, *Tarantula* resembles T.S. Eliot's *The Waste Land*, which it quotes, focused on the wandering thoughts of a deposed king adrift in a forest of symbols, religious and secular, devoid of meaning but unified by an alienated, anti-heroic bardic voice.

Self-conscious mockery of grandiose misinterpretations and by extension academic pretentiousness is *Tarantula*'s oxygen and one of the major sources of its high-jinks. Teachers and professors appear and disappear, nonsensical lectures on literature or history are delivered, tests are anticipated, and when you "get B's / in the ivanhoe tests and A minuses / in the silas marners ... then you / wonder why you flunked the hamlet / exams" (70). The assumption that all knowledge lies in books and that such knowledge can be evaluated in multiple-choice questions drafted by over-paid, self-important professors in love with the sound of their own voices and their comfortable lecterns is held up for ridicule.

Dylan's examples here seem to anticipate an awareness that his own work, including *Tarantula*, would be studied in coming decades less in departments of musicology than in departments of English literature (Lee Marshall 100–2). Moreover, as Susan Wheeler writes within the edited collection *Do You Mr Jones? Bob Dylan with the Poets and Professors*: "In writing about any aspect of Dylan, a fan runs the risk of becoming his *Tarantula* character, Scholar, 'his body held together by chiclets … not even talking to anybody,' and of course this is magnified when the subject is Dylan's jokes" (176). The hyper-self-awareness of the narrative, however, does sometimes seem to be weary from its own somewhat belabored, nonsensical cleverness and its anticipation that misreading will be the inevitable result of the "drag" of "writing for this chosen few" who presumably will not be a mass audience (11). In this respect, *Tarantula* is an anti-*erziehungsroman* or novel of education and instead an interrogation of the value of formal schooling vs that of creative miseducation. This theme may have emerged from Dylan's dismay as a university student for one semester or from his being pursued from early in his career by hipster-wanna-bes in corduroy jackets or university presidents offering honorary doctorates in exchange for celebrity walk-ons at graduation ceremonies as he mentions in *Chronicles*, when Dylan's real education began with his study of popular music (132–4).

Songs

Dylan's songs, he writes in *Chronicles*, "come from an autobiographical place," but inevitably there are exceptions when "I wasn't in the song" (199, 166).[29] His songs primarily bring together European art song, Anglo-American ballads, and the folk protest tradition. Folk songs are tied to Dylan's sense of identity, as we have seen, and even constitute a kind of secular religion for him, surpassing "all human understanding" and presenting "life magnified" (*Chronicles* 236). Only some of his songs, such as "If Dogs Run Free," suggest the Beats' practice of rhyming over freeform jazz, though there are other signs of Beat influence. Especially in his most famous early and mid-1960s work, his songs introduce a personal mythology, which, if not as systematic and coherent as that in for example William Blake's apocalyptic epics, does contribute to a unified vision. Amid a range of allusions to biblical and classical mythology, Hollywood and Americana, French symbolist poetry, and esoteric tradition, Dylan has crafted a unique folk expression. Dylan as a songwriter and also self-fashioning

Dylanologist was partly honed in the collective which created the *Broadside* song-writing bulletin, modeled on the broadside sheets of Shakespeare's era, addressed to urgent, local problems and designed to provoke outrage and social change. Dylan wrote songs but also song critiques demonstrating an early version of his later role as a self-reflexive, personal-archive-constructing Dylanologist. Influenced by the anti-totalitarian art of Brecht, Weill, and folksinger poets like Federico Garcia Lorca—directing anti-fascist sentiments against post-McCarthyite conformity—Dylan generalized and romanticized "topical" song. As he would say in *Chronicles*, topical or protest songs readily become "preachy and one-dimensional," and to correct this tendency, "[y]ou have to show people a side of themselves that they don't know is there" (54). Dylan's famous protest-style art songs, as a result, locate solutions to social problems or direct listeners to locate them not in specific actions but, instead, in the wind or the hard rain, freedom's chimes or the changing times.

It is difficult to address Dylan's songs without cliché and platitude, though he used these devices to open up his dense, image-laden lyrics, showing that "you can have your cake and eat it too," as he sings in "Lay Lady Lay," its chorus based on "La…le —ly labials" (Ricks 158). Dylan's songs extended moon/June pop lyrics—the declensions of "love me do" and "she loves you"—into evocations of Columbus's arrival in America, wrongful imprisonment, and the plight of immigrants; denunciations of xenophobia and military arrogance; and love songs to death at heaven's door. It is no small achievement to score a hit with references to Leviticus, Deuteronomy, and Sodom and Gomorrah, as he would in 1983's beautiful, reggae-inflected "Jokerman," while still facing every aging rock star's nightmare: being outsold by your son's band (The Wallflowers). Dylan has been a popular people's poet and songwriter, and everyone may have their own Bob Dylan,[30] though some are united by loathing for his gravely, late-career voice; for his "imagine that," "Siamese cat," "Where it's at" rhymes in "Like a Rolling Stone"; or for his sometimes misogynistic lyrics, such as the venomous, personal, accusative, you're-not-good-enough-for-me sentiments of "Positively 4th Street" or "It Ain't Me, Babe." There are many Bob Dylans, and he's been an enigmatic chameleon, who by the late 1960s had produced virtually a life's work of songs.

Dylan is a troubadour rock star poet, seemingly on a never-ending tour, but he is also a scholar and archivist of the great American song tradition. In *Chronicles*, Dylan claims to be more devoted to conveying the essence of a traditional song rather than his interpretation of it: "Most of the other performers [in Greenwich folk clubs] tried to put themselves across .... With me, it was about putting the song across" (18). He overlooks his early Chaplinesque, country bumpkin stage antics, as well as his deployment of second order parody, imitating Ramblin' Jack Elliott's imitation of Woody Guthrie, presumably part of the "trick or two" needed to compete (17). He used Britain's ballad tradition in recasting "Lord Randall" as "A Hard Rain's A-Gonna Fall," but he may have drawn more extensively on the American tradition, and his *Self Portrait* revealingly began as an album of covers like two more recent albums, *Good As I Been to You* and *World Gone Wrong*. Most of Dylan's hits, of course, were cover versions by other artists. One of Dylan's most moving vocal performances, showing the often discounted emotional power of his singing, is his simple, piano-accompanied cover of "Spanish is the Loving Tongue," the B-side of 1971's Leon Russell-propelled "Watching the River Flow" which perhaps anticipated Lennon's 1980 "Watching the Wheels." Greil Marcus's recent exploration of three songs that appear in their unique timelessness as if they wrote themselves and have always existed, singles out Dylan's "Ballad of Hollis Brown." He refers to Dylan's borrowing freely from the great American songbook, noting Dylan's remark that "[m]ost of my songs aren't original" (*Three Songs* 28). Even his greatest songs' melodies, however simple, draw on often mournful roots in the trance melodies of the blues, the gospel tradition, and W.E.B. Du Bois's "sorrow songs," the musical inheritance of the transit across the Black Atlantic (Du Bois 204). Dylan's early protest songs, like those of Guthrie and Pete Seeger, are rooted in the legacy of a collective tragedy of dispossession, his own American *Wretched of the Earth*. Dylan also drew on the more contemporary social critique in the work of the Beat writers, even making Allen Ginsberg something of a video star, in the promotional footage for "Subterranean Homesick Blues," taken from D.A. Pennebaker's cinema verité parody *Dont Look Back*.[31] As Robbie Robertson writes in his autobiography, Dylan shared the Beats' artistic "fearlessness" (200), with a lyrical disrobing. He embraced the trans- or pan-American epic of *On the Road*, especially in his hymn-like "Sad Eyed Lady of the Lowlands." He shares Kerouac's preoccupation with outlaws, eccentric prophets of the open road, and dharma bums. In this way, he also embraced the love affair with the idea of America we find in Whitman's long lines, of which Ginsberg would make a career. From Burroughs, Dylan borrowed the cut-up, slicing and dicing text into collage. Dylan's songs' intertextual borrowing, from the British-American tradition via Paris and Tangier, and from the French symbolists, lead indirectly to that "elementary penguin singing Hari Krishna" in Lennon's "I Am the Walrus," the Beatles' lyrical experimentation being perhaps the clearest extension of Dylan's global cultural influence.[32]

"My Back Pages," composed during a brief songwriting sabbatical in Greece in 1964, marks Dylan's move from highly successful public protest, "finger-pointing songs" to more introspective material (Dylan qtd. in Hentoff). Its melody resembles a somewhat more waltz-like version of that in "With God on Our Side." It announces his farewell to the job of being a folk singer songwriter of topical, "rebellion," or protest songs and a popular public intellectual (*Chronicles* 83). He is a poet of individual lines, highly memorable and often paradoxical. The evocative, memorable chorus of "My Back Pages"—"I was so much older then, I'm younger than that now"—contains the knowing paradox for which Dylan had become famous but with a new strain of humility. The responsible moral seriousness of his young adulthood and his early songs like "A Hard Rain's A-Gonna Fall" and "The Times They Are A-Changin'" are being renounced, though, at least for Joan Baez, writing songs had always encompassed the entirety of Dylan's "active commitment to social change" (*And a Voice* 95).[33] By extension, he abandons the assumed or imposed role of generational mouthpiece and prophet of the coming apocalypse. The song's emphasis is on the ethical convolutions of the past and his overly portentous youth, rather than on severing ties or sketching a post-protest future. In this respect, "My Back Pages" may be "a parable of antigrowth," like Rimbaud's "Alchemy of the Word," and the "aesthetic counterpart" to 1965's "Like a Rolling Stone"—itself possibly extracted from Dylan's *Tarantula* manuscript (Wilentz 296)—which "turn[s] abjection into emancipation" (Hampton 89, 102, 105). In comparison with another "autobiographical" song from 1965, the Beatles' very popular and much loved, and also possibly Dylan-inspired "In My Life" (Jones 83), Dylan's song is remarkable for its complexity of sentiment and tone.[34] Rather than simply stating that fond memories of past places and faces, and particularly—as per popular song convention—one face, remain a poignant memory, "My Back Pages" addresses the specter of youthful folly in a wise and wrathful yet self-deprecating fashion.

Dylan may suggest the source of "My Back Pages" in his remark in *Chronicles* that "[i]n *Beyond Good and Evil*, Nietzsche talks about feeling old at the beginning of his life ... I felt like that, too" (73). While some have contended that "My Back Pages" dissects the collapse of Dylan's relationship with Suze Rotolo (Margotin and Guesdon 126), and Rotolo herself writes that the *Another Side of Bob Dylan* album, on which the song appears, caused her distress (288), the song does not only refer to a romance's collapse. Rotolo, however, did introduce Dylan to many of the aesthetic and political forces that influenced his songwriting, and just before the single night of recording the entire album, Dylan said to journalist Nat Hentoff, that "[i]f I haven't been through what I write about, the songs aren't worth anything" (Hentoff). Nietzsche stresses in *Beyond Good and Evil* that philosophy is personal—both "confession" and "memoir" (19)—and that even philosophers are subject to self-delusion. He draws attention in section 31 to young people's characteristic zeal for absolute moral distinctions between "Yes and No," or Dylan's "black and white" and "good and bad," which distort the truth.[35] Adherence to such binaries is unworthy of "genuine artists of life," but its worst consequence is making individuals distrust their own moral judgement and question even the best aspects of their nature (44). In addition, a more insidious consequence is that individuals blame youth itself, when, as Nietzsche suggests, people all remain youthful in their tendency toward simplistic judgement, blaming others, and self-delusion. Dylan in "My Back Pages" announces a break from delusion rather than cautioning that self-delusion may be inevitable and ongoing, but he also expresses anger at being separated from a more artistic perspective. In the song, a veritable chorus of ministers, professors, teachers, soldiers, sailors, and guards represent institutions or society collectively, or they may represent self-monitoring aspects of the self. These forces are both deceitful and demanding of total commitment, and even the singer becomes his own "enemy" when he "preaches" or pontificates. The song does not point clearly to a point of resolution or an acceptance of the danger of ongoing delusion, as in Nietzsche's analysis, but particularly in its deftly crafted chorus, it announces a moment of profound self-understanding and presumably a resolution about not being pressed into service by others in such a way as to compromise artistic integrity.

Archive

The Bob Dylan Archive, created in 2016, at the Gilcrease Museum in Tulsa, Oklahoma—site of the Woody Guthrie Center—with a Bob Dylan Center to follow in 2021, is a type of institutionalized autobiography. Created before Dylan became Nobel laureate, the Archive acknowledges origins and sources, and emphasizes proximity to both the Beat writers, with their archival drive, and the roots of American folklore. It may constitute a second volume of memoir, after

Chronicles, or a deflection from autobiographical self-reflection in writing.[36] Unlike *Chronicles*, the Archive, given its focus on song manuscripts, at least aspires to being the record of a self defined by music. Celebrity monuments, like Jim Morrison's grave in Père Lachaise, Paris, offer sites for reverence or Dionysian irreverence, but the archive is distanced from memorial or place of pilgrimage, though lying still further from the commercial celebrity theme park such as Dolly Parton's Dollywood. Significantly, the documents at the Dylan Archive, its website cautions, are available only to researchers whose applications for access are vetted by the Archive, and not merely to fans, though this may differ at the forthcoming Center. Departing from the fan-friendly Woody Guthrie Center, the Dylan Archive stays closer to Beat poet Ginsberg's site at Stanford University.

The Allen Ginsberg Project houses the Beat poet, promoter, editor, and documentarian's archives that include his musical recordings (including "Father Death Blues" and "Hard-On Blues"), some of them with Dylan, and also his correspondence with Dylan whose celebrity Ginsberg valued for the exposure it afforded for all manner of causes and its access to different publics unmoved by poetry. Publisher and Beat poet Lawrence Ferlinghetti felt that Ginsberg's artistry declined as a result of "deciding early on that he wanted to be a rock star, like Bob Dylan" (qtd. in Sounes, *Down* 154). Ginsberg represented a radicalized version of engaged celebrity, but he also institutionalized literary fame. Ginsberg was Dylan's connection to the jazz- and Zen-inflected literary heritage of the Beats, their embrace of the saints and prophets of Whitman's and Kerouac's open road, and their hard-won fame in the canon of American literature. In his connection with Dylan, "Ginsberg waxed paternal, adopting Dylan as a sort of … little brother, though he made no secret of a lust for Bob that rivaled that of Paul Clayton …. [and] would have gladly played Verlaine to Dylan's Rimbaud" (McDougal 105). Ginsberg would anoint Dylan as his successor and in effect as the last member of the Beats, by backing Dylan's nomination for the Nobel Prize in Literature (Thomas 292–3). The Dylan Archive was created in 2016, prior to his being named Nobel laureate, when Dylan had become a self-interpreting, self-branding Dylanologist—fame itself, he noted in *Chronicles*, having become a career (123). He had begun acquiring his scattered 1960s papers in the 1980s during a career slump when the success of his retrospective compilation *Biograph*—with a sixty-three-page booklet by Cameron Crowe and including a photograph of Dylan's parents—drew attention to his papers' and his legacy's value (M. Davidson 329). Dylan's donation of his papers earned him approximately $20 million (Spencer 52).

Museums are self-interrogating, interpretative sites for narrating, defining, and commodifying—while ostensibly celebrating—nations, cultures, and also individuals, as contemporary museology studies have shown (Dudley 3–14; Janes 13–25; Knell 3–9). However, for artists in our celebrity-obsessed, postmodern, posthuman present, the dedicated, single-artist museum also entails a distinct autobiographical gesture, especially when constructed by the artist. The single-artist museum denotes an anticipation of archaeological memory work (Barthel and Kunze), while performing something resembling a living wake. Like the various popular music halls of fame and awards museums, as well as sites such as the Jimi Hendrix Experience Museum, the dedicated museum demonstrates the individual artist's renown while simultaneously and inevitably establishing an official "object biography" or, in Dylan's case, something closer to a notional kind of "institutional autobiography" (Whitehead 157–70). While art or history museums select artifacts and episodes to collectivize, de-individualize, and even dehumanize their original owners, the dedicated museum's selection memorializes the individual as a leviathan. In musical artifacts, recordings, and writings, the dedicated, stationary museum is a history or my-story of the present with an eye fixed on posterity's retrospection (Morin 139; Nemec 279–93). The archival autograph makes the artist history. Dylan's Archive shows how far Dylan's self-construction has shifted away from audience identification as the marker of an authentic musical identity, as in his very early 1960s persona,[37] but it has not morphed into the interactive, democratizing "presentational regime," in Marshall's terminology ("New Media" 637, 634–44), characteristic of celebrities in the new social mediascape. The Dylan Archive was created at a time of crisis for museums, due to declining audiences and a not-unrelated concern with public perceptions of appropriation and irrelevance. In critical museological discourse, moreover, museums have become regarded less as static warehouses than as active sites of exclusion, in terms of race, gender, and sexual orientation, for example (Reilly 17–23), reinforcing ahistorical masternarratives. The Dylan Archive engages with this critique in an unusual way by actively excluding the public, disdaining monetizing opportunities, and focusing on written texts. It enacts a type of anti-self-promotion, while subtly staging a style of autobiographical self-fashioning.

The Archive, however inadvertently, may demonstrate some of the accommodations and assumptions lying behind its creation. Its creation coincided with the ongoing releases of Dylan's "Bootleg Series," documenting virtually every take of his songs, and in *More Blood, More Tracks, The Deluxe Edition*, reproducing a notebook.[38] Signaling recognition of the value of the archive, however, this reproduced manuscript "notebook" is a fair copy, and lacks any deletions or alterations. It is a sanitized version of the archive for public consumption rather than a glimpse into the musician's working practices. A few years later, Dylan, like other rock stars, would launch a line of whiskey, with labels reproducing designs from his sculptures, indicating the distance traveled from 1960s visions of strident counterculture anti-capitalism. Inadvertently, the Archive itself appears as a bid for self-legitimation within established, literary registers as if to validate Dylan's elevation as Nobel laureate, which to a degree rebrands Dylan as a unique cultural hybrid and also a fetishized, Euro-style artist-intellectual (Braun 320–34). The Archive's proximity to the Guthrie Center also inadvertently reinforces a dominant national narrative of whiteness in locating the roots of American folk or vernacular music, though Tulsa has had a fraught interracial history, indicated by 1921's Tulsa Race Massacre. The Archive's proximity at least downplays debts, fully acknowledged in *Chronicles*, to what Dave Van Ronk's memoir calls the "authentically ethnic" or "neo-ethnic" music of the African American tradition (47). The focus thus remains on the legacy of European immigrants whose music and its vocal inflections carried survivals of ancestral voices, but even this music is far from being an unalloyed legacy. What originated as the private music of the voiceless underclass became suspicious in the 1950s. Senator Joseph McCarthy and his legal sidekick, the gay and homophobic Roy Cohn, mentor to Donald Trump (Brenner 84–9, 120–3), ensured that "country" folk music, with its sorrowful blues roots, prevailed over "folk" due to folk music's guilt by association with communism during the 1950s' Red Scare (Peterson 198–9). In the emerging myth of this music as America's theme song, Appalachia was elevated into a national homeland, its people configured as "noble relics of Elizabethan England" (Peterson 215), among whom "[s]inging was almost as universal a practice as speaking" (Cecil Sharp qtd. in Mancuso 157). This notion of a living archive of cultural memory representing the origin of the national narrative would be exploited to legitimate the nation's ownership by white European immigrants. This music could in turn be manipulated by right-wing populists as an ethnic signifier, an unbroken circle of rightful possession.

For most of his career, Dylan probably would have resisted establishing a Mount Rushmore-like monument in the Dylan Archive and the forthcoming Dylan Center. He declared in 1965, for example, that "[m]useums are cemeteries" (qtd. in Shelton 150). He refers to himself in *Chronicles* as having been "frozen in the temple of a museum" with his fame and his audience's expectations: "[w]herever

I am, I'm a '60s troubadour, a folk-rock relic, a wordsmith from bygone days, a fictitious head of state from a place nobody knows. I'm in the bottomless pit of cultural oblivion. You name it. I can't shake it" (161, 147). *Chronicles* gives some indication of the Archive's file of letters from political leaders, folk legends, school teachers, and fans asking for favors or jobs for relatives, contributions, donations, or participation in order to tap into Dylan's enduring fame and influence. *Chronicles* details Archibald MacLeish seeking songs from Dylan as someone whose "work would be a touchstone for generations" and Princeton University's President introducing Dylan at an honorary degree ceremony as "the authentic expression of the disturbed and concerned conscience of Young America" (*Chronicles* 111, 133). Producer Daniel Lanois wants new songs like Dylan's most famous ones, Robbie Robertson asks him his plans for the future of "the whole music scene," and Joan Baez calls on him to "lead the masses" (195, 117, 119).

However, in *Chronicles*, there is another, more positive evocation of an archive's power. Dylan recalls Guthrie directing him to the cache of songs without melodies in the basement of his Coney Island home which Dylan is unable to access. This invitation appears to designate Dylan as Guthrie's musical heir. Dylan clearly regrets having lost the opportunity to work on this material, an opportunity much later afforded to Billy Bragg and Wilco. Wilco's Jeff Tweedy in his memoir remembers this project as "wildly liberating" as if he were sonically "vacationing from the future," while resisting the aura of Guthrie's "legacy" and the stereotype that authenticity resided in "backwoods chic" (157–60). Tweedy particularly appreciated Guthrie's practical injunctions to himself scattered among the songs: "drink less," "womanize less," and "[w]rite a song every day" (158). The location of the Woody Guthrie Center in Tulsa, Oklahoma was one of the reasons for Dylan's Archive being housed there. Dylan acknowledged the fitness of this location (Cogley), if only because his own artistic vocation was fueled by reading Guthrie's autobiography and inspired by his songs, and no doubt he did not want a memorial in his birthplace or in New York or in Malibu. The funders of the Dylan Center, the George Kaiser Family Foundation, partly hoped to re-make Tulsa to rival Nashville, one of the homes of Americana music, though Nashville itself had resisted this designation in the 1940s when country music was treated with derision (Escott 50; Pecknold 23–35). The Guthrie Center also houses the papers of Dylan's compatriot in writing protest songs, Phil Ochs who suffered a very different fate. It displays Ochs' gold lamé suit, which he wore in a final, misguided attempt to parody Vegas-era Elvis before Ochs' bipolar disorder and alcoholism led him to suicide. Guthrie's own perception of the contradictions of an archival legacy may be revealed in the story of his most famous song, set out in a display at the Center: "This Land Is Your Land" was originally composed as a bitterly ironic comment on "America the Beautiful" and not as an unalloyed democratic paean to a national benevolence and triumphalism in which he did not participate and could not believe.

Notes

1 In his Nobel lecture, Dylan compares himself with Shakespeare, though he does not seek to establish himself as a giant of the literary tradition, because Dylan's Shakespeare is less an artistic giant than a worker in theater who happened to write plays. Literature for Dylan, however disingenuously, draws on the oral tradition of the folk. Literature or "litorature" is grounded in the oral culture of the people (Ngũgĩ 3) and not the product of a particular education or upbringing, genius, ambition, or celebrity. As he said in an early interview with Ralph Gleason, Dylan was not a poet but merely a "song and dance man" (qtd. in Cott 66), but he would ultimately and selectively fashion himself into a "song and dance" Shakespeare. In time, Dylan would perfect his "identityless identity" (Cheyette 354, n.5).

2 Joni Mitchell dismisses Dylan as a "plagiarist" (qtd. in McCarron 27), but for American poet and Trappist monk Thomas Merton, Dylan is a "prophetic voice" (Hudson 8). Bruce Springsteen writes in his memoir that "Bob Dylan is the father of my country," offering hopeful assistance "in making your way through the new wilderness America had become" (166, 167). Christopher Ricks claims that Dylan "is the greatest living user of the English language" (qtd. in Hudson 1). Ricks' learned *Dylan's Visions of Sin* appeared before *Chronicles*, and it offers an insistently anti-biographical reading of Dylan's songs in light of Ricks' own Olympian range of reference: "It is easy to make the mistake of supposing that a Dylan song is about Dylan" (192). For Ricks, a daily reading of Dylan functions as a spiritual practice. While Dylan was a magpie, possibly a plagiarist, perhaps a conduit for the zeitgeist, and an industrial-strength cultural and intellectual vacuum, overblown assessments may tell us more about the listener or critic than the work.

3 Huxley was something of a shaman in the 1960s—the Doors took their name from Huxley's book on mescaline—and part of a well-respected intellectual lineage in England. Huxley explored psychedelic drugs seriously towards the end of his life and was injected with LSD on his deathbed. Dylan refers to Huxley in passing in *Chronicles* (91). LSD's use in palliative care is again being researched after

such work was derailed in the late 1960s. Due to its coinciding with Kennedy's assassination, Huxley's passing received relatively little attention.

4   Even Richard Fariña would write a "worship liturgy" about Dylan and his sister-in-law Joan Baez for *Mademoiselle* (Hajdu 198). Baez's 1968 memoir *Daybreak* in its brief account is more cryptic and hostile to Dylan, "the dada king," "a bizarre liar," and "a huge transparent bubble of ego," who is, however, "fragile" and beloved by the author (qtd. in Shelton 136).

5   Baez and Rotolo, and also Britta Lee Shain two decades later as she details in *Seeing the Real You at Last*, noted Dylan's exasperating fondness for what Donovan Leitch refers to in a different context as "the game of musical beds" (Leitch 279) or maintaining simultaneous relationships with different women.

6   Dylan recorded La Farge's "The Ballad of Ira Hayes" on 1973's *Dylan* and performs the song in Martin Scorsese's *Rolling Thunder Revue: A Bob Dylan Story*. Ochs committed suicide before that tour, which his biographer suggests originated as a joint tour idea, but one from which Ochs was excluded (Schumacher 298-9, 339), "[o]ne of his final disappointments" (Sounes 302). He was in a severe psychotic state, exacerbated by alcoholism, in this period. Clayton's "Gotta Travel On" appears to have been played as an encore, but it is not in the film. Suze Rotolo mentions Ramblin' Jack Elliott as yet another who was "left unacknowledged in the dust of Bob's hard and fast drive out of the picture" (127).

7   George W. Williams, Clayton's graduate colleague at Virginia working with musicologist Arthur Kyle Davis in the 1950s and later Professor of English at Duke University, was unaware of Clayton's self-identification as gay; he also noted that musicology in the 50s was tolerated but not encouraged in English departments (personal communication). Clayton's good friend Stephen Wilson says that, via experiments with pot and LSD, Clayton exploded from the "closet" after about 1960 when Wilson was put off by his aggressive advocacy (personal communication).

8   Stephen Wilson (personal communication).

9   Tim Dunn's *The Bob Dylan Copyright Files 1962-2007* provides an extensive account of Dylan's debt to Clayton's song (126) and the copyright agreements for the song over the following decades (126-9). Copyright law, originating in England in 1556, focuses on publishers', not creators', rights, according to Avron Levine White (170).

10 Timothy Hampton points to important musical distinctions between Clayton's and Dylan's versions (60-1).

11 *Chronicles* does not address charges of plagiarism, "a ball and chain on Dylan's career as a songwriter … as his fame was growing" (Rotolo 135), but he frequently refers to musicians freely adapting and transforming older material. In particular,

he notes putting his own words to one of Len Chandler's melodies and the blasé reaction: "Len didn't seem to mind" (87).

12   Bob Coltman's invaluable 2008 biography of Clayton focuses on folksong genealogy and the contexts of the revival, and it both underplays the importance of Clayton's sexuality and advocacy, and suggests he was doomed by his queer identity. Larry Mollin's 2013 play *Search: Paul Clayton, The Man Who Loved Bob Dylan* in dramatic terms is at best modest, styling itself a "Wiki=musical" (2). The historical record is treated very freely with Dylan arriving in New York with songs in hand, and Clayton's suicide involving an electric guitar. Biographical details seem chosen to reinforce stereotypes of gay identity formation in a bullying father and overprotective mother, and the play can't resist tropes of gay sexual mania. Mollin's Clayton frankly expresses an erotic obsession from the start with Dylan reinforced by Clayton's outré remarks: "I gave head ahead of my time" (3), "I've always been a sucker for a hot mouth organist" (9), and "Is that a harmonica in your pocket or are you just happy to see me?" (28). While Dylan has never been a gay rights advocate, though claiming to have worked as a male prostitute on his arrival in New York (McDougal 137, n.165), he recently sang "He's Funny That Way" on *Universal Love: Wedding Songs Reimagined* (2018) which shifts pronouns for effect.

13   The recording sounds more like a cluttered demo than a finished master, and its melody is taken from "My Creole Belle," a song from 1900 by George Sidney and J. Bodewalt Lampe and popularized by Mississippi John Hurt.

14   They are housed at the Howard T. Glasser Archives of Folk Music and Letters at the University of Massachusetts.

15   John Sebastian said to Robert Shelton: "[y]ou can't get too close to Dylan. He burns with such a bright flame you can get burned" (qtd. in Shelton 46).

16   Even some of Dylan's lecture for the Nobel Prize for Literature, ironically crediting literary influences, may have been plagiarized from SparkNotes (Spencer 53; English 309–10).

17   Dylan claims to have witnessed "one of the last blackface minstrel shows at a country carnival" (*Chronicles* 234).

18   See Timothy Gray on the dangers to "roots" biographers of unlimited access to their subjects (52–3). For Dylan biographer Dennis McDougal, "Shelton abandoned whatever remained of his journalistic objectivity" when he encountered Dylan (137).

19   Rimbaud's assertion appears in a long letter of 1871 to Paul Demeny on the poet's vocation, enjoining self-awareness, for which he uses musical creation as a metaphor, and famously asserting that the poet must become a visionary via "a long, boundless, and systematized *disorganization of all the senses*" (Rimbaud 102), a statement Dylan references in his statement that "I might have to disorientate

myself" (*Chronicles* 71). Martin Buber's *I and Thou*, advancing a dialogical philosophy based in the mystical Hasidic tradition, is focused on the relationship of self and other; it was popular in the 1960s: "I require a You to become; becoming I, I say You. All actual life is encounter" (62). In the fallout from the media exposure of his background in 1963, Dylan read Buber and almost certainly *I and Thou* (Shelton 139).

20 On *Bound for Glory*'s impact on Dylan, see Petrus and Cohen (255) and Shelton (62–3).

21 Lanois has recently noted that "Bob says his songs can be done in any time signature, in any key with any chord. It's really about the lyric" (Lanois qtd. in "Dylan at 80" 71).

22 *Tarantula* is termed a novel by Neil Corcoran (15), Tudor Jones (111), Alex Abramovich (150), and Shelton (15). Echoing *Heart of Darkness*, Shelton calls *Tarantula* "an enigma wrapped in a question mark," and he cites Gabrielle Goodchild's remark that "the book wrote him as much as he wrote it" (qtd. in Shelton 166, 167). *Tarantula* is often ignored in critical work on Dylan, even in discussions of Dylan's status as a "literary artist" within *The Cambridge Companion to Bob Dylan* (Dettmar 3). Similarly, famous Joyce scholar Sean Latham, within a perceptive study of Dylan's historically grounded musical invention, refers to *Tarantula* briefly as Dylan's "largely abandoned novel" ("Songwriting" 40), as if it were unfinished and unworthy of sustained critical attention.

23 Will Self suggests a connection with Lennon's prose works when he calls *Tarantula* a "Lennon-esque poetic grab bag" (vii). See, too, Clinton Heylin's *The Double Life of Bob Dylan* (303–7).

24 Jeff Tweedy more recently has acted as a kind of comic go-between for Dylan and Staples, whose Grammy-winning *You Are Not Alone* (2010) Tweedy produced (265). Tweedy's memoir presents a facetious, self-deprecating linkage between the author's often bathetic *bildungs* narrative and superstar moments such as Springsteen's smash hit, Dylan's motorcycle crash, Strummer's post-marriage Telecaster, and Richards' heroin addiction—the Nowheresville, USA equivalents of the rock 'n' roll stations of the cross.

25 Dylan said that it lacked a "framework" or "structure" and "it just wasn't a book," having been assembled "like a collage of scraps of paper" (qtd. in Shelton 262, 167). According to David Hajdu, Dylan coveted the novelistic abilities of Richard Fariña, recognized by Thomas Pynchon, and Fariña in turn was jealous of Dylan's $10,000 advance and his ease in securing a book contract due to his musical fame (222, 217).

26 Lisa O'Neill Sanders of Saint Peters University (personal communication). Shelton refers briefly to an earlier manuscript of *Tarantula* (167).

27 Louis A. Renza notes that "Dylan here turns the black female singer/song into a trope for an unself-conscious mode of both composing and performing lyrics from which he himself feels socially but not spiritually barred" (167, n.3).
28 Nietzsche's *Thus Spoke Zarathustra* may also be a source (Heylin, *Behind* 195–6).
29 Renza importantly reminds us of the fundamental distinction between songwriters and their songs (xii).
30 This is the sort of sentiment Dylan loathed, as evidenced by his exasperation at the Weavers' Ronnie Gilbert's introduction at the Newport Folk Festival: "take him ... he's yours" (*Chronicles* 115); George Harrison would introduce him similarly at the Concert for Bangladesh as "a friend of us all."
31 Hajdu points out that Pennebaker's film is a cinema verité parody of *A Hard Day's Night*, itself a cinema verité parody (250).
32 See Tudor Jones on Dylan's influence on Lennon (49–50).
33 According to Hajdu, Dylan would later disavow the sincerity of his protest songs in his fury at *Newsweek*'s November 1963 exposé of his inauthenticity (277–8, 192–5), and Dylan's vitriol would extend to his cruel rejection of Baez and his refusal to reciprocate the career boost she had offered him (246–7, 252–4). Dylan was and continues to be perceived as politically radical. The extremist Weathermen took their name from Dylan's "Subterranean Homesick Blues": "You don't need a weatherman / To know which way the wind blows" (Ayers 145, 232), with the member who suggested the name, Terry Robbins, dying in the explosion of a bomb intended for an NCO dance at Fort Dix (Rudd 146). The Weathermen would write their own parodic "Weather songs," such as "I'm dreaming of a white riot" and "We all live in a Weatherman machine," and eventually and expediently embrace counterculture hedonism, which they had previously dismissed for its apolitical stance, as "inherently revolutionary" (Rudd 188, 226).
34 "In My Life," however, as Kit O'Toole and Kenneth Womack argue, may effect a transformation of simple nostalgia (1). Lennon and Dylan battled in Dylan's "4th Time Around" response to Lennon's "Norwegian Wood," and Lennon's "Serve Yourself" response to Dylan's "Gotta Serve Somebody" (Womack, *John* 61–2, 66); while a fervent admirer, Lennon was biting about some of Dylan's rhymes: "I'm stuck inside of a lexicon with the *Roget's Thesaurus* blues again" (Lennon qtd. in Womack, *John* 63).
35 Nietzsche writes: "In our youthful years we respect and despise without that art of nuance which constitutes the best thing we gain from life, and, as is only fair, we have to pay dearly for having assailed men and things with Yes and No in such a fashion. Everything is so regulated that the worst of all tastes, the taste for the unconditional, is cruelly misused and made a fool of until a man learns to introduce a little art into his feelings and even to venture trying the artificial: as

genuine artists of life do. The anger and reverence characteristic of youth seem to allow themselves no peace until they have falsified men and things in such a way that they can vent themselves on them—youth as such is something that falsifies and deceives. Later, when the youthful soul, tormented by disappointments, finally turns suspiciously on itself, still hot and savage even in its suspicion and pangs of conscience: how angry it is with itself now, how it impatiently rends itself, how it takes revenge for its long self-delusion, as if it had blinded itself deliberately! During this transition one punishes oneself by distrusting one's feelings; one tortures one's enthusiasm with doubts, indeed one feels that even a good conscience is a danger, as though a good conscience were a screening of oneself and a sign that one's subtler honesty had grown weary; and above all one takes sides, takes sides on principle, *against* 'youth'.—A decade later: and one grasps that all this too—was still youth!" (44).

36 See Hilary Edwards' "Protecting Life from Language" on the opposite process, moving from self-fashioning museum to written autobiography, in the work of John Ruskin.
37 Heylin's *The Double Life of Bob Dylan*, however, remarks on the paucity of pre-1966 manuscripts in the Archive (14–5, 304), though Mark A. Davidson details the cornucopia of what is present and the various constraints on the collection (325–34).
38 Dylan's 1973 *Writings and Drawings* earlier reproduced a few MS pages and line drawings.

Conclusion

As this inevitably preliminary, selective intervention in the ever-growing though still under-examined field of popular music autobiography has attempted to show, music people's lives increasingly constitute a vital part of the digital, textual, and visual experience of listening to music in the twenty-first century. They deserve attention as a kind of generational autobiography reflecting the paradigm shift in the history of popular music in the 1960s with musicians performing and recording music they had written themselves as well as with popular music's accelerating global circulation. Though embedded in our celebrity obsessed present, they also offer meditations on disability and mortality. Some, as we have seen, treat drug addiction as fame's analgesic, while others disdain rock star style celebrity altogether for the renown afforded by more traditionally sanctioned genres. A number also construct and interrogate performative selves, paradoxically reclaiming the private self in a public forum. They often embrace a relational identity. Increasingly, popular music autobiographies incorporate hyper-self-conscious meta-textuality reflecting humorously on their own place in what is rapidly becoming a well-established tradition. Taken together, popular music autobiographies indicate the mainstreaming of popular culture and particularly popular music, and the broader acceptance of popular musicians as artists and the work of the singer-songwriter-performer-musician as a distinct art form. They offer a portrait of an outsider class whose members often were raised in poverty and disadvantage. Along the same lines, they often portray an alternate meritocracy, and set out a methodology, however unsystematic, for escaping the determinations of social caste. Some of them may indicate a sub-set of working class autobiography.

These works also register the sweeping influence of the social and cultural revolution of the 1960s and its afterlives, despite its wacky stereotypes. Recent advances in cognitive science, for example, as much as the sadly wasted talents of Syd Barrett or Alexander (Skip) Spence,[1] show some of the lost opportunities of the 1960s and attempts at contemporary redress. Ryan Walsh explains the early failure of the promise of psychedelic drugs in the 1960s with the excesses of Timothy Leary (190–209) in an account of Van Morrison's and popular music's embrace of the occult as well as the East Coast version of Manson's family in Mel Lyman's commune, associated with Jim Kweskin's Jug Band. A "psychedelic renaissance" may be emerging in the twenty-first century, researching and re-evaluating the use of LSD in treating addictions, PTSD, and end-of-life care, after the official demonization of psychedelics in the early and mid-1960s due to horror at some of the catastrophic effects of approved drugs like Thalidomide and the inflammatory, insurrectionist pronouncements of counterculture figures like Leary (Dyck "Psychedelic").[2] Advances in cognitive science, moreover, suggest that while there is no individual gene, isolated DNA sequence, "single 'music center'" (Sacks xi), or "specific neural module" (G. Marcus 142) in the human brain for appreciating a song like "Yesterday," for example, music may be a kind of brain food (Marcus 195). Moreover, many of the neural reactions that take place in the brain when listening to music also occur when the music is recalled silently (Sacks xii). Even Charles Darwin recognized, as Daniel Levitin points out, that the ability to carry a tune, if not to look good holding a guitar, indicates a fitness for courtship (251). David Byrne, in his exploration of neurological explanations for the appreciation of music, reminds us that silence or "sonic fresh-air" is not merely an aural palate cleanser but a fundamental human right (327).

Theodore Roszak, in the late 1960s, recognized the potential of the "counter culture," a phrase he almost certainly coined, to confront the juggernaut of an urban-industrial "technocratic totalitarianism" and to effect transformative, systemic social and cultural change (*Counter* xiii). Comprising a small minority of the massive post-war boomer generation—in 1967, half of America's population was under twenty-five (*Counter* 27)—this alienated counterculture, which Roszak endorsed somewhat reluctantly as a pampered, infantalized voice of dissent, was fomenting a revolution in consciousness. The heterogeneity and esotericism of their demands and the dominant culture's expertise in co-opting critics restricted their achievements beyond, importantly, ending the Vietnam war and recognizing the rights of women, African Americans, and gays, and warning of approaching ecocide (*Elder* 19–40).[3] Roszak's work, as he acknowledged, was deeply influenced by Paul Goodman, the curmudgeonly professional provocateur and polymath artist, musician, sociologist, and founder of Gestalt therapy, who was almost as famous in the 1960s as he is forgotten today.[4]

Goodman's views and practices illustrate contemporary attitudes. His *Growing Up Absurd* (1960) addressed the "youth problems" of the late 1950s (213), the anxiety-inducing manifestations of a demographic time bomb. For Goodman, these problems were rooted in a type of generational existentialist crisis, a sane, moral response to an insane, absurd society which alienated young men from meaningful work and lifeways. These problems were the consequences of "the missed and compromised revolutions of modern times" (*Growing* 194). Women had no place in Goodman's formulation because he saw marriage and maternity as supplying them with social meaning (*Growing* 21). Goodman was an out bisexual, as announced in his published personal notebooks *Five Years*,[5] who "made passes at literally everyone" (Rorem 303), and outrageously declared "my homosexual needs have made me a nigger" ("Politics" 216), anticipating Lennon and Ono's controversial single "Woman is the Nigger of the World" (1972). Goodman's Reichian propensity for attempting to seduce students and colleagues largely terminated his teaching career. Goodman was a self-taught musician, composer, influencer of the music of others, and critic, who, for example, dismissed the Beats' "Negro jazz" as "childish" and "thin," advocating they pursue Balinese music instead (*Growing* 63, 64, 165). Composer and memoirist Ned Rorem, some of whose art songs have been performed by Judy Collins, acknowledged that Goodman had an "inestimable" influence on his music; Rorem also acknowledged, "I went to bed unsentimentally with Paul as long as he wanted but never initiated it" (*Knowing* 301, 304). Elton John's 2019 autobiography *Me*, detailing losing his virginity to his manager, John Reid, establishing an international AIDS foundation, and marrying as well as having children with his husband, David Furnish, shows some of the monumental advances of the past fifty years which Goodman could not have imagined.

By 2009, Roszak was anticipating a "longevity revolution" led by aging baby boomers living unprecedented long lives and positioned to realize the counterculture's social and spiritual dreams, "a second chance to reshape history" (*Elder* 180, 33). This revolution would entail accepting mutual dependence and putting away the things of youth by the generation which had created the cult of youth in the first place (*Elder* 183). While rarely referring to popular music, an absence he later regretted,[6] Roszak had located the counterculture's revolutionary zeitgeist in poetry, and particularly that of Shelly and Ginsberg, and he traced some of Ginsberg's values in Dylan's songs (*Counter* 63). The "[g]erontocracy" of aging rockers as a cohort manifested in their autobiographies may be less motivated to advance a revolutionary agenda other than, as with

Dylan or the Stones, vowing to continue writing and performing to the end (*Elder* 7).[7] "I can't retire until I croak," boasts Keith Richards (545), or as Tom Jones puts it with tongue in cheek: "I'm an 80-year-old sex symbol! ... More than likely I will die on stage" (qtd. in S. Dalton 27). "Getting old ... is such a bitch," remarks Rob Halford, contemplating his mother's, bandmate Glenn Tipton's, and fellow metal meister Ozzy Osborne's diagnoses of Parkinson's disease (323). Marianne Faithfull was hospitalized with Covid-19 in early 2020 and still suffers its devastating after-effects, though she "managed not to die" (qtd. in Barton 50). Some rock stars, from Ozzy to Elton John, have long enjoyed second careers in announcing retirements from touring or launching endlessly repeated farewell tours. After detailing life-threatening complications from a radical prostatectomy at the end of his autobiography, Elton John launches into grandiose plans for a three-year final tour as well as multiple post-tour projects, making it apparent that a work addiction might be added to those previously treated for cocaine, alcohol, and food (343–54). Before a definitive retirement from touring due to the physical demands of jazz-inflected, prog-rock drumming with Rush, after having for "forty years of touring ... played through a lot of pain" (156), Neil Peart published his autobiographical *Far and Wide* in 2016 and in January 2020 died of brain cancer. A year later, in January 2021, David Crosby—whose "notorious" 1967 song "Triad" about a ménage a trois contributed to his ouster from the Byrds—announced his erectile dysfunction in *Rolling Stone*: "It's one of those milestones you don't want to get to. ... It's not the end of the world, it's just the end of sex" ("Ask" 14).

In terms of generational dynamics, popular music autobiographies document a move away from popular music's being considered exclusively the province of the young or merely a Proustian sonic madeleine triggering memories of the heady days of the 1960s' post-war demographic explosion.[8] Producer and musician Daniel Lanois, whom Dylan writes about extensively in *Chronicles*, indicates in his memoir that Dylan's Grammy-winning *Time Out of Mind* (1997) "shattered" the time-worn "myth that rock 'n' roll belonged only to youth" (145). Dylan no doubt would agree with Jeff Tweedy—both with children in the music business—that popular music is not always merely a soundtrack or medium for "generational warfare" (qtd. in Marchese 2). However, David Keenan, from a different perspective, has argued that "[r]ock 'n' roll is an adolescent art form," "a relatively safe conduit" for burning off youthful energy and particularly testosterone, a theory for which he finds evidence in Paleolithic art (viii, ix). As a result, he regards rock as a conservative control mechanism, and perhaps the contemporary equivalent of a necessary stage in human development and social evolution. Hence, rock 'n' roll may be one of the later stages Piaget forgot or the adolescent stages he didn't investigate. It also may be that popular music time stamps the period when it was first heard or continues to evoke an energetic response. "[W]hatever age you may be," insists Rob Halford, " when you go to a heavy metal gig, you're a teenager again" (353).

Those 1960s musicians who died young, such as Brian Jones, Jimi Hendrix, Janis Joplin, Jim Morrison, and others are a specter that looms over the legacy of especially post-1960s rock music, a specter that has been interpreted as signifying the ultimate commitment to the music and to absolute authenticity, despite the woefully pathetic circumstances of their deaths. Rilke's *Duino Elegies*, something of a backpackers' classic in the 1960s—though never as popular as *On the Road*, *The Prophet*, or *Steppenwolf*—muses that reflecting on those who died young—and thus who never lived to write their autobiographies—fosters an appreciation of our transitional place in the world; moreover, mourning the death of a seemingly godlike youth, Rilke reflects, inaugurated the birth of music itself, in at least one myth of its origin (Leishman and Spender 104, 142).[9] "When young people die," however, wrote Cicero (106-43 BCE), "nature rebels and fights against this fate. A young person dying reminds me of a fire extinguished by a deluge" (147, 149). Popular music autobiographies perhaps register a movement away from fascination to horror in contemplating these deaths. If rock music's 1960s mythology has an uncomfortable association with death, then this association also darkens the summing up near the end of life which is an autobiographical convention. This association may also develop an awareness of physical limitation, *meditation mortis* or intimations of death, due to disability, age, or the passing of others.

Popular music autobiographies of the last few decades have coincided with "the golden age of pathography," a species of life writing devoted to documenting living with an acute illness (Laqueur).[10] They also show a certain humility in the face of mortality, the Senecan precept of a good death being one that follows living well and preferably post-dates the attainment of wisdom (Seneca 50). The notion of such humility or modesty, however, might elicit a colorful riposte from an Iggy Pop still performing and modeling, partly nude, in his seventh decade (Kent, "Four Ages" 244-66), or from counterculture filmmaker John Waters who muses pragmatically that the secret to, if not a good life, then at least graceful aging is to "never go to a nude beach" (98).[11] For Seneca (4 BCE-65 CE), who lived amid the spectacular violence of Caligula and Nero in Rome—which may have at least some resemblance to our post-truth, global pandemic-engulfed present—dying is a fundamental human right. While it should be prepared for—though it can't be rehearsed—it is certainly also a performance, and Seneca revered displays of courage or indifference at the last. As if anticipating an autobiographical account or the climax of a rock concert, he writes that "[j]ust as with storytelling, so with life: it's important how well it is done, not how long. … [O]nly put a good closer on it" (47). Though he died in the bath after opening his veins and finally taking poison, his suicide was ordered by Nero and he was sanguine and lucid till his demise, which was a very different end to that reported of Jim Morrison with a toxic dose of heroin in a Paris suite or of Paul Clayton who took a final bath with an electric heater in New York. They died in circumstances anything other than creative, original, or heroic—never attaining a comforting wisdom about their lives—reinforcing Thomas Laqueur's uncomfortable adage, "death, like youth, is wasted on the young" (Laqueur).

We are witnessing a period of crisis for musicians and the music industry with greatly diminished returns for recordings and possibly a generational shift away from popular music constituting the soundtrack of one's life, a trend exacerbated in the time of a global Covid-19 pandemic and other companion pandemics of fake news, conspiracy theories, domestic violence, toxic drug supply, and climate crisis. One result has been a renewed interest in concert attendance contingent upon a post-pandemic return to whatever will constitute the new normal and hence a return to appreciation for unique live performance vs "definitive" and endlessly repeatable recordings. This eventuality also entails a shift from solitary and mobile music consumption to communal and stationary listening to music. Whether the digital revolution has enabled popular music to break free and return to the spheres or whether its algorithmic logic and infinite choice have counterintuitively inaugurated popular music's death throes remains to be seen. Has unlimited internet access and illegal streaming that have made a universe of music available in the palm of the hand devalued music?[12] Has popular music's importance diminished with so much competition for clicks and cash within entertainment's distraction economy? Is the popular music autobiography merely a book-length requiem for popular music's revolutionary explosion in the 1960s, a verdict on the cultural revolution of that rapidly receding decade, or a personal reminder that music is intellectual property but also a human activity rooted in a time when it was composed of voices, woodwinds, and strings, and not strings of zeros and ones blowing in the wind or stuck inside a cloud.[13]

Notes

1. LSD probably exacerbated Pink Floyd's Barrett's underlying mental health condition (Kent, "Cracked" 105–14), and this may also be true for Moby Grape's Spence, whose solo album *Oar*, recorded after a stay in New York's Bellevue asylum in 1968, following a catastrophic drug binge and a psychotic break, may be a type of autobiography or confession. Jud Cost remarks in an essay in *Oar*'s 1999 reissue booklet, "[t]he songs on *Oar* are the work of a repentant sinner" ("Through a Glass Darkly").
2. See, too, Dyck's *Psychedelic Psychiatry*.
3. The largely disillusioned 1960s radical Osha Neumann, for whom "revolution" was as much "therapy" as politics, laments, "[t]he hippy counter-culture of the Sixties has melted away. What's left is a residue of trivial curiosities: tie-dyed shirts, psychedelic posters, aging rock stars—hardly an impressive legacy" (151, 149). Former Weatherman Mark Rudd regrets the Weather Underground's destruction of the SDS and hence its undermining of anti-Vietnam war protest, despite the cautions of the Vietnamese (156, 168, 190–1), as well as its embrace of cult-like, sexist, and Stalinist practices. Designating all white Americans as legitimate targets for violence in order to bring the war home was similarly counterproductive. He does feel nostalgic for the revolutionary zeal of the 1960s, however ineffective, in comparison with the apolitical attitudes he perceives in young people in the early 2000s: "The seductions of the entertainment and consumer cultures, fueled by cheap goods and easy credit, have achieved almost total hegemony as the purpose of individual life" (312).
4. He was admired by Noam Chomsky, and Susan Sontag called him "our Sartre, our Cocteau" ("On Paul" 9). See Jonathan Lee's documentary *Paul Goodman Changed My Life* (2011).
5. Amid despairing notes on his circumstances, Goodman acknowledges that his same-sex affairs have "damaged my reputation" and his pursuit of men has exposed him to danger: "occasionally being knocked down, threats of blackmail, or possibility of arrest" (*Five Years* 8, 248). He appears to disregard the possibility of long-term gay relationships, as he says, perhaps facetiously, "the meaning of homosexual love is that we both have penises and engage in sex" (50).
6. Roszak's 1995 "Introduction" noted this absence given that music "inspired and carried the best insights of the counter culture" (xxxiv), though *The Making of the Counter Culture* does refer somewhat oddly to Dylan's "psychedelic" songs and the Doors' "acid-rock" (63, 75), just as elsewhere it refers to virtually all drugs, from glue and marijuana to LSD, as "psychedelics" (155, n.1).

7 The Sex Pistols' Steve Jones includes "[b]eing old" in his "list of rock 'n' roll no-nos" (303–4).
8 Proust's novel refers to involuntary audio memory triggers, in addition to taste-related ones, and he subscribed to "Théâtrophone, a service that held a telephone receiver up at a concert, which allowed people to stay at home and hear live music on their receivers" (White, *Marcel Proust* 111).
9 Rilke writes that, lamenting the death of Linus, "the daring first notes of song pierced through the barren numbness; / and then in the startled space which a youth as lovely as a god / had suddenly left forever, the Void felt for the first time / that harmony which now enraptures and comforts and helps us" (Rilke 9).
10 See G. Thomas Couser on "autopathography" (*Memoir* 43–4).
11 As Jon Savage puts it, as a possible alternative, "dying young is the perfect way of retaining your youth" ("Juvenilia").
12 See Reynolds' *Retromania* (86–128).
13 Whatever its origins or modes of transmission, music like "the story of your life ... must / Take the ear strangely" (V.i.314–15). These are Alonso's words to Prospero about anticipating hearing the story of his life on the magical, musical island near the end of Shakespeare's *The Tempest*—not Dylan's inspiration for *Tempest*—where the chastened insurrectionist Stephano had earlier anticipated, "I shall have my music for nothing" (III.ii.150).

Acknowledgments

An earlier version of Chapter 1 first appeared in *a/b: Auto/Biography Studies* (26.2; January 2011) and is used by permission of Taylor & Francis: https://www.tandfonline.com. An earlier version of Chapter 2 first appeared in *Popular Music & Society* (38.2; March 2015) and is used by permission of Taylor & Francis: https://www.tandfonline.com. The cover image, "Paul Thek, Nude, Astride Zebra," 1965, by Peter Hujar is used with the permission of the Peter Hujar Archive. All errors are mine.

This book is dedicated to Marie Loughlin and Mark Lovesey, and in loving memory to Ryan Douglas Thomson (2003–21). *Resurgam*!

Works Cited

"3 Teens Kill 4." 12-page insert. *No Motive*. 3 Teens Kill 4. Remastered 1982 vinyl LP, Dark Entries, 2017.
3 Teens Kill 4. *No Motive*. Executive Producers. Robert Bradley and Alan Mace. 1982 vinyl LP remastered and reissued by Dark Entries, 2017.
Abramovich, Alex. "The Basement Tapes (1967; 1975)." *The Cambridge Companion to Bob Dylan*. Ed. Kevin J.H. Dettmar. 150–4.
Ackerley, J.R. *Hindoo Holiday* (1932). New York: New York Review Books, 2000.
Ackerley, J.R. *We Think the World of You* (1960). New York: New York Review Books, 2000.
Ackerley, J.R. *My Father and Myself* (1968). New York: New York Review Books, 1999.
Adorno, Theodor W. "On Popular Music." *Essays on Music*. Theodor Adorno. Ed. Richard Leppert. Trans. Susan H. Gillespie. Berkeley, CA: University of California Press, 2002. 437–69.
Aers, David. *Community, Gender, and Individual Identity: English Writing 1360–1430*. London: Routledge, 1988.
Ahmad, Salman with Robert Schroeder. *Rock & Roll Jihad, A Muslim Rock Star's Revolution*. New York: Free, 2010.
Aletti, Vince. "Interview with Vince Aletti." *Peter Hujar*. Ed. Thomas Sokolowski. New York University: Grey Art Gallery & Study Center, 1990. 33–40.
Aletti, Vince. *The Disco Files, 1973–78: New York's Underground, Week by Week*. New York: D.A.P., 2018.
Aletti, Vince. "No Part of Me Is Remote, My Dear." *Peter Hujar: Love and Lust*. Ed. Jeffrey Fraenkel. n.p.
Almond, Marc. *Tainted Life, The Autobiography*. London: Sidgwick & Jackson, 1999.
Ambrosino, Giancarlo, ed. *David Wojnarowicz: A Definitive History of Five or Six Years on the Lower East Side*. Los Angeles: Semiotext(e), 2006.
Anderson, Brett. *Coal Black Mornings*. London: Little, Brown, 2018.
Anderson, Brett. *Afternoons with the Blinds Drawn*. London: Little, Brown, 2019.
Anderson, Linda. *Autobiography*. 2nd ed. New York: Routledge, 2011.
Ant, Adam. *Stand & Deliver: The Autobiography*. London: Pan Macmillan, 2006.
Artaud, Antonin. "Appeal to Youth: Intoxication—Disintoxication." *Antonin Artaud: Selected Writings*. Antonin Artaud. Ed. Susan Sontag. Trans. Helen Weaver. New York: Farrar, Straus and Giroux, 1976. 338–40.
Artaud, Antonin. *Collected Works*. Antonin Artaud. Trans. Victor Corti. Vol. 4. London: Calder, 1999.

Artaud, Antonin. "An Affective Athleticism." *Collected Works*. Antonin Artuad. 100–6.
Artaud, Antonin. "Letters on Cruelty." *Collected Works*. Antonin Artaud. 77–9.
Artaud, Antonin. "No More Masterpieces." *Collected Works*. Antonin Artaud. 56–63.
Artaud, Antonin. "Theatre and Cruelty." *Collected Works*. Antonin Artaud. 64–67.
Artaud, Antonin. "The Theatre of Cruelty (*First Manifesto*)." *Collected Works*. Antonin Artaud. 68–76.
Augustine. *Confessions*. Trans. R.S. Pine-Coffin. London: Penguin, 1961.
Augustine. *The City of God against the Pagans*. Ed. and Trans. R.W. Dyson. Cambridge: Cambridge University Press, 1998.
Aurelius, Marcus. *Meditations*. Trans. Martin Hammond. London: Penguin, 2006.
Auslander, Philip. "Watch That Man: David Bowie: Hammersmith Odeon, London, July 3, 1973." *Performance and Popular Music: History, Place and Time*. Ed. Ian Inglis. Aldershot, Hampshire: Ashgate, 2006. 70–80.
Auslander, Philip. *Liveness: Performance in a Mediatized Culture*. 2nd ed. New York: Routledge, 2008.
Ayers, Bill. *Fugitive Days: Memoirs of an Antiwar Activist*. Boston: Beacon, 2009.
Babitz, Eve. "Jim Morrison Is Dead and Living in Hollywood." *I Used to Be Charming: The Rest of Eve Babitz*. Eve Babitz. Ed. Sara J. Kramer. New York: NYRB, 2019. 221–34.
Baez, Joan. *And A Voice to Sing With, A Memoir*. New York: Summit, 1987.
Bailey, Blake. *Cheever, A Life*. New York: Vintage, 2009.
Baker, Ginger with Ginette Baker. *Ginger Baker, Hellraiser: The Autobiography of the World's Greatest Drummer*. London: John Blake, 2009.
Barber, Lynn. "Lady Rolling Stone." *The Observer* (February 24, 2008). Available online: http://www.guardian.co.uk/film/2008/feb/24/1 (accessed July 9, 2021).
Barthel, Wolfgang and Max Kunze, eds. *Literary Memorial Museums*. Frankfurt: ICOM National Committee of the GDR, 1986.
Barton, Laura. "Marianne Faithfull: 'I Managed Not to Die.'" *Uncut* Take 289 (June 2021): 49–53.
Baudrillard, Jean. *The Transparency of Evil: Essays on Extreme Phenomena*. Trans. James Benedict. London: Verso, 1990.
Baudrillard, Jean. *Baudrillard Live, Selected Interviews*. Ed. Mike Gane. New York: Routledge, 1993.
Baudrillard, Jean. *Simulacra and Simulation*. Trans. Sheila Faria Glaser. Ann Arbor, MI: University of Michigan Press, 1994.
Baudrillard, Jean. *Fragments: Cool Memories III, 1991–95*. Trans. Emily Agar. London: Verso, 1997.
Baudrillard, Jean. *Paroxysm. Interviews with Philippe Petit*. Trans. Chris Turner. London: Verso, 1998.
Becker, Adam H. "Augustine's *Confessions*." *The Cambridge Companion to Autobiography*. Eds. Maria DiBattista and Emily O. Wittman. 23–34.

Becker, Jane S. *Selling Tradition: Appalachia and the Construction of an American Folk, 1930–1940*. Chapel Hill, NC: University of North Carolina Press, 1998.

Bedford, David. "The Beatles in Liverpool." *The Beatles in Context*. Ed. Kenneth Womack. 19–27.

Bennett, Andy. "Subcultures or Neotribes?: Rethinking the Relationship Between Youth, Style and Musical Taste." *The Popular Music Studies Reader*. Eds. Andy Bennett, Barry Shank, and Jason Toynbee. New York: Routledge, 2006. 106–13.

Bennett, Andy. "Identity: Music, Community, and Self." *The Routledge Reader on the Sociology of Music*. Eds. John Shepherd and Kyle Devine. New York: Routledge, 2015. 143–51.

Berridge, Virginia. *Opium and the People: Opiate Use and Drug Control Policy in Nineteenth and Early Twentieth Century England*. London: Free Association Books, 1999.

Bérubé, Michael. "Afterword." *Disability Studies: Enabling the Humanities*. Eds Sharon L. Snyder, Brenda Jo Brueggemann, and Rosemarie Garland-Thomson. New York: MLA, 2003. 337–43.

Bidlo, Mike. "Collaborators: Mike Bidlo [interviewed by Sylvère Lotringer]." *David Wojnarowicz*. Ed. Giancarlo Ambrosino. 27–33.

Black, Joel. "National Bad Habits: Thomas De Quincey's Geography of Addiction." *Thomas de Quincey: New Theoretical and Critical Directions*. Eds. Robert Morrison and Daniel Sanjiv Roberts. New York: Routledge, 2008. 143–64.

Blake, Mark, compiler. *Stone Me: The Wit and Wisdom of Keith Richards*. London: Aurum, 2008.

Blinderman, Barry. "Daniel S. Berger and Barry Blinderman in Conversation." *David Wojnarowicz: Flesh of My Flesh*. David Wojnarowicz. 78–99.

Bohlman, Philip. *The Study of Folk Music in the Modern World*. Bloomington: Indiana University Press, 1988.

Boyd, Pattie with Penny Junor. *Wonderful Tonight: George Harrison, Eric Clapton, and Me*. New York: Harmony, 2007.

Brackett, David. *Interpreting Popular Music*. Cambridge: Cambridge University Press, 1995.

Bramwell, Tony with Rosemary Kingsland. *Magical Mystery Tours: My Life with the Beatles*. New York: Thomas Dunne, 2005.

Brantley, Will and Nancy McGuire Roche, eds. *Conversations with Edmund White*. Jackson, Mississippi: University Press of Mississippi, 2017.

Braudy, Leo. *The Frenzy of Renown: Fame & Its History*. New York: Oxford University Press, 1986.

Braun, Rebecca. "Fetishising Intellectual Achievement: The Nobel Prize and European Literary Celebrity." *Celebrity Studies* 2.3 (2011): 320–34.

Brennan, Jake. *Disgraceland: Musicians Getting Away with Murder and Behaving Very Badly*. New York: Grand Central, 2019.

Brenner, Marie. "Deal with the Devil." *Vanity Fair* (Aug. 2017): 84–9, 120–3.

Breslin, David and David Kiehl. "Acknowledgments." *David Wojnarowicz: History Keeps Me Awake at Night*. Eds. David Breslin and David Kiehl. New York: Whitney Museum of American Art, 2018. 10–13.

Brinkley, Douglas and Johnny Depp. "Introduction." *House of Earth, A Novel*. Woody Guthrie. xi–xliv.

Brodie, Janet Farrell and Marc Redfield, eds. *High Anxieties: Cultural Studies in Addiction*. Berkeley, CA: University of California Press, 2002.

Brown, Peter and Steven Gaines. *The Love You Make*. New York: NAL, 2002.

Brown, Steve. "Collaborators: Steve Brown [interviewed by Sylvère Lotringer]." *David Wojnarowicz*. Ed. Giancarlo Ambrosino. 39–45.

Browne, David. *Dream Brother: The Lives & Music of Jeff and Tim Buckley*. New York: HarperCollins, 2001.

Bruss, Elizabeth. *Autobiographical Acts: The Changing Situation of a Literary Genre*. Baltimore: Johns Hopkins University Press, 1976.

Buber, Martin. *I and Thou*. Trans. Walter Kaufmann. New York: Charles Scribner's Sons, 1970.

Buckley, Jeff. *Jeff Buckley: His Own Voice: Journals, Objects & Ephemera*. Eds. Mary Guibert and David Browne. New York: Da Capo, 2019.

Buckton, Oliver S. *Secret Selves: Confession and Same-Sex Desire in Victorian Autobiography*. Chapel Hill, NC: University of North Carolina Press, 1998.

Bullock, Darryl W. *The Velvet Mafia: The Gay Men Who Ran the Swinging Sixties*. London: Omnibus, 2021.

Burgher, Elijah. "'Saint' Wojnarowicz." *David Wojnarowicz: Flesh of My Flesh*. David Wojnarowicz. 14–21.

Burroughs, William S. *Junky*. Ed. Oliver Harris. 50th Anniversary Definitive ed. New York: Penguin, 2003.

Burroughs, William S. "Prologue." *Junky*. William S. Burroughs. xxxvii–xli.

Byrne, David. *How Music Works*. San Francisco: McSweeney's, 2012.

Cale, John and Victor Bockris. *What's Welsh for Zen: The Autobiography of John Cale*. London: Bloomsbury, 1999.

Cappello, Mary. "Wending Artifice: Creative Nonfiction." *The Cambridge Companion to Autobiography*. Eds. Maria DiBattista and Emily O. Wittman. 237–52.

Carlisle, Belinda. *Lips Unsealed, A Memoir*. New York: Crown, 2010.

Carr, Cynthia. *Fire in the Belly: The Life and Times of David Wojnarowicz*. New York: Bloomsbury, 2012.

Carroll, Jim. *Forced Entries: The Downtown Diaries 1971–73*. New York: Penguin, 1987.

Cheever, Benjamin H. "Introduction." *The Journals of John Cheever*. John Cheever. vii–xi.

Cheever, John. *The Journals of John Cheever*. New York: Knopf, 1991.

Cheever, Susan. *Note Found in a Bottle, My Life as a Drinker, A Memoir*. New York: Washington Square, 1999.

Cheyette, Bryan. "On the 'D' Train: Bob Dylan's Conversions." *Do You, Mr Jones? Bob Dylan with the Poets & Professors*. Ed. Neil Corcoran. 221–52.

Cicero, Marcus Tullius. *How to Grow Old: Ancient Wisdom for the Second Half of Life*. Trans. Philip Freeman. Princeton: Princeton University Press, 2016.

Cinque, Toija. "Digital Shimmer: Popular Music and the Intimate Nexus between Fan and Star." *A Companion to Celebrity*. Eds. P. David Marshall and Sean Redmond. 440–55.

Clancy, Liam. *The Mountain of the Women: Memoirs of an Irish Troubadour*. New York: Doubleday, 2002.

Clapton, Eric. *Clapton*. New York: Broadway, 2007.

Clarke, Gary. *Elton, my Elton*. London: Smith Gryphon, 1995.

Clayton, Martin, Trevor Herbert, and Richard Middleton, eds. *The Cultural Study of Music: A Critical Introduction*. 2nd ed. New York: Routledge, 2012.

Clayton, Paul. *Nine Rare Traditional Ballads from Virginia*. University of Virginia MA in English Diss., 1957.

Cobain, Kurt. *Kurt Cobain: Journals*. New York: Riverhead Books, 2002.

Cocks, H.G. *Nameless Offences*. London: I. B. Tauris, 2003.

Cogley, Bridget. "Olson Kundig Reveals Plans for Bob Dylan Center in Oklahoma." *Dezeen* (June 28, 2018). Available online: https://www.dezeen.com/2018/06/28/olson-kundig-reveals-plans-for-bob-dylan-center-in-oklahoma/ (accessed July 9, 2021).

Cohen, Ronald D. *Rainbow Quest: The Folk Music Revival and American Society, 1940–1970*. Amherst, MA: University of Massachusetts Press, 2002.

Colacello, Bob. *Holy Terror: Andy Warhol Close Up*. New York: HarperCollins, 1990.

Coleman, Ray. *The Man Who Made The Beatles: An Intimate Biography of Brian Epstein*. New York: McGraw-Hill, 1989.

Collins, Shirley. *America Over the Water*. London: SAF, 2005.

Collins, Shirley. *All in the Downs: Reflections on Life, Landscape and Song*. London: Strange Attractor, 2018.

Colls, Robert and Katie Palmer Heathman. "Music of Englishness: National Identity and the First Folk Revival." *Handbook of Musical Identities*. Eds. Raymond Macdonald, David J. Hargreaves, and Dorothy Miell. Oxford: Oxford University Press, 2017. 751–69.

Coltman, Bob. *Paul Clayton and the Folksong Revival*. Lanham, Maryland: Scarecrow, 2008.

Cook, Matt. *London and the Culture of Homosexuality, 1885–1914*. Cambridge: Cambridge University Press, 2003.

Cooke, John Byrne. *On the Road with Janis Joplin*. New York: Berkley Books, 2014.

Coolidge, Rita with Michael Walker. *Delta Lady, A Memoir*. New York: Harper, 2016.

Cooper, Alice with Keith and Kent Zimmerman. *Alice Cooper, Golf Monster: A Rock 'n' Roller's Life and 12 Steps to Becoming a Golf Addict.* New York: Three Rivers, 2007.

Corcoran, Neil, ed. *Do You, Mr Jones? Bob Dylan with the Poets & Professors.* London: Vintage, 2017.

Corcoran, Neil. "Introduction: Writing Aloud." *Do You, Mr Jones? Bob Dylan with the Poets & Professors.* Ed. Neil Corcoran. 7–23.

Cornwall, Richard. "Incorporating Social Identities into Economic Theory." *A Queer World.* Ed. Martin Duberman. New York: New York University Press, 1997. 477–501.

Cosgrave, Bill. *Love Her Madly: Jim Morrison, Mary, and Me.* Toronto: Dundurn, 2020.

Cost, Jud. "Through a Glass Darkly." *Oar.* Alexander Spence. [CD] reissue booklet, 1991. n.p.

Cott, Jonathan. "The Lost Lennon Tapes." Interview with John Lennon. *Rolling Stone* 1120/1121 (Dec. 23, 2010–Jan. 6, 2011): 89–96, 120–1.

Cott, Jonathan, ed. *Bob Dylan: The Essential Interviews.* New York: Simon & Schuster, 2017.

Couser, G. Thomas. *Recovering Bodies: Illness, Disability, and Life Writing.* Madison, WI: University of Wisconsin Press, 1997.

Couser, G. Thomas. *Memoir, An Introduction.* Oxford: Oxford University Press, 2012.

Coyle, Michael and Jon Dolan. "Modeling Authenticity, Authenticating Commercial Models." *Reading Rock and Roll: Authenticity, Appropriation, Aesthetics.* Eds. Kevin J.H. Dettmar and William Richey. New York: Columbia University Press, 1999.

Crosby, David. *Since Then: How I Survived Everything and Lived to Tell About It.* New York: G.P. Putnam's Sons, 2006.

Crosby, David. *David Crosby: Remember My Name.* [DVD] Prod. Cameron Crowe. Sony Pictures Classics, 2019.

Crosby, David. "Ask Croz." *Rolling Stone* Issue 1347 (Jan. 2021): 14.

Crosby, David and Carl Gottlieb. *Long Time Gone: The Autobiography of David Crosby.* New York: Doubleday, 1988.

Cross, Charles R. *Cobain Unseen.* New York: Little, Brown, 2008.

Culley, Amy and Rebecca Styler. "Lives in Relation: Editorial." *Life Writing* 8.3 (Sept. 2011): 237–40.

Cunnell, Howard. "Fast This Time: Jack Kerouac and the Writing of *On the Road*." *On the Road: The Original Scroll.* Jack Kerouac. New York: Penguin, 2008. 1–52.

Dalton, David. *Who Is That Man? In Search of the Real Bob Dylan.* New York: Hachette, 2016.

Dalton, Stephen. "Revelations." *Uncut* Take 288 (May 2021): 27.

Daniel, Drew. *33 1/3: Twenty Jazz Funk Greats.* New York: Bloomsbury, 2020.

Danis, Melissa. "Moby Finds Inspiration in Cheever for Memoir." *Boston Globe* (May 12, 2016). Available online: http://www.bostonglobe.com/arts/books/2016/05/12/obsessing-cheever-and-percy/hWtKtjpCxOSKK73WBEL/story.html (accessed July 9, 2021).

Davidson, Guy. "'Just a Couple of Fags': Truman Capote, Gore Vidal, and Celebrity Feud." *Celebrity Studies* 7.3 (2016): 293–308.

Davidson, Mark A. "The Bob Dylan Archive." *The World of Bob Dylan*. Ed. Sean Latham. 325–34.

Davies, Dave. *Kink: An Autobiography*. New York: Hyperion, 1996.

Davies, Dave. "Kinks Legend: Dave Davies talks about his life, the music industry …" *YouTube* Sept. 20, 2013.

Davis, Clive with Anthony DeCurtis. *The Soundtrack of My Life: Clive Davis*. New York: Simon & Schuster, 2013.

Davis, Lennard J. *Bending Over Backwards: Disability, Dismodernism, and Other Difficult Positions*. New York: New York University Press, 2002.

Davis, Miles with Quincy Troupe. *Miles: The Autobiography of Miles Davis*. New York: Simon & Schuster, 2011.

DeAngelis, Michael and Mary Desjardins. "Introduction." *Celebrity Studies* 8.4 (2017): 489–92.

DeCurtis, Anthony. "Bob Dylan as Songwriter." *The Cambridge Companion to Bob Dylan*. Ed. Kevin J.H. Dettmar. 42–54.

DeCurtis, Anthony. *Lou Reed, A Life*. New York: Little, Brown, 2017.

De Man, Paul. "Autobiography as De-Facement." *Modern Language Notes* 94.5 (Dec. 1979): 919–30.

DeNora, Tia. *Music in Everyday Life*. Cambridge: Cambridge University Press, 2000.

DeNora, Tia. *Music Asylums: Wellbeing Through Music in Everyday Life*. New York: Routledge, 2016.

Dettmar, Kevin J.H., ed. *The Cambridge Companion to Bob Dylan*. Cambridge: Cambridge University Press, 2009.

Dettmar, Kevin J.H. "Introduction." *The Cambridge Companion to Bob Dylan*. Ed. Kevin J.H. Dettmar. 1–11.

DiBattista, Maria and Emily O. Wittman, eds. *The Cambridge Companion to Autobiography*. New York: Cambridge University Press, 2014.

DiBattista, Maria and Emily O. Wittman. "Introduction." *The Cambridge Companion to Autobiography*. Eds. Maria DiBattista and Emily O. Wittman. 1–20.

Dickinson, Bruce. *What Does This Button Do? An Autobiography*. New York: Dey St., 2017.

Didion, Joan. *The White Album*. New York: Farrar, Straus and Giroux, 2009.

Doggett, Peter. *Lou Reed*. London: Omnibus, 1991.

Doggett, Peter. *You Never Give Me Your Money*. New York: It Books, 2011.

Doughton, Steve. "Collaborators: Steve Doughton [interviewed by Sylvère Lotringer]." *David Wojnarowicz*. Ed. Giancarlo Ambrosino. 46–53.

Driver, Jim, ed. *The Mammoth Book of Sex, Drugs and Rock 'n' Roll*. New York: Carroll & Graf, 2006.

Duberman, Martin. *Cures*. New York: Dutton, 1991.

Du Bois, W.E.B. *The Souls of Black Folk*. New York: Penguin, 1996.
Dudley, Sandra H. "Museum Materialities: Objects, Sense and Feeling." *Museum Materialities: Objects, Engagements, Interpretations*. Ed. Sandra Dudley. London: Routledge, 2010. 1–17.
Dunn, Tim. *The Bob Dylan Copyright Files 1962–2007*. Bloomington, IN: AuthorHouse, 2008.
Dyck, Erika. *Psychedelic Psychiatry: LSD on the Canadian Prairies*. Winnipeg: University of Manitoba Press, 2012.
Dyck, Erika. "Psychedelic Research in 1950s Saskatchewan." *The Canadian Encyclopedia* (July 16, 2019). Available online: https://www.thecanadianencyclopedia.ca/en/article/psychedelic-research-in-1950s-saskatchewan (accessed July 9, 2021).
Dyer, Richard. *Stars*. London: BFI, 1979.
Dylan, Bob. *Writings and Drawings by Bob Dylan*. New York: Knopf, 1973.
Dylan, Bob. *Biograph*. [CD] Sony Music. 1985.
Dylan, Bob. *Chronicles, Volume One*. New York: Simon & Schuster, 2004.
Dylan, Bob. *Tarantula*. New York: Scribner, 2004.
Dylan, Bob. *The Lyrics: 1961–2012*. Eds. Christopher Ricks, Lisa Nemrow, and Julie Nemrow. New York: Simon & Schuster, 2014.
Dylan, Bob. *The Nobel Lecture*. New York: Simon & Schuster, 2017.
Dylan, Bob. *More Blood, More Tracks, The Deluxe Edition*. The Bootleg Series, Vol. 14. Columbia Records, Legacy, 2018.
"Dylan at 80." *Uncut* Take 289 (June 2021). 60–73.
Eakin, Paul John. *Living Autobiographically: How We Create Identity in Narrative*. Ithaca: Cornell University Press, 2008.
Edgar, Robert, Fraser Mann, and Helen Pleasance. "Introduction." *Music, Memory and Memoir*. Eds. Robert Edgar, Fraser Mann, and Helen Pleasance. New York: Bloomsbury, 2021. 1–9.
Edwards, Hilary. "Protecting Life from Language: John Ruskin's Museum as Autobiography." *Biography* 32.2 (Spring 2009): 297–315.
Eells, Josh. "Eminem: The Road Back From Hell." *Rolling Stone* Issue 1118 (Nov. 25, 2010): 48–54.
Elliott, Anthony. *The Mourning of John Lennon*. Berkeley, CA: University of California Press, 1999.
Ellis, Geoffrey. *I Should Have Known Better*. London: Thorogood, 2004.
Eminem. *The Way I Am*. New York: Plume, 2009.
English, James F. "The Nobel Prize: The Dramaturgy of Consecration." *The World of Bob Dylan*. Ed. Sean Latham. 299–312.
Epstein, Brian. *A Cellarful of Noise*. New York: Pocket Books, 1998.
Eribon, Didier. *Michel Foucault*. Trans. Betsy Wing. Cambridge: Harvard University Press, 1991.
Escott, Colin. *I Saw the Light: The Story of Hank Williams*. New York: Back Bay, 2015.

Fairchild, Charles and P. David Marshall. "Music and Persona: An Introduction." *Persona Studies* 5.1 (2019): 1–16.

Faithfull, Marianne with David Dalton. *Faithfull*. London: Penguin, 1994.

Faithfull, Marianne with David Dalton. *Memories, Dreams and Reflections*. London: Harper Perennial, 2008.

Fariña, Richard. *Long Time Coming and A Long Time Gone*. New York: Random House, 1969.

Faulks, Sebastian. *The Fatal Englishman*. New York: Vintage, 1996.

Ferguson, Moira. "Introduction." *The History of Mary Prince*. Mary Prince. Ed. Moira Ferguson. 1–51.

Filene, Benjamin. *Romancing the Folk: Public Memory and American Roots Music*. Chapel Hill, NC: University of North Carolina Press, 2000.

Flannery, Joe with Mike Brocken. *Standing in the Wings*. Stroud, Gloucestershire: History Press, 2013.

Flea [Michael Balzary]. *Acid for the Children, a Memoir*. New York: Grand Central, 2019.

Ford, Simon. *Wreckers of Civilisation*. London: Black Dog, 1999.

Foucault, Michel. "Contemporary Music and the Public." Discussion with Pierre Boulez. *Politics, Philosophy, Culture: Interviews and Other Writings, 1977–1984*. Michel Foucault. Ed. Lawrence D. Kritzman. New York: Routledge, 1988. 314–22.

Foucault, Michel. "Technologies of the Self." *Technologies of the Self: A Seminar with Michel Foucault*. Eds. Luther H. Martin, Huck Gutman, and Patrick H. Hutton. Amherst, MA: University of Massachusetts Press, 1988. 16–49.

Foucault, Michel. "Truth, Power, Self: An Interview with Michel Foucault." Foucault interviewed by Rux Martin. *Technologies of the Self: A Seminar with Michel Foucault*. Eds. Luther H. Martin, Huck Gutman, and Patrick H. Hutton. Amherst, MA: University of Massachusetts Press, 1988. 9–15.

Fowlie, Wallace. "My Journal on the Two Rebel Artists." *Rimbaud and Jim Morrison: The Rebel as Poet, A Memoir*. Wallace Fowlie. Durham: Duke University Press, 1993. 1–34.

Fox, Michael J. *Lucky Man: A Memoir*. New York: Hyperion, 2003.

Fox, Pamela. "*Born to Run* and *Reckless: My Life as a Pretender*. Rewriting the Political Imaginary of Rock Music Memoir." *Popular Music and the Politics of Hope: Queer and Feminist Interventions*. Eds. Susan Fast and Craig Jennex. New York: Routledge, 2019. 123–42.

Fraenkel, Jeffrey, ed. *Peter Hujar: Love and Lust*. San Francisco: Fraenkel Gallery, 2014.

Frank, Arthur W. *The Wounded Storyteller: Body, Illness, and Ethics*. Chicago, IL: University of Chicago Press, 1995.

Frank, Arthur W. *The Renewal of Generosity: Illness, Medicine, and How to Live*. Chicago, IL: University of Chicago Press, 2004.

Frantz, Chris. *Remain in Love: Talking Heads, Tom Tom Club, Tina*. New York: St. Martin's Press, 2020.

Frawley, Maria H. *Invalidism and Identity in Nineteenth-Century Britain*. Chicago, IL: University of Chicago Press, 2004.

Freedman, Jean R. *Peggy Seeger: A Life of Music, Love, and Politics*. Urbana, IL: University of Illinois Press, 2017.

Freeman, Philip. "Introduction." *How to Grow Old*. Cicero. Trans. Philip Freeman. Princeton, NJ: Princeton University Press, 2016. vii–xvii.

Frith, Simon. "'The Magic that Can Set You Free': The Ideology of Folk and the Myth of the Rock Community." *Popular Music* 1 (1981): 159–68.

Frith, Simon. "The Cultural Study of Popular Music." *Cultural Studies*. Eds. Lawrence Grossberg, Cary Nelson, and Paula A. Treichler. 174–86.

Frith, Simon. *Performing Rites: On the Value of Popular Music*. Cambridge, MA: Harvard University Press, 1998.

Frith, Simon. "Music and Everyday Life." *The Cultural Study of Music: A Critical Introduction*. Eds. Martin Clayton, Trevor Herbert, and Richard Middleton. 149–58.

Frith, Simon and Howard Horne. *Art Into Pop*. London: Routledge, 2016.

Gamson, Joshua. *Claims to Fame: Celebrity in Contemporary America*. Berkeley, CA: University of California Press, 1994.

Garland-Thomson, Rosemarie. "Integrating Disability, Transforming Feminist Theory." *Gendering Disability*. Eds. Bonnie G. Smith and Beth Hutchison. New Brunswick: Rutgers University Press, 2004. 73–106.

Gass, William. "The Art of Self: Autobiography in an Age of Narcissism." *Harper's Magazine* (May 1994): 43–52.

Gefter, Philip. *Wagstaff: Before and After Mapplethorpe, A Biography*. New York: Liveright, 2015.

Geller, Deborah and Anthony Wall. *The Brian Epstein Story*. London: Faber & Faber, 2000.

Gibb, Barry. "The Mojo Interview." Gibb interviewed by Jim Irvin. *Mojo* Issue 328 (March 2021): 28–33.

Giorno, John. *Great Demon Kings: A Memoir of Poetry, Sex, Art, Death, and Enlightenment*. New York: Farrar, Straus and Giroux, 2020.

Glass, Loren. "Brand Names: A Brief History of Literary Celebrity." *A Companion to Celebrity*. Eds. P. David Marshall and Sean Redmond. 39–57.

Glissant, Édouard. *Poetics of Relation*. Trans. Betsy Wing. Ann Arbor, MI: University of Michigan Press, 1997.

Goldberg, Danny. *Bumping into Geniuses: My Life Inside the Rock and Roll Business*. New York: Gotham, 2008.

Goldsmith, Lynn. "Talking Heads." *Uncut* Take 277 (June 2020): 100–5.

Goldstein, Kenneth S. *A Guide for Field Workers in Folklore*. Hatboro, PA: Folklore Associates, 1964.

Goodman, Lizzy. *Meet Me In The Bathroom: Rebirth and Rock and Roll in New York City 2001–2011*. New York: Dey St., 2017.

Goodman, Paul. *Five Years: Thoughts During a Useless Time*. New York: Vintage, 1969.

Goodman, Paul. "The Politics of Being Queer." *Nature Heals: The Psychological Essays of Paul Goodman*. Paul Goodman. Ed. Taylor Stoehr. Gouldsboro, ME: Gestalt Journal Press, 1991. 216–25.

Goodman, Paul. *Growing Up Absurd: Problems of Youth in the Organized Society* [1960]. New York: New York Review Books, 2012.

Gopnik, Blake. *Warhol*. New York: Ecco, 2020.

Gordon, Kim. *Girl in a Band, A Memoir*. New York: Dey St., 2015.

Goss, Nina and Eric Hoffman. "Introduction." *Tearing the World Apart: Bob Dylan and the Twenty-First Century*. Eds. Nina Goss and Eric Hoffman. Jackson: University Press of Mississippi, 2017. 3–11.

Gottlieb, Robert. "Editor's Note." *The Journals of John Cheever*. John Cheever. 397–99.

Gray, Timothy. *It's Just the Normal Noises: Marcus, Guralnick, No Depression, and the Mystery of Americana Music*. Iowa City: University of Iowa Press, 2017.

Green, Robin. *The Only Girl: My Life and Times on the Masthead of Rolling Stone*. London: Virago, 2018.

Greene, Andy. "A Brief History of Love and Theft." *Bob Dylan: The Complete Album Guide*. Editors of *Rolling Stone*. 2017: 94–5.

Greene, Andy. "The Mix: Billy Joel." *Rolling Stone* Issue 1327 (May 2019): 38.

Greenslade, William. *Degeneration, Culture and the Novel 1880–1940*. Cambridge: Cambridge University Press, 1994.

Grossberg, Lawrence, Cary Nelson, and Paula A. Treichler, eds. *Cultural Studies*. New York: Routledge, 1992.

Guattari, Felix. "David Wojnarowicz." *In the Shadow of Forward Motion*. David Wojnarowicz. New York: P.P.O.W. 1988, n.p. Reprinted by Primary Information, 2020.

Guthrie, Woody. *Bound for Glory*. London: Penguin, 2004.

Guthrie, Woody. *House of Earth, A Novel*. New York: Harper Perennial, 2013.

Gutting, Gary. "Introduction: Michel Foucault: A User's Manual." *The Cambridge Companion to Foucault*. Ed. Gary Gutting. 2nd ed. Cambridge: Cambridge University Press, 2005. 1–28.

Hackett, Pat. "Introduction." *The Andy Warhol Diaries*. Andy Warhol. x–xxi.

Hagan, Joe. "Question & Answer: Joe Hagan on His Explosive Biography of *Rolling Stone*'s Jann Wenner." Joe Hagan interviewed by Elon Green. *Columbia Journalism Review* (Oct. 19, 2017). Available online: https://www.cjr.org/the-feature/jann-wenner-biography.php (accessed July 9, 2021).

Hagan, Joe. *Sticky Fingers: The Life and Times of Jann Wenner and Rolling Stone Magazine*. New York: Knopf, 2017.

Hair, Julie. "Collaborators: Julie Hair [interviewed by Sylvère Lotringer]." *David Wojnarowicz*. Ed. Giancarlo Ambrosino. 18–25.

Hajdu, David. *Positively 4th Street: The Lives and Times of Joan Baez, Bob Dylan, Mimi Baez Fariña, and Richard Fariña*. New York: North Point, 2002.

Halford, Rob with Ian Gittins. *Confess, the Autobiography*. New York: Hachette, 2020.

Halperin, David M. "Why Gay Shame Now?" *Gay Shame*. Eds. David Halperin and Valerie Traub. Chicago, IL: University of Chicago Press, 2009. 41–6.

Halpern, Jake. *Fame Junkies: The Hidden Truths Behind America's Favorite Addiction*. New York: Houghton Mifflin, 2007.

Hamm, Charles. "Review." Review of Richard Middleton's *Studying Popular Music*. *The Journal of Musicology*. 9.3 (Summer 1991): 376–98.

Hampton, Timothy. *Bob Dylan's Poetics: How the Songs Work*. New York: Zone, 2019.

Harkins, Anthony and Meredith McCarroll. "Introduction: Why This Book?" *Appalachian Reckoning*. Eds. Anthony Harkins and Meredith McCarroll. Morgantown, WV: West Virginia University Press, 2019. 1–15.

Harris, Oliver. "Introduction." *Junky*. William S. Burroughs. ix–xxxiii.

Harrison, George. *I, Me, Mine*. New York: Simon and Schuster, 1980.

Harry, Debbie, in collaboration with Sylvie Simmons. *Face It*. New York: Dey St., 2019.

Hayes, Patrick. "Human 2.0? Life-Writing in the Digital Age." *On Life-Writing*. Ed. Zachary Leader. Oxford: Oxford University Press, 2018. 233–56.

Hell, Richard. *I Dreamed I Was a Very Clean Tramp, An Autobiography*. New York: Ecco, 2013.

Hell, Richard. *Massive Pissed Love: Nonfiction 2001–2014*. Berkeley: Soft Skull, 2015.

Hell, Richard. "CBGB as a Physical Space." *Massive Pissed Love: Nonfiction 2001–2014*. 154–7.

Hell, Richard. "'Punk' Couture: Insides Out." *Massive Pissed Love: Nonfiction 2001–2014*. 117–20.

Hentoff, Nat. "The Crackin', Shakin', Breakin' Sounds." *The New Yorker* (Oct. 24, 1964). https://www.newyorker.com/magazine/1964/10/24/the-crackin-shakin-breakin-sounds.

Heron, Mike and Andrew Greig. *You Know What You Could Be*. London: Riverrun, 2017.

Hersh, Kristin. *Paradoxical Undressing*. London: Atlantic, 2011.

Heylin, Clinton. *Bob Dylan: Behind the Shades*. 20th Anniversary ed. London: Faber & Faber, 2011.

Heylin, Clinton. *The Double Life of Bob Dylan: A Restless, Hungry Feeling, 1941–1966*. New York: Little, Brown, 2021.

Hilburn, Robert. *Paul Simon, The Life*. New York: Simon & Schuster, 2018.

Hill, Mary. "1972-Film Culture No. 76, 1992 [Harry Smith interviewed by Mary Hill]." *Think of the Self Speaking: Harry Smith—Selected Interviews*. Ed. Rani Singh. Seattle: Elbow/Cityful Press, 1999. 166–79.

Hocquenghem, Guy. *Homosexual Desire*. Trans. Daniella Dangoor. Durham: Duke University Press, 1993.

Hofler, Robert. *The Man Who Invented Rock Hudson*. New York: Carroll & Graf, 2005.

Holiday, Billie with William Dufty. *Lady Sings the Blues*. London: Penguin, 1984.

Hontiveros, Romeo. "Daily Readings with Reflections" (Oct. 15, 2016). www.pagadiandiocese.org/2016/10/14/readings-reflections-saturday-of-the-twenty-eighth-week-in-ordinary-time-st-teresa-of-avila-october-152016/.

Hook, Peter. *Unknown Pleasures: Inside Joy Division*. London: Simon & Schuster, 2012.

Houlbrook, Matt. *Queer London*. Chicago, IL: University of Chicago Press, 2005.

Hoye, Jacob. *Smoke, Snort, Swallow, Shoot: Legendary Binges, Lost Weekends, and Other Feats of Rock 'n' Roll Incoherence*. New York: Lesser Gods, 2017.

Hudson, Robert. *The Monk's Record Player: Thomas Merton, Bob Dylan, and the Perilous Summer of 1966*. Grand Rapids, MI: William B. Eerdmans Publishing Company, 2018.

Hultberg, Jesse. "Jesse Hultberg Interview." *QMH* (May 2005). Available online: www.queermusicheritage.com/may2005s.html (accessed July 9, 2021).

Hutcheon, Linda. *A Theory of Parody: The Teaching of Twentieth-Century Art Forms*. New York, Methuen, 1985.

Hynde, Chrissie. *Reckless: My Life As a Pretender*. Toronto: Random House, 2015.

Igliori, Paola, ed. *American Magus Harry Smith: A Modern Alchemist*. New York: Inanout Press, 1996.

Jameson, Fredric. *Postmodernism, or, The Cultural Logic of Late Capitalism*. Durham, NC: Duke University Press, 1991.

Janes, Robert R. *Museums in a Troubled World: Renewal, Irrelevance or Collapse*. London: Routledge, 2009.

Jarnow, Jesse. *Wasn't That A Time: The Weavers, the Blacklist, and the Battle for the Soul of America*. New York: Da Capo, 2018.

John, Elton. *Me*. New York: Henry Holt, 2019.

"John Mayer's Penis Speaks!" *Huffpost* (April 14, 2010). Available online: http://www.huffpost.com/entry/john-mayers-penis-speaks_n_459842 (accessed July 9, 2021).

Jones, Steve with Ben Thompson. *Lonely Boy: Tales From a Sex Pistol*. New York: Da Capo, 2017.

Jones, Tudor. *Bob Dylan and the British Sixties*. New York: Routledge, 2019.

Kaag, John. *Hiking with Nietzsche: On Becoming Who You Are*. New York: Picador, 2018.

Kane, Larry. *When They Were Boys*. Philadelphia: Running Press, 2013.

Keenan, David. *England's Hidden Reverse: A Secret History of the Esoteric Underground: Coil, Current 93, Nurse With Wound*. Expanded ed. London: Strange Attractor, 2016.

Keightley, Keir. "Long Play: Adult-Oriented Popular Music and the Temporal Logics of the Post-War Sound Recording Industry in the USA." *Media, Culture & Society* 26.3 (2004): 375–91.

Kellein, Thomas. *The Dream of Fluxus: George Maciunas: An Artist's Biography*. London: Edition Hansjörg Mayer, 2007.

Kempe, Margery. *The Book of Margery Kempe*. Trans. Barry Windeatt. London: Penguin, 1994.

Kent, Nick. *The Dark Stuff: Selected Writings on Rock Music*. Cambridge, MA: Da Capo, 2002.

Kent, Nick. "The Cracked Ballad of Syd Barrett." *The Dark Stuff*. 98–114.

Kent, Nick. "The Four Ages of a Man Named Pop: Pictures of Iggy." *The Dark Stuff*. 244–66.

Kern, Richard. "Collaborators: Richard Kern [interviewed by Sylvère Lotringer]." *David Wojnarowicz*. Ed. Giancarlo Ambrosino. 62–73.

Kiedis, Anthony with Larry Sloman. *Scar Tissue*. New York: Hyperion, 2004.

Klein, Joe. *Woody Guthrie, A Life*. New York: Delta, 1980.

Knell, Simon J. "Museums, Reality and the Material World." *Museums in the Material World*. Ed. Simon Knell. London: Routledge, 2007. 1–28.

Koch, Stephen. *Stargazer: The Life, World, and Films of Andy Warhol*. Revised and updated. New York: Marion Boyars, 2002.

Koch, Stephen. "If You're Vincent, You've Got To Have Your Theo." Interview with Stephen Koch by Matthew Leifheit. Matte 2013. Available online: Artfcity.com/2013/10/15/Stephen-koch-peter-hujar-if-youre-vincent-youve-got-to-have-your-theo/ (accessed July 9, 2021).

Koch, Stephen. "The Pictures: Securing Peter Hujar's Place Among the Greats." *Harper's Magazine* (2018). Available online: https://harpers.org/archive/2018/05/the-pictures/ (accessed July 9, 2021).

Kramer, Lawrence. "Subjectivity Unbound: Music, Language, Culture." *The Cultural Study of Music*. Eds. Martin Clayton, Trevor Herbert, and Richard Middleton. 395–406.

Kramer, Wayne. *The Hard Stuff: Dope, Crime, the MC5 & My Life of Impossibilities*. New York: Hachette, 2020.

Kravitz, Lenny with David Ritz. *Let Love Rule*. New York: Henry Holt, 2020.

Lahr, John. *Prick Up Your Ears: The Biography of Joe Orton*. New York: Avon, 1980.

Lahr, John. "Introduction." *The Orton Diaries*. Joe Orton. Ed. John Lahr. London: Methuen, 1989. 11–31.

Lanegan, Mark. *Sing Backwards and Weep, A Memoir*. Ed. Mishka Shubaly. New York: Hachette, 2020.

Lanois, Daniel with Keisha Kalfin. *Soul Mining: A Musical Life*. New York: Farrar, Straus and Giroux, 2011.

Laqueur, Thomas. "Nothing Becomes Something." Review of Paul Kalanithi's *When Breath Becomes Air*. *London Review of Books* 38.18 (Sept. 22, 2016). Available online: https://www.lrb.co.uk/the-paper/v38/n18/thomas-laqueur/nothing-becomes-something (accessed July 9, 2021).

Latham, Sean, ed. *The World of Bob Dylan*. Cambridge: Cambridge University Press, 2021.

Latham, Sean. "Songwriting." *The World of Bob Dylan*. Ed. Sean Latham. 31–45.

Lebowitz, Fran. "To Me They Look Like Peter: An Interview with Fran Lebowitz by Thomas Sokolowski." *Peter Hujar: Love and Lust*. Ed. Jeffrey Fraenkel. n.p.

Lee, Jonathan. *Paul Goodman Changed My Life*. [DVD] Zeitgeist Films, 2011.

Lee, Laura. *Oscar's Ghost: The Battle over Oscar Wilde's Legacy*. Stroud, Gloucestershire: Amberley, 2017.

Leibovitz, Annie. *A Photographer's Life 1900–2005*. Ed. Mark Holborn. New York: Random House, 2006.

Leishman, J.B. and Stephen Spender. "Commentary." *Duino Elegies*. Rainer Maria Rilke. Trans. J.B. Leishman and Stephen Spender. London: Chatto & Windus, 1977. 101–47.

Leitch, Donovan. *The Autobiography of Donovan: The Hurdy Gurdy Man*. New York: St. Martin's, 2005.

Lejeune, Philippe. *On Autobiography*. Trans. Katherine Leary. Ed. John Paul Eakin. Minneapolis, MN: University of Minnesota Press, 1989.

Lennon, Cynthia. *John*. London: Hodder & Stoughton, 2005.

Lennon, John. *Skywriting by Word of Mouth and Other Writings, including The Ballad of John and Yoko*. New York: HarperPerennial, 1996.

Lerner, Jonathan. *Alex Underground*. PenPowerPublishing, 2009.

Lerner, Jonathan. *Swords in the Hands of Children: Reflections of an American Revolutionary*. New York: OR Books, 2017.

Levithan, Robert. *The New 60: Outliving Yourself and Reinventing a Future*. North Charleston, SC: CreateSpace, 2012.

Levitin, Daniel J. *This Is Your Brain On Music: The Science of a Human Obsession*. New York: Plume, 2007.

Lewisohn, Mark. *Tune In. The Beatles: All These Years*. Vol. 1. New York: Crown, 2013.

Light, Alan. *The Holy or the Broken: Leonard Cohen, Jeff Buckley and the Unlikely Ascent of "Hallelujah."* New York: Atria, 2012.

Lindon, Mathieu. *Learning What Love Means*. Trans. Bruce Benderson. South Pasadena, CA: Semiotext(e), 2017.

Linton, Simi. "Reassigning Meaning." *The Disability Studies Reader*. Ed. Lennard J. Davis. 2nd ed. New York: Routledge, 2006. 161–72.

Lloyd, Richard. *Everything is Combustible: Television, CBGB's, and Five Decades of Rock and Roll: The Memoirs of an Alchemical Guitarist*. Mount Desert, Maine: Beech Hill, 2019.

Lochrie, Karma. "*The Book of Margery Kempe*: The Marginal Woman's Quest for Literary Authority." *Journal of Medieval and Renaissance Studies* 16.1 (Spring 1986): 33–55.

Lomax, Alan. *The Land Where the Blues Began*. New York: Delta, 1993.

Lomax, John A. *Adventures of a Ballad Hunter*. Austin: University of Texas Press, 2017.

Long, April. "Patti Smith." Patti Smith interviewed by April Long. *Uncut* Take 281 (October 2020): 52–7.

Love, Courtney. *The Diaries of Courtney Love*. London: Faber & Faber, 2006.

Lovesey, Oliver. "Anti-Orpheus: Narrating the Dream Brother." *Popular Music* 23.3 (October 2004): 331–48.

Lovesey, Oliver. "The 'World' Before Globalization: Moroccan Elements in The Incredible String Band's Music." *Popular Music* 30.1 (January 2011): 127–43.

Lovesey, Oliver. "Decolonizing the Ear: Introduction to 'Popular Music and the Postcolonial.'" *Popular Music and the Postcolonial*. Ed. Oliver Lovesey. New York: Routledge, 2019. 1–4.

Lovesey, Oliver. "The British Invasion of the Wild West: Country Parody in the Rolling Stones and Other British Bands." *The Routledge Companion to Popular Music and Humor*. Eds. Thomas Kitts and Nick Baxter-Moore. New York: Routledge, 2019. 169–76.

Lovesey, Oliver. "Introduction to 'Woodstock University': The Idea of Woodstock." *Popular Music and Society*. Special Issue: Woodstock University. Ed. Oliver Lovesey 43.2 (May 2020): 121–5.

Lovesey, Oliver. "Pop Art at Woodstock: Sha Na Na." *Popular Music and Society*. Special Issue: Woodstock University. Ed. Oliver Lovesey 43.2 (May 2020): 158–62.

Lovesey, Oliver. "The Victorian Guitar: Exoticism and Extinction Discourse from Radcliffe to Wilde." *Music & Letters* 101.3 (August 2020): 489–511.

Lowenthal, Leo. "The Triumph of Mass Idols." *The Celebrity Studies Reader*. Ed. P. David Marshall. 124–52.

Lure, Walter with Dave Thompson. *To Hell and Back*. Guilford, CT: Backbeat, 2020.

Lydon, Michael. "The Doors." *Guardian* (May 22, 2013). Available online: http://www.theguardian.com/music/2013/may/22/the-doors-rocks-backpages-classic-interview (accessed July 9, 2021).

MacColl, Ewan. *Journeyman, An Autobiography*. Re-edited by Peggy Seeger. Manchester: Manchester University Press, 2009.

MacDonald, Raymond, David J. Hargreaves, and Dorothy Miell, eds. *Handbook of Musical Identities*. Oxford: Oxford University Press, 2017.

Macey, David. *The Lives of Michel Foucault*. London: Vintage, 1993.

Machado de Assis. *The Posthumous Memoirs of Brás Cubas*. Trans. Flora Thomson-DeVeaux. New York: Penguin, 2020.

MacIsaac, Ashley with Francis Condron. *Fiddling with Disaster: Clearing the Past*. Toronto: Warwick, 2003.

Madden, Patrick. "The 'New Memoir.'" *The Cambridge Companion to Autobiography.* Eds. Maria DiBattista and Emily O. Wittman. New York: Cambridge University Press, 2014. 222–36.

Mallinder, Stephen. "Foreword." *Assimilate: A Critical History of Industrial Music.* S. Alexander Reed. ix–xiv.

Mancuso, Chuck. *Popular Music and the Underground: Foundations of Jazz, Blues, Country, and Rock, 1900–1950.* Dubuque, IA: Kendall/Hunt, 1996.

Marchese, David. "Jeff Tweedy's Family Affair." *Rolling Stone* Issue 1217 (September 11, 2014): 20–1.

Marcus, Gary. *Guitar Zero: The Science of Becoming Musical at Any Age.* New York: Penguin, 2012.

Marcus, Greil. *Bob Dylan By Greil Marcus, Writings 1968–2010.* New York: Publicaffairs, 2010.

Marcus, Greil. *Three Songs, Three Singers, Three Nations.* Cambridge: Harvard University Press, 2015.

Marcus, Laura. *Autobiography, A Very Short History.* Oxford: Oxford University Press, 2018.

Margotin, Philippe and Jean-Michel Guesdon. *Bob Dylan: All the Songs.* New York: Black Dog & Leventhal, 2015.

Marr, Johnny. *Set the Boy Free, The Autobiography.* New York: Dey St., 2017.

Marshall, Lee. "Bob Dylan and the Academy." *The Cambridge Companion to Bob Dylan.* Ed. Kevin J.H. Dettmar. 100–9.

Marshall, P. David. "The Celebrity of the Beatles." *The Beatles, Popular Music and Society: A Thousand Voices.* Ed. Ian Inglis. Macmillan, 2000. 163–75.

Marshall, P. David, ed. *The Celebrity Culture Reader.* New York: Routledge, 2006.

Marshall, P. David. "Introduction." *The Celebrity Culture Reader.* Ed. P. David Marshall. 1–15.

Marshall, P. David. "New Media—New Self: The Changing Power of Celebrity." *The Celebrity Culture Reader.* Ed. P. David Marshall. New York: Routledge, 2006. 634–44.

Marshall, P. David. "The Celebrity Legacy of the Beatles." *The Celebrity Culture Reader.* Ed. P. David Marshall. 501–9.

Marshall, P. David. "The Meanings of the Popular Music Celebrity." *The Celebrity Culture Reader.* Ed. P. David Marshall. 196–222.

Marshall, P. David. "Introduction: Celebrity in the Digital Age." *Celebrity and Power.* P. David Marshall. 2nd ed. Minneapolis: University of Minnesota Press, 2014. xi–xlvi.

Marshall, P. David and Sean Redmond, eds. *A Companion to Celebrity.* Chichester, West Sussex: John Wiley & Sons, 2016.

Marshall, P. David and Sean Redmond. "Introduction." *A Companion to Celebrity.* Eds. P. David Marshall and Sean Redmond. 1–13.

Marshall, Scott M. *Bob Dylan: A Spiritual Life.* Washington, DC: WND Books, 2017.

Martyn, Beverley. *Sweet Honesty: The Beverley Martyn Story*. Guildford, Surrey: Grosvenor House, 2011.

Maymudes, Victor. *Another Side of Bob Dylan: A Personal History on the Road and Off the Tracks*. Co-written and ed. by Jacob Maymudes. New York: St. Martin's/Griffin, 2014.

McCarron, Andrew. *Light Come Shining: The Transformations of Bob Dylan*. Oxford: Oxford University Press, 2017.

McCooey, David. "The Limits of Life Writing." *Life Writing* 14.3 (2017): 277–80.

McCormick, Carlo. "Afterword." *Seven Miles a Second*. David Wojnarowicz and James Romberger. 60–4.

McCormick, Carlo. "Collaborators: Carlo McCormick [interviewed by Sylvère Lotringer]. *David Wojnarowicz*. Ed. Giancarlo Ambrosino. 11–16.

McDougal, Dennis. *Dylan: The Biography*. New York: Wiley, 2014.

McNeil, Legs and Gillian McCain, eds. *Please Kill Me: The Uncensored Oral History of Punk*. 20th Anniversary ed. New York: Grove Press, 2016.

Melley, Timothy. "A Terminal Case: William Burroughs and the Logic of Addiction." *High Anxieties. Cultural Studies in Addiction*. Berkeley, CA: University of California Press, 2002. 38–60.

Mendelssohn, Michèle. *Making Oscar Wilde*. Oxford: Oxford University Press, 2018.

Middleton, Richard. *Studying Popular Music*. Milton Keynes: Open University Press, 1990.

Middleton, Richard. *Voicing the Popular: On the Subjects of Popular Music*. London: Routledge, 2006.

Miles, Barry. *Many Years From Now*. London: Vintage, 1998.

Miller, James. *The Passion of Michel Foucault*. New York: Simon & Schuster, 1993.

Miller, Merle. *On Being Different: What It Means to Be a Homosexual* [1971]. New York: Penguin, 2012.

Moby. *Porcelain, A Memoir*. New York: Penguin, 2017.

Moby. *Then It Fell Apart*. London: Faber & Faber, 2019.

Mollin, Larry. *Search: Paul Clayton, The Man Who Loved Bob Dylan*. Los Angeles: Steele Spring Stage Rights, 2013.

Montagu, Lord Edward. *Wheels Within Wheels*. London: Weidenfeld & Nicolson, 2000.

Montaigne, Michel de. *Essays*. Trans. J.M. Cohen. London: Penguin, 1993.

Moore-Gilbert, Bart. *Postcolonial Life-Writing: Culture, Politics and Self-representation*. London: Routledge, 2009.

Morin, Peter. "My Life as a Museum, or, Performing Indigenous Epistemologies." *Embodied Politics in Visual Autobiography*. Eds. Sarah Brophy and Janice Hladki. Toronto: University of Toronto Press, 2014. 137–52.

Morrison, Robert. *De Quincey The English Opium Eater: A Biography of Thomas*. London: Weidenfeld & Nicolson, 2009.

Morrissey. *Autobiography*. London: Penguin, 2013.

Morrissey. *List of the Lost*. London: Penguin, 2015.
Motion, Andrew. *The Lamberts*. London: Chatto & Windus, 1986.
Munro, John Neil. *Some People Are Crazy: The John Martyn Story*. Edinburgh: Polygon, 2008.
Muzak, Joanne. "'They Say the Disease is Responsible': Social Identity and the Disease Concept of Drug Addiction." *Unfitting Stories: Narrative Approaches to Disease, Disability, and Trauma*. Waterloo, Ontario: Wildrid Laurier University Press, 2007. 255–64.
Myers, Paul. *It Ain't Easy*. Vancouver: Greystone, 2007.
Nalbantian, Suzanne. *Aesthetic Autobiography*. Houndmills, Basingstoke: Macmillan, 1994.
Napier-Bell, Simon. *You Don't Have To Say You Love Me*. London: Ebury, 1998.
Napier-Bell, Simon. *Black Vinyl White Powder*. London: Ebury, 2001.
Neil, Vince with Mike Sager. *Tattoos & Tequila: To Hell and Back with One of Rock's Most Notorious Frontmen*. New York: Grand Central Publishing, 2010.
Neill, Ben. "Collaborators: Ben Neill [interviewed by Sylvère Lotringer]." *David Wojnarowicz*. Ed. Giancarlo Ambrosino. 112–15.
Nemec, Belinda. "Autobiographical Museums." *Museums and Biographies: Stories, Objects, Identities*. Ed. Kate Hill. Martlesham, Suffolk: Boydell & Brewer, 2012. 279–93.
Neumann, Osha. *Up Against the Wall Motherf**ker: A Memoir of the '60s, with Notes for Next Time*. New York: Seven Stories, 2008.
Ngũgĩ wa Thiong'o. "Orature in Education." *Approaches to Teaching the Works of Ngũgĩ wa Thiong'o*. Ed. Oliver Lovesey. New York: MLA Publications, 2012. 1–4.
Nicholson, Virginia. *How Was It For You: Women, Sex, Love and Power in the 1960s*. New York: Viking, 2019.
Nietzsche, Friedrich. *Beyond Good and Evil: Prelude to a Philosophy of the Future*. Trans. R.J. Hollingdale. Harmondsworth, Middlesex: Penguin, 1984.
Nietzsche, Friedrich. *Ecce Homo*. Trans. R.J. Hollingdale. London: Penguin, 2004.
Nolan, David. *Bernard Sumner: Confusion: Joy Division, Electronic and New Order Versus the World*. Church Stretton, Shropshire: Independent Music Press, 2007.
Norman, Philip. *John Lennon*. Toronto: Doubleday, 2008.
Northcutt, William M. "The Spectacle of Alienation: Death, Loss, and the Crowd in *Sgt. Pepper's Lonely Hearts Club Band*." *Reading the Beatles: Cultural Studies, Literary Criticism, and the Fab Four*. Eds. Kenneth Womack and Todd F. Davis. 129–46.
Nuttall, Jeff. *Bomb Culture*. Ed. Douglas Field and Jay Jeff Jones. London: Strange Attractor Press, 2018.
Ono, Yoko. *Grapefruit*. New York: Simon and Schuster, 1970.
Orton, Joe. *The Orton Diaries*. Ed. John Lahr. London: Methuen, 1986.
O'Toole, Kit and Kenneth Womack. "Introduction: The Act You've Known for All These Years." *Fandom and the Beatles*. Eds. Kenneth Womack and Kit O'Toole. New York: Oxford University Press, 2021. 1–16.
Pang, May with Henry Edwards. *Loving John*. New York: WarnerBooks, 1983.

Parker, Peter. *Ackerley, A Life of J.R. Ackerley*. London: Constable, 1989.
Peart, Neil. *Far and Wide: Bring That Horizon to Me!* Toronto: ECW, 2016.
Pecknold, Diane. *The Selling Sound: The Rise of the Country Music Industry*. Durham: Duke University Press, 2007.
Pescatello, Ann M. *Charles Seeger, A Life in American Music*. Pittsburgh, PA: University of Pittsburgh Press, 1992.
Peterson, Richard A. *Creating Country Music: Fabricating Authenticity*. Chicago, IL: University of Chicago Press, 1997.
Petridis, Alexis. "Straight and Narrow: How Pop Lost Its Gay Edge." *Guardian* (February 28, 2012). Available online: https://www.theguardian.com/music/2012/feb/28/how-pop-lost-gay-edge (accessed July 9, 2021).
Petridis, Alexis. "Music." Review of Bob Dylan's *Rough and Rowdy Ways*. *The Guardian Weekly* 203.2 (June 26, 2020): 56.
Petrus, Stephen and Ronald D. Cohen. *Folk City: New York and the American Folk Music Revival*. Oxford: Oxford University Press, 2015.
Phillips, John. *Papa John, An Autobiography*. New York: Dell, 1987.
Phillips, Mackenzie with Hilary Liftin. *High on Arrival*. New York: Simon Spotlight Entertainment, 2009.
P-Orridge, Genesis Breyer, ed. *Painful But Fabulous: The Lives & Art of Genesis P-Orridge*. Brooklyn, NY: Soft Skull, 2002.
P-Orridge, Genesis Breyer. *Brion Gysin: His Name Was Master: Texts & Interviews by Genesis Breyer P-Orridge with Peter Christopherson and Jon Savage*. Ed. Andrew M. McKenzie. Stockholm: Trapart Books, 2018.
P-Orridge, Genesis Breyer. *Sacred Intent: Conversations and Travels with Carl Abrahamsson, 1986–2019*. Stockholm, Sweden: Trapart Books, 2020.
P-Orridge, Genesis Breyer. *Nonbinary, A Memoir*. New York: Abrams, 2021.
Postcards From America. [DVD] Dir. Steve McLean. Strand Releasing, 2001.
Prince, Mary. The *History of Mary Prince*. Ed. Moira Ferguson. Ann Arbor, MI: University of Michigan Press, 1997.
Pringle, Thomas. "Preface." *The History of Mary Prince*. Mary Prince. 55–6.
Quayson, Ato. *Aesthetic Nervousness: Disability and the Crisis of Representation*. New York: Columbia University Press, 2007.
Rak, Julie. *Boom! Manufacturing Memoir for the American Public*. Waterloo, Ontario, Canada: Wilfrid Laurier University Press, 2013.
Rauffenbart, Tom. "Introduction." *Seven Miles a Second*. David Wojnarowicz and James Romberger, 2.
Rauffenbart, Tom. "Collaborators: Tom Rauffenbart. [interviewed by Cynthia Carr]." *David Wojnarowicz*. Ed. Giancarlo Ambrosino. 143–53.
Redfield, Marc and Janet Farrell Brodie. "Introduction." *High Anxieties: Cultural Studies in Addiction*. Eds. Janet Farrell Brodie and Marc Redfield. Berkeley, CA: University of California Press, 2002. 1–15.

Reed, Lou. "Fallen Knights and Fallen Ladies." *No-one Waved Good-bye: A Casualty Report on Rock and Roll*. Ed. Robert Somma. London: Charisma, 1973. 81–92.

Reed, S. Alexander. *Assimilate: A Critical History of Industrial Music*. Oxford: Oxford University Press, 2013.

Rees, Helen. "'Temporary Bypaths'? Seeger and Folk Music Research." *Understanding Charles Seeger, Pioneer in American Musicology*. Eds. Bell Yung and Helen Rees. 84–108.

Reeve, Christopher. *Still Me*. New York: Ballantine, 1998.

Reiff, Corbin. *Total F*cking Godhead: The Biography of Chris Cornell*. New York: Post Hill, 2020.

Reilly, Maura. *Curatorial Activism: Towards an Ethics of Curating*. London: Thames & Hudson, 2018.

Renza, Louis A. *Dylan's Autobiography of a Vocation: A Reading of the Lyrics 1965–1967*. New York: Bloomsbury, 2019.

Repsch, John. *The Legendary Joe Meek*. London: Woodford House, 1989.

Reynolds, Simon. *Rip It Up and Start Again: Post-punk 1978–1984*. London: Faber & Faber, 2006.

Reynolds, Simon. *Retromania: Pop Culture's Addiction to Its Own Past*. New York: Farrar, Straus and Giroux, 2011.

Richards, Keith with James Fox. *Life*. New York: Little, Brown and Company, 2010.

Ricks, Christopher. *Dylan's Visions of Sin*. New York: Ecco, 2005.

Riley II, Charles A. *Disability and the Media: Prescriptions for Change*. Hanover: University Press of New England, 2005.

Rilke, Rainer Maria. *Duino Elegies and The Sonnets to Orpheus*. Trans. Stephen Mitchell. New York: Vintage, 2009.

Rimbaud, Arthur. *Arthur Rimbaud: Complete Works*. Trans. Paul Schmidt. New York: Harper & Row, 1976.

Robertson, Robbie. *Testimony*. New York: Knopf, 2016.

Roessner, Jeffrey. "Revolution 2.0: Beatles Fan Scholarship in the Digital Age." *New Critical Perspectives on the Beatles: Things We Did Today*. Eds. Kenneth Womack and Katie Kapurch. 221–40.

Rogers, Jude. "Not the Only One: How Yoko Ono Helped Create John Lennon's Imagine." *Guardian* (October 6, 2018). Available online: https://www.theguardian.com/culture/2018/oct/06/how-yoko-ono-helped-create-john-lennon-imagine (accessed July 9, 2021).

Rojek, Chris. *Celebrity*. London: Reaktion, 2001.

Rojek, Chris. *Frank Sinatra*. Cambridge: Polity, 2004.

Rojek, Chris. *Pop Music, Pop Culture*. Cambridge: Polity, 2011.

Rorem, Ned. *Knowing When to Stop, A Memoir*. New York: Simon & Schuster, 1994.

Rosebud. "Rosebud." Rosebud Feliu-Pettet interviewed by Paola Igliori (October 12, 1995). *American Magus Harry Smith*. Ed. Paola Igliori. 97–105.

Rosenberg, Neil V. "Introduction." *Transforming Tradition: Folk Music Revivals Examined*. Ed. Neil V. Rosenberg. Urbana, IL: University of Illinois Press, 1993. 1–25.

Roszak, Theodore. *The Making of a Counter Culture: Reflections on the Technocratic Society and the Youthful Opposition*. Berkeley, CA: University of California Press, 1995.

Roszak, Theodore. "Introduction." *The Making of a Counter Culture: Reflections on the Technocratic Society and the Youthful Opposition*. Theodore Roszak. xi–xxxvii.

Roszak, Theodore. *The Making of an Elder Culture: Reflections on the Future of America's Most Audacious Generation*. Gabriola Island, BC: New Society Publishers, 2009.

Rotolo, Suze. *A Freewheelin' Time: A Memoir of Greenwich Village in the Sixties*. New York: Broadway, 2008.

Rousseau, Jean-Jacques. *Confessions*. Ed. Patrick Coleman. Trans. Angela Scholar. Oxford: Oxford University Press, 2008.

Rousseau, Jean-Jacques. "Preface to the Neuchâtel Edition of *Confessions*." *Confessions*. Jean-Jacques Rousseau. 643–9.

Rowell, Margit, ed. *Antonin Artaud: Works on Paper*. New York: Museum of Modern Art, 1996.

Rowell, Margit. "A Conversation with Patti Smith." *Antonin Artaud: Works on Paper*. Ed. Margit Rowell. 141–3.

Rudy, Jill Terry. "Transforming Audiences for Oral Tradition: Child, Kittredge, Thompson, and the Connections of Folklore and English Studies." *College English* 66.5 (May 2004): 524–44.

Rudd, Mark. *Underground: My Life with SDS and the Weathermen*. New York: Harper, 2010.

Sacks, Oliver. *Musicophilia: Tales of Music and the Brain*. Rev. ed. Toronto: Vintage, 2008.

Saint Teresa of Ávila. *The Life of Saint Teresa of Ávila by Herself*. Trans. J.M. Cohen. London: Penguin, 1957.

Salinger, J.D. *The Catcher in the Rye*. New York: Little, Brown, 1991.

Savage, Jon. "Juvenilia and Other Delinquencies: An Interview with Jon Savage." Savage interviewed by Andrew Gallix. *3:AM Magazine* (May 16, 2007). Available online: https://www.3ammagazine.com/3am/juvenilia-and-other-delinquencies-an-interview-with-Jon-Savage/ (accessed July 9, 2021).

Savage, Jon. *England's Dreaming: Sex Pistols and Punk Rock*. London: Faber & Faber, 2016.

Savage, Jon. "Introduction." *As Time Goes By*. Derek Taylor. London: Faber & Faber, 2018. 1–13.

Scaduto, Anthony. *Bob Dylan*. New York: Grosset & Dunlap, 1971.

Schemel, Patty with Erin Hosier. *Hit So Hard, A Memoir*. New York: Da Capo, 2017.

Schumacher, Michael. *There But For Fortune: The Life of Phil Ochs*. New York: Hyperion, 1996.

Seaman, Frederic. *The Last Days of John Lennon, A Personal Memoir*. New York: Dell, 1991.

Sedgwick, Eve Kosofsky. *Tendencies*. Durham: Duke University Press, 1993.

Sedgwick, Eve Kosofsky. *Between Men: English Literature and Male Homosocial Desire*. 13th ed. New York: Columbia University Press, 2016.

Seeger, Charles. "Tradition and the (North) American Composer: A Contribution to the Ethnomusicology of the Western World (1967)." *Studies in Musicology II: 1929–1979*. Charles Seeger. Ed. Ann M. Pescatello. Berkeley, CA: University of California Press, 1994. 411–26.

Seeger, Peggy. *First Time Ever, A Memoir*. London: Faber & Faber, 2018.

Self, Will. "Foreword." *Do You, Mr Jones? Bob Dylan with the Poets & Professors*. Ed. Neil Corcoran. vii–xv.

Sell, Mike. *Avant-Garde Performance & the Limits of Criticism: Approaching the Living Theatre, Happenings/Fluxus, and the Black Arts Movement*. Ann Arbor, MI: University of Michigan Press, 2005.

Seneca, Lucius Annaeus. *How to Die: An Ancient Guide to the End of Life*. Ed. and Trans. James S. Romm. Princeton, NJ: Princeton University Press, 2018.

Shafer, David A. *Antonin Artaud*. London: Reaktion, 2016.

Shain, Britta Lee. *Seeing the Real You at Last: Life and Love on the Road with Bob Dylan*. London: Jawbone, 2016.

Shakespeare, William. *The Tempest*. Ed. Robert Langbaum. New York: Signet, 1998.

Shapiro, Harry. *Jack Bruce: Composing Himself, The Authorised Biography*. London: Genuine Jawbone, 2010.

Shaw, Philip. *33 1/3: Horses* [2008]. New York: Bloomsbury, 2020.

Shears, Jake. *Boys Keep Swinging, A Memoir*. New York: Atria, 2019.

Shelton, Robert. *No Direction Home*. Revised ed. Elizabeth Thomson and Patrick Humphries. London: Omnibus, 2011.

Shepherd, John. "Music and Social Categories." *The Cultural Study of Music: A Critical Introduction*. Eds. Martin Clayton, Trevor Herbert, and Richard Middleton. 239–48.

Shepard, Sam. *The One Inside*. New York: Knopf, 2017.

Shields, Andrew. "TopperPost #228: Paul Clayton." 2014. Available online: http://www.toppermost.co.uk/paul-clayton/ (accessed July 9, 2021).

"Silence is Golden." Letter to the Editor. *The Globe and Mail* (October 28, 1978): 7.

Silverstein, Charles and Felice Picano. "Introduction: A Brief History of *The Joy of Gay Sex*." *The Joy of Gay Sex*. Charles Silverstein and Felice Picano. 3rd ed. New York: HarperResou, 2006. xv–xx.

Simon, Carly. *Boys in the Trees, A Memoir*. New York: Flatiron Books, 2015.

Simpson, Rose. *Muse, Odalisque, Handmaiden: A Girl's Life in the Incredible String Band*. London: Strange Attractor, 2020.

Simpson, Rose. "Scattered Brightness: A Performer's View of Woodstock 1969." *Popular Music and Society*. Special Issue: Woodstock University. Ed. Oliver Lovesey. 43.2 (May 2020): 126–37.

Sinfield, Alan. *The Wilde Century*. New York: Columbia University Press, 1994.

Sixx, Nikki with Ian Giffins. *The Heroin Diaries: A Year in the Life of a Shattered Rock Star*. New York: Pocket, 2007.

Slash with Anthony Bossa. *Slash*. New York: HarperCollins, 2007.

Slick, Grace and Andrea Cagan. *Grace Slick: Somebody to Love? A Rock-and-Roll Memoir*. New York: Grand Central Publishing, 1999.

Smith, Joel. "A Gorgeous Mental Discretion." *Peter Hujar: Speed of Life*. Ed. Joel Smith. Barcelona, Spain: Fundación MAPRE, 2017. 10–33.

Smith, Joel and Martha Scott Burton. "Chronology." *Peter Hujar: Speed of Life*. Ed. Joel Smith. Barcelona, Spain: Fundación MAPRE, 2017. 229–38.

Smith, Patti. "A Note to the Reader." *The Petting Zoo*. Jim Carroll. New York: Viking, 2010. v–vi.

Smith, Patti. *Just Kids*. New York: Ecco, 2010.

Smith, Patti. *The Coral Sea*. New York: Norton, 2012.

Smith, Patti. "How Does It Feel." *The New Yorker* (December 14, 2016). Available online: https://www.newyorker.com/culture/culturalcomment/patti-smith-on-singing-at-bob-dylans-nobel-prize-ceremony (accessed July 9, 2021).

Smith, Patti. *M Train*. New York: Vintage, 2016.

Smith, Patti. *Devotion*. New Haven: Yale University Press, 2017.

Smith, Patti. "Foreword." *The One Inside*. Sam Shepard. New York: Knopf, 2017. ix–xii.

Smith, Patti. *Year of the Monkey*. New York: Knopf, 2019.

Smith, Paul. *Discerning the Subject*. Minneapolis, MN: University of Minnesota Press, 1988.

Smith, Sidonie. "Performativity, Autobiographical Practice, Resistance." *Life Writing in the Long Run*. Sidonie Smith and Julia Watson. 261–82.

Smith, Sidonie and Julia Watson. *Reading Autobiography: A Guide for Interpreting Life Narratives*. 2nd ed. Ann Arbor, MI: University of Minnesota Press, 2010.

Smith, Sidonie and Julia Watson. *Life Writing in the Long Run*. Ann Arbor, MI: Maize, 2016.

Smith, Sidonie and Julia Watson. "A Personal Introduction to *Life Writing in the Long Run*." *Life Writing in the Long Run*. Sidonie Smith and Julia Watson. xix–li.

Snyder, Sharon L. and David T. Mitchell. *Cultural Locations of Disability*. Chicago, IL: University of Chicago Press, 2006.

Sontag, Susan. "Photographic Life/Death." *Vogue* vol. 166. Issue 9. (September 1976): 348–9.

Sontag, Susan. *Illness as Metaphor and AIDS and Its Metaphors*. New York: Anchor, 1989.
Sontag, Susan. *Regarding the Pain of Others*. New York: Picador, 2003.
Sontag, Susan. *As Consciousness Is Harnessed to Flesh: Journals & Notebooks 1964–1980*. Ed. David Rieff. New York: Picador, 2012.
Sontag, Susan. "Against Interpretation." *Susan Sontag: Essays of the 1960s & 70s*. Ed. David Rieff. New York: Library of America, 2013. 10–285.
Sontag, Susan. *The Complete Rolling Stone Interview*. Sontag interviewed by Jonathan Cott. New Haven: Yale UP, 2013.
Sontag, Susan. *Susan Sontag: Later Essays*. Ed. David Rieff. New York. Library of America, 2017.
Sontag, Susan. "Approaching Artaud." *Susan Sontag: Later Essays*. Susan Sontag. 11–53.
Sontag, Susan. "On Paul Goodman." *Susan Sontag: Later Essays*. Susan Sontag. 5–10.
Sounes, Howard. *FAB*. New York: Doubleday, 2010.
Sounes, Howard. *Down the Highway: The Life of Bob Dylan*. New York: Grove, 2011.
Spencer, Neil. "The Dylan Industry." *The Guardian Weekly* 204.15 (April 2, 2021): 51–4.
Springfield, Rick. *Late, Late at Night, A Memoir*. New York: Touchstone, 2010.
Springsteen, Bruce. *Born to Run*. New York: Simon & Schuster, 2017.
Stairway to Heaven: The Final Resting Places of Rock's Legends. J.D. Reed and Maddy Miller. New York: Wenner, 2005.
Stein, Daniel and Martin Butler, eds. "Musical Autobiographies." Special Issue. *Popular Music and Society* 38.2 (May 2015).
Stekert, Ellen J. "Cents and Nonsense in the Urban Folksong Movement: 1930–66." *Transforming Tradition*. Ed. Neil V. Rosenberg. Urbana, IL: University of Illinois Press, 1993. 84–106.
Stevens, Norma and Steven M.L. Aronson. *Avedon: Something Personal*. New York: Spiegel & Grau, 2017.
Sting. *Broken Music, A Memoir*. New York: Dial, 2003.
Stobart, Henry. "Introduction." *The New (Ethno)musicologies*. Ed. Henry Stobart. Lanham, Maryland: Scarecrow, 2008. 1–20.
Stratton, Jon. *Jewish Identity in Western Pop Culture*. New York: Palgrave Macmillan, 2008.
Street, John. "'This is your Woodstock': Popular Memories and Political Myths." *Remembering Woodstock*. Ed. Andy Bennett. Aldershot, Hampshire: Ashgate, 2004. 29–42.
Sturgis, Matthew. *Oscar, A Life*. London: Head of Zeus, 2018.
Sumner, Bernard. *Chapter and Verse: New Order, Joy Division and Me*. New York: Thomas Dunne, 2014.
"Sweet Inspiration." *Mojo* Issue 333 (August 2021): 58–65.
Swiss, Thomas. "That's Me in the Spotlight: Rock Autobiographies." *Popular Music* 24.2 (2005): 287–94.

Szwed, John. *Alan Lomax, the Man Who Recorded the World: A Biography*. New York: Penguin, 2010.

Tagaq, Tanya. *Split Tooth*. New York: Viking, 2018.

Tanner, Michael. *Nietzsche, A Very Short Introduction*. Oxford: Oxford University Press, 2000.

Tennyson, Alfred. "In Memoriam A.H.H." *Tennyson's Poetry*. Ed. Robert W. Hill. 2nd ed. New York: Norton, 1999. 205–91.

Tessitore, Carol. "Painful But Fabulous (An Interview on the Dematerialization of Identity)." *Painful But Fabulous: The Lives & Art of Genesis P-Orridge*. Ed. Genesis P-Orridge. 139–49.

Thomas, Richard F. *Why Bob Dylan Matters*. New York: Dey St., 2017.

Thompson, Chris. *Felt: Fluxus, Joseph Beuys, and the Dalai Lama*. Minneapolis, MN: University of Minnesota Press, 2011.

Tick, Judith. "Ruth Crawford, Charles Seeger, and 'The Music of American Folk Songs.'" *Understanding Charles Seeger, Pioneer in American Musicology*. Eds. Bell Yung and Helen Rees. 109–29.

Townshend, Pete. *Who I Am, A Memoir*. Toronto: HarperCollins, 2012.

Tuite, Clara. *Lord Byron and Scandalous Celebrity*. Cambridge: Cambridge University Press, 2015.

Turner, Graeme, Frances Bonner, and P. David Marshall. *Fame Games: The Production of Celebrity in Australia*. Cambridge: Cambridge University Press, 2000.

Turner, Graeme. *Understanding Celebrity*. London: Sage, 2004.

Turner, Tina with Kurt Loder. *I, Tina: My Life Story*. New York: It Books, 2010.

Tutti, Cosey Fanni. *Art Sex Music*. London: Faber & Faber, 2017.

Tweedy, Jeff. *Let's Go (So We Can Get Back): A Memoir of Recording and Discording with Wilco, etc*. New York: Dutton, 2018.

Uncle Howard. [DVD] Dir. Aaron Brookner. Pinball London, 2018.

United in Anger: A History of ACT UP. [DVD] Dir. Jim Hubbard. United in Anger, Inc. 2014.

Van Ronk, Dave with Elijah Wald. *The Mayor of MacDougal Street, A Memoir*. Philadelphia, PA: Da Capo Press, 2013.

Veyne, Paul. *Foucault: His Thought, His Character*. Trans. Janet Lloyd. Cambridge: Polity, 2010.

Voynovskaya, Nastia. "How It 'Fell Apart': Moby Talks New Memoir, Addiction and Trauma." *KQED* (April 23, 2019). Available online: https://www.kqed.org/arts/13855452/how-it-fell-apart-moby-talks-new-memoir-addiction-and-trauma (accessed July 9, 2021).

Wade, Simeon. *Foucault in California*. Berkeley, California: Heyday, 2019.

Walsh, Ryan H. *Astral Weeks: A Secret History of 1968*. New York: Penguin, 2018.

Warhol, Andy. *a*. New York: Grove, 1968.

Warhol, Andy. *The Andy Warhol Diaries*. Ed. Pat Hackett. New York: Twelve, 2014.

Warhol, Robyn R. "The Rhetoric of Addiction from Victorian Novels to AA." *High Anxieties: Cultural Studies in Addiction*. Eds. Janet Farrell Brodie and Marc Redfield. Berkeley, CA: University of California Press, 2002. 97–107.

Waters, John. "The Last Word." *Rolling Stone* (June 27, 2019): 98. Available online: http://www.rollingstone.com/movies/movie-features/john-waters-interview-last-word-848050/ (accessed July 9, 2021).

Watson, Julia. "Patti Smith Kicks In the Walls of Memoir: Relational Lives and 'the Right Voice' in *Just Kids*." *a/b: Auto/Biography Studies* 30.1 (March 2015): 131–51.

Watson, Julia and Sidonie Smith. "De/Colonization and the Politics of Discourse in Women's Autobiographical Practices, Introduction." *De/Colonizing the Subject: The Politics of Gender in Women's Autobiography*. Eds. Sidonie Smith and Julia Watson. Minneapolis, MN: University of Minnesota Press, 1992. xiii–xxxi.

Watson, Laura. "*Born to Run*: The Transmedia Evolution of the Bruce Springsteen Memoir from Book to Stage and Screen." *Popular Music and Society*. Forthcoming.

Weeks, Jeffrey. *Against Nature*. London: River Oram, 1991.

Weeks, Jeffrey. *The World We Have Won: The Remaking of Erotic and Intimate Life*. London: Routledge, 2007.

Weeks, Jeffrey and Kevin Porter, eds. *Between the Acts*. London: River Oram, 1998.

Welch, Brian "Head." *Save Me From Myself: How I Found God, Quit Korn, Kicked Drugs, and Lived to Tell My Story*. New York: HarperOne, 2007.

Weller, Sheila. *Girls Like Us: Carole King, Joni Mitchell, Carly Simon—and the Journey of a Generation*. New York: Atria Books, 2008.

Werth, Barry. *The Scarlet Professor: Newton Arvin, A Literary Life Shattered by Scandal*. New York: Nan A. Talese, 2001.

Wesołowski, Adrian D. "Beyond Celebrity History: Towards the Consolidation of Fame Studies." *Celebrity Studies* (October 18, 2018). Available online: http://doi.org/10.1080/19392397.2018.1527705 (accessed July 9, 2021).

Wheeler, Susan. "Jokerman." *Do You, Mr Jones? Bob Dylan with the Poets & Professors*. Ed. Neil Corcoran. 175–91.

White, Avron Levine. "Popular Music and the Law—Who Owns the Song." *Lost in Music: Culture, Style and the Musical Event*. Ed. Avron Levine White. London: Routledge, 1987. 164–90.

White, Edmund. "*Publishers Weekly* Interviews: Edmund White." Edmund White interviewed by William Goldstein, 1982. *Conversations with Edmund White*. Eds Will Brantley and Nancy McGuire Roche. 3–6.

White, Edmund. *Marcel Proust*. New York: Viking, 1999.

White, Edmund. *Arts and Letters*. San Francisco: Cleis, 2004.

White, Edmund. *My Lives*. London: Bloomsbury, 2006.

White, Edmund. *Rimbaud: The Double Life of a Rebel*. New York: Atlas, 2008.

White, Edmund. "An Interview with Edmund White." Edmund White interviewed by Carlos Motta, 2011. *Conversations with Edmund White*. Eds. Will Brantley and Nancy McGuire Roche. 158–72.

White, Edmund. "Q&A with Edmund White." Interview by Jon Wiener, 2014. *Conversations with Edmund White*. Eds. Will Brantley and Nancy McGuire Roche. 184–6.

Whitehead, Christopher. "Institutional Autobiography and the Architecture of the Art Museum." *Museums and Biographies*. Ed. Kate Hill. Rochester, NY: Boydell & Brewer, 2013. 157–70.

Whitman, Walt. "Song of Myself." *The Complete Poems*. Walt Whitman. Ed. Francis Murphy. London: Penguin, 2004. 63–124.

Wilde, Oscar. *De Profundis and Other Prison Writings*. Ed. Colm Tóibín. London: Penguin, 2013.

Wilde, Oscar. "Letter to the Home Secretary (1896)." *De Profundis and Other Prison Writings*. Oscar Wilde. 16–20.

Wildeblood, Peter. *Against the Law*. New York: Julian Messner, 1959.

Wilentz, Sean. *Bob Dylan in America*. New York: Anchor, 2011.

Wills, Garry. *Saint Augustine*. New York: Viking, 1999.

Windeatt, Barry. "Introduction." *The Book of Margery Kempe*. Margery Kempe. 9–28.

Winters, John J. "Alt Country." Review of Jeff Tweedy's *Let's Go (So We Can Get Back)*. *TLS: Times Literary Supplement* (June 14, 2019): 30–1.

Wojnarowicz, David. *Close to the Knives: A Memoir of Disintegration*. New York: Vintage, 1991.

Wojnarowicz, David. *In the Shadow of the American Dream: The Diaries of David Wojnarowicz*. Ed. Amy Scholder. New York: Grove, 1999.

Wojnarowicz, David. *Memories That Smell Like Gasoline*. 3rd ed. San Francisco: Artspace, 2016.

Wojnarowicz, David. *David Wojnarowicz: Flesh of My Flesh*. Ed. Daniel S. Berger. Chicago, IL: Iceberg Projects, 2018.

Wojnarowicz, David. *The Waterfront Journals*. London: Peninsula, 2018.

Wojnarowicz, David. *Weight of the Earth: The Tape Journals of David Wojnarowicz*. Eds. Lisa Darms and David O'Neill. South Pasadena, CA: Semiotext(e), 2018.

Wojnarowicz, David and Cynthia Carr. "Biographical Dateline." *David Wojnarowicz: History Keeps Me Awake at Night*. Eds. David Breslin and David Kiehl. New York: Whitney Museum of American Art, 2018. 285–308.

Wojnarowicz, David and James Romberger. *Seven Miles a Second*. New York: DC Comics, 1996.

Wojnarowicz, David and Nan Goldin. "David Live: David Wojnarowicz interviewed by Nan Goldin." *David Wojnarowicz*. Ed. Giancarlo Ambrosino. 196–211.

Wojnarowicz, David and Sylvère Lotringer. "David Live: David Wojnarowicz interviewed by Sylvère Lotringer." *David Wojnarowicz*. Ed. Giancarlo Ambrosino. 156–95.

Womack, Kenneth. "Reconsidering Performative Autobiography: Life-Writing and the Beatles." *Life Writing* 1.2 (2005): 47–70.
Womack, Kenneth. *Long and Winding Roads: The Evolving Artistry of the Beatles*. New York: Continuum, 2007.
Womack, Kenneth. *Maximum Volume: The Life of Beatles Producer George Martin, the Early Years, 1926–1966*. Chicago, IL: Chicago Review Press, 2017.
Womack, Kenneth. *Solid State: The Story of Abbey Road and the End of the Beatles*. Ithaca, NY: Cornell University Press, 2019.
Womack, Kenneth. *John Lennon 1980: The Last Days in the Life*. London: Omnibus, 2020.
Womack, Kenneth, ed. *The Beatles in Context*. Cambridge: Cambridge University Press, 2020.
Womack, Kenneth and Katie Kapurch, eds. *New Critical Perspectives on the Beatles: Things We Did Today*. London: Palgrave Macmillan, 2016.
Womack, Kenneth and Kit O'Toole, eds. *Fandom and the Beatles*. New York: Oxford University Press, 2021.
Womack, Kenneth and Todd F. Davis, eds. *Reading the Beatles: Cultural Studies, Literary Criticism, and the Fab Four*. Albany, NY: State University of New York Press, 2006.
Wood, Ronnie. *Ronnie*. London: Pan Macmillan, 2007.
Yung, Bell and Helen Rees, eds. *Understanding Charles Seeger, Pioneer in American Musicology*. Urbana, IL: University of Illinois Press, 1999.
Zappe, Florian. "'When Order is Lost, Time Spits': The Abject Unpopular Art of Genesis (Breyer) P-Orridge." *Unpopular Culture*. Eds. Martin Lüthe and Sascha Pöhlmann. Amsterdam: Amsterdam University Press, 2016. 129–45.

Index

3 Teens Kill 4 (3TK4) 96, 150, 151

AA/NA (12-step programs) 53, 54–5, 57, 60, 63, 66, 91 n.26
abuse
    child 52, 55, 67 n.4, 91 n.26
    domestic 91 n.21, 103–05, 100, 101, 102, 133 n.26, 134 n.27
Ackerley, J.R. 120, 141
    Hindoo Holiday 120
    My Father and Myself 120, 141
    We Think the World of You 120
ACT UP 37, 150, 155–6
addiction
    in autobiography studies 36, 47–8
    in celebrity career trajectory 49–51
    and claims to rock authenticity 69 n.13
    copycat 49–50
    in disability studies 36, 48–9
    as illness 48–9, 53, 68 n.6–7
    in rock 'n' recovery autobiography 4, 36, 47–71, 68 n.6
Adorno, Theodor (*On Popular Music*) 12, 13
Ahmad, Salman (*Rock & Roll Jihad: A Muslim Rock Star's Revolutions*) 39 n.15
AIDS 12, 37, 48, 89 n.9–10, 137, 141, 143, 156–7, 158, 168 n.37
    and the AIDS memoir 141, 155–6
Albarn, Damon 110
Aletti, Vince 151, 167 n.33, 169 n.40
Almond, Marc (*Tainted Life*) 74
Anderson, Brett 36, 108–15, 135 n.35–6, 137
    Afternoons with the Blinds Drawn
        addiction in 114
        identity, construction and performance of 108, 109, 114
        influences on Anderson's music in 109
        Justine Frischmann 109
        style and voice 114
        Suede, disintegration of 114–15
        Suede, song-by-song analysis in 114–15
    Coal Black Mornings
        allusions to canonical writers in 108, 110
        androgyny/gender transformation 109, 112–13
        autobiography, traditional 108, 110
        class envy in 110
        father 108, 111–12, 113
        Justine Frischmann 109–10
        identity, construction and performance of 108–09, 110, 112–14
        mental health 111, 112, 113
        Morrissey and the Smiths 108–09
        mother 111–12
        prostitution, male 112–13
        Suede 113–14
        style and voice 110–11, 113
        trauma 111–12
Anderson, Linda 2
Ant, Adam 53, 61–2
    Stand and Deliver: The Autobiography 62
    as rock 'n' recovery autobiography 62–3
Appalachia
    and African-American music 173, 191
    mythologized 16, 23, 42–3 n.44, 44 n.52, 173, 191
Appalachia Reckoning 173
Arlen, Harold 179
Artaud, Antonin 138–41, 148, 164 n.5
    addiction 139, 164 n.7
    counterculture and 165
    electroshock 139, 165 n.10
    performance, new modes of 140, 165 n.13
    rebellion, emblem of 139
    sexuality, fear of 139
    theatre of cruelty 139–41, 165 n.11

Augustine of Hippo, Saint
    City of God 7
    Confessions 6–7, 12, 40 n.20, 40 n.21, 105
    De Musica 7
    importance of music to 7
Aurelius, Marcus (*Meditations*) 50, 68 n.4–5, 147
authenticity 5, 12, 29, 34–5, 69 n.13, 102
    and inauthenticity, deliberate 93–4
    and integrity, musical and artistic 61–3, 115
    and live performance 46 n.67
autobiography (autobiography studies)
    history of 6–12
    and memoir 38–9 n.8
    popular music autobiography in 2, 6, 7, 8, 32, 37–8 n.2
    as problematic term 5–6, 13, 39–40 n.16, 38–9 n.8
    spiritual 7–9
    theories of 5–6
autobiography, popular music. *See also* celebrity; fame; rock 'n' recovery autobiography; rock star/popular musician
    academic dismissal of 42 n.41
    addiction 35, 36
    authenticity nexus 5
    in celebrity studies 32–4, 38 n.2–3
    celebrity vs. fame in 35
    collaborative authorship of 8, 25 n.41, 54, 79–80
    cross-marketing of 33
    critical studies of 38 n.4
    and de-celebrification 35
    as generational lifewriting 3, 199–204
    genres 3–5, 54
    and listening experience 4, 35
    literary seriousness of 2, 35, 38 n.7
    multi-media products 2, 3, 4, 5, 18, 29, 33, 40 n.18, 68 n.6
    reader expectations and response 2, 6, 33, 38 n.3
    as self-therapy 17, 25
    as supplemental souvenir 33
    witness 3
Avedon, Richard 151, 152
Ayers, Bill 68 n.4

Baez, Joan 58, 133 n.26
    Bob Dylan, relationship with 15, 29, 172, 173, 174, 187, 192, 194 n.4–5, 197 n.33
    Bob Dylan on 177, 178
    folk tradition and 29
    Rose Simpson 22
    And a Voice to Sing With 172
Baez, Mimi 133 n.26
Baker, Ginger (*Hellraiser*) 56
Balance, John 134 n.30
Baldry, Long John 77
    as gay musician 77
Ballard, J.G. (*Crash*) 96
Barraqué, Jean 12
Bataille, George (*My Mother*) 96
Baudelaire, Charles 138, 182
Baudrillard, Jean 61, 63, 64–5, 69 n.12, 70 n.15
The Beatles 22, 50, 84, 85, 98, 175, 187. *See also* Harrison, George; Lennon, John; McCartney, Paul
    Anthology 81
    celebrity, new type of 29, 79
    A Cellarful of Noise (Epstein), depiction in 79, 80, 81, 83
    Epstein, Brian, relationship with 73, 81, 86
    A Hard Day's Night 87
    "In My Life" 187
    image creation and control of 81, 175
The Beats 178, 179–80, 182, 184, 186, 188, 189, 201. *See also* Ginsberg, Allen; Kerouac, Jack
Berridge, Virginia (*Opium and the People*) 48
Best, Pete 85
Bible 6, 8, 111, 122, 123, 130, 184, 185
blackface 176, 195 n.17
Blake, William 143, 184
Blind Faith 56
the blues 178, 180
    mythology of 51, 56
Blur 24, 108, 110, 135 n.39
    "Girls and Boys" 112
    "Modern Life Is Rubbish" 112
The Bob Dylan Archive 171, 175, 182, 188–93, 198 n.37
Bohlman, Philip 14, 42–3 n.44

Bolaño, Roberto 147
Bono (*U2*) 30, 161, 177
Boswell, James (*The Life of Samuel Johnson*) 27
Boulez, Pierre 12
Bowie, David 20, 109, 112, 113, 115, 116, 125, 130
BOY Boutique 100
Boyd, Joe 22, 24, 104
Boyd, Patti
   Wonderful Tonight 21, 56
     divorce settlement 57
     on Eric Clapton's and George Harrison's drug addiction 57
     as muse to Eric Clapton and George Harrison 21, 56
Brainard, Joe 142
Braudy, Leo 63, 64, 65, 70 n.15
   The Frenzy of Renown 27
Brecht, Bertolt 142, 180, 182, 185
Bressler, Doug 157
Brookner, Howard 168 n.37
Buber, Martin 176, 195–6 n.19
Buckley, Jeff 9, 125, 134 n.33
   bipolar 49
   and Tim Buckley 125
   drug use 49
   Grace 125
   Jeff Buckley: His Own Voice 41 n.30
   Journals 9
   performing overdose deaths 125
Bunyan, John (*Grace Abounding to the Chief of Sinners*) 7
Bunyan, Vashti 22
Burroughs, William 37, 40 n.21, 137, 138, 143, 149, 150, 158, 160
   as celebrity addict role model 50–1
   Junky 50–1
   Nova Express 160
Bush, George 158
Butler, Bernard 109, 113, 134 n.32
Butterick, Brian 152, 157, 161, 163. *See also* 3TK4
Butthole Surfers 125
Byrne, David 4, 157. *See also* Talking Heads
   How Music Works 39 n.13
Byron, Lord 28
   Childe Harold's Pilgrimage 28

Don Juan 28
   as first international celebrity 38, 46 n.64

Cage, John 97, 132 n.13
Cale, John 9, 31, 60, 90 n.16, 143. *See also* Velvet Underground
   on Lou Reed 90 n.16
Cameron, David 117
Capote, Truman 182
Carlisle, Belinda 25
   Lips Unsealed 25, 45 n.58
   as rock 'n' recovery autobiography 68 n.8
Carr, Cynthia 154, 160, 162–3
Carroll, Jim 94, 131 n.7
   Patti Smith, relationship with 140, 142–3, 166 n.17
   performance art 94
   The Petting Zoo 166 n.17
Carter, Chris 99, 100, 107, 132 n.12. *See also* Throbbing Gristle; Tutti, Cosey Fanni
celebrity. *See also* fame.
   the Beatles and the 'new' celebrity 29
   and celebrity studies 1, 4–5, 9, 27, 34, 38 n.2, 59
   definition 35
   fabricated 64
   difference from fame 35
   history of 27–32
   popular music 28–35
   postmodern industry of 64–5
   the Rolling Stones contributions to 29–30
   Victorian musical 28
Chambers, Paddy 77
Chandler, Len 176
Cheever, John (*Journals*) 52, 118
   homosexual desires and homophobia in 120–1, 135 n.40, 135–6 n.41
   influence on Moby 118–21
Cheever, Susan (*Note Found in a Bottle: My Life as a Drinker*) 52
Child, Francis James 14, 15, 16, 42–3 n.44
   English and Scottish Popular Ballads 43 n.45, 173
   and ethnomusicological classism 16
   and romanticism 43 n.46

Chopin, Frédéric 14
Christopherson, Peter (Sleazy) 99, 110,
    107, 132 n.12, 134 n. 30. *See also*
    Throbbing Gristle (TG)
The Clancy Brothers 20, 44 n.53
Clancy, Liam 20
    Diane Guggenheim, relationships with
        44 n.52
    folksong field research 44 n.52
    *The Mountain of the Women, Memoirs
        of an Irish Troubadour* 44 n.52
Clapton, Eric 2, 21, 47, 55–9, 64
    Clapton
        anti-disability memoir 55–9
        childhood trauma in 55
        comic conclusion 60
        mythology of the blues 56
        Patti Boyd, relationship with 56
        rock 'n' recovery autobiography 36,
            52, 55–9, 61
    "Wonderful Tonight" 21
Clapton, Eric and Jim Gordon ("Layla")
    21, 56, 57
CBGB 90 n.17, 125, 145, 166 n.19
The Clash 26
Clayton, Paul 14, 15
    biographies of 195 n.12
    drug use 194 n.7
    Bob Dylan, relationship with 14, 15,
        172–3, 174–5, 194 n.9–10, 195 n.12
    education
        ethnomusicology 44 n.52, 172–3
        field research/collection 44 n.52,
            173
        MA thesis on Child ballads 173
    in folk scene, Greenwich Village, 1960s
        172–3, 179
    gay identity 172, 173, 189, 194 n.7, 195
        n.12
    legal action against Dylan 174, 194 n.9
    music
        Dulcimer Songs and Solos, liner
            notes for 173
        "Gingerbreadd Mindd" 175
        "Gotta Travel On" 173, 194 n.6
        "Who's Gonna Buy you Ribbons"
            174
    performance, content and style 173–4
    suicide 175, 204

Clinton, George 62
Clinton, Hillary 130, 148
Cobain, Kurt 25, 49, 70–1 n.18, 158
    authenticity and fame 61, 64, 65–6
    drug addiction 66
    In Utero 65–6
    Journals 65, 66
    multi-media life-writings 65, 66
    self-marketing/promotion 65–6
    suicide 49, 61, 64, 71 n.19
    William Burroughs, as celebrity addict
        role model 60
Cohen, Leonard ("Hallelujah") 9, 41 n.29
Coil 134 n.30
Collins, Dolly 24
Collins, Judy 24, 29, 58
Collins, Phil 127
Collins, Shirley 3, 23
    Alan Lomax, relationship with 23
    All in the Downs 23
    America Over the Water 23
    Ashley Hutchings, relationship with 24
    The Ballad of Shirley Collins 23
    Folk Roots, New Routes 24
    folk tradition and innovation 24
    humiliation and silencing 24
    Incredible String Band, assessment of
        24
    Lodestar 24
    muse, rejection of role of 23–4
Coolidge, Rita 21
    Delta Lady 21
    "Layla" 21
    muse 21
Cooper, Alice 52
Copland, Aaron 17
Cornell, Chris 4, 30, 159. *See also*
    Soundgarden
Corso, Gregory 143
Cotten, Elizabeth 18
COUM Transmissions 96, 97, 98, 99, 107,
    133 n.24. *See also* Throbbing Gristle
    (TG)
counterculture, American 1960s 21–2,
    30, 129
counterculture, British 1960s
    Swinging London/60s 73
Coxon, Graham 24. *See also* Blur
Crabtree, Lee 144

Cream 56. *See also* Baker, Ginger; Clapton, Eric.
Creedence Clearwater Revival 129
Croland, David 143
Crosby, David 3, 39, 52, 50
   David Crosby: Remember My Name 39
   erectile dysfunction 202
   Long Time Gone 52
Current 93 24
Curtis, Ian 129, 132 n.17. *See also* Joy Division

The Damned 26
Danceteria 130, 157
Davies, Dave. *See also* The Kinks.
   being gay in the Swinging 60s 84–5
   Long John Baldry, relationship with 84
Davies, Ray 26, 84
Davis, Clive 18, 90 n.13
Davis, Miles 50, 56, 125
Delage, Jean-Pierre 159, 161
Denny, Sandy 22, 49
De Quincey, Thomas 59
   Confessions of an Opium Eater 59
disability (disability studies)
   addiction as 48–51, 68 n.6
Dohrn, Bernardine 68 n.4. *See also* Weathermen; Weather Underground
Dollywood 189
Dont Look Back (dir. D.A. Pennebaker) 181, 186
The Doors 144
Doughton, Steve 161
drag 151, 157
Drake, Nick 22, 104
drugs
   alcohol 4, 52, 53, 55, 60, 61, 67 n.1, 67–8 n.4, 68 n.6, 68 n.8, 69 n.13, 86, 89 n.9, 91 n.21, 107, 118, 119, 122, 124, 126, 128–9, 202
   ayahuasca 69 n.13
   cocaine 45 n.58, 57, 58, 59, 63, 68 n.6, 68 n.8, 78, 89 n.9, 128, 129, 202
   crack 53, 62, 67–8 n.4, 69–70 n.14, 68 n.8
   ecstasy (MDMA) 117, 118, 126, 128, 149
   heroin 20, 49, 50, 51, 52, 53, 55, 56, 57, 58, 59, 60, 62, 63, 66, 67 n.3, 67–8 n.4, 69 n.9, 70 n.18, 78, 91 n.26, 114, 125, 139, 142, 152, 159, 165 n.10, 166–7 n.24, 196 n.24, 204
   LSD/psychedelics 12, 24, 42 n.39, 86, 119, 129, 142, 143, 193–4 n.3, 194 n.7, 200, 205 n.1, 205 n.6
   overdose 67 n.3, 73
   pills 69 n.13, 85, 128, 129
   pot (marijuana) 126, 129, 164 n.4, 194 n.7
Du Bois, W.E.B. 186
Duchamp, Marcel 94, 106, 157
Dylan, Bob 2, 3, 21, 27, 29, 104, 137, 143, 171–98.
   Anthology of American Folk Music (Harry Smith), influence on 15
   assessments of 193 n.2
   the Beats, influence on 178, 179–80
   The Bob Dylan Archive 171, 175, 182, 188–93, 198 n.37
   and celebrity monument 189, 191–2
   contexts, cultural and musical 190–3
   creation of 190–1
   as institutionalized autobiography 188–9, 190–3
   and museology studies 190
   self-construction and 190–1
   charisma 172, 173
   Paul Clayton, relationship with, personal and professional 14, 15, 172–3, 174–5, 194 n.9–10, 195 n.12
   on Leonard Cohen 41 n.29
   Dylanology 171, 172
   fame
      collateral damage 172, 174–5, 194 n.6, 195 n.12, 195 n.15
      pathology of 28, 174
   and fans 178
   films of
      Eat This Document 183
      Renaldo and Clara 183
   in folk scene, Greenwich Village, 1960s 44 n.52, 172–3, 179–80
   and manager Albert Grossman 105, 176
   Woody Guthrie, influence of 172, 177–8, 192–3
      on *Bound for Glory* 14–15, 177–8

identity
- archive and archival activity 172, 185, 188–93, 190–3
- construction of 175–80, 187–8
- as Dylanologist 184–5, 189
- in interviews 175, 188
- and Nietzsche 187–8
- relational 176–7
- and acknowledgement of sources and influences 175–81, 182–3, 184–9
- and Peter La Farge 172, 194 n.6
- music of
  - American history, engagement with 172
  - *Another Side of Bob Dylan* 187
  - apocalypticism in 172, 178, 184, 187
  - autobiographical 184, 185, 187, 189
  - "Ballad in Plain D" 174
  - "Ballad of Hollis Brown" 186
  - *Biograph* 189
  - characteristics of 184, 185–7
  - "Don't Think Twice, It's All Right" 174
  - *Good As I Been To You* 186
  - "Gotta Travel On" 173
  - "A Hard Rain's A-Gonna Fall" 186, 187
  - "I Contain Multitudes" 176
  - "I Dreamed I Saw St. Augustine" 40 n.19
  - "If Dogs Run Free" 184
  - influences and sources 184–8
  - "It Ain't Me, Babe" 185
  - "Jokerman" 9, 185
  - "Lay Lady Lay" 185
  - "Like a Rolling Stone" 185, 187
  - *More Blood, More Tracks: The Deluxe Edition* 190
  - "My Back Pages" 187–8
  - "Positively 4th Street" 185
  - *Rough and Rowdy Ways* 176
  - "Sad Eyed Lady of the Lowlands" 186
  - *Self Portrait* 173, 186
  - "Spanish is the Loving Tongue" 186
  - *Time Out of Mind* 202
  - "The Times They Are A-Changin" 187
  - "With God On Our Side" 113, 187
  - *World Gone Wrong* 186
- Nobel Prize for Literature, recipient of 2, 37, 137, 171, 188, 189, 191, 193 n.1, 195 n.16
- and Phil Ochs 172, 192–3, 194 n.6
- originality 186
- performance, content and style 173, 174, 177, 178, 180
- plagiarism, charges against 174, 176, 193 n.2, 194 n.9, 194–5 n.11, 195 n.16
- radicalism of 197 n.33
- Arthur Rimbaud, influence on 151, 176, 195–6 n.19
- Carla Rotolo, relationship with 174, 175
- Suze Rotolo, relationship with 172, 176, 177, 187–8
- as scholar and archivist, of American song tradition 185–7
- Mike Seeger, respect for 17, 177
- Frank Sinatra, influence on 29, 179
- Patti Smith, relationship with 148
- treatment of women 21, 172, 194 n.5, 195 n.12
- writings, autobiographical
  - *Chronicles* 5, 17, 38 n.3, 126, 171, 172, 173, 175–80, 188–9, 192, 202; allusions, cultural, literary and musical in 187; archetypes in 176–7; critical interpretations of 175–6; identity in 176–8, 187–8; influences and sources, literary and musical 177–80; as counterculural radical 178–9; on American song tradition 185–6; songwriting education 179–80
  - Nobel Lecture 193 n.1
  - *Tarantula* 175, 187; academia, satire of 183–4; allusions, literary and popular music in 181, 182, 183; as autofiction/anti-autobiography 183–4; composition of 181–2; critics on 196 n.22–23; as experimental

fiction 181, 182–3; genre 180–1;
as homage to African-American
music 181; misinterpretation
of self and work, as central
theme 181, 183–4; structure and
style 181

Eakin, Paul John 6
East Village 154, 155
Edgar, Robert 2
Eliot, T.S. 123, 183
  The Waste Land 123, 183
Elliott, Ramblin' Jack 186
Ellis, Geoffrey 89 n.11
Elton John 31
  domesticity, marriage and parenthood 74, 201
  gay identity 74, 77, 201
  illness 202
  Jewel Box (8-CD set) 33
  Me 33, 74, 89 n.9, 201
Elvis 115, 192
Eminem 69 n.13, 130
Eno, Brian 4
Epstein, Brian 30, 36, 73–92
  addiction 86
  anti-Semitism of and towards 73, 80, 83, 90–1 n.18
  artistic interests 82
  Beatles as alter-ego projection 87–8
  bipolar, undiagnosed 86
  Peter (Bette) Bourne, lover of 84
  A Cellarful of Noise 36, 73–5, 79–83, 85–88
    anti-*bildungs* narrative 82
    anti-Semitism 83
    on the Beatles 79, 80, 81–2
    contexts, legal, social, and sexual for gay identity in 74, 75–77
    fame, pathology of 86
    family business, record merchandising in 82, 83
    ghostwritten (with Derek Taylor) 36, 79–80
    identity; class 80–1; conflicted exposure and concealment in 75, 79, 80, 81–3, 87–8, 88 n.5; as fan 87; gay, erasure of 79–80, 84, 85–6; Jewish 80–1; reticence and disguise in 79–81, 82; self-representation as heterosexual 83–4
  internalized homophobia in 74, 75
  management talent 79, 80, 81
  as quasi late-Victorian autobiography 36, 74, 81–2
  'retitling' of, by Lennon 74
  theatre and acting 82–3
  'Diaries' 75, 89 n.12
  as fan 87–8
  family origins, birth, upbringing 73, 75, 78, 81–3
  family shame 83, 84
  as 'fifth' Beatle 73, 81
  and Joe Flannery 85
  Diz Gillespie, abusive intimate partner of 85
  homosexuality
    and army, expulsion from 82
    arrest and conviction for 83
    assault and/or robbery 80, 85
    blackmail of 77, 80, 85, 91 n.21, 91 n.23
    confession of 79
    cruising 82, 89 n.11
    diagnosed as illness 82
    homoerotic attraction to Lennon and the Beatles 73–4, 85, 86, 92 n.30
    homophobia against 73–4, 80, 91 n.21
    homophobia, internalized 84, 85, 89 n.17
    Lennon's troubled relationship with, and 73, 91 n.21
    psychiatric treatment for 80, 82, 83
    rough trade (dangerous, anonymous sex), attraction to 73, 74, 84, 85, 86, 88 n.3, 88 n.6, 89 n.11
    young, straight men, attraction to 77–8
  insomnia, chronic 86
  manager 73, 81, 86, 87
  Joe Orton film script for Beatles, commissioned by 87
  post-Beatles life 87
  suicide attempt 85

Faithfull, Marianne 2, 47, 49, 109, 115
   William Burroughs, as celebrity addict role model 50, 59
   Bob Dylan, relationship with 53
   Faithfull
      addiction to heroin 58–60
      bifurcated self 58–60
      marriage to John Dunbar 59
      gothic/romantic tropes 58–9
      homelessness 59
      1960s rock milieu 59–60
      rock 'n' recovery autobiography 36, 58–9
      self-criticism/diagnosis 59–60
      suicide, attempted 59
   illness 202
   Memories, Dreams, and Reflections 58–9
      breast cancer 58
      gothic/romantic tropes 58–9
   Mick Jagger, relationship with 20, 58, 59
   muse, rejection of role of 20–1
   1960s pop milieu, on reactionary sexual politics of 54
   "Sister Morphine" 58
   trauma 55
fame. *See also* celebrity
   and authenticity/musical integrity 61–3
   and celebrity career trajectory 47, 49
   difference from celebrity 35
   junkies 65
   pathology of 47–8, 63–7
   postmodern 3, 64–5
   self-construction and 61–3
fans
   adulation of popular musicians 7
   devotion to music 11
   fan scholars 34
   managers as 88
   readers as 2, 6
   rock stars as 2, 63
   postmodern 65
Fariña, Richard 133 n.26, 174, 194 n.4, 194 n.6
Farndon, Peter 26
fashion 32, 39 n.12, 151
Ferlinghetti, Lawrence 189

Fillmore East 151
Flea 62, 125. *See also* Red Hot Chili Peppers.
   Acid for the Children, A Memoir 62, 69–70 n.14
Fluxus movement 96, 97, 150
folksong/folk music, American. *See also* Clayton, Paul; Dylan, Bob; Lomax, Alan; Lomax, John; Seeger, Charles; Seeger, Peggy; Smith, Harry
   and African-American music 43 n.47, 191
   anonymity of 17
   authenticity 20
   and class struggle 16, 17
   collection of 14–15, 23
   communism, association with 43 n.48, 191
   and early ethnomusicology 14–19, 43 n.44, 173–4
   and life writing 14, 15
   originality and plagiarism in 20, 174, 179
   revival 20, 24, 173–4
Ford, Simon 132 n.14
Foucault, Michel 42 n.37–40
   autobiographical allegory 12
   on music 12
Franklin, Aretha 182, 183
Frantz, Chris (*Remain in Love*), 4, 134 n.27, 136 n.43, 157. *See also* Talking Heads
Frischmann, Justine 109–10, 111, 112
Frith, Simon 14, 73, 94
Frith, Simon and Howard Horne 12–13
Frusciante, John 62
Fugs 151
Furnish, David 74, 201

Geffen, David 65, 90 n.13
Genet, Jean 138, 143, 150
Gibb, Barry 77
   on gay management in 1960s London 77
Gillespie, John 'Diz' 77. *See also* Epstein, Brian
Gilmore, Gary 98
Ginsberg, Allen 143, 146, 182, 186, 201
   Bob Dylan 189

The Allen Ginsberg Project 189
"Howl" 182
Giorno, John 142, 166 n.22
Glissant, Édouard (*Poetics of Relation*) 6
The Go-Go's 25, 45 n.58
Goldin, Nan 156, 159, 168 n.40
   David Wojnarowicz at Home, NYC, 1990 159
   Witnesses: Against Our Vanishing 156
Goldstein, Kenneth S. 14
Goodman Paul, 22, 44 n.55, 200–1
   Gestalt therapy 201
   Growing Up Absurd 201
   homosexuality 200–1, 205 n.5
Gordon, Jim (Derek and the Dominos) 21, 56, 57
Gordon, Kim 25, 45 n.57, 130
   Girl in a Band 25, 41 n.28
   Thurston Moore, relationship with 25, 41 n.28
   and Sonic Youth 25, 130
Gosse, Edmund (*Father and Son*) 81, 141
Graham, Davy 24
The Grateful Dead 94
Grauerholz, James 149
Green, Robin 25, 45 n.59
   The Only Girl: My Life and Times on the Masthead of Rolling Stone 25, 45 n.59
Grossman, Albert 105, 176
Guattari, Felix 150, 154
Gunn, Tom (*The Man with Night Sweats*) 155
Guns N' Roses 36, 52, 60, 62, 63, 65
Guthrie, Woody 14–15, 18, 97, 171, 179, 183, 186. See also Dylan, Bob; The Woody Guthrie Center
   Bound for Glory 15, 171, 177–8
   Bob Dylan, influence on 177–8
   House of Earth 15
   "This Machine Kills Fascists" 97
Gysin, Brion 97, 98, 132 n.15

Hagan, Joe 27, 30
Hair, Julie 154, 157
Halford, Rob 4, 39 n.12, 74, 202. See also Judas Priest
   Confess 74, 89 n.10, 202, 203
Hall, Richard Melville. See Moby

happenings 94, 131 n.6
Harrison, George 21, 79, 114
   All Things Must Pass 29
   Concert for Bangladesh 35
   I, Me, Mine 81, 114
   "Something" 21
Harry, Debbie (Blondie) 20–1, 27
   Face It 20–1
   and Chris Stein 20–1
   feminist critique of 1970s rock milieu 20
Hell, Richard 139, 145, 149, 159, 166–7 n.24
   "Love Comes In Spurts" 149
   style 164 n.6, 165 n.8
Hendrix, Jimi 24, 49, 54, 144, 146, 203
   The Jimi Hendrix Experience Museum 190
Hentoff, Nat 188
Heron, Gil Scott 97
   "The Revolution Will Not Be Televised" 97
Heron, Mike 22–3, 24
   You Know What You Could Be 45 n.56
Hersh, Kristin (*Paradoxical Undressing*) 21
Hester, Carolyn 133 n.26
Hipgnosis 100
Hirst, Damien 101
Holden Caulfield (*A Catcher in the Rye*) 124
Hole 25, 70–1 n.18. See also Courtney Love
Holiday, Billie (*Lady Sings the Blues*) 13, 42 n.43
   "Strange Fruit" 42 n.43
Holly, Buddy 177
Holocaust 83, 98, 176
   Auschwitz 176
Honeyman-Scott, James 26
Hook, Peter 135 n.39. See also Joy Division
Hubbard, Jim (*United in Anger: A History of ACT UP*) 155
Hujar, Peter 1, 37, 137, 150. See also Wojnarowicz, David
   AIDS 155
   life 151
   on Robert Mapplethorpe 168 n.38
   music and performance, interests in 151
   photography of

Catacombs at Palermo 152
Candy Darling, death of 152
fashion and rock 'n' roll 151
Portraits in Life and Death 152
photographic subject, of David Wojnarowicz 152
self-saboteur, professional 161, 167, 169 n.42
sex and sexuality 151, 167
Susan Sontag on 152
personal and professional relationship with David Wojnarowicz 151, 152, 159
Hultberg, Jesse 150, 157, 158, 159, 167 n.27. *See also* 3TK4
Huxley, Aldous 172, 193–4 n.3
Hynde, Chrissie 25–7, 116
    addiction 26
    The Pretenders 25
    sexually abused 105
        Reckless 26–7, 45–6 n.62; sexual fantasies 46 n.63

identity 5–6, 38 n.5
    Enlightenment 5–6
    performative 3, 5, 36, 37, 93–5, 101–2, 108
    in persona studies 38 n.6
    queer 36, 39 n.12
    relational 5, 6
    in rock 'n' recovery autobiography 57–61, 64, 65–6
    and self-renunciation 12, 102
Iggy Pop 1, 20, 27, 46 n.63, 125, 151, 203
illness, psychiatric
    alcoholism 48, 49, 52, 53, 55, 57, 64, 67 n.1–2, 68 n.6, 68 n.8, 70 n.18, 77, 78, 91 n.26, 111, 118, 119, 121, 128, 129, 130, 159, 193, 194 n.6
    anorexia 68 n.8
    bipolar disorder 49, 53, 62, 86
    depression 8, 67 n.3, 68 n.7, 88, 175
    depression, post-partum 8
    dissociative affective disorder 21
    psychosis (drug-induced) 57, 59
    suicide (attempted) 59, 68 n.7
    suicide 49, 61, 64, 66, 71 n.19
Incredible String Band 21–3, 24, 104. *See also* Heron, Mike; Simpson, Rose

DIY ethos 22–3
The Hangman's Beautiful Daughter 24
Scientology 23
U 94
Institute of Contemporary Art (ICA) 100

Jagger, Mick 20, 58, 60, 145. *See also* The Rolling Stones
    gay sex 78
    Performance 60, 113
    "Sister Morphine" 58
Jameson, Fredric 69 n.12–13
Jane Eyre (Charlotte Brontë) 145
Jansch, Bert 104
Joel, Billy 69 n.11
Johnny Rotten 26
Johnson, Robert 56, 177, 180
Jones, Brian 49, 51, 144, 164 n.3, 203
    The Pipes of Pan at Joujouka 144
Jones, Steve. *See also* The Sex Pistols
    addiction 91 n.26
    sexual abuse of 91 n.26
    sexual experimentation of 91 n.26
Jones, Tom 202
Joplin, Janis 22, 45 n.59, 49, 151
Joyce, James 115, 180, 181, 196 n.22
    Finnegan's Wake 181
    Ulysses 180, 181
Joy Division 61, 29, 132 n.17, 135 n.39
    Nazi imagery 98, 135 n.39
    post-WWII working class dispossession 97–8
    compared to Throbbing Gristle (TG) 97–8
Judas Priest 89 n.10
Julian of Norwich 8

Karpeles, Maud 16, 43 n.47
Kaye, Lenny 144, 145, 148, 149
Kempe, Margery 7–8
    influence on Cosey Fanni Tutti 101–2
    The Book of Margery Kempe 7–8, 41 n.26–27
Kern, Richard 150
Kerouac, Jack 158, 179, 182, 186, 189
    On the Road 179, 182, 186, 203
Kiedis, Anthony 47, 52, 53, 58, 62, 69–70 n.14, 125. *See also* Red Hot Chili Peppers

Blood Sugar Sex Magik 62
Scar Tissue 62-3
King, Carol 105
King Missile
  "Detachable Penis" (music video) 150
The Kinks 26
The Kingston Trio 179
Kittredge, George 15
Klein, Allen 73, 88 n.2
Kneller, Richard. *See* Pride, Dickie
Koch, Stephen 151, 168 n.38
Kraftwerk 150
Král, Ivan 145
Kramer, Wayne 50, 67-8 n.4 *See also* MC5

Labouchere Amendment (1885) 74, 75
La Farge, Peter 172, 194 n.6
Lambert, Kit 36, 77, 78, 79
  aborted autobiography 78
  addiction 79
  death 79
  homophobia, internalized 78-9
  as manager of the Who 78
  masochism 78
  Mick Jagger, sexual encounter with 78
  on the Who's homoerotic appeal 78
  the Who's style and performance, contributions to 78
Lanegan, Mark 3
Lanier, Allen 144
Lanois, Daniel 179, 202
Lawrence, T.E. (Lawrence of Arabia) 110, 111
Leadbelly 14, 15, 18
  "Goodnight Irene" 14
Led Zeppelin 22, 129
  "Going to California" 129
Leibovitz, Annie 45 n.58, 70 n.17, 152
Leitch, Donovan 3
Lennon, John 7, 29-30, 57, 59, 67-8 n.4, 91 n.19, 164 n.3
  autobiographical writings, models for 30
  anti-Semitism of 73-4, 91 n.21
  disabled, mocking of 47, 74, 88 n.4
  Double Fantasy 44 n.53
  Brian Epstein, assault on and relationship with 73-4, 92 n.29, 92 n.21

homophobia of 73-4, 91 n.21
"I Am the Walrus" 186
"Imagine" 21
In His Own Write 73
Lennon Remembers 81
"Mother" 97
persona 85
and the rock star imaginary 47
sex and sexual desires, homoerotic 92 n.29
Skywriting by Word of Mouth 30
violence of, in relationships 91 n.21
"Watching the Wheels" 186
and Yoko Ono as muse 44 n.53
Lennon, John and Yoko Ono
  "Two Virgins" 30
Lerner, Jonathan (*Alex Underground*) 68 n.4
Levithan, Robert 151
  account of Hujar 167 n.32
Liszt 110, 111
Lloyd, Richard 4, 77, 90 n.17
Lomax, Alan 14, 15
  relationship with Shirley Collins 23
Lomax, John 14, 15
  Adventures of a Ballad Hunter 15
  Cowboy Songs 15
Lomax, John and Alan
  oral autobiographies, collectors of 15-16
  American Ballads and Folk Songs 14
  folksongs, ethnological field collection and publication of 15-16
  The Land Where the Blues Began 16
Lorca, Federico Garcia 185
Love, Courtney 25, 65, 70-1 n.18
  Diaries 65
  Pretty on the Inside 25

MacColl, Ewan 18, 19, 20, 24, 44 n.51
  "The First Time Ever I Saw Your Face" 19, 20
MacColl, Kirsty ("Fairytale of New York") 19
Machado De Assis (*The Posthumous Memoirs of Brás Cubas*) 10, 41 n.31
MacIsaac, Ashley (*Fiddling with Disaster*) 53
managers, rock

desire for stardom 78
  as fans 88
  gay 75, 77–8, 90 n.13
Manson, Charlie 23, 98
Mapplethorpe, Robert 37, 106, 137, 138
  photographic works 156, 166 n.17
  plagiarism 168 n.38
  sex work 142
  relationship with Patti Smith 137, 138, 141–3
  relationship with Andy Warhol 143–4
Marcus, Greil 176, 186
Marr, Johnny 109, 135 n.39. *See also* the Smiths.
  Set the Boy Free 109
    growing up in Manchester 117
    music writing, arranging and performing 117
    the Smiths' disintegration 117
Martyn, Beverley (Kutner) 104–5, 134 n.27
  Sweet Honesty 104
    domestic abuse 104–5
Martyn, John 104–5, 134 n.27
Maymudes, Victor 174
McCartney, Paul 81, 91 n.20, 106, 117, 164 n.3
MC5 67–8 n.4, 146
McKechnie, Licorice 22
McLaren, Malcolm 27, 100, 165 n.8
McLean, Steve 155
Meek, Joe 36
  gay seducer 77
  relationship with partner Lionel Howard 78
  murder/suicide 78
  dangerous sexual encounters, attracted to 78
Megson, Neil. *See* P-Orridge, Genesis Breyer
memory 2, 31, 54, 58, 68 n.6, 122–3, 138, 142, 146–7, 148, 187, 206 n.8
  and forgetting 54, 56, 69 n.9, 152
  institutionalized 190–1
Metallica
  group therapy, parodic music video of 61
  Some Kind of Monster 61
Middleton Richard 13, 42 n.42
Mississippi Fred McDowell 23

Mitchell, Joni 20, 29, 146
  "Both Sides Now" 20
  "Coyote" 148
Moby 4, 33, 36, 130
  Porcelain
    alcoholism 121
    allusions, literary and pop culture in 123, 124–5, 127
    Animal Rights 122, 128
    celebrity encounters 125
    John Cheever's *Journals*, influence on 118–20, 130
    childhood sexual abuse in 119
    comic mode 123–4
    electronic music scene of 1980s and 1990s 122, 126–7
    "Go" 121, 126, 127
    identity, performative 118–20
    Herman Melville's *Moby-Dick; or, The Whale*, influence on 118–19, 130
    mental health 121–2
    persona, construction of 33, 94, 118, 119, 120, 121–4, 125–8
    "Play" 126, 128
    poverty 122, 126
    style and voice 123–5
    suicide, contemplated 119
  Then It Fell Apart 118
    addiction as focus 128, 129, 130
    alcoholism 128, 129, 130
    allusions, literary in 128
    childhood sexual abuse in 119
    electronic music scene, as community 129
    father, suicide of 129
    identity, performative 128
    1960s music, contempt for 129
    "Play", success of 130
    as rock 'n' recovery autobiography 118, 128–30
Monette, Paul (*Borrowed Time*) 155
Montagu, Lord 75, 76
  and Inquiry into Homosexual Offences and Prostitution (Wolfenden Commission) 75–6
  and the Montagu Case of 1953 75–6, 80

Peter Wildeblood, homosexual
  relationship with 75–6
Montaigne, Michel de
  Confessions 7
  Essays 10
  life-writing, experimental 9–10
Moon, Keith 49
Moore, Thurston 25, 41 n.28
Morello, Tom (*Whatever It Takes*) 4
Morrissey 108, 109, 115
  Autobiography 108–9
  Johnny Marr, relationship with 115–16
  music, influences on 115
  persona, construction of 109, 116–17
  the Smiths, formation and development of 115–16
  style, voice, and structure 116–17
  and Oscar Wilde 116–17
Morrison, Jim 1, 49, 67 n.1, 144, 146, 151, 189, 203, 204
Mötley Crüe 36, 61, 62, 68 n.6
  The Dirt 119
music industry 21, 34, 56, 57, 65–6, 114–15, 116
  crisis in 204
  homophobia in 74–5, 77–8
  sexual abuse/sexism in 19–27, 77, 105
musicology (and ethnomusicology)
  field research 14, 15, 16, 19
  life writing in 14–19
  popular music in 12–19
  salvage 16

Napier-Bell, Simon 86
  on The Beatles as homoerotic fantasy 92 n.30
  on Epstein, closeted homosexuality of 92 n.30
Nazis
  addiction, treatment of 48
  concentration camps 16
  disabled, treatment of 165 n.10
  folk music, treatment of 42–3 n.44
  imagery 61, 98, 135 n.39, 156
Neill, Ben 150
Neil, Vince 68 n.6. See also Mötley Crüe

Neumann, Osha 131 n.8, 205 n.3
Neuwirth, Bob 144, 176, 177
Newby, Christine Carol. *See* Tutti, Cosey Fanni
Nico 22
Nietzsche, Friedrich 41 n.34, 187–8, 197 n.35
  Beyond Good and Evil 187–8
  Ecce Homo 11–12, 41 n.35
  music composition 11
Nirvana 66. *See also* Cobain, Kurt.
  "Smells Like Teen Spirit" (music video) 66
Nobel Prize for Literature. *See* Dylan, Bob.
Nuttall, Jeff 94

Oasis 108, 135 n.39
Ochs, Phil 172, 192–3, 194 n.6
Oldham, Andrew Loog 50, 60, 77
Ono, Yoko 21, 31, 59, 109
  "Cut-Dress" 97
  and the Fluxus movement 97
  Grapefruit 21
  "Imagine" 21
  John Lennon, relationship with 44 n.53
  as muse 21, 44 n.53
  "Why" 97
opera 10–11, 94, 98, 147, 151, 183
Orton, Joe 87
Osbourne, Ozzy 50, 61, 202

Paganini, Niccolò 28
Pallenberg, Anita 60, 69 n.9
Pang, May 44 n.53
parody 61–2, 69 n.12, 93, 96–7, 98
Parton, Dolly 189
pastiche 61, 69 n.12
The Patti Smith Group 138, 145, 146
Patton, Charlie 143
Peart, Neil 4
  brain cancer 202
  Far and Wide 202
Pennebaker, D.A. (*Dont Look Back*) 181, 186
Phillips, John 52
  Papa John: An Autobiography 52
Phillips, Mackenzie 52, 58
  High on Arrival 52, 69 n.9
The Police 69 n.13

P-Orridge, Genesis Breyer
   as abuser, domestic 102, 103–4, 105
   appropriation of others' work 107, 132 n.14
   autobiographies by 134 n.29
   body modifications 95
   William Burroughs, influence on 98
   criminal record 132 n.16
   Aleister Crowley, influence on 98
   cult leader 95, 103, 107, 134 n.30
   Brion Gysin, influence on 98
   identities, experimental 95
   performance, artistic, as self-therapy 95
   pornography 97, 132 n.16
   Psychic TV 107, 134 n.30
   punk rock-star posturing 100, 107–8
   Sacred 106, 132 n.13
      on John Cage 132 n.13
      early life in Manchester 132 n.17
      and Joy Division 132. n.17
      Throbbing Gristle, 2004 reunion 106–7
      Virgin Records incident 133 n.20
      on Andy Warhol 132 n.13
   writer 95, 96
Postcards from America 155
Pride, Dickie 50, 67 n.3
Prince, Mary 8, 40–1 n.24
   The History of Mary Prince 40–1 n.24
prostitution 70 n.18, 78, 84, 88 n.6, 90 n.17, 112, 122
Prostitution action (19–26 Oct. 1976), ICA, London 97, 100–1
   tampon art 97, 101
Proust, Marcel (*Remembrance of Things Past*) 10, 202

Quigley [Quickly], Tommy 87

Rauffenbart, Tom 163
Reagan, Ronald 158
recording studios
   Electric Lady Studios 144
   penitentiary 15, 18, 23
Red Hot Chili Peppers 36, 62–3, 125. *See also* Flea; Kiedis, Anthony
   "Knock Me Down" (music video) 125

Reed, Lou 4, 31, 46 n.63, 46 n.72, 130, 136 n.43, 142. *See also* Velvet Underground
   homosexuality, electroshock treatment for 76, 139, 165 n.10
   identity, gay 90 n.16
   and Patti Smith 142, 144
   Andy Warhol, relationship with 131–2 n.9
Reed, S. Alexander 96
rehabilitation clinics 57, 59, 60
Reich, Matthew 144
Reid, John 74
Reynolds, Simon 96
Reznor, Trent 125
Richards, Keith 137, 144, 164 n.3
   addict, model celebrity 50, 51, 60, 63
   aging 201
   drug offences 76
   Mick Jagger, relationship with 78
   Life (with James Fox) 8, 38 n.2, 38 n.7, 51, 59, 115
   addiction 50
   recovery narratives, contempt for 47
   African-American music, debt to 51
Rilke (*Duino Elegies*) 203
Rimbaud, Arthur 37, 137, 138, 142, 143, 150, 151–2, 161, 164 n.5, 165 n.14, 176, 187, 189
Robertson, Robbie (*Testimony*) 6, 33, 172, 186, 192
rock 'n' recovery autobiography
   and addiction as disability 48–51, 55
   in autobiography studies 47
   confessional motives 52–3
   in disability studies 47
   fame, pathology of 63–7
   fractured identity 63–7
   generic hybridity 52, 54–7
   Junky (William Burroughs) as model of 50–1, 66
   as postmodern form 66–7
   rehabilitation and recovery 53, 54–5
   Keith Richards' *Life* as model of 51
   self-fashioning in 57–61
rock star/popular musician
   activism 35

aging 201–2, 206 n.7
  as romantic artist 36
  authenticity 34–5
  disdain for celebrity 34–5
  dying young 203, 205 n.11
  fame, desire for 35
  illness 201–2
  mortality 49, 203–04
  myths related to 1, 34–5, 36, 47, 49–50, 63, 67, 67 n.2, 203–4
  post-glam 36, 93
  post-punk 36, 93
  rebel 34–5, 47, 49–50
  youth and 202–3
Rojek, Chris 27–8, 34
Rolling Stone Magazine 27, 32, 45 n.58–59, 138, 202
  celebrity, construction of 29–30
  covers 66
  'Jesus Christ Pose,' on covers of 29–30
The Rolling Stones 22, 50, 51, 59, 60, 77, 132 n.15. *See also* Jagger, Mick; Richards, Keith
  'bad boy' image 60
  Love You Live (album cover) 31
  Our Own Story 67 n.4
  Sticky Fingers (album cover) 31
  "Sympathy for the Devil" 142
Ronk, Dave Van 172, 176, 177, 191
  "House of the Rising Sun" 176
Rorem, Ned 201
Roszak, Theodore 200, 201–2
Rotolo, Carla 15, 174, 175
Rotolo, Suze 15, 21, 172, 174, 176, 177, 187–8, 194 n.5–6
  A Freewheelin' Time 21, 187–8, 194 n.6, 194 n.11
  abortion 176
  rejects role as Dylan's muse 21
Rousseau, Jean-Jacques 8, 10–11
  Confessions
    music in 10–11
    somatic experience in 11
Rudd, Mark 94, 205 n.3
Rundgren, Todd 144
Russell, Leon
  "Delta Lady" 21
  "A Song for You" 21

"Superstar" 21
"Watching the River Flow" 186

Sainte-Marie, Buffy 115
Sandburg, Carl 15, 178
Scemama, Marion 153, 161
Schemel, Patty
  rock 'n' recovery autobiography 70–1 n.18
Schult, Emil 150
Scissor Sisters 74
Sedgwick, Eve Kosofsky 57, 174
Seeger, Charles 15, 16, 43 n.45, 174
  American folksong tradition, shifting views on 16–17
  "Barbara Allen" 16
  class struggle and folk tradition 17
  FBI investigation of, for HUAC 43 n.48
  "Lenin, Who's That Guy?" 17
  originality of 174
Seeger, Mike 17, 18, 177
Seeger, Peggy 4, 43 n.44, 43 n.50
  in American folksong tradition 17, 24, 43 n.49
  First Time Ever, A Memoir 17–18
  abuse, sexual, in music industry 105
  family 17–19
  "The First Time Ever I Saw Your Face" (MacColl), views on 19–20
  folksong, ethnographic field research 19, 43 n.17
  Ewan MacColl, relationship with 18–19, 20
  muse, view on role of ("muse-axes") 19–20
  music, revolutionary politics and 18, 19
  as therapy 17–18, 19
Seeger, Pete 17, 18, 24, 186
  House Un-American Activities Committee (HUAC) 43 n.48
Serrano, Andres (*Piss Christ*) 156
The Sex Pistols 26, 91 n.26, 135 n.39. *See also* Jones, Steve; Sid Vicious
Sid and Nancy 63, 139
Sexual Offences Act (1967) 36, 74
Sharp, Cecil 16, 43 n.47
Shears, Jake 74

Shelton, Robert (*No Direction Home*) 176
Shepard, Sam 144, 145, 147–8
   The One Inside 148
   Renaldo and Clara (with Bob Dylan and Patti Smith) 148
Sid Vicious 26–7, 63
Simon, Carly 105
Simpson, Rose 21. *See also* Heron, Mike; Incredible String Band
   Muse, Odalisque, Handmaid: A Girl's Life in the Incredible String Band
   muse 21–3
Sinatra, Frank 28, 29, 67 n.1, 179
Sinclair, John 67–8 n.4
Sixx, Nikki 47, 50, 52, 55, 58, 63, 68 n.6
   The Heroin Diaries: A Year in the Life of a Shattered Rock Star 52–3
   addiction, copycat 63
   childhood trauma 55
   fame, pathology of 63
   rock 'n' recovery autobiography 63
Slash 47, 50, 63. *See also* Guns N' Roses
   Slash 52, 63
   as rock 'n' recovery autobiography 63
Slick, Grace 53
The Slits 26
Smith, Fred "Sonic" 146. *See also* MC5
Smith, Harry 15, 143, 153, 166 n.20
   Anthology of American Folk Music 15, 143
Smith, Patti 3, 4, 9, 51, 116, 137–49, 151, 157, 161, 164 n.2
   androgyny 138, 144
   autobiographical fiction of 10
   art and intimate relationships 142, 143
   Artaud's theatre of cruelty and performance 138–41
   contexts, cultural, literary, geographic, musical and spiritual 140, 143–4, 165 n.14
   DIY aesthetic 37, 137, 145
   drugs, rejection of 138, 139, 164 n.4
   and Bob Dylan 144
   as fan 137, 164 n.3
   Jimi Hendrix, influence on 144, 146
   influences, musical and literary on 37, 137–44, 149

   life-writing, experimental and paratextual 5, 9
   Jim Morrison, influence on 144
   muse, role of 20
   performance, aesthetic, theory and praxis 145–6, 149, 166 n.19, 166–7 n.24
   performances
      at opening for Gerard Malanga, Poetry Project 142
      at Nobel Prize for Literature presentation (for Bob Dylan) 137
      with the Patti Smith Group 145; "Gloria" 145; "Hey Joe" 145; "My Generation" 145
   photographer 37, 137
   photographic subject, of Mapplethorpe 37, 137
   recordings
      Antonin Artaud's *The Peyote Dance* (with Soundwalk Collective) 138–9
      "Because the Night" 100
      Horses 138, 144, 157, 167 n.25; "Gloria" 7, 140
   and rock 'n' roll Jesus 7, 142
   Arthur Rimbaud, influence on 165–6 n.14–15
   writings
   The Coral Sea 165 n.14
   Cowboy Mouth 7
   Just Kids 38 n.7, 138, 141, 144–6, 149
      AIDS memoir 141
      Jim Carroll, relationship with 142–3
      as dual autobiography 141
      DIY aesthetic in 145
      gender roles 142–3
      homage, musical 144–6
      identity, construction of 141, 142, 143, 145, 149
      influences, literary and musical in 145–6
      Mapplethorpe, relationship with 138, 141–4
      on Mapplethorpe's aesthetic 141, 142
      performative self 144–6
      on recording 146

M Train 138, 141, 146–7, 148, 164 n.2
  allusions, literary in 145, 147
  as elegy 146–7, 166 n.21
  as homage, literary 146–7
  identity, construction of 146–7
  Sylvia Plath in 147
  premonitions and signs 147, 165–6 n.15
  Fred "Sonic" Smith in 146
 music reviews 138
  Year of the Monkey 10, 138, 147–8;
    allusions, literary, high culture, and pop culture in 147–8;
    hybrid genres of 147–8; death/impermanence in 147–8, 149;
    identity, construction of, as archivist 147–8; premonitions and signs in 148; Sandy Pearlman in 147–8; Sam Shepard in 147–8
  on writing 164 n.5
The Smiths 108, 109, 112, 113, 115, 116, 134 n.33
Smith, Sidonie 2, 3, 6, 39–40 n.16
Sonic Youth 9, 25, 125, 150, 157, 164 n.1
  "Death Valley '69" (music video) 150
Sontag, Susan 1, 48, 54, 63, 70 n.15, 70 n.17
  on Antonin Artaud 139, 141, 165 n.9
  on Richard Avedon 152
  Death Kit 152
  death, photographed by Annie Leibovitz 70 n.17, 151
  on Peter Hujar 152
  On Photography 152
Sor, Fernando 28
Soundgarden 30, 159
Spectre, Phil 20
Spinal Tap 61, 62
Springfield, Rick 68 n.7
Springsteen, Bruce 4, 18, 34
  Born to Run 33, 46 n.74
Sterne, Laurence (*Tristram Shandy*) 10
Stigwood, Robert 77
Stradlin, Izzy 51
Suede 108, 109, 110, 111, 112
Sumner, Bernard 135 n.39. *See also* Joy Division

Sun Pie 177
Sussex Pistols 24
Sutcliffe, Stu 91 n.19, 117

Tagaq, Tanya (*Split Tooth*) 105
Talking Heads 4, 39 n.13, 134 n.29, 157, 158, 166 n.19
  "Psycho Killer" 158–9
Television 145, 166 n.19, 166–7 n.24
Teresa of Ávila, St. (*Life*) 9
Terkel, Studs 153
Thek, Paul 1
Throbbing Gristle (TG) 8, 95, 132 n.17
  anti-rock 99–100, 133 n.19
  audience, terrorizing of 99–100
  authenticity 96–7, 133 n.20
  body and bodily fluids in performance by 96, 97, 99–100, 101
  commodifying of, post-2004 reunion 107–8
  and COUM Transmissions 96–9
  fans 133 n.20
  Fluxus movement 96, 97
  launch of, at *Prostitution* action 100–1, 106
  mail art 97
  "Music from the Death Factory" (concert poster) 98
  music, industrial 132 n.10
  Nazi imagery 98
  reunion, 2004 96–7, 106, 107
  Tate Britain 107, 108
  as transgressive art performance band 96–7, 98, 99–101, 102
  "Zyklon B" 98
Throwing Muses 21
Thunders, Johnny 63, 90 n.17
Tibet, David 24
Townshend, Pete (*Who I Am*) 78, 96
trauma 3, 23, 58, 112, 153, 163
  childhood 3, 5, 55, 66, 71 n.19, 83, 105, 118, 121, 128
Tress, Arthur 161
Trump, Donald 30, 130, 148, 173, 183, 191
Turing, Alan 75
Turner, Tina 105

Tutti, Cosey Fanni 8, 36, 95–108, 138. *See also* P-Orridge, Genesis Breyer; Throbbing Gristle
   abused by P-Orridge 100–1
   abused women in popular music autobiographies, compared with 104–5
   Art Sex Music 95, 98
      abuse, by father 105
      abuse, by P-Orridge 102, 103–4, 105
      Chris Carter, relationship with 100, 106, 107, 134 n.29
      childhood 98
      identity, construction in 101–2, 105–6
      Margery Kempe as influence 133 n.22
      post-2004 Throbbing Gristle reunion 107–8
      sex work and pornography in life and art 103, 105–6
      Throbbing Gristle, account of music and aesthetic 99
      works, appropriation of, by P-Orridge 107, 133 n.24
   identity, construction of 94
   music, industrial 95, 132 n.10
   "My Life Is My Art. My Art Is My Life" 106
   origins of name 97, 98
   precocity, sexual of 132–3 n.18
   sex work and pornographic film 95, 100, 101, 106–7
   *Self*lessness 101, 102
   Throbbing Gristle, early account of 132 n.14
   Throbbing Gristle, participation in 95, 106–7
Tweedy, Jeff 4, 33, 192, 196 n.24, 202
   persona 33, 192, 196 n.24

Up Against the Wall Motherfuckers 68 n.4, 94, 131 n.8

Velvet Underground 30–1, 46 n.72, 143. *See also* Cale, John; Reed, Lou
Verlaine, Paul 143, 151, 189
Verlaine, Tom 145, 146, 166–7 n.24
Vienna Aktionists 96

Wagner, Richard 11, 28, 33, 41 n.33, 150
   gesamtkunstwerk 33, 150
Wagstaff, Sam 143, 165–6 n.15
The Wallflowers 185
Walters, Jake 116
Warhol, Andy 20, 101, 132 n.13, 136 n.43, 142, 143, 164 n.3, 169 n.41
   aesthetic, homoerotic/queer, of 31–2
   art, commercialization of 131 n.9
   art, hybrid and multi-media 94–5
   celebrity culture, contributions to 30–2, 64
   Diaries 31, 32, 46 n.71–2
   Exploding Plastic Inevitable 31, 94–5
   Factory 31, 32, 143, 151, 152
   identity, gay 31–2
   homophobia of 31–2
   rock album covers, design of 31, 32
   self-promoter 31–2, 161
   and Velvet Underground 30, 31, 46 n.72, 131–2 n.9
   as writer 31, 181
Watson, Julia 2, 3, 6, 39–40 n.16
Weathermen 94, 197 n.33, 205 n.3. *See also* Ayers, Bill; Rudd, Mark; Weather Underground
Weather Underground 68 n.4, 205 n.3
Weill, Kurt 180, 185
Welch, Brian (*Save Me From Myself*) 54
Wenner, Jann 30, 44 n.53, 90 n.13
Westwood, Vivienne 26, 100
Weymouth, Tina 4
Whitman, Walt 120, 121, 176, 182, 186, 189
   "Song of Myself" 176
The Who 78, 85, 94, 166 n.23. *See also* Townshend, Pete
   Tommy 94
Wilco 192
Wildeblood, Peter
   homosexual relationship with Lord Montagu 76
   imprisonment 76
   and the Montagu Case of 1953 75–6
   Wolfenden Commission, testimony for 76
Wilde, Oscar 130, 152
   "The Ballad of Reading Gaol" 117
   in celebrity, development of 28, 46 n.45

De Profundis 76, 135-6 n.41, 136 n.44
  as gay martyr 115, 116, 117, 121
  homosexuality, trial, conviction, and imprisonment for 75, 76, 135 n.41, 136 n.44
  as mythic role model 115, 116-17
Williamson, Robin 22, 24
Winwood, Steve 56
Wojnarowicz, David 32, 100, 130, 149-64
  ACT UP 37, 150, 155-7
  aesthetic modes of 149-50
  AIDS 150, 154, 155
  alt rock stardom, contempt for 159
  art, activist theory and praxis of 37, 150, 154-7
  art, multi-media of 149-50
    Fuck You Faggot Fucker, 1984 (collage: photography/painting)
    influences on 161
    ITSOFOMO: In the Shadow of Forward Motion (multi-media performance with music); 150 (with Ben Neill)
    Roach Bunnies (art installation) 150
    Untitled (One Day This Kid ...), 1990 (text/photograph)
    Untitled (Sometimes I Come to Hate People), 1992 (text/photograph)
    'Warhol Factory, 1984' (art installation) 150
    When I Put My Hands on Your Body, 1990 (text/photograph) 154, 168 n.36
  autobiographical writings 153-6
  art as autobiography 154
  child sexual abuse in 153
  Close to the Knives 150, 152, 153, 155-6, 160, 162; as AIDS memoir 155-6
  fact and fiction in 160-1
  identity, doubled construction of 160-1
  In the Shadow of the American Dream 158, 160, 162-3, 168 n.37
  love in 162-3
  Memories That Smell Like Gasoline 153, 155, 162
    as montage 153-4
    rape in 153, 155
    self-mythologizing in 160-1
  Seven Miles a Second (collaborator, James Romberger) 153, 168 n.36
  sex and sexuality in 160
  Sounds in the Distance 153
  The Waterfront Journals 153
  William Burroughs, influence on 37, 137
  3 Teens Kill 4 (3TK4) 150, 154, 157-9; *No Motive* 158-9
  child sexual abuse of 155, 159, 161, 162, 163
  and Cinema of Transgression 150
  death, as artistic theme 152-3
  death of 156-7, 163-4, 168 n.40
  DIY aesthetic 37, 137, 152
  drugs 159
  Peter Hujar, personal and professional relationship with 150, 151, 152, 159, 161, 163
  identity, construction of 94, 137, 150, 162-3
  influences, literary, musical, artistic on 150-1
  music of
  no wave 137, 164 n.1
  as photographer 37, 137, 151-2
  as photographic subject 151, 152-3
  photography of
    Arthur Rimbaud in New York (1978-9) 151-2, 154, 161
    'Peter Hujar's head, feet and hands, post-mortem' 152
    Sex Series (for Marion Scemama) 161 (photomontages)
    "*Silence=Death*", 1989 153, 161
    Untitled (Face in Dirt), 1991 153
  and *Postcards from America* (dir. Steve McLean) 155

Arthur Rimbaud, influence on 37, 137, 151–2
self-saboteur, in personal relationships 163
sexual encounters, dangerous 162
on signifying systems, linguistic, visual, and musical 154, 157–9
in *United in Anger: A History of ACT UP* (dir. Jim Hubbard) 155
Wolfenden Commission 75, 76–7
Wolfenden, Jeremy 76–7
Wolfenden, John 76
Wolfenden Report (1957) 36, 74
Womack, Kenneth 40 n.23
Wood, Ronnie 47, 50, 54
Ronnie
    comic conclusion 60–1
    as rock 'n' recovery autobiography 60–1
    Keith Richards, imitation of 60
Woodstock 22, 93, 104, 131 n.2, 151
    generation 56, 131 n.2
    reunion 62
The Woody Guthrie Centre 171, 183, 188, 189, 191, 192, 193
Wordsworth, William (*The Prelude*) 11, 82

The Yardbirds 86
Young, La Monte 97, 143
    Dream Syndicate 143

Zimmerman, Robert Allen 171. *See* Dylan, Bob

www.ingramcontent.com/pod-product-compliance
Lightning Source LLC
Chambersburg PA
CBHW062131300426
44115CB00012BA/1885